EXPERIENCE AND SUBSTANCE

EXPERIENCE AND SUBSTANCE

AN ESSAY IN METAPHYSICS

BY

DeWITT H. PARKER

UNIVERSITY OF MICHIGAN

GREENWOOD PRESS, PUBLISHERS
NEW YORK   1968

TO THE MEMORY OF
DeWitt Webster Parker
BORN IN BOSTON SEPTEMBER 4, 1910
DIED IN ACTION AT BELCHITE,
SPAIN, MARCH 10, 1938

Preface

SOME years ago I began to investigate certain topics in the metaphysics of value, but soon found that I could not proceed without a preliminary study of general metaphysical problems. As this study grew it took the shape of an independent essay in metaphysics. I am now publishing the essay in the hope that— despite manifest shortcomings—it may prove to be a contribution to a way of thinking the fundamental style of which was initiated by Plato, Aristotle, and Plotinus, recast by Berkeley, Leibniz, and Fichte, and immensely enriched in our time by the insights of Bergson, James, and Whitehead. If the auspices are favoring, the projected work on the metaphysics of value should follow, for which the short and polemical Chapter XV, "The Nature of Value," of this book is in no sense intended to be a substitute or introduction.

In writing this essay I have sought to achieve brevity and simplicity by limiting myself so far as possible to the presentation of a single point of view—broadly idealist, finitist, and monadistic in character—saying no more on any theme than its positive development seemed to require, instead of complicating its rhythm by the consideration of every possible alternative theory. I have, moreover, wherever feasible, subordinated epistemological to ontological discussion. It was sometimes obviously impossible, nevertheless, not to take specific account of the contrasting ideas of thinkers from whom I have learned much. I have also found it necessary to give particular attention to well-known contemporary writers on the philosophy of logic and mathematics, including the philosophy of probability and the method of science. To all of these I have tried to make due acknowledgment in the course of my text or in footnotes, although I fear there may be some whose names and publications I may have overlooked. I owe a heavy debt to my colleagues in the department of philosophy for the benefit which I have derived from informal discussions with them or from their writings.

Small portions of this essay have already appeared in print, although not in quite the same language, in the *International Journal of Ethics* (XLIV [1934], No. 3 : 293–312), in *Ethics* (XLVIII [1938], No. 4 : 475–486), and in my book *The Self and Nature*, published in 1917. From the last—a work of my philosophic youth—I have borrowed most in the chapters on "The Theory of Relations," but whatever I have borrowed has been revised in the light of recent knowledge or my own reflection.

I wish to express my thanks to the Regents of the University of Michigan for their generosity in providing the funds for the publication of this essay; to Dr. Frank E. Robbins, Managing Editor of the University of Michigan Press, for his interest in the enterprise; and to Dr. Eugene S. McCartney and Miss Grace Potter for their sympathetic and unerring help in revising my manuscript and preparing it for the printer.

D. H. P.

ANN ARBOR, MICHIGAN
October 16, 1940

Contents

EXPERIENCE AND SUBSTANCE

I

Definition of Subject Matter

S TANDING out in contrast with man's passionate interest in
the transient objects and events of his environment is his
metaphysical interest in the Eternal. We have no need to enquire
into its psychological roots and origins. Whatever these be, there
can be no doubt of its profundity in view of the historic fact that
the metaphysical interest maintains itself in competition with
ordinary purposes and in the midst of stirring conflicts in the
political and social worlds. Socrates and Plato pursue their investigations into the nature of the good and the real despite the
defeat and decay of their city; and Hegel composes the symphony
of his thoughts within hearing of the guns of the Battle of Jena.
In our day, all the while that opposing national and social causes
prepare for a decisive struggle which may bring the end of an
epoch in our civilization, we witness a revival of speculative
philosophy. It is as if, fearful and confused by his own close passions, man were looking for some far horizon where his mind
might rest.

Although not identical with any one of them the metaphysical
interest is akin, as Hegel taught,[1] to the scientific, the religious,
and the artistic interests, and in our culture the destiny of all
three has been intertwined. Like science, metaphysics is a mode
of intellectual endeavor aiming at truth, and so provides the
same sort of satisfaction in appeasing the larger ranges of curiosity that science provides; only the truth it aims at is more
universal than any that science seeks. It is like religion in trying
to discern man's place in the universe; yet unlike religion it does
not rely on traditional faith or the vision peculiar to mystics, but
on the candid examination of aspects of experience public to all.
Dry and conceptual in its methods, it seems the antithesis of art;

[1] Georg Wilhelm Friedrich Hegel, *Aesthetik,* Erster Theil, "Die Idee des
Kunstschoenen oder das Ideal," in *Werke* (Berlin: Verlag von Duncker und
Humblot, 1832) , Bd. 10, 1 Abth., pp. 131 ff.

3

but when we look at one of Rembrandt's portraits of some old
Jew and see there depicted the tragedy not merely of a race and
of humanity, but of all that is finite, or when we read Shakspere's
lines

> Golden lads and girls all must,
> As chimney-sweepers, come to dust

and find there stated the transiency not of youth alone, but of
all things golden, all things precious, we appreciate how little
difference there is between the subject matter of metaphysics and
the deeper meanings of art.   The kinship of these interests, which
one might expect to bring coöperation among them, has led,
unfortunately for all, to jealousy and recrimination.   Again and
again in the name of science metaphysics has been condemned
as barren and fruitless; in the name of religion, dismissed for
coldness and moral inefficacy; and in the name of art, scorned
for its intellectual asceticism; yet all three are found borrowing
from it.   In arranging basic ideas science is helpless without it;
the men of religion turn to it during those recurring crises of
faith to which Christianity is subject when the mystic vision
fades; and the artists owe to it the "depth meanings" that underlie their intuitions.   Its doom is constantly foretold by positivists
and specialists, yet its perennial history continues.   The present
treatise is another effort to feed this ancient and peculiar interest
and to meet the challenge that comes today from a newer, "logical," positivism which sees philosophy at a crossroads ready to
abandon its traditional task, and from a newer, secularized
religion that has lost all feeling for the Eternal.
    The traditional conception of the province of metaphysics
was defined once and for all by Aristotle as the study of being as
being.   That is, metaphysics investigates those properties which
pertain to anything and everything that exists: properties which
we can know that a thing has as soon as we know that it exists;
universal or generic characters, the conjunction of which make
up the common denominator or essence of existence; categories.
Metaphysics does not increase knowledge by increasing the number of particulars we know, but by increasing the depth of our
knowledge of any particular.   Progress in metaphysics does not
wait upon the opening up of new frontiers of fact by the inven-
tion of novel technical instruments and methods of research, such

as the telescope, microscope, or cyclotron, as is the case with science, for since the generic characters of being are as surely present in a single fact as in many facts, the careful analysis of any facts will serve. Not so much learning as the ability to attend to matters so obvious that they commonly escape notice, together with the gift to devise a language in which to express them, is required of the philosopher. The Greeks, who from the standpoint of scientific knowledge were very ignorant men, could make important discoveries in metaphysics because of their endowment in both observation and language: the analysis of being in *Philebus* 23 and the philosophical parts of the *Timaeus* are still significant, even though the scientific parts of the latter dialogue are obsolete; Aristotle's Four Causes and his discussion in *Metaphysics* α maintain their value, though his Astronomy is worthless. As illustrations of generic characters of existence we may take the following: individuality, universality, time, space, cause, relation, value. Everything that exists is concrete and unique, yet possesses aspects that are found the same in other things; everything is a process and is related to every other thing in the complex fashion we call "space," is both determined by other things and determines them and itself, this determination issuing out of a striving and culminating in a satisfaction (value). These generic characters were familiar to Plato and Aristotle and can be discerned by anyone who will take the trouble to reflect upon the world as it is known to him. Progress in speculative philosophy occurs through bringing such characters to reflection, discovering their interrelations, and expressing them in increasingly clear and adequate language.

The study of the categories, however, is no mere analysis of existence, but involves, in addition, a synthetic activity terminating in a picture of the world as a whole. Obviously this picture can be no detailed map, but only an outline of basic structure. The study of many of the categories leads inevitably to synthesis, for they are themselves essentially forms of organization. Space is indisputably such a form; time and causality, which underlie space, are organizing principles. Even those categories which, in Heracleitean fashion, present a vivid polarity, and appear to have a disruptive function in being, prove to be founded on an underlying unity. I have in mind such well-known categorial opposites as fact and value, form and substance, mind and matter, subject and object, necessity and freedom, individuality and universality. Superficial philosophies leave these pairs side by side, joined in mechanical fashion, but a more profound reflection reveals their mutual dependence.

If the British empirical movement, together with Kant, had not occurred, introducing into philosophy a new approach to the problem of knowledge and putting it on an equal footing with the problem of being, the statement just given of the task of metaphysics would suffice. But as matters have stood ever since, the relation of the categories to reality cannot be studied apart from their relation to experience. It is now clear that in any investigation we do not open our eyes like windows on to reality, but perceive it through the medium of our own minds. Corresponding to every category is a belief that the category applies to reality. The categories are not discovered by the mere analysis of reality, but, as we have just noted, there is required in addition a synthetic act transcending anything directly findable. These acts must present their credentials. We are thus impelled to view the task of metaphysics not so much objectively—as the study of observable, existential form—as subjectively—as a criticism of beliefs. Metaphysics becomes the attempt to discover necessary beliefs. A necessary belief is one that is foundational for other beliefs, the metaphysical being the most basic that we possess. Our persuasion of the existence of other selves is a necessary and also a metaphysical belief, because it is foundational not only for our faith in rights and duties, but, as we shall show, for our belief in causality and space, and therefore for the whole common-sense picture of the world. A belief such as this is so elementary that no one except a philosopher thinks of looking for a justification of it; yet even such convictions cannot be taken for granted in metaphysics. Metaphysics achieves the complete sophistication of belief. The search for necessary beliefs involves the purging of the mind of gratuitous ones. Berkeley's criticism of the conception of matter and Hume's attack on causality—the prelude to the contemporary attack—are the classical examples of metaphysical catharsis. Very often, however, the issue of metaphysical criticism has been to provide a negative proof of the necessity of one or another fundamental conception: the fruitless effort to prove a conception unnecessary has established its necessity. It is true, moreover, that no conception that has won wide acceptance in philosophy is wholly factitious or gratuitous. In all the dross which the conception of matter contains there is a strain of pure metal: the recognition of the dependence of given experience on an enclosing reality. A good metaphysics must provide a place for whatever functions were performed by otherwise unnecessary beliefs.

In the search for necessary beliefs we shall make use of two principles. The first I shall call the empirical principle. This principle, in its corrected and purified statement, is the great contribution of the eighteenth century to metaphysics. Following closely the thought of Hume, but substituting for his term "impression" our richer and more adequate term "experience," we may express it thus: For the elements and the principle of construction of every concept that we employ in metaphysics we must be able to find a corresponding experience which illustrates them.[1] Negatively applied, this principle rules out all transcendental concepts: the absolutely simple "reals" of Herbart, the windowless monads of Leibniz, the unconscious matter or "stuff" of the materialist, the "neutral" entities of Sheffer and Russell, as well as such physical concepts as "action," and other "working" concepts of science; for nothing in experience illustrates them, either with regard to their elements or their method of construction. The principle will lead us straight to the recognition that only concrete experience can be accepted as reality and that the only valid picture of the world must be an empirically idealistic or "spiritualistic" one. The principle may also be called the "principle of concreteness" (after Berkeley). By fidelity to it metaphysics becomes the most empirical of all forms of enquiry, more empirical in this respect than physics, which employs transcendental concepts without hesitation. The reason for the principle is partly the traditional caution of metaphysics, initiated by Descartes, and partly the conviction, which

---

[1] We could not write simply, "For every concept we must find the corresponding experience," for suppose we wished to use a very large number, larger than the number of any class of which we had experience? Such a number concept would, however, be metaphysically valid because we have experience of the elements of number, namely, unit classes, and we know by experience, also, the principle of the construction of larger classes, namely, "plus one."

investigation confirms, that given experience is representative of all reality.

The empirical principle must, however, be supplemented by what I shall call the speculative. This principle is the formulation of our procedure in applying concepts derived from our own experience to a reality extending beyond our experience. The range of application of a concept is not limited to its base or source. The principle is illustrated in our everyday social experience. If seeing the drawn face of a companion I make the judgment, He is in distress, I am employing a concept obviously derived from my own experience of sorrow to characterize—not that experience itself—but an analogous experience, the existence of which I acknowledge. Creatively, speculatively, I move away from my base and claim cognizance of something that transcends it. But the speculative element in knowledge is not limited to extending the range of application of concepts; it includes, in addition, the use of new concepts, which, although based on given experience, do not, as I can see, apply to my own experience. Again our social experience provides the best examples. For whenever a companion tells me of an experience of his which I have never had, I find myself possessed of a concept or complex of concepts to the whole of which nothing in my experience corresponds although to each element of the concept something does correspond; and I am not merely seized with this new creation, but make use of it to affirm and to characterize an existence not my own. When we read history the same process occurs: a complex of concepts arises in the mind, impossible of application to our own experience and referred beyond it. "Every learned and confident stranger was enriched by the bounty and flattered by the conversation of the monarch; he nobly rewarded a Greek physician by the deliverance of three thousand captives; and the sophists who contended for his favor were exasperated by the wealth and insolence of Uranius, their more successful rival." [1] Who that reads this sentence would think of applying it to himself, and who does not, nevertheless, accept it as valid? The use of the speculative principle in metaphysics is not essentially different from the uses which I have illustrated

[1] Edward Gibbon, *Decline and Fall of the Roman Empire* (New York: First Modern Library Edition, 1932), p. 259.

from our everyday experience. In a former publication I described the procedure of metaphysics in a single phrase which brings together the empirical and the speculative principles—"radical empiricism extended by the imagination," the term "imagination" being used to signify the activity of combining the elements of given experience into new conceptual pictures and applying them to acknowledged existences that are not given.[1] A good metaphysics admits the transcendent, but not the transcendental.

Our empirical principle is in accord with the doctrines of positivism, "logical" or other, although our speculative principle might be disputed by its most recent adherents. For it is characteristic of positivism that it not only demands, as we do, that concepts have a base in given experience, but that the application of concepts also be given experience. If experience were used in some interpersonal or social sense we should have no quarrel—in fact we might then call ourselves positivists—but it appears to be used in the narrow, personal sense of "my" experience, thereby denying the speculative use of the concept away from its base. To judge by what some positivists say, it is even denied that the concept has meaning when so used, with the result that such an obviously meaningful expression as, A has a toothache, would have no significance. It is an easy matter, however, to point to a seeming inconsistency in this doctrine, for all positivists admit that meaning belongs to propositions regarding their own future experience, which, as future, is still not yet "my" experience. If meaning can transcend its base in the case of future experience why cannot it do so in the case of the experience of another mind? And to deny meaning to such a proposition as, A has a toothache, is, prima facie at least, preposterous. A proposition is preposterous when to be consistent with himself the person who believes it must disbelieve other propositions which he would not be able to disbelieve. For not even a logical positivist can disbelieve the meaningfulness of the concepts which underlie his social relations: the affirmation of rights and the acknowledgment of duties, his love for his family and friends, his coöperation with other logicians, his controversies with them, the significance

1 DeWitt H. Parker, *The Self and Nature* (Cambridge: Harvard University Press, 1917) , p. vi.

of the books and articles he writes and reads. In rebuttal the
positivist may assert that, whatever significance such concepts
have for life, only those concepts that can be verified have meaning for science; and only concepts relating to one's own experience can be verified. A dentist can verify the tissue changes at the
root of a tooth, or the increased blood pressure of his patient, but
cannot verify his pain. Yet how, when science itself is so obviously a part of life, depending at all points on social coöperation,
this distinction between science and life can be maintained has
never been shown. It is a distinction which, whatever be its
value as a working conception, no philosopher who aims at a final
interpretation could accept.[1]

For all this, the contemporary positivist has called attention
anew to a problem that has haunted metaphysics ever since
Descartes looked for the ground of certainty within the mind
and then found difficulty in justifying belief in an external world.
As we now see it, the problem is how to justify belief in propositions which we cannot completely verify, as we can verify propositions regarding our own experience. It comes to a focus with
regard to the simplest of all "metaphysical" propositions, that
which affirms the existence of centers of experience other than
oneself.[2] The logical status of this proposition is different from
that of predictive propositions concerning events in one's own
future experience because, whereas the latter can eventually be
verified in detail by confrontation with the experiences foretold,
the former cannot be verified thus. How significant this simple
proposition is we have noted. I should maintain, indeed, that
the credibility of all speculative philosophy is no different in kind

1 Among the many discussions of logical positivism see especially Rudolf
Carnap's *Logical Syntax of Language* (London and New York: The Macmillan Co., 1937) ; "Testability and Meaning," *Philosophy of Science*, III
(1939) , No. 4, and IV (1940) , No. 1; and the Psyche Miniature, *Philosophy
and Logical Syntax* (London: K. Paul, Trench, Trubner and Co., 1935) . An
article by L. J. Russell, "Communication and Verification, II," *Proceedings
of the Aristotelian Society*, Supplementary Vol. XIII (1934): 174–193, is of
crucial importance.

2 Compare the discussion by C. I. Lewis in "Experience and Meaning,"
from which I quote the following: "The conception of other selves as metaphysical ultimates exemplifies the philosophical importance that may attach
to a supposition which is nevertheless unverifiable on account of the limitations of knowledge" (*Philosophical Review*, VII [2] : 146).

from that of this banal belief.   If we can show the reasonableness of the one, we can show the reasonableness of the other; but to do so will require of us that we consider certain phases of the general problem of knowledge.   Here in this first chapter we shall do no more than offer a sketch of fundamental theory, leaving to the following pages all matters of detail.

The instrument of knowledge is the concept.   Efforts have been made in recent times to substitute the sentence for the concept; but since the same "knowledge" may be expressed through different sentences, German, French, or English, it is clear that there must be something that remains the same through translation from a sentence in English to one in French or German: now that which remains the same through translation is the concept, or meaning of the sentence.[1]   Or to put the matter differently: to be language a sentence must be "understood"; the concept or meaning of a sentence is the difference between the sentence understood and the sentence when it is not understood.   It is true that in certain stages of an investigation every element of a symbolic process need not be understood—as in the use of calculating machines or shorthand mathematical devices—but for knowledge to exist, the first and the last steps must be understood: the mechanical process or symbolic device must be put to a definite use, which requires understanding; and the result of its use, the final interpretation, is also a matter of understanding. If we were constantly in the presence of the objects to which our sentences are applied, they might be used without any meaning; we could set up one–one relations between the sentences and the objects; the relations would then be the meanings.   But since we are not always in the presence of the objects to which we apply our sentences, the meaning must be something embodied in the sentence which is neither the object nor the sentence, something as it were *between* the sentence and that to which the sentence is applied.

The assertion that all knowledge is borne by the concept is opposed to the familiar view that there are two kinds of knowl-

---

[1] I owe this definition of the meaning of the sentence to my colleague, Professor C. H. Langford.   Of course for limited purposes sentences with the same meaning, when they are defined as equivalent, may be substituted for the meaning.

edge—knowledge by description, or conceptual knowledge, and knowledge by acquaintance, or intuition.[1]   It is said that when I smell the odor of saffron or experience a sharp pain, I am knowing "sensa" by acquaintance; or it is sometimes said that I have an intuition of myself as an enduring object, and that knowledge of this kind is a very different sort of thing from the knowledge of saffron that one might have who had never smelled it, derived from a mere description of it, or of myself in comparison with the knowledge that another person has of me derived from what I might tell him of myself.   But this will not do.   Saffron and pain are not known merely by being factors in the totality of given experience; they are not known until some concept is applied to them; they must at least be recognized as odor or as pain, and then the knowledge of them is borne by the *concepts* "odor" and "pain."   Even the knowledge that I have of myself is conceptual knowledge: it is borne by a whole complex of concepts which form the connotation of my name when I apply it to myself.   Experience becomes knowledge only through conceptual interpretation.   The differentia of intuition is not the absence of the concept, but the presence along with it of that to which the concept is applied.   Intuitive knowledge seems to be the most certain of all knowledge because it is instantly confirmed and because the presence of the object shuts off, while it is there, the possibility of error.   On the other hand, it must not be overlooked that objects may be present and yet not be known because no concepts are available at the time through which they can be known.   Our impulses and feelings are always with us, and man's generic nature and the metaphysical structure of the world are ever at hand, yet they are still incompletely known to us for this reason.

Many philosophers have thought that intuitive knowledge is not only the most certain, but the only really credible knowledge, and in this regard they approach the views of the positivists. Wishing to rescue the belief in the other self and the physical world, they have striven to show that our knowledge of them is intuitive.   And yet it is certain that our knowledge neither of the physical world nor of the fellow mind is wholly intuitive; it is

[1] Bertrand Russell, *The Problems of Philosophy* (New York: Henry Holt and Co., 1912) , chap. v.

partly descriptive, and partly intuitive. In the case of the physical world we shall try to show that its given sensuous "surface" belongs at once to the mind of the perceiver and to the thing, and that the forces issuing from the "external" reality play through this surface within the mind itself. The mind is not, as conceived by some philosophers, cut off from the world in which it lies, but is in contact with it, so that, with regard to the immediate environment, our concepts can confront what they know. Yet it is clear that we never confront the whole of any physical thing, however neighborly, but only surfaces here and there at a time; we have to build up constructively a plan of the whole. We are in the situation of a visitor in a vast cathedral: he cannot see the whole at once, but now the façade, now the towers, now the nave or the choir; it is a work of imagination, not of vision, to picture the whole. The matter is not notably different in the case of our knowledge of our fellow men. Through our contact with their bodies we are also in contact with the forces of control exerted by their minds over their bodies. When you wrestle with a man you apprehend directly the pressure of his will against your own; or in the embrace of the beloved you feel a will concrescent with your own. And when you communicate with a fellow being the universal "minimum" meanings are the same in his mind and in yours. But there the contact ends; the rest is interpretation. Unless this were so it would be impossible to understand how constantly mistaken our judgments of another mind are.

That there is a nonintuitive factor even in science has long been recognized. In prediction, if a concept or description refers to a unique future event, the concept can confront its object once, but never again. Now only a memory of it exists, which tells us that it was. The memory can be confirmed in indirect ways, through records and testimony and by showing its general consistency with other beliefs, but not by confrontation: you cannot confront the nonexistent. Only concepts that refer to repeatable aspects of experience can be confirmed by confrontation; and even such concepts are not at every moment being confronted with their objects, yet at such moments they are believed. The *possibility* of confirming these concepts by confrontation—the inductive principle—cannot itself be instantly confirmed by confrontation. And nothing in the realm of historical knowledge, since it has to do with what is both unique and nonexistent, can be confirmed by confrontation.

There is, therefore, an ineradicable speculative element in all knowledge, not distinctively in metaphysics. Ideas function unconfronted and unconfrontable with their objects. The skeptic uses this fact to impugn the credibility of all knowledge and especially of metaphysical knowledge; or else, recognizing the necessities of life, takes refuge in some form of voluntaristic "escapist" theory—the "will to believe," the "as-if," "animal," or religious faith. But this skepticism is without foundation, and the refuge, therefore, without excuse. It would have reason if the mind were separate from its environment, or if ideas were factitious entities generated from within by the mind alone. But the foundation is cut away from all such forms of skepticism by our intuition of the mind's contact with its world and the coöperation of the world with the mind in the formation of concepts. There are no purely factitious concepts. When the subjective factor of selection in accordance with interest is allowed for, the concept is revealed as the effect, the child of the object. We can easily see how this is so in the case of knowledge of our own experiences, where the concept is obviously the product of the primary experiences which it recognizes and knows. The concept "red" is the product of our experiences of red things. The concept of an enduring ego is the echo, as we shall show, of the actual identical self. And even when we do not have complete intuition of the object, an elephant, for example, our knowledge is the product of our elephant experiences, as controlled in us by the elephant himself, and when we recognize an elephant as an elephant, we are describing him by his own products. The concept of the other self is constructed after the analogy of our personal experience, but under the directly felt pressure exerted by the other self. The facial expressions, actions seen, and words heard, on the basis of which we form our conception of what is going on in the mind of another person, are caused by that person. All communication between two minds occurs in this way. If a man says to me, "I am hurt," I construct the judgment, He is hurt, as a consequence of his very intention to let me know his distress. In order to confirm them, we do not need to confront our concepts of the experience of the other self with his experience, for the other self has produced them in us. Now all knowledge is a "communication" between reality and the mind, an offspring of their interaction. Our necessary beliefs—in the fellow mind, the physical world, the order of space, the stability of nature, the Eternal—are of this sort. The final justification of these beliefs is our experience of the world building up its own image in our minds.

It is true that this image usually comes to us woefully distorted, and we cannot be too critical in our realism. Nevertheless, every concept offers some knowledge, because of its very derivation, and has a prima-facie claim on our acceptance. Even fictitious concepts and absurd combinations of concepts contain some knowledge. There is knowledge of human nature in Becky Sharp, and of the structure of a woman and of a fish in a mermaid. Even false judgments are not wholly false, for when the predicate concept is wrong, there is some truth in the subject concept; unless this were so the reference of the predicate would be unintelligible. And every false concept contains some knowledge of the general facts of the world. If I say, The house is red, and that is wrong because the house is blue, nevertheless the following items of knowledge at least are embodied in my judgment: first, knowledge implied from the fact that the subject concept, "house," is true; second, knowledge that although the concept "red" is false, the house has some color; third, deeper, metaphysical items of knowledge, of space and causality.

Another recent type of antimetaphysical theory is behaviorism, or, as it is being called in Europe, "physicalism," [1] according to which knowledge is concerned solely with behavior. The theory may take two forms, one recognizing specific and irreducible types and levels of behavior, the other recognizing only one type, that studied by the physicist, to which all seemingly different types are supposed to be reducible; the latter makes physics the sole comprehensive science. We are not now concerned with the differences between the two schools, but only with the general point of view. In Europe the theory appears to have come as a reaction against the epistemological solipsism of the earlier logical positivists. It was perceived that for science the trained perceptions of any individual are as good as those of any other, and that a reliable recording instrument is as good as the perception or memory of a human being. We may in fact treat the human

<hr/>

[1] Cf. O. Neurath, "Physikalismus," *Scientia*, L (1931) : 297–303.

organism as a physical instrument and science, reduced to a set of symbols, as a physical process going on in the organism. As a corrective of epistemological solipsism, this theory—which is only the twentieth-century version of the eighteenth-century slogan *l'homme machine*—is useful, but as philosophy it is absurd. For philosophy cannot ignore any aspect of reality; it cannot ignore itself as a system of conscious meanings and emotions, created by philosophers, who cannot treat themselves—or their companions—as mere behaving mechanisms. If the philosopher cannot ignore his own feelings he cannot ignore the feelings lodged in other organisms. If it be iterated that of other organisms and of the physical world we know only behavior, that we know nothing of the feelings supposed to lie behind, we are brought back again to the question of what knowing is. And if we recall that each investigator knows his own behavior, and a fortiori the behavior of other organisms and physical things only by way of patterns of sensa of his own, we find ourselves involved in the epistemological problems we have been studying; and if we ignore the results just reached, we are back in epistemological solipsism, with the "Viennese circle" complete. However, although behaviorism cannot be philosophy, it finds a place within philosophy, because for each center of experience any other center fills a spatiotemporal shape—that is to say, is a behavior pattern. But to suppose that the abstract behavior pattern is all there is, or that because physics limits itself to the study of this pattern all science must so limit itself, is the sheerest error. Alongside behavioristically oriented psychology and sociology is needed an interpretation of behavior in terms of motives and ends; alongside exact quantitative studies in biology, the natural history of plants and animals, for which a plant or an animal is no mere behavior pattern but a concretely enduring and developing existence. And alongside these are needed history, biography, memory, art, and philosophy, to clothe the skeleton of behavior with the life of experience.

The result of these reflections is to put the epistemological burden upon ideas and at the same time to reëstablish their credibility. This credibility is especially great precisely where it has been called in question, namely in metaphysics. For particularly with regard to the analytic part of metaphysics, since the subject matter is the universal aspects of experience, the object of knowledge is always present, and our ideas of it may therefore be verified at any time. The idea and the object are always capable of being confronted with each other, and any defects may be corrected. The idea can conjugate with its object and receive from it life and refreshment. Hasty ideas, appealing dogmas taken uncritically from tradition, prejudices devised to serve some ulterior end of desire, can be revised into accuracy. For example, in order to possess a good notion of time it is not necessary, as is so often the case in science, to hunt for the object in some hidden recess of reality, for the object is given in any happening, in any example of coming to be and passing away. And even with regard to the speculative, synthetic task of metaphysics, the materials upon which construction is based are all empirical and accessible. For the theory of space, of the order of time and causality, and of the Eternal, we need assume nothing besides other centers of experience, generically similar to ourselves. The world of cosmology is the social situation, magnificently enlarged.

Metaphysical knowledge has the same general character as other knowledge. Aristotle has put the mystery of knowledge finely in a passage of the *De Memoria:*

. . . when one remembers, is it the impressed affection that he remembers, or is it the objective thing from which the impression was derived? If the memory image, it would follow that we remember nothing which is absent; if the objective thing, how is it possible that, though perceiving directly only the impression, we remember that absent thing which we do not perceive? Granted that there is in us something like an impression or picture, why should the perception of the mere impression be memory of something else, instead of being related to this impression alone? For when one actually remembers, this impression is what one perceives. How then does he remember what is not present? One might as well suppose it were possible to see or hear that which is not present. In reply we suggest that this very thing is quite conceivable, nay actually occurs in experience. A picture painted on a panel is at once a picture and a likeness: that is, while one and the same it is both of these, although the being of both is not the same, and one may contemplate it either as a picture or a likeness. Just in the same way we have to conceive that the mnemonic presentation within us is something which by itself is merely an object of contemplation, while in relation to something else, it is also a presentation of that other thing. In so far as it is regarded in itself, it is only an object of contemplation, or a presentation,—but when considered as relative to something else, for example as its likeness, it is also a mnemonic token.[1]

[1] Aristotle *De Memoria* 450*b*, in *The Works of Aristotle Translated into English*, ed. by J. A. Smith and W. D. Ross (Oxford: At the Clarendon Press, 1931), Vol. III.

The mystery is how through an idea present in the mind information may be conveyed about something not in the mind. Now notice that Aristotle does little more than tell us that the mystery is fact. We may take the image as a likeness; when we do so it is knowledge. The taking of it as a likeness is the fact of knowledge. There is no explaining away or getting around this fact. You cannot reduce knowledge to any other sort of fact; you can distinguish its components and you can exhibit its relations, but, even so, its specificity will remain. Aristotle is, of course, thinking in terms of the primitive seal-and-wax, effluvium, or image theory of knowledge, according to which the instrument of knowledge is a sort of peeling or skin which the object gives off and the sense organs receive. He sees that a mere image or skin of an object does not make knowledge; the imprint on the wax does not know what impressed it; a picture does not know its original. Knowledge occurs only when the mind uses the impression as a picture. Today we no longer conceive of knowledge in terms of pictures but in terms of concepts, although everyone would grant that pictures have their use in knowledge, whether they are plans, diagrams, mechanical or other models, or photographs, moving or static. The concept is not a picture but an anticipation of a character or essence. If I judge, The earth is round, I do not necessarily have in mind a circle or a globe, but I am prepared to find or to construct something either in sensuous or imaginal material that will illustrate the elements of the system of relations embodied in either. The concept need not itself embody the character which it ascribes to the object: the concept "round" is not round; but it does involve knowing how to get before the mind the character ascribed, the term "knowing how" being used in the same sense as when I say that I "know how" to swim or walk. And even as knowing how to swim does not involve swimming all the time, so to have knowledge does not involve a continual contacting of a character, but only the consciousness of being able to do so. To know a thing is, therefore, to be prepared to confront the essence predicated of the thing; it is virtual contact with the essence, readiness to experience the like of what is ascribed to the object. The concept is a pointer or signpost showing the way. The significance for knowledge of models and pictures is that they provide means through which the characters predicated of the object may be contacted; but of these pictures we use only what we need, only the relevant characters: from the rest we abstract. A system of concepts is a set of directions on how to get a foretaste, the very tang, of reality. The reality may be remote from us, yet knowledge puts us in the way of experiencing its like. The judgment says, The object is such as this, where by "this" is meant an experience in which is embodied the essence ascribed to the object. The *this* is the base of the concept.

Since metaphysical knowledge has the same general character as all knowledge, the difficulties that beset it—the theme of so much discussion through the ages—are partly difficulties that attend upon knowledge of any kind. Of this sort is the problem of the time locus of the object of knowledge. If the ideas of some philosophers are correct the only objects to which we can refer our concepts are either past or future, and since neither the past nor the future exists, we seem faced with the unwelcome conclusion that we never know reality. In Whitehead's system, where the "actual occasions," which are the sole realities (exception being made of God), are perpetually perishing, we can refer only to the settled world of the past; for the pragmatists, who think of knowledge in terms of practical action, which is always veered to the future, the object of knowledge lies in the future. And it must be admitted that a large part of what we know and talk about lies in the past or the future. The pragmatic analysis of everyday propositions of a certain type has proved this with regard to the future. If I judge that my house is brown, what I am really saying is that it will be brown for any normal eye; or if I say that so-and-so loves me I am saying that she will perform gracious deeds for me when I ask her, and feel kindly toward me when she thinks of me: I am not saying that she *is* performing such deeds or having such feelings. Usually when I ascribe a predicate to a "thing," I am referring to the thing as it will behave in the future—"is" is equivalent to "will be." And this is so not merely because I am more interested in the future than in the present, but rather because there is no reason to suppose that the "thing" has these predicates now. Very often, on the other hand, propositions which seem to ascribe predicates to the present are in fact historical. I make an observation: I say, perhaps, It is snowing, but all that I am justified in saying is, It was snowing, for since there was a time interval between the event of snowing and my perception of the snowing, it may have ceased snowing when the "message" from the snow reached me; and in any case, what I actually perceived was merely a past phase of the process of snowing. Even when, perhaps verifying a prediction, I am observing elements of my own experience, their rapid evanescence makes false or makes historical the most certain judgments I can utter. I say, Here is cold, when lo! that cold sensation has vanished. In the end, owing to "all-devouring time," most of the propositions I think I am asserting about the present, about reality, are true only of the past. The solid world thus seems to slip under our feet.

An adequate philosophy will, however, exhibit a way out of these difficulties. For—to begin with the seemingly historical character of much of our knowledge—it will demonstrate that even when our knowledge is frankly and explicitly historical, we are knowing the present in knowing the past. It will show that every event leaves its echo in the present, and through this echo belongs to reality forever. The world is a vast self-recording mechanism generating out of the Heracleitean flux an eternal basis for historical truth. Mussolini's march on Rome has disappeared, but its echoes are held undying in the structure of the world. The historian can know of the march only because he has first known its echoes. The historical judgment is not itself about these echoes, but a knowledge of them is its basis; it looks through them, as it were, to the historical fact that caused them. Crusoe must first see the living footprint in the sand before he can know that a man has walked there; and his memories in the present are his witnesses of the past that vanished with the shipwreck. So when I judge that it is snowing I make the judgment looking through the echoes of the physical process, the white and shiny sensa in my mind. Always when I am knowing the past I am knowing the present too. This present will vanish, it is true; the memories will fade; the snows of today will become the snows of yesteryear; yet a new present is always born of the old one, conserving something out of the past; and amidst the quicksands of experience the self that is spectator of its flux cannot slip away with it. There is no substance apart from experience, but there is, we shall prove, substance within it.

With regard to propositions about the future it can be shown that they, also, presuppose as their basis a present enduring reality. For it will be noticed that they are all conditional and therefore only probable. The proposition, The house is brown, becomes, as we have seen, The house will be brown; but this is true only if I can see, and if . . . and if . . . . The proposition is therefore not certainly true, hence must read, The house will probably be brown. But why even probably? What ground have I for asserting that it will probably be brown? Of course it was often brown before, brown whenever, in fact, I saw it; but that cannot be the meaning of the proposition; for if so it would be a pure historical proposition equivalent to, The house was often brown. And I cannot get out of, The house was often brown, the proposition, The house will probably be brown. Only if there are in nature permanent tendencies or forces making for its brownness can I assert that it will probably be brown. The very meaning of "probably," we shall see, is that such forces exist. Whoever claims that he has knowledge of the future claims, therefore, that he has knowledge of the present. Apart from knowledge of the present, there is no prophecy, even as there is no history. The flux of events is deployed against the background of an enduring matrix, the acknowledgment of which is the forgotten premise of propositions concerning past and future.

Special difficulties, however, stand in the way of any attempt to characterize this matrix of reality. We can, to be sure, always characterize it negatively. This was well understood by Plotinus [1] and the Christian philosophers,[2] who believed that only negative propositions are wholly true of the supreme reality. Something exists, something is here and now, which at the least prevents us from saying certain things about it. This holds even with regard to the situations of ordinary experience. I may find it difficult adequately to characterize a classroom scene before me, but at least I can say of it that it is not a wedding, not a funeral, not a circus. And much of metaphysics must consist in determining what we shall not say about reality. So to us it is clear that we should not say that it is changeless, or indifferent to value, or composed of "neutral stuff." And if metaphysics could do nothing else, that would be a great deal. But it would hardly be enough. One important difficulty is the seeming indeterminateness of reality in contrast to the determinateness of our con-

[1] *Fifth Ennead* V, 6, 10–15.
[2] See, for example, Dionysius, *De divinis nominibus, passim.*

cepts: the fact that reality, although it excludes a concept within a range of concepts, sometimes does not permit us to decide, of the remainder, which should be applied. I may know that this thing is not inorganic, but may not know whether it is plant or animal; I may know that it is not red or yellow, but not whether it is green or blue. I may not even be able to determine as between two contradictories which should be applied—whether, for example, this man is bald or not bald, boy or not boy, or whether this electron is here or not here. Interesting as this limitation is for the general theory of knowledge, it is, however, not equally a difficulty for metaphysics; for although I may be left in doubt as between specific concepts, I am not left in doubt regarding the underlying generic concepts with which metaphysics is concerned. Any indeterminateness of experience is a surface phenomenon overlying a basic generic determinateness.[1] For even though I do not know whether this thing is plant or animal, I do know that it is alive; if I do not know whether it is green or blue, I do know that it is colored; and if I do not know whether this man is bald or not bald, I do know that he has a head. Since the difference between genus and species is relative, except at the extremes, the difficulty may, of course, break out afresh at a deeper level: as when I do not know whether a certain object is living or not living, or whether it has color or not; nevertheless, when I reach the deepest stratum of genera—the metaphysical stratum—I am below alternatives, I have arrived at certainty. For whether living or not living, this thing is at least material, and whether colored or not, it has quality; whether man or boy, it is changing; whether here or not here, it is within a certain volume. We may, indeed, use this circumstance as a definition of metaphysical concepts.

Other difficulties attaching to the positive characterization of reality have often been cited, in our own time notably by Bergson and Bradley. I wish to call attention to two that have a special interest and relevance for us. They arise from opposed defects in our concepts: the too great concreteness of some, the insufficient concreteness of others. As an illustration of the former I would cite the following circumstance. There is truth in saying that reality is spatial, but not that it has, as a whole, the spread-

[1] It follows that, although what I confront is always individual, I am more certain of its generic than of its specific characters.

outness, the extendedness characteristic of shapes in the visual fields of human beings; it is doubtless also true that the physical earth is round, but it does not follow that the earth looks like a ball, even though its shadow on the moon does look so for any eye that can see. The mathematical and metaphysical meanings of extension and roundness carry no such implications, and these are the only ones valid in this case, as we shall show. Although given experience is their base, we cannot always use its full concreteness in our concepts. Even our critical realists are not critical enough, by reason of their acceptance of unduly concrete concepts taken over unscrutinized from common sense and popular science for the description of the physical world. It will become one of our tasks to purge such concepts of their irrelevant concreteness, leading us into a *more critical realism,* that will end in a kind of spiritualism.

If some concepts are too concrete for the use that is made of them, there are others that are not concrete enough. For the descripion of the final units of reality we need the most concrete of all concepts, concepts of personality and society, which alone are capable of introducing us to the full individuality of existence, with its unity of stability and change. How any concepts can do this has been a problem for certain philosophers who have thought of the concept as existing separate from the things it means and made of different stuff; but for the philosophy that I am expressing, one which keeps the concept tied to its base in experience, this difficulty has no weight. Consider the question as to how the concept can be referred to this rather than to that object when, as indicating a character unavoidably general, it is potentially applicable indifferently to any one of numberless objects which it might describe. This problem would not exist if reality were a disjunction of Platonic Ideas or Universals, for knowledge would then be the simple intuition of these Ideas through concepts referring directly and unequivocably to one or a group of them. But if reality consists of individuals any one of a class of which may embody a given character, the problem stands. Or again, if the object of knowledge were no other than the given, the problem would not exist, for then every judgment would have the form, This is so-and-so, "this" indicating directly some item of given experience; but since in knowledge we are often referring to objects that are not given, wholly or in part, the problem remains once more. The avoidance of the problem depends upon noticing that the *this,* the given, is always an element in the object of knowledge, however transcendent, to which a concept is applied, and through this relation to the given, its individuality is captured. Thus if I apply the concept "John," the concept, taken by itself, might refer to any man who is called "John," but when I use it, it means "the one and only one entity that controls these and these sensa of mine" (facial appearance, sound of voice, touch of hand, and the like). And you can understand who the individual is to whom I refer because you mean by "John" the one and only one entity that controls, not only such and such given sensa of mine, but also such and such sensa, the same in kind, of yours. Even so, if I use the metaphysical concept "world" or "universe," it is not any whole of reality in general to which I refer, but my world, the world that includes me, stretching out from me as a given center, possessed therefore of an equal concreteness and uniqueness. In ordinary discourse we are apt to omit explicit reference to the connection with the given, but this connection is always implied. In metaphysics the connection of all discourse with the given is made explicit. If, therefore, the stuff of all reality is such as this given experience, then our concepts will suffice not only to express its individuality, but faithfully to provide a foretaste of its generic characters. For, being items in this experience, our concepts have the generic characters of all experience, and metaphysical concepts which mean precisely such characters will themselves have the characters that they mean. Philosophers who make an issue out of the supposed contrast between the changefulness of reality and the rigidity of concepts forget this. The very concept "change" itself possesses the changefulness to which it refers. The concept in use possesses the life, plasticity, and resilience of reality itself.

These considerations enable us to reject a final criticism of the claims of metaphysics. It is often objected that, no matter how far the generality of philosophical concepts may reach, there may yet be realms of being unknown to us, possessed of very different characters from any of which we are aware or could be aware. "There are more things in heaven and earth, Horatio, than are dreamt of in your philosophy." But—while accepting the admonition to humility—we must remind the critic that in metaphysics we are not concerned with any unknowable or vaguely possible world, but with our own world. The absolute generality claimed for metaphysics is an absoluteness relative to ourselves. We seek the universal form of our own or knowable world. And it is difficult to see how any part of the still unknown world could ever become known to us unless it had the most general characters of the known world. For we could know it only through our own concepts, which would direct us to construct its like in our experience; therefore, if we could not do this, we could not know it. Or if in coming into our world, the hitherto unknown reality completely transformed our experience, there would no longer be any we to greet it and hail it as ours.

II

Preliminary Description of Some Aspects of Experience

W E HAVE committed ourselves to a metaphysical philosophy that shall be more empirical than common sense or science through a franker, more consistent, and rigorous acceptance of experience as the basis for interpretation. But in so doing we have not established a genuine starting point. The example of the classical empirical philosophies of Locke, Berkeley, and Hume, or the subsequent example set by the Mills, James, Mach, Bergson, and Whitehead, should warn us that experience, although the basis, is not the starting point of a philosophy. For if these thinkers had proceeded from the same data they would have come out with the same results; but how discordant are their conclusions! Discordant because, while they may have thought they were beginning with the same thing, experience, they were actually beginning with descriptions of experience which were very different! In some systems the preliminary description is not explicitly stated and has to be divined from the finished philosophy, but it is always presupposed, and by it the mistakes and the insights are determined. We shall therefore establish our own starting point with a description of some general aspects of experience. This description will not pretend to completeness, but should be viewed as supplemented by all the chapters to follow and especially by those on "Experience as Substance," "Universals and Experience," and "The Temporal Experience."

CENTRICITY

We shall begin by calling attention to a familiar fact with regard to experience which I shall call "centricity"—the fact that experience falls into distinct wholes. This implies, first, that there are items in each whole which do not belong in any other; and from the fact that an item belongs in one it does not follow that it belongs in any other. The joy which is in the whole that I call "you" is not in the whole that I call "me," but sorrow perhaps is there. Or you perhaps are blind but can hear, while I have sight and yet am deaf; then for me exist all the colors of the rainbow, and for you the multitudinous sounds of the Stravinsky ballet, but no sound for me and no color for you. Or you are perhaps a learned geometrician and have knowledge of all the propositions in the First Book of Euclid; while I know not one of these, but do know the dates of the English kings, of which you know few. The distinctness of the wholes of experience does not imply, however, that there may not be items common to two or more wholes. Common to you and to me, for example, are the minimum meanings of the sentences which, when I read aloud to you, we both understand. This may not be evident and doubtless demands discussion, but we shall be content now to enter it here as a fact, to be validated in a subsequent chapter. But what I am calling the centricity of experience does imply, in the second place, that there is no addition operation between wholes of experience; that you cannot put any two together and get a new whole which includes both, as you can add an area to an area or a length to a length and get an area or a length that includes the original areas or lengths. It is not possible to combine the experience of a deaf man who can see with that of a blind man who can hear, and get a new whole of experience capable of both hearing and seeing.[1] Or if one child knows the alphabet from A to K, and another child from K to Z, you cannot put the two children together and get one that knows all his letters! Following Bradley, I shall call the distinct wholes of experience "centers" of experience, and sometimes, without implying all that Leibniz implied when he used the term, I shall call them "monads." We may sum up the facts that I am calling centricity by saying that centers of experience are like circles that are never concentric or co-incident, never lie wholly one within another, but may overlap or be tangential. And from the facts of centricity it is clear that the term "experience" is a general term like "water"; for even as, not *water*, but this pool or this cupful exists, so, not *experience*, but this or that center of experience exists.

[1] Cf. Franz Brentano, *Psychologie vom empirischen Standpunkt* (Leipzig: F. Weiner, 1874) , I, 226, 227.

The usual way of stating the centricity of experience is to say that experience is either mine or yours, that it stands in a peculiar relation to something unique called a "self" or "ego." If this were in fact so, centricity would be the same as egocentricity. But I use the term "centricity" instead of "egocentricity" with intent, for it is not immediately evident that the fact that experience falls into distinct centers of the kind described is the same as the fact that the centers are personal. Whether or not this is the case cannot be decided until we have reached some conclusion as to the nature of the self.

ACTIVITIES AND SENSA

If now we begin to raise the question, What is the self? and remain faithful to the method of empiricism, we can rule out from the start any theory of the self as an existence outside experience. We must, on the contrary, follow the procedure of Hume, as expressed in a famous passage of the *Treatise of Human Nature,* and look for the self within experience. The passage will bear recall once more:

> . . . For my part, when I enter most intimately into what I call myself, I always stumble on some particular perception or other, of heat or cold, light or shade, pain or pleasure; I can never catch myself at any time without a perception, and can never observe anything but the perception. When my perceptions are removed at any time as by sound sleep, so long am I insensible of myself, and may truly be said not to exist. And were all my perceptions removed by death, and could I neither think nor feel nor love nor hate after the dissolution of my body, I should be entirely annihilated, nor do I feel what is further necessary to make a perfect nonentity.[1]

If we examine this passage, and remember that Hume uses the term "perception" in a sense almost, if not quite, identical with the present use of the term "experience," we notice that, in addition to affirming—most explicitly in the last sentence—the empirical thesis with regard to the self, Hume begins, in the first sentence, by identifying the self with certain particular perceptions—of heat or cold, light or shade, pain or pleasure. But this identification is certainly an error: the self cannot be identified with such elements as these. It is true that on a summer's day I may *say* that I am hot, or on a winter's day that I am cold—

---

[1] David Hume, *Treatise of Human Nature,* Part IV, Sec. 6; ed. by T. H. Green and T. H. Grose (London: Longmans, Green and Co., 1898), I, 534.

hardly, however, that I am light or shade—but I cannot *mean* that hotness and coldness are myself, any more than that I am green or yellow, loud or soft, round or square. It is, to be sure, true that when I say that I am hot or cold, there is a very intimate connection between myself and heat or cold; but the heat and cold are not myself. As for pain or pleasure, if by them Hume meant sensations—by pain the specific sensations that come to us by way of pain spots in the skin, and by pleasure any sensation that is pleasurable—I should say regarding them what I have said regarding heat and cold, light and shade; but if, on the contrary, he meant by pain a frustrated impulse, and by pleasure an impulse that is being appeased, that is a different matter, which leads us directly to an interesting observation on this same passage from the *Treatise*.

It is notable, namely, that in the last sentence quoted Hume identifies himself with a new set of experiences—thinking, feeling, loving, hating—which elsewhere he has called "impressions of reflection" and contrasted with other items, which he calls "impressions of sensation," such as the heat and cold, light and shade mentioned first in the quoted passage. Hume makes the mistake of identifying the self with the latter class of impressions, and then—so at least it seems—corrects himself and makes the identification, this time properly, with the former class.[1] For although I am certainly not the light or shade, heat or cold, or (we may add) sweet or bitter taste, loud or soft sound, or the like, which may be present as items of my experience, I am just as certainly the love or the hate, the thought or the feeling that is there. My mind or consciousness, my total field of experience, includes items of both kinds; but the self, whose mind this is, is not made up of sensa, but of what Hume called "impressions of reflection," and which we shall term "activities." If we enter most intimately into what we call ourselves, we do find that apart from the activities there is no self. All that we mean by the self is covered by them. Take away our thoughts,

---

[1] Hume made the further mistake of regarding "impressions of reflection" (our "activities") as secondary to "impressions of sensation." See the whole discussion in Hume, *op. cit.*, Part I, Sec. 11. My distinction between activities and sensa corresponds, of course, to Berkeley's distinction between ideas and notions. See George Berkeley, *The Principles of Human Knowledge* (1711), Sec. 1.

our feelings, our loves, and our hates, and there is no least part of us left.

In the life of any center the activities are seemingly number-less and of most various kinds. They are, nevertheless, capable of classification, and, following closely, although not adopting, a well-known tripartite division, I shall propose a classification of the activities into what I shall call "expressions," "concepts," and "volitions." [1] Some illustration and explanation of each type will throw light on the general nature of experience.

First let us consider expression, or the giving of meaning—language or symbolism in its many forms. I am myself when I talk or read, when I create a work of art or appreciate one. That meanings do not belong of their own right to whatever possesses them, but are given, and given by someone, is evident. The symbol has meaning only for me or for you or for us, and as used by me, or you, or us. Apart from its use a word is nothing but a color or sound pattern, the flag of our country, a piece of bunting blowing in the breeze, the decoration, a bit of cloth on the lapel of a man's coat. The meaning may seem to lie in the word, as if it belonged there, but that is illusion; it is there because someone has put it there. The concept "two" may seem incarnate in the word "two," but someone had to devise the second as a symbol of the first, and I had to learn to use and recognize it as such. When we think of symbolism we usually have in mind language in the ordinary sense, but per-ception is an equally important example. For perception is the activity of giving "thing" meanings to sensa, which then become symbols of those meanings: a certain pattern of color and line means a man; another pattern means a rose. Perception is, as Berkeley called it, a natural language, with ordinary sensa taking the place of words. In themselves these sensa have no mean-ings: a pattern of light is just a pattern of light; a colored oval is just a colored oval; the one is not a planet or the other a flower. It is we who give them their meanings. By reason of symbolism experience is forever transcending itself. There is no item, no

[1] The division to which I refer is Brentano's. Compare also Benedetto Croce's classification of the "forms of the spirit," in his *Aesthetic as Science of Expression and General Linguistic*, tr. by Douglas Ainslie, Second Edition (London: Macmillan and Co., 1929), chaps vi–vii.

least shred of sensation, that is not made symbolic of something beyond its own immediacy. The activity of language is everywhere; a sensation or image without meaning is a fiction of analysis. And since every symbol not only means what it means (its primary meaning), but carries the implication of having a meaning for you as well as for me, the experience of each center is lived as a center among other centers—a one among many.

A second type of activity is conception. In the first chapter conception was considered in its dependence on its object; I wish now to consider briefly its other, subjective, side—conception as an activity of the self. The activity involved in conception shows up most clearly in the attitudes, which are always personal, of belief, disbelief, or make-believe that accompany it. A concept is never a mere picture on a panel, but a live thing which someone makes and uses for a purpose. Basically every concept is a mode of belief, a judgment saying: There are things of such and such a character. "Blue" says: There are blue things; "God" says: There is an eternal being; "moon" says: There exists an entity which controls this disk that I see in the sky. The concept is at once a description and an affirmation of existence. Its effect is to enlarge experience vicariously by presenting absent existences as if they were here and past ones as if they were present. When, for example, I read a book of history or oceanography the strange cities and peoples described or the colorful forms of life on the bed of the sea seem to be now before my eyes. But because of the repeated failure of concepts to prove true, and their free multiplication beyond the necessities of use for their sheer appeal to desire (imagination), conception must be distinguished from what is ordinarily called "judgment," which is really "second" judgment, in contrast to which conception is "first" judgment and by which it is critically affirmed or denied as true or false. A proposition, as distinguished from a judgment, is a universal or essence, the single "what" or content affirmed or denied, which may be the same in the many acts of judgment of one or several persons. Make-believe is a peculiar attitude toward concepts, characteristic of play and art, a species of disbelief "willingly suspended" in favor of the original attitude of belief, by reason of which, although rejected for not presenting reality, concepts may yet arouse in

us the emotions appropriate to reality.[1] The cat does not believe in the wooden mouse or the child in the china baby, yet
to the cat the spool is as if it were a mouse and to the child the
doll is as if it were a baby, and both cat and child enjoy themselves
accordingly. And while the spectator does not critically accept
the actor Forbes-Robertson as Hamlet, the actor is as if he were
Hamlet and so moves to pity and fear. Even ordinary perception becomes for the sophisticated person a kind of play or art,
for the objects of naïve belief—the house, the tree, the mountain
seen—retain their original feeling of reality long after they have
been rejected by scientific or metaphysical criticism.

A third type of activity belonging to the self is volition.
Volition is the guidance of experience from within. It is I who
express myself and judge, but also I who control experience in
eating and drinking, buying and selling, dreaming and playing.
The most elementary form of guidance is impulse; when developed this becomes deliberate, an intention pointed toward a pre-
conceived goal, and the goals of different impulses become elements in a total plan. Volition fulfils itself in two ways: either
through action, which is the process of realizing a goal in sense
experience involving control over the real things of the environment; or, vicariously, through mere concepts of action and
images of objects freely created in dream, play, and art (for example, the dream image, the doll, the statue). The fulfilment
of volition is value; its frustration is evil. "Volition" corresponds to Plato's "*eros*," Schopenhauer's "will," Brentano's "Love
and Hate," Bergson's "*élan vital*," Freud's "*libido*" or "wish";
"instinct," "habit," "desire," "interest," "sentiment," "reaction
tendency" also denote it or its manifestations. What is ordinarily called feeling, including pleasure and emotion, are phases
of volition. The difference between mere wish and desire fulfilling itself in action is not intrinsic to either, but is due to the
failure in the case of the wish to secure the coöperation of forces
external to the body necessary for action.

Although the activities may be classified in the three ways
indicated it would be a mistake to suppose that they are independent or exist in a pure state. The fact is that every unit of

[1] For further discussion of make-believe, or the "as-if" attitude, see my
Human Values (New York and London: Harper and Brothers, 1931),
chap. xiv.

action involves all three types at once; we call an action one of conception or volition or expression according to the dominance of one or another of the types, or according to our interest. Thus talking illustrates action that is at once expression, as giving meaning to word sounds, conception, as an expression of opinions, and volition, as fulfilling an interest. Eating illustrates volition since it is guided by an impulse due to hunger, conception since it involves the judgment on the food presented that it is good to eat, and symbolism in so far as the colored, odorous shapes perceived signify food. Moreover, one kind of activity may be foundational for another. Since expression is either of feelings or concepts or both, volition and conception are foundational for it. The relation between volition and conception is complicated. On the one hand, it is certain that conception is foundational for the usual forms of volition. Thus the simple voluntary action of eating bread involves the thing concept "bread" and the objective or goal concept "that I shall eat bread," the realization of which yields the satisfaction or the value in the process. The situation in higher forms of volition involving choice is similar to that which exists in "second" judgment, only in place of alternative concepts to be accepted or rejected as showing forth reality, there are alternative thing meanings and objectives to be selected for action, each with its "call" issuing from desire. Since, therefore, desire is always *for* some sort of action on some sort of object and choice is always between actions or objects, it would seem clear that desire and choice cannot exist independently of conceptions of objects to be acted on and goals to be pursued. Nevertheless there are acts of volition that appear not to involve concepts—the most rudimentary impulses and also curious manifestations associated with high mental development: objectless hate and love, desire for we know not what, elation and depression unformulated. The existence of such volitions independent of concepts proves that conception is not essentially foundational for volition. Not only is this the case, but there are reasons for believing that even when volition stands above conception, in articulate desire and action, it also stands below as a basis for conception. There are reasons for believing that all acts are acts of volition.

The reasons for this belief are as follows. First, there can be no doubt of the fact in the realm of imagination—in dream, play,

and art. For in that realm we both conceive what we want to
conceive and believe or make believe what we wish. The daydream is a series of object- and event-meanings and make-believe
attitudes, all determined by some obvious love wish or wish
of ambition, or sometimes by a recreational wish, as when
the tired workman daydreams that he is home smoking his pipe;
in the night dream the determination by desire is equally certain,
only there the desires are disguised or repressed; in art, say in a
novel, what we shall imagine, what concepts we shall accept as
if they were true, are determined by the creative wish of the
artist; in play the wax image means a baby, because, in the end,
the child wishes so to mean and make believe. Outside the
realm of imagination, however, the prima_y of volition may seem
to be more difficult to establish, first, because, while the attitude
within imagination is make-believe, freely taken for the sake of
some value, the attitude outside imagination is belief or disbelief which seems to be forced upon us by evidence whether we
wish to take it or not, as when, unwillingly, we come to accept
bad news; and secondly because, while in the case of imagination
the sensuous material that functions as symbol for conception is
either image stuff (in a dream) or sensuous stuff, of which the
quality and shape are freely determined (as the colors and lines
of a picture are freely determined by the painter), outside imagination, on the other hand, the symbols are sensa whose quality
and form are determined not by us, but for us (as when I see a
visual shape and it means to me a tree, or hear a sound and it
means to me the ocean). But these considerations are not decisive. For it does not follow that because the quality and form
of a symbol, as in perception, are determined for us, the interpretation of the symbol and the attitude taken toward the interpretation are also determined for us, in independence of desire.
Interpretation and belief are one thing; sense data, however
determined, are another; the latter are given, the former are not
given but made; they are our own act and deed; and the only
question is whether this deed is a free one, a deed expressive of
desire, or whether it is forced upon us against or independent
of desire. That there is constraint laid upon us to mean and to
judge when we interpret given sense data as things and believe
in their existence is a fact emphasized in the first chapter; this
constraint, however, is not the constraint of brute force, but the

constraint of suggestion, of solicitation, almost, one might say, of temptation, to which we consent, because, in the end, we wish to consent. It is a form of docility, not of mechanism or slavery. We make our concepts conform to the evidence, first because in the long run it is to our obvious advantage to do so, since otherwise we perish (the pragmatic reason), and secondly because we have a specific interest that is satisfied in conforming. This interest, whether called "love of truth," the "sentiment of rationality," "docility," or the "reality feeling," is a desire as real as hunger. It is of the essence of sanity, and may be lost in lunacy. It is a phase of sociality, for the love of truth is one with the love of company: the acknowledgment of a world beyond the self is, as we shall see, the acknowledgment of a larger society, and the person who is indifferent to truth is content with a world that is merely his. It is this desire that constrains us to accept a concept as showing reality even when the concept is distasteful. Thus volition, not conception, is established as the basic activity. Through concepts the world builds up its image in our minds, but this occurs only with our coöperation and consent. Conception is volition seeking virtual contact with the surrounding world; true judgment is success and false judgment is failure in this endeavor. The thesis of Schopenhauer and Fichte is thus established—the primacy of will.

While the suggested classification of activities has points of contact with Brentano's, there is one important particular in which it diverges from his. For Brentano, hearing, seeing, smelling, and the like—sensing—are activities, whereas I should agree with most recent writers in holding that there are no such activities. It is true that I *say* that *I* see the color, hear the sound, and so on, and whatever is said about experience deserves the most respectful consideration; but what passes for the supposed activity of sensing is really one or another or all of the activities distinguished—expression, conception, volition—which attend the emergence of a sensum into experience. When I perceive the blue of the sky, the blue means to me the sky, and that is expression; this interpretation I accept, and that is judgment or conception; and I feel its mystic quietness, and that is volition. The presence of the activities along with the sensum is mistaken for a specific activity of sensing. The emergence of the sensum is not itself an activity but an event, even though determined by an activity, as in the case of action. It is equally a mistake to distinguish (as G. E. Moore once did [1]) the consciousness of a sensum from a sensum, if by consciousness be meant something over and above the activities that penetrate the sensum, on its emergence. There is no such thing as pure mind or consciousness. On the other hand, if by consciousness be meant concrete experience, there is a difference between blue, say, and the consciousness of blue, because the "consciousness of blue" means now the whole composed of blue and of the activities that penetrate it, while "blue" means nothing but a quality abstracted from the complex.

Our analysis of experience has issued in a sharp distinction of factors in experience which we are calling activities from other factors commonly called sensa and images. The activities have in common a trait which we can best designate by the very word we use to name them, to wit, "activity." What we mean by "activity" in this connection is so ultimate that we can convey it only by citing examples of items to which it applies and contrasting them with items to which it does not apply. Compare a desire with a color, or believing with a perfume! To point this contrast between activities and sensa we may characterize the latter as "passive." A sensum may seem to be active—red passionate, the scent of violets alluring—but only because certain activities, aroused when the sensum emerges, penetrates it. Red may seem to *demand* green, and orange, blue; the sequence of tones *C–E–G* may seem to demand *C* again; but this seeming activity is also illusory, for red in itself, as pure sensum, does not demand green, or orange, yellow, or any tone in itself any other tone, but only so far as the feeling that penetrates a sensum demands the balancing or completing feeling—the quiet that embraces the blue seeks the complementary feeling that embraces the yellow. Brentano thought that reference to an object was the common and distinctive mark of psychical activities, but this trait belongs to them solely in so far as they are founded on conception. Expressions of mere feeling, such as "alas!" or a musical phrase, have no such reference, nor, as we have seen, have objectless volitions. It is true, however, that by themselves sensa never do refer to objects; they are completely self-contained, being just

---

[1] G. E. Moore, "The Refutation of Idealism," reprinted in *Philosophical Studies* (New York: Harcourt, Brace and Co., 1922), chap. i.

what they are, blue or soft or sweet; they acquire reference only as they are given meaning, when they become blue of sky, soft of bed, sweet of cherry. Of the activities of volition and conception, polarity is a well-known characteristic: positive against negative, acceptance against rejection of concepts in judgment; attraction against repulsion, appeasement against frustration in the case of volition. In the realm of sensa, on the other hand, there is no polarity, except by way of volition and judgment. Yellow and blue, hard and soft, light and dark are polar opposites not in themselves but through contrasting attitudes embodied in them. Seriality, not polarity, belongs to sense qualities: we may have series of pitches of sound, of saturations and intensities of color, and of the like.

Despite the contrast between activities and sensa they are inextricably interwoven—so closely that simple-minded analysts have not seldom mistaken the warp of sensa for the woof of activities. Our desires are always found hugging some image of shape and color, or, when put into action, inwrought with sensa from muscle and tendon; our concepts go not naked, but clothed in symbols visual or auditory or encrusted with images from any department of sense, which give us at times a foretaste of the object meant, as when, meaning *ocean,* we see and hear and taste it through imagery. There are no pure activities; there is no disembodied self. Some sensa seem closer to the self than others, namely, those which accompany specific types of activity—as the sound and feel of a beating heart when one is afraid, or sensations from relaxed muscles when overjoyed, and, in general, most sensations and images referred to the body, since these are constant attendants of elementary actions. This fact accounts for the vulgar belief that the self is the phenomenal body. Seemingly objective and distant on the other 'hand are those sensa whose origin and course are determined in relative independence of the self—the colors and sounds and shapes and smells that we refer to the outer or external world. Tastes, touches, heat and cold, muscle and tendon sensations, and pain appear for the most part more subjective or near. But even the sensa referred to the so-called "external" world are not in the physical sense of the word at a distance from the self, for they too are penetrated by the conceptual activity of recognition and reference to an object and arouse some vague emotions. There are no self-less sensa.

CONTROL AND COUNTERCONTROL

Of decisive importance metaphysically is another distinction, namely, the distinction between sensa under the control of the self and those not under control.[1] Items under control are those subject to what I have been calling "guidance"—the melody that sings when I play the piano, the kinesthetic sensations that arise in my experience when I walk, and the like. Exempt from control are those sensa that are not subject to my guidance—the unbidden hurry of the white shapes of the snowflakes and the headache that threatens to envelop my consciousness. This distinction is the foundation of our conception of a world beyond our own experience. If our experience were all daydream, where images and meanings are under the control of desire, we should never reach the idea of physical things or of other selves. Or, equally, if sensations were as completely under control as they are in certain actions, such as the lifting of a finger, then also the idea of an external world would not arise. In either case we should live in a completely solipsistic world, for the whole of our experience would be dominated from the central focus of our desires. We should be the source, and know ourselves to be the source, of its entire content. But while the contrast between items of experience under control and items exempt from control would give us a concept, it would not suffice to give us an intuition, of the external world. We actually come into contact with that world through a distinctive experience, which I shall call "countercontrol." We get this experience when, during action, which is experience under control, we find action limited, or deflected, or made to conform. Any adaptive action, any action which takes its form not wholly from within, but partly from without, gives us this experience. When the sailor alters his course before the breeze, or when, grasping the handle of a jar, our fingers bend to conform to its shape—in such experiences as these we have the intuition of countercontrol. There are always the two aspects: the experience of our own control as we guide the course of sensa and the experience of a control counter to this. The intuition of countercontrol is an original element of our total experience, impossible of derivation from or reduction

[1] Cf. Berkeley's *Principles of Human Knowledge*, Sec. 27.

to anything else—the empirical evidence for our concept of the external world.[1] Our conception of countercontrol bears an obvious resemblance to the traditional conception of "resistance" as the source of belief in an external world, and is analogous to Spencer's and Santayana's "shock" and to Fichte's "*Anstoss.*"[2] But before identifying these concepts I wish to offer certain explanations and make certain reservations. In the first place, the experience of countercontrol must not be identified with mere strain sensations. These may be present, but they are not the whole of the experience. There must be an experience of action, of the governance of a course of experience by desire or purpose, and the deflection or conformity of the purpose. In this experience we intuit at once our own control and foreign control. Secondly, the experience of countercontrol occurs in connection with sensations of all types, not merely with those of muscle and tendon derivation. We have a striking experience of it in sound sensations which capture and deflect our attention, whether they are the disagreeable and insistent kind, like the noise of a neighboring drill, or the charming kind, the music that attracts and holds and will not let our minds go. We have the same vivid experience in visual sensations, of an annoying flickering light or a fair compelling form, or in connection with the sense of olfaction, when we react to the nauseous odor of rank vegetation or the alluring perfume of the orchid. In fact, the awareness of countercontrol pervades every item of sensory experience, for the mere presence of a sensum invites the conformity of interest, and every effort to get rid of or to change it makes us aware of a control counter to our own.

In discussing countercontrol I have used the expressions "intuition" and "experience" interchangeably, and I have wished to be taken literally, for I have meant that countercontrol is exercised directly, within experience. I mean that in this experi-

---

[1] In biological language this fact is expressed by the concept of adaptation.

[2] Herbert Spencer, *Principles of Psychology*, Third Edition (New York: D. Appleton and Co., 1896), Vol. I, Sec. 60; George Santayana, *Scepticism and Animal Faith* (New York: Charles Scribner's Sons, 1923), p. 193; J. G. Fichte, *Grundlage der gesammten Wissenschaftslehre*, Zweiter verbesserte Ausgabe (Jena und Leipzig: Gabler, 1802), Dritter Theil, Sec. 5.

ence we are actually in contact with the forces of the external world, that here the self and the not-self touch each other. The reality surrounding each center of experience is, therefore, no mere concept which we accept as a matter of inference or animal faith, but is as much "given" as ourselves.[1] But if this is true, we seem to be confronted with the paradox of a consciousness containing data that are not our own. How can what is mine be also not mine? what is the mind's be also nature's? The answer is that this is possible at the boundary of the mind. In all cases where there is a boundary, inside and outside meet and touch each other, and whatever is there belongs to both. If we consider a plane surface with genuine contiguity of elements—as contrasted with the sham "continuity" of a Dedekind continuum—and suppose a circle inscribed thereon, then the boundary of the area determined by the circle belongs both to the circle and to the area. This becomes impressively evident if we suppose the area determined by the circle to be of one color, say red, and the rest of the plane of another color, say blue, for in that case whatever exists on the boundary is both red and blue. So when control meets countercontrol, there is a genuine contact between the self and nature, and at the point of contact whatever is the mind's is also the environment's. Hence to the question often raised, How can we get outside our own minds, the answer is, We are already on the outside, when we are on the boundary. It is like asking the question, How can we see over our garden wall? To which the answer is, We can if we sit on the top of the wall; for there we can look both ways, both inside and outside.

The view that there is real contiguity between the mind and nature will seem strange, not because of any disparity between it and the facts, for it is a simple rendering of the facts of experience, but because of the acceptance of the theory of a shut-in mind. This theory is vividly set forth by Karl Pearson in his *Grammar of Science*,[2] where he compares the mind to a telephone exchange. Being inside the telephone exchange, we can see or

---

[1] This, of course, distinguishes my concept of countercontrol from Santayana's "shock," which is supposed to be an occurrence within consciousness only—whereas countercontrol is, I believe, an occurrence within nature also.

[2] Karl Pearson, *The Grammar of Science*, Second Edition (London: Adam and Charles Black, 1900), p. 44.

hear nothing that goes on in the world outside; we know only what we derive from the messages that come to us over the wires. The messages themselves, when we get them, are events within the telephone exchange; the information we obtain is the interpretation we put on them. There may be a correspondence between this information and events in the world without, but being prisoners in the exchange, we never really get out. But this whole way of viewing the situation is false. The mind is not shut out from the world as if there were something like a wall shutting it out; there is nothing between it and the external world. The mind extends right up to and on to the boundary between itself and nature. Physiologically, also, the view is false, for, again, the body does not shut the mind out from its environment as if it were an enclosing rampart; the mind, we shall see, is in the same place with the brain, and at the brain the mind and the environment intersect.

FOCAL AND MATRIX SELF

The result at which we have arrived has affinities not only with the views of Hume, but also with those of James and Mach.[1] In his *Principles of Psychology* James proclaimed that "the thoughts are the thinker" and later on denied that consciousness as such exists, meaning by consciousness something over and above the empirical constituents of the center. If we could substitute what we are calling activities for what he called thoughts, there would so far be little difference between us. For Mach, also, *"Die Elemente bilden das Ich"*; only Mach, adhering to the sensationalistic tradition, would not have distinguished, as we have, between activities and sensa. But to all such views there is this important objection, that they seem to reduce the self, which is intuitively a unity, to a bare multiplicity of factors. For, whether these factors be denominated thoughts, activities, elements, or impressions, they are many, and if we view the self as made up out of them it appears to be, as Plato said of it, a society rather than a unity, in fact, almost a crowd. Moreover,

[1] William James, *Principles of Psychology* (New York: Henry Holt and Co., 1904), Vol. I, chap. x, and "Does Consciousness Exist?" in *Essays in Radical Empiricism* (New York: Longmans, Green and Co., 1922), p. 1; E. Mach, *Analyse der Empfindungen*, Fuenfte Auflage (Jena: Gustav Fischer, 1906), p. 19.

the self possesses intuitively a stability, a self-sameness, contrasting strongly with the manifest flux of activities—this act of expression succeeding that, this judgment replacing that one, this flash of desire fading before the satisfaction which consumes it. Thus we reach what appears to be a crisis in the analysis of the self. For on the one hand, empirically, the self consists of the activities we have been describing, but if so it is a mere manyness, a mere collection, an unstable series of members that come and go. On the other hand, and just as empirically, it is a unified and enduring thing.

That this difficulty is not, however, as serious as it seems becomes clear when we reflect that in no phase of experience or reality is manyness incompatible with unity, and that there is no such thing as an absolutely simple unity. We may perhaps think of the point as such a unity, but in forgetfulness of the fact that the point is nothing except a center of relations, not merely many, but infinite, in number; it is a perfect example of a many-in-one. Accordingly, whatever unity the self possesses must be a unity out of manifoldness. This unity is itself not simple. The most basic form of unity is to be described as "compresence"—a with-each-other and in-each-other (German *"miteinander* und *ineinander"*) of activities and sensa. In so describing this unity we recognize, however, that the words used are mere instruments for calling attention to something so aboriginal that, although we may compare and contrast it with other forms of unification, we can in no sense and by no method reduce it to any other mode. We have already seen how activities of different types interpenetrate when they are foundational for each other; we have also noted how activities are interwoven with sensa; we have just observed how in the experience of countercontrol the activities are in contact with forces of the environment; we may now remind ourselves how the most diverse kinds of activities, not in any way necessary to each other, and sensa of the most diverse provenance and quality may be present together and interpenetrate. So a sorrow may exist not only side by side with but compenetrating each member of a series of reflections on the latest important European crisis, or equally compenetrating a medley of sounds coming in from the busy traffic of the city streets, and mingling and commingling with the odors that enter by the window, together with the colors of the landscape and the pressure of the arms as they rest upon the table. All these elements, the similar as well as the diverse in quality, the phenomenally near with the far, are compresent: the sound with the odor, the "distant" blue of the sky with the red of the curtain "close" at hand. Every item of experience is as it were diaphanous to every other, and passes through it. Yet despite this compenetration the individuality of elements remains intact, so that we readily discriminate sorrow from anxious reflection, our own control from countercontrol, and a sound from an odor or a color. This basic mode of unification is to be distinguished from further connections among the items of experience, in particular from logical and axiological bonds. There is no intelligible connection between the sounds from the street and reflections on the current crisis in Europe. It is to be noted, furthermore, that this type of unity does not hold among all the elements of different monads, but only among the elements of single monads and the boundary forces of their contiguous environments. The fact that it does not hold among all the elements of different monads is one aspect of what we have called the centricity of experience: it does not hold between what the blind man hears and what the deaf man sees, or between your secret thoughts about me and mine about you. It is the basic mode of unification not only for the self but for the total field of experience of the self, for what is often called mind or consciousness.

Upon the primary mode of unification, compresence, other modes, more luminous, more intelligible, are founded. In order to understand how this is so, two phases of the self, which we shall call the focal and the matrix self, must be distinguished. The former consists of that activity, or complex of compresent activities, now in operation: the present thought, the present impulse, the present dream, whatever is going on in the life of the self—its point of concentration or growth, its cambium layer. The focal self is an event, coming and going, one of a series of events flashing into and out of existence. These events do not, however, rise from a vacuum, but appear against a background more stable than themselves, and whatever intelligible relations they possess among themselves they derive from the matrix from which they emerge. For illustration consider the fact that I have just performed the act of interwoven conception, expression, and volition embodied in the writing of the last three words.

This act while it was going on constituted at least a part of what I am calling my focal self. But these words would never have been written, nor could they have had the significance they possess—a significance that was their essence as mental activities —had there not been a matrix of meaning, the root idea which I am trying to formulate and express in this paragraph, out of which they issued. Furthermore, the concept expressed in this paragraph is itself incomplete except in relation to the meaning of the whole chapter and, in a measure, in relation to the meaning which will be the whole book, already existing in germ in my mind; and the intention to write the paragraph is part and parcel of the intention to write the chapter and the book. Or take an example from the field of practical life. A young man is embarking on a highly ambitious political career, yet accepts appointment to a relatively humble post; clearly his action can be explained only in relation to his long-time goal, as an effort to get a start. Beneath his interest in the post is his interest in ultimate success. Or consider a trivial matter: a man is driving a car at a high speed, an action belonging to what I am calling the focal self; but this action is intelligible only in relation to a schedule of appointments which clarifies the dominant interests operating through the entire day. Or, for a final illustration, consider a man of science who accepts a certain hypothesis as true: his activity occurs because of, in the light of, a whole set of beliefs into which it fits and through which it is validated. The ongoing activity in the three spheres of expression, conception, and will overlies a relatively deeper and larger background of expression, conception, and volition of a relatively systematic character, out of which it springs and to which it contributes. Underneath each sentence written or uttered is a course of expression remembered and anticipated which the sentence carries on; presupposed by each judgment is a world picture tacitly acknowledged; enveloping each plan is a life plan that formulates a system of interests, or, as we may call it, a "system interest," since the system possesses a wholeness constituting it a single entity, within which, as in a net, all our acts are caught.

The matrix self provides the stability which we know to belong to the self and which we looked for in vain among the flux of ongoing activities making up the focal self. I do not wish to imply that the matrix self is changeless; but the fact is that it moves more slowly than the pulse of focal activities. The matrix self alters because each focal activity enriches it and causes an inner adjustment. Every sentence we use modifies the latent fund of accumulated and interrelated symbols available for future employment; every judgment either renders more certain or in some fashion transforms the world picture of the individual; every action reëstablishes or modifies the life plan. But that the matrix self never changes entirely—that there is a core which remains the same over long periods of time, indeed as long as the self endures, which we shall call the essential self —we shall show in the next chapter. Yet despite this contrast in stability between the focal self and the matrix self it would be a mistake to suppose that the matrix self exists apart from the focal self. There is but one self: the focal self and the matrix self are only two aspects of a single fact. The matrix self is a layer of deeper significance that continues and endures from one ongoing activity to another, but it cannot exist unless there is a focal activity that carries it on. The use of the term "significance" does not, however, imply that the matrix self has a merely logical or Platonic existence or subsistence. Its genuine existence is shown by the impossibility just noted of separating the activity, as an event, from its significance at a deeper level. It would also be a mistake to think of the matrix self as existing in the subconscious, since it is directly embodied and fully alive in every focal activity of symbolism, judgment, or volition, where anyone can find it who looks for it. The matrix self bears the focal self in its bosom; but, equally, the focal self is the growing point, or even the burning point, of the latter.

That through the matrix self the activities form an intelligible unity has already been indicated. Every judgment a man makes is connected with others through the world picture which he accepts; each symbol, with other symbols through the system of symbols that is carried over from one focal phase of the self to another; and every desire and act that fulfils desire, with others through the life plan into which it fits, or, as the case may be, which it disrupts. A false judgment or a mistaken or wrong action belong within the intelligible unity of the self together with true judgments and right actions, because a judgment is false or an action wrong through inconsistency with the world picture or incompatibility with the life plan. Apart from the background of the matrix self they are not false or wrong. Yet while there is this intelligible unity within the self through the matrix, the question might still be raised whether such unity is precisely the oneness that we have in mind when we think of the unity of the self. This may seem to be a more intimate thing than a system of judgments and a simpler thing than a life plan. No matter how rudimentary the world picture or how childish the life plan, there is a spread about the latter and a seeming impersonality about the former that may appear to stand in contrast with the felt warmth and indescribable univocality of the self. But such doubts can arise, I believe, only when certain matters already established have been forgotten. With regard to simplicity, it is forgotten that neither the world picture nor the life plan exists at any moment except as embodied in an ongoing act of thought or impulse; now this ongoing activity provides the concentration missed in the matrix. The simplicity that we intuit so vividly is the simplicity of the pulsing activity; there, in the living thought or deed, the entire matrix is focussed. As regards warmth, it is forgotten that volition holds the primacy over all modes of activity. The central core of the self is desire: it underlies all symbols and judgments, it creates the world picture, and the life plan is a formulation of what it seeks.

We are now in a position to answer, and answer affirmatively, the question which we asked at the beginning of this chapter, to wit, whether what we have been calling the centricity of experience is the same as egocentricity. For, from the nature of the matrix self and its relation to the whole of experience, it is evident that there cannot be an addition operation among centers. This can easily be shown with regard to both belief and desire. A hypothetical inclusive self might possess all the truth possessed by two or more included selves, yet could not believe what both believed, unless both had the same beliefs. It could not, with the child, believe in Santa Claus, and with the adult not so believe, or believe that the earth is flat and also believe that it is round. The world pictures of the child and the adult are exclusive—the latter does not simply include the former. And a hypothetical inclusive self could not have both a desire to see Santa Claus and, doubting his existence, no desire to see him (although it could, of course, pretend to such a desire—

but that is something else). Or love of native land could not unite in one whole of experience with the hate felt by an enemy; such polar affections cannot interpenetrate. The world picture and the life desire are correlative, each depending upon the limitations of the other; a self with a narrow world view falls outside, not inside, one with a wider view. The well-known ambivalence of love does not pertain to the same, but to different traits in the object of love. Centricity and egocentricity are, therefore, identical. I wish, however, to insist that the disparateness of centers is not absolute, for they have universals in common and, although they cannot together form a single self, they do form a single system with each other and with nature, which is contiguous with them.[1]

[1] For the criticism of the notion of an inclusive self, as well as for the theory of the contiguity, direct or indirect, of centers of experience I am obviously indebted to the writings and teaching of William James. See especially his *A Pluralistic Universe* (New York: Longmans, Green and Co., 1909), chaps. v, vii–viii.

III

Experience as Substance

IN OUR last chapter we made a preliminary study of some basic aspects of experience. In this we shall raise the crucial question as to the substantiality of experience—to put the matter in an untechnical, yet not misleading fashion: Does experience stand, as it were, on its own feet, or is it supported by, undergirded by, something that is not experience? By the answer given to this question is defined the great divide among philosophers, between idealists and materialists. Our own position is with the idealists, but we think, nevertheless, that idealists have taken their position too lightly or too haughtily, not giving themselves the trouble to establish it or to consider the objections of their opponents. They have relied too exclusively on what to them, as to us, is an indefeasible intuition, namely, that in experience we are acquainted with the stuff of reality, as directly acquainted with it as we are with the taste of a lemon when we suck it; so that to exist and to be a center of experience, or an element of a center, are one and the same, and cannot be other than one and the same. But there are two parts to a philosophy: systematic expression of intuition, and defense against objections, the latter amounting finally to the clarification of difficulties upon which objections are based; and it is with regard to this second part, I claim, that idealists have been neglectful. This chapter will, accordingly, be devoted primarily to defense; in the fifth chapter, however, we shall take the offensive and show that if one looks for substance where those who deny substance to experience always do look, namely, among things perceived by the senses, one cannot find it there.

Before proceeding to our argument, however, we must explain the meaning which we shall attach to "substance." This is especially necessary because of recent attacks on the concept of substance which have led some thinkers to wish to dispense with it altogether. The aversion to "substance" has been particularly notable among philosophers of the natural sciences, who discarded it first from psychology after the well-known attacks upon the concept of soul substance, and are now discarding it in the physical sciences, where they substitute the notion of event. Of course the whole movement goes much further back, having its inception in Hume. But a careful consideration will show, I think, that these attacks were effective only in destroying certain applications of the concept of substance; they did not demolish the concept itself. Thus, while the advocates of "psychology without a soul" destroyed the notion of an underlying psychical substance supposed to be distinct from mental life, they did not refute the application of the concept of substance to experience itself, and they continued to ascribe substance to material things; and those who attack the concept in the physical field have never seriously considered the possibility of its legitimate application to the field of experience. Moreover, the notion of event, which is substituted for "substance," performs many of the functions of the latter concept. To anyone who has reflected deeply on fundamental categories this situation will cause no surprise, for the concept of substance is so basic, that is to say, so deeply rooted in experience, that it is indispensable. And this is true, not of some new and reformed concept of substance, but of the concept as it has been developed by the great masters of metaphysical philosophy in the past; not the concept, but the application of it to certain purely hypothetical entities, is outmoded.

As developed historically, the concept of substance yields, upon analysis, four moments: to be substance means to be subject but never predicate, to be independent, to be causally efficient, and to be conserved through change. These moments are closely interrelated, yet each contributes something unique to the definition of the concept. A brief explanation of each will prove useful before we examine the possibility of applying it to experience.

The first is the most original and characteristic of the many contributions of Aristotle to this matter.[1] There are, Aristotle observed, certain terms of discourse that are properly used as

[1] Aristotle *Categories* V; *Metaphysics* V. ix, VII. iii, etc.; *Analytics* 83a 1–17.

predicates, although they may sometimes be used as subjects also, and certain other terms that are properly used as subjects, but never as predicates—these designate substances. Thus the term "white" is used as a predicate when I say that Socrates is white, but is subject when I say that white is a color; whereas the term "Socrates," in the first sentence, is used as subject, but can never be used as a predicate. Of course, I may say, Such and such a one is a Socrates, when "Socrates" seems to be used as a predicate; but "a Socrates" is not Socrates, for "a Socrates" means certain characteristics of the man Socrates, which, although unusual, might be attributed to at least one other individual besides Socrates, and hence are not unique, while "Socrates" designates something absolutely unique. To say, therefore, that substance is the subject is the same as to say that substance is the individual. This, as Aristotle recognized, is the significance of his distinction between the absolute subject and all predicates, and thus interpreted it remains a valid distinction and expresses a fundamental element in the concept of substance.

There are, however, some well-known objections to the distinction. Most radically, it may be argued that it rests on the subject–predicate logic, now outgrown and already replaced by a relational point of view. That is to say, instead of conceiving of existence as made up of subjects and predicates, we ought to view it as consisting of elements in relations, and when so viewed the whole distinction between subjects that can and cannot be predicates becomes meaningless. Now, fully to discuss this matter would lead to anticipations of the material of Chapters X and XI; I shall, therefore, at the risk of seeming dogmatic, merely state what I believe to be the answer to this type of objection, leaving the justification of it to the sequel. The answer is this: However you view the nature of existence, whether through the categories of terms and relations or of subjects and predicates, you cannot avoid the distinction between repeatable and nonrepeatable factors or aspects. Any inventory of existence will reveal repeats: in fifth-century Athens, Plato as man, Socrates as man, Theodorus as man, Theaetetus as man—even perhaps Socrates as a Socrates and someone else as also a Socrates, Plato as a Plato and someone else also as a Plato—but never two of Socrates, two of Plato, two of Theaetetus, two of Theodorus; or again, I find this rose red and that rose red, red here and red there, but never another instance of this red rose. Furthermore, we observe that the repeatable factors are never discerned by themselves, but always intertwined with the nonrepeatable. Thus, although we find man here, man there, and man elsewhere, we never find merely man, man, man, but Socrates as a man, Plato as a man, and the like; and we never find mere red, red, red, but this rose as red or that rose as red, and the like. We may therefore build concepts or descriptions on the basis of the repeatable factors and apply these to the individuals that possess both repeatable and nonrepeatable factors, thus characterizing Socrates as a man, Plato as a man, and so on. But clearly we cannot build a description on the basis of the nonrepeatable factors and apply it to any individual. The one type of factor yields a description that has multiple application; the other does not yield a description at all. When, therefore, we assert that substance is absolute subject, we mean and can justly mean that there are factors of existence that are unique; hence, while substances may be designated by proper names and partly described, they cannot be adequately described.

The second characteristic of substance, independence, we also owe to Aristotle; but the meaning which he attached to it has been enlarged by modern philosophers. For Aristotle it meant self-existence, that is to say, existence that is not intrinsically—as distinguished from causally—founded on the existence of other things in the way that the existence of relations and universals is founded on the existence of individuals.[1] Thus, white cannot exist by itself, but only as, for example, the white of a white man, and one could not find "greater than" lying loose in reality, although one could find Athens greater than Corinth; on the other hand, Socrates has self-existence. It will be noticed that this qualification for substance is very close to the preceding one, for only individuals have self-existence of this sort. But, as I have said, independence now means more than this: it means, in addition, absence of causal determination from outside. I do not say, of course, that the Aristotelian conception of independence has lost its significance for modern philosophy. A typical use of it is the Lockian conception, inherited by way

[1] Aristotle, *loc. cit.*

of the Scholastics, of the dependent nature of the properties of physical things: the properties could not exist by themselves, but only as they inhered in an underlying substance. The concept of substance employed by Descartes and Spinoza [1] was also, formally at least, the same as Aristotle's. And we shall find that it still has significance for us. But with the emphasis on causality typical of modern ways of thinking, the meaning of independence cannot be limited to the intrinsic nature of a thing: it must include its relations to other things. When thus enlarged, however, the meaning of the concept becomes unworkable for our purposes if independence is interpreted as *absolute* independence. For, as Spinoza claimed, only the universe or God is independent of things outside itself; hence, only God or the universe could be substance in this sense. If, therefore, we are to raise the question of the application of the concept to the parts of the universe, in particular to centers of experience, the notion of independence cannot be taken in an absolute sense but must be softened to mean absence of *complete* determination from outside. And in a universe such as ours, consisting of a plurality of mutually determining and determined entities, that is all the independence or substantiality anything could possibly have.

The third qualification for substantiality is causal efficacy. This is already recognized by Plato in the *Sophist*, where he criticizes the "friends of the Ideas" for their failure to attribute activity to the Ideas,[2] and by Aristotle, who gives to his substances both final and efficient causation. One might be tempted to think that this third moment was the same as the second, but it is rather the supplement, for the second requires that substance be itself a source of determination. A Leibnizian monad partly fulfils this requirement by being the source of internal events, but does not completely do so since it is not also a source of events outside.[3]

The fourth qualification, conservation through time, we also owe to Aristotle, for his notion of substance was devised in order to make possible the conception of a thing's maintaining its

---

[1] René Descartes, *Principles of Philosophy* (1644), Principles 51, 52; Baruch Spinoza, *Ethics* (1677), Part I, Def. 3 and Prop. 14.
[2] Plato *Sophist* 248.
[3] Gottfried Wilhelm von Leibniz, *Monadology* (1714), Sec. 11.

identity despite the alteration of its attributes. But the Aristotelian concept is not sufficiently refined for contemporary philosophical purposes, and extreme caution is required in order to give a satisfactory definition of it. We shall find it expedient to postpone the fine analysis of the concept until we approach the problem of its application to experience, when many established prejudices will have to be abandoned. At this point we must, however, insist that conservation does not necessarily mean absolute conservation; that is to say, we cannot deny substance to an entity because it is not eternal; all that we can rightfully demand is that it should persist through a succession of events, in relation to which it may be said to endure. If there are eternal substances we shall have to follow Aristotle and distinguish them from the transient.

Such, then, is the concept of substance whose application to experience is now in question. Materialists deny the possibility of applying it in all four moments of its meaning. First, and most radically, they deny that experience is properly subject. Experience, they insist, is a mere attribute, property, or "variant" of the body or the brain. In a certain state of motion or tension the brain is qualified by color or sound, by emotion or desire, and these qualities can no more exist by themselves without the underpinning of the brain than any other attribute, say size or weight, can exist without a subject in which it inheres. Accordingly, whenever experience enters into discourse, in order to be correctly expressed it should enter as predicate to the brain or the body as subject. It is the brain that wishes, desires, hopes or fears, hears and sees, smells and tastes. The brain puts on or takes off these attributes according to its condition at the moment, much as a man puts on or takes off, according to the particular social occasion, now his street clothes, his night garments, or his evening wear. And experience is declared to emerge with an equal lack of necessity in the biological series [1] when matter has attained to a certain degree of complexity, appearing there as an additional attribute which the investigator cannot understand in terms of the material system but must nevertheless accept with natural piety because he finds it there.

[1] R. W. Sellars, *Evolutionary Naturalism* (Chicago and London: The Open Court Publishing Co., 1922); C. Lloyd Morgan, *Emergent Evolution* (New York: Henry Holt and Co., 1924), *passim*.

There are several ways of showing that this cannot be true. In the first place, if it were true, the materialism upon the basis of which it is believed to be true could not be true. For, if experience is an attribute of the brain, a description of the brain in terms of this attribute must be possible, and the brain itself would be describable in terms of experience. Or, to put the same proposition in another way: an attribute qualifies its subject; there is no way of separating the nature of a thing from the qualities or description of it; the thing may, to be sure, be richer than any description can reveal, but the description, if it applies, must at least disclose what sort of thing it is. A brain, therefore, to which smelling, hoping, tasting, and thinking belong as attributes is no mere brain, in the materialistic sense; it has all the attributes of a monad, and differs from one not in anything which the brain lacks, but in other attributes which the monad lacks. The brain itself becomes a monad—only more than a monad—and the concept of matter is so enriched that it no longer means matter.[1]

But the argument above is no refutation of the view that experience is a predicate, for it merely points out a consequence that would follow if experience were a predicate; and both the antecedent and the consequent of the hypothetical proposition involved might, for anything which we have shown, be true. It has force only against the unregenerate materialist who is unwilling to modify his view a jot or a tittle. However, in admitting for the sake of argument that experience might be a predicate, we have granted too much, for an examination of experience shows that it is no mere predicate. As we have seen, it is characteristic of a predicate that it may become' the basis of a description that can apply to other subjects besides the subject to which it does in fact apply; in other words, a predicate is not intrinsically unique. But a subject is intrinsically unique. Now it is clear that a monad, as well as its constituent elements or parts, is unique, and that no complete description either of a monad or of the elements of a monad can be the basis of descriptions that have multiple application. Consider, for example, the song that I hear. We may significantly say of it that

---

[1] This, I think, can fairly be said of the "stuff" of Professor R. W. Sellars. See his discussions of the mind–body problem in *The Philosophy of Physical Realism* (New York: The Macmillan Co., 1932), chaps. xiii, xvi.

you also hear it, in which case it would seem to function as a quality of your subject; but the song that you and I both hear is only the rhythmic and melodic pattern of the song that each of us hears. The one is a universal; the other is a concrete event. And since the latter is a concrete event it is unique and therefore cannot be a predicate. The same is true of an activity like thinking: you may think the same thought that I think, in the sense of having in mind the same universal that I have in mind; but the thought process itself, as an element in your concrete experience, cannot be the same as my thought process. The song and the thought, as concrete events, are therefore subjects, not predicates. The monad as a whole is also unique, and is therefore subject, not predicate, for while there might possibly be another person just like myself—although this is doubtful[1]—there could not be another me.

A final argument may be employed against the materialist who holds that the brain is subject, of which experience is predicate, as follows: First, we premise the general principle, stated in the language of the Aristotelian logic, that the predicates of a predicate are also the predicates of its subject. Thus, if the subject *x* is red, it is also colored, for color is a predicate of red; or if Socrates is a man, he is also mortal, for mortality is a predicate of man. Next, we observe that there are certain predicates, especially value predicates, which apply to a monad or its concrete elements that would also apply, in accordance with the logical principle just laid down, to the brain, if the brain is the subject of which experience is a predicate. But these in fact do not apply, from which it follows that the brain cannot be subject. For example, a purpose may be morally good or bad, but not a brain; a judgment may be true or false, but not a brain.[2] The sole way to avoid the force of this argument is to identify the brain and experience, which means relinquishing the point of view of the materialist.

To summarize: with regard to the first moment in the analysis of substance, we have discovered no reason why experience should not be substance; on the contrary we have found that we know intuitively that experience is subject, and we have found that the theory of the materialist to the effect that experience is

1 See the discussion on pp. 87–88.
2 See Plato's arguments against the corporealists in the *Sophist* 247.

a predicate of the brain, if true, would entail the consequence that the brain would not be the brain as ordinarily conceived, for, having experience as a predicate, it would have the same nature as experience.

As for the second moment in the analysis of substance, independence, we have seen that it may not mean absolute independence, but may mean partial independence, that is to say, the absence of complete determination from without. And this in turn may mean either that experience is not founded, intrinsically, upon anything outside itself, or that it is not completely determined causally by anything without. The second meaning merges, as we have seen, with the problem of the third requirement for substance—causal efficacy. We may therefore treat it in connection with that and confine our attention at this point entirely to the first meaning. With regard to this, if we view experience strictly from the inside, ignoring what we may know about it through its discoverable relations to other things, it does not reveal itself as being intrinsically based on anything other than itself, either as a whole monad or in its elements. A sound heard comes to us as completely self-existent; it shows nothing of any underlying or underpinning reality such as the auditory apparatus in the ear or the vibration of sound waves in the air or commotions in the brain are supposed to be. So a color is just a color seen, and does not reveal within itself any dependence on the visual center in the brain or on the electromagnetic wave; it is only by experiments which take us beyond the given sense impression that any such dependence is revealed. Again, while it may be evident that hunger and thirst are impossible without certain disturbances in the *experienced* body, these impulses together with the somesthetic experiences with which they are connected do not reveal any dependence on the *physical* body. Experience comes to us not like a relation, like an adjective that needs its perch on a substantive, but as a self-subsistent kind of entity, standing on its own feet. The only intrinsic dependence that a monad reveals is dependence on other monads—social dependence—the *I* on the *you;* the *you* on the *me,* but the entire circle of monads is not revealed as depending on anything known to be different in kind from experience.

In order to show that causal efficacy belongs to experience we must follow the twofold procedure suggested at the beginning of this chapter: we must appeal to intuition and we must silence the doubts of the skeptics. Without the testimony of intuition the assumption of causality would be arbitrary; without the refutation of objections it would be insecure. Now looking within experience we find causal efficacy in two broad classes of events: events inside a monad determined by something in that same monad, and events in one monad determined by something in another monad. In both cases it is certain that causal efficacy belongs to experience, but the first type is preëminent because we not only know that causality is present there, but we also know how it is present there: we have a revelation of its essential mechanism. For consider the following typical experiences: On a cold, damp, and sunless Michigan day, in the pauses of his work, there arise in the mind of the student images of a boat in which he sits and listlessly floats down a warm and sunlit stream. Or it may happen that the student will turn to the piano and, obedient to his impulse, sound after sound will arise in his consciousness. Or, finally, he may seize his hat and go for a walk, which means that a succession of patterned kinesthetic sensa rise and fall, fall and rise in his consciousness. We shall have to reserve the complete analysis of such phenomena for our chapter on causality, but at this point we wish to call attention to the following common and decisive feature of all of them: the coming to be and passing away, within consciousness, of a series of events, chiefly images in the daydream, chiefly sensations in the other two experiences (sounds in the one, kinesthetic patterns in the other), all following upon a relatively constant item of experience, and not merely following upon it, but following upon it in such a way as to fulfil its objective or intent. In the daydream the relatively constant item is a certain restlessness, of which the intent is to get away from the present situation; in the last two illustrations there is the intention, as we put it, to do something—to make music, to take a walk. And in each case the presence of the item is a condition both of the occurrence and of the succession of events; not only is it a condition *sine qua non* of their occurrence, but it is besides a condition of such a kind that we can understand why only such and such events occur. That is to say, the relatively constant item—the restlessness, with the connected plan or intent—is a condition *sine qua non* not only of the existence of the events, but of the quality or character of the events.

The consequent follows not only after the antecedent, but from the antecedent.   By all the criteria for cause—being a condition, being a necessary condition, and being something from which the consequent can be deduced—what we have called the relatively constant factors in the experiences analyzed are causes. And they all lie within experience and are not exceptional, but typical.   In every phase of experience we find a relatively constant factor generating events within experience which fulfil its intent.   To any unprejudiced mind the operation of this factor is an utterly luminous fact and is, as we shall see, the paradigm from which our very concept of causality is derived.   In this fact we are witnesses of the process of creation itself.

To show that there is causal efficacy between monads, as well as within the experience of a single monad, let us consider two of the illustrative cases cited.   When our student takes his walk there arise not only in his mind patterns of kinesthetic sensa, but also, subsequently yet correspondingly in mine, patterns of visual sensa; and when the musician plays, there may arise in my mind sound for sound the tonal pattern that arises in his.   Let us add another illustration.   You wish to speak to me, and, obedient to your intention, sounds embodying your thoughts appear in your mind—but similar sounds appear in my mind also. And not only are certain existences in your mind regular antecedents of events in my mind, but they are necessary antecedents for such events.   I cannot see you walk unless you intend to walk, or hear you play unless you desire to play, or hear you speak unless you wish to speak.   There is no possible way of producing from within my own mind exactly the same events as are produced through the agency of your mind; and these effects are equally impossible through what are popularly called purely natural processes. To use a more telling illustration, perhaps: when I listen to the impassioned orator or the inspired creative musician I experience sounds that no intention of mine could possibly produce.   And all communication, if on a lower plane, is of the same nature: a creative process starting in one mind yet having effects in another mind, through which it is understood. It is true that I cannot experience the tie that binds the intention in one mind with the effects in another, as I can witness the tie that binds intention and effect when both lie within the same mind; yet that there is genuine causality there cannot be doubted, since the intention is not only a condition but an indispensable condition of the effect.

Despite the overwhelming lucidity of the evidence for the efficacy of consciousness, this evidence has been called into question by philosophers—not, I think, because they have not appreciated its force, but because they have been under the sway of certain purely theoretical dogmas derived from sources extraneous to the situation. One ground of doubt is very easy to eliminate. It is often objected that the efficacy of consciousness is illusory because voluntary action is impossible without intact neuromuscular paths, which are thus shown to be the real conditions for action. The musician's intention to play a sonata is absolutely ineffective if his fingers are paralyzed. But all that this argument proves is that an intention or volition is never the sole or sufficient determinant of action; it does not prove that a volition is not a necessary determinant. And it is not noticed that the logic of this argument would destroy the efficacy of every agent, for no agent can work without the coöperation of other agents; every effect is the resultant of a multiplicity of causes. One can indeed show, as has been so often shown by physiologists and psychologists, that all voluntary action is determined by stimuli external to the mind of the individual—for example, hunger is determined by certain stimulations in the muscle walls of the stomach—but this does not prove that these stimuli are the sole determinants of the actions that follow, in particular, that in the case of man an intention is not a determinant and a necessary determinant. And it is clear that certainly in the case of no civilized man are the resulting acts merely the resultant of somatic stimulations.

The second objection, due to Hume, is really an objection— it is his famous objection—to all causality, and, by proving too much, is similar in its weakness to the first. Hume tried to show, it will be recalled, that there is no tie, no link, no necessary connection between, let us say, the desire to make music and the sounds that subsequently emerge into consciousness. But the answer is that while it is true that in all other instances of what we believe to be causality we find no necessary connection but only a constant association of cause and effect, in exactly this case of succession, where desire is an indispensable antecedent, we do in fact actually observe the tie. In the daydream, for example, we are eyewitnesses of the emergence of the dream images *under the control* of desire, and see that not only their existence but their character is such as to fulfil its intention. One wonders what stronger tie, what more obvious necessitation could be sought than is found here. And it seems to me clear that Hume never examined this case on its merits—to judge by the hesitating and fumbling paragraph on the matter added in the Appendix to the *Treatise of Human Nature* [1]—but was merely repeating without thought what he had found to be true of the other alleged causal sequences.

We come, finally, to the study of the fourth criterion of substantiality, conservation. This would mean, if application could be made to experience, that the obvious flux of thoughts, sensations, and passions is not absolute, but that something is preserved in the midst of the flow, and carried over, as it were, from moment to moment. Now there are two modes, we can show, in which this is true. First, we can show that what we have already distinguished as the repetitive aspect of experience is literal fact with regard to time as well as to space. The universals embodied in particular momentary phases of experience recur, so that, not to be sure the snows, but the generic whiteness and coldness of the snows of yesteryear are here in the snows of today. But because of the fact that many philosophers have questioned the reality of universals and in view of the general difficulty of the whole subject, we shall find it wise to leave this mode of conservation to a chapter by itself. We may remark in passing, however, that conservation through universals is the basis for everything that we mean by tradition and culture—our inheritance and comprehension of the language, the customs, the moralities, the art, and the music of our past selves and our ancestors.

The second manner in which experience is conserved is through the matrix self. We have already given reasons for believing that in the matrix self we find something within experience that is preserved from moment to moment, but we must examine the testimony afresh with regard to the whole question of substantiality. The problem is much the same as the traditional problem of personal identity. Before entering upon the

---

[1] David Hume, *Treatise of Human Nature*, Part III, Sec. 14; ed by T. H. Green and T. H. Grose (London: Longmans, Green and Co., 1898), I, 455.

full examination of the question, however, we must try to define precisely what "identity" means. Identity is usually assumed to be a universal relation holding somehow between a thing and itself, and the statement of this relation that A is identical with A has been numbered among the three august Laws of Thought. Yet there have not been wanting irreverent persons to call into question the very meaning of this law and the very sense of the notion of identity. Hegel called the law of identity a silly proposition,[1] and Wittgenstein has written, "To say of two things that they are identical is nonsense, and to say of one thing that it is identical with itself is to say nothing." [2] Identity, as traditionally defined, shares the absurdity of all so-called reflexive relations, in being supposed to hold between a thing and itself— could we say *between* itself?—when the essence of relationship requires that it shall hold between at least two things. If, therefore, the concept of identity is to be preserved, the traditional definition must be abandoned and a new definition found. A careful analysis of all actual uses of the concept discloses, in fact, that it is never a relation between a thing and itself, but a relation between at least three things. Thus I may say of two words or expressions that they are the same (for example, *"blau"* and "blue," $p \supset q$ and $\sim p \vee q$), when what I am really saying is that both have one meaning; or I may say that a thing described in one way is the same as a thing described in another way (Scott is the author of *Waverley*, or the author of *Waverley* is the same as the author of *Marmion*), when what I am really saying is that both descriptions apply to a given thing; or, finally, I may say that two things, x and y, are the same in quality, when what I am indicating is that a certain characteristic characterizes x and characterizes y (symbolically, $F(x)$ and $F(y)$). In all these cases, and they are typical, it will be observed that at least three things are involved—two expressions and what they express, two descriptions and what they describe, two objects and their common predicate—and that what is asserted is the possession by something of a relation to two other things—the meaning to the words or expressions, the object to the two descriptions of it, the

[1] Georg Wilhelm Friedrich Hegel, "Die Logik," Sec. 115, in *Encyclopaedie* (Berlin, 1840).

[2] L. Wittgenstein, *Tractatus Logico-philosophicus* (New York: Harcourt, Brace and Co., 1922), 5.5301.

predicate to the two objects which it characterizes. Generalizing from two to many, we notice that identity is a case of a one–many relationship, and not a reflexive relation at all. I have elsewhere suggested that, in fact, the so-called principle of identity is really the principle of one–many relations: it affirms their possibility.[1]

The application of this analysis to personal identity is simple. Personal identity is also seen to be a one–many relation between the self and many moments, events, or situations. To believe in personal identity is to believe that the self may be present at these many moments, along with the rise and fall of these many events, "in" these many situations, and hence conserved in the midst of their coming to be and passing away. An examination of some typical assertions implying personal identity shows this. Thus when I assert that I was born on such a date so many years ago I am asserting the presence of the self both now and then, hence that it was not subject to the transiency of the past moment. Or when I affirm that it is I who wrote a certain book I am implying that my self, which obviously exists now when I make the assertion, also existed then when the book was written, and hence has relation to both the present and the past and is conserved despite the transiency of the action of writing. Or when a judge sentences a man for a crime, he assumes the existence of the man as both the agent of the crime and the sufferer of the penalty. If this were not true, if the man did not somehow carry over and be preserved from the situation of the crime to the situation of the courtroom, there would be no sense, no justice, in punishing *him*. A similar case is that of the man who receives an honor, let us say the Nobel prize for work in physics: he must have been present as an agent in the situation where the work was done, and must carry over from that situation into the present situation, where the prize is given. Or suppose I feel remorse for some act—then the remorse is meaningless unless the I that feels sorry also committed the deed. Finally, consider the fact of memory:

> I remember, I remember
> The house where I was born,
> The little window, where the sun
> Came peeping in at morn.

---

[1] See my article "Reflexive Relations," *Philosophical Review*, XLII (1933). No. 3 : 303–311.

The significance of memory is completely destroyed unless the self that lives now lived also in that little house of long ago and watched the sunrise there, as it might watch the sunrise here, and so was conserved from house to house and from boyhood to manhood.

The self we claim, the self we know to be the same from moment to moment, but clearly not all the self, is conserved. What we have been calling the focal self is not conserved. This passing thought, this agony of pain or ecstasy of joy, these we know are not conserved; they are events that are, then are not, that come to be and pass away. Only what we have called the matrix self is conserved, the matrix self that lives within the passing thought or passion, but carries over from this thought and that passion to the thought or passion that follows. Only the life plan, the world picture remain the same. But although the matrix self is constant in relation to the flux of activities that bear it, it, too, slowly alters: our concepts become enriched and enlarged, our world picture matures and sometimes suffers revolutionary changes, our life plan undergoes a slow evolution. Nevertheless, the verbal expression of experience and the report of intuition which assert that in some sense the person is identical throughout sane and conscious life are not in error. In order to show how this can be so I am going to distinguish within the matrix self what I shall call its *essence* from the remainder, retaining in this term something of the original Aristotelian flavor: by the "essence" of the matrix I shall mean that part without which the person ceases to be himself. Thus there is a set of beliefs—in the existence of the persons with whom one's life is intimately connected, father, mother, wife, children, and friends, in the existence of the familiar physical objects of one's immediate environment, house, furniture, and landscape, together with certain feelings toward these objects—and in addition certain beliefs regarding our own past, and certain intentions and expectations regarding our own future—enough to provide at least a framework of orientation—without which one could not be or know oneself to be the same. For let us make the following *Gedankexperiment* [1] and suppose that we cease to believe in the house and town in which we live; let us say that we fail entirely to remember our past, or if we remember cease to believe

---

[1] The expression is Ernst Mach's.

that it was ours; let us imagine further that we have lost all affection and interest in these things; and, finally, let us suppose that we have no design or expectation regarding our own future, no thought of tomorrow's sunrise, no plan for tomorrow's work or bread: Would not you or I have ceased to be? Would not the issue be either death or lunacy? With all the changes of detail in our world picture or life plan, the fundamental background of belief and feeling which I am calling the essential self remains invariant.

But until we have shown how baseless are the doubts which have been raised by philosophers against the evidence of intuition, the possibility still remains open that personal identity may not be a fact but an illusion comparable to the illusions of perception which come to us with all the lucidity of intuition but dissolve when we apply to them the corrective of reflection. There have been several grounds for these doubts. The first which I shall consider we have already disposed of by implication—the seeming evanescence or "eventness" of experience. To judge by what they say of it, experience appears to some thinkers to be like the foam on the crest of the wave, or the shimmer and play of light, something essentially momentary, elusive, and unsubstantial. But we have shown that this is true only of the focal self, and is precisely not true of the matrix. The difficulty arises, then, from a singularly one-eyed view of experience, accurate so far as it goes, but half blind. Yet to point this out is not enough; we must explain how the concept of the essential evanescence of experience could have arisen against the evidence. The idea originated, I believe, out of a false contrast between the genuine evanescence of the activities that constitute the focal self and the purely hypothetical invariance of the material substrata conceived to underlie phenomenal physical objects, and especially the phenomenal physical body or brain. Consciousness is thus pictured as being like the changing, ephemeral shadows which accompany the relatively unchanging material objects that cast them. But in our fifth chapter we shall try to show (1) that there are no grounds for believing in the existence of material objects, and (2) that the supposed identities there revealed are identities not of "things," but of types of purely phenomenal objects that recur, in accordance with certain laws, in the experience of various centers. Thus, for example, if I undertake the action called "boiling water," the phenomenal water does not remain constant but in time disappears altogether and is replaced by another phenomenal object which we call "steam"; this, by means of certain well-defined actions, may now give place in turn to some new phenomenal water. But this new phenomenal water is the same as the old in type only: the hypothetical identical water is no more than a construction built up on the basis of certain recurring species of sensa which have no existence outside the minds that contain them. And with regard to what we shall call the scientific objects—molecules, atoms, electrons, electromagnetic waves, and the like—supposed to underlie the phenomenal objects, they are themselves not things at all, but schemes of relations which serve as plans of action enabling us to generate desired phenomenal objects or to control such phenomenal objects as are not wholly subject to our manufacture. It is true, as we shall see, that we have good reason for believing in the existence of a reality more permanent than the human mind, correlated in some way with these schemes of relation; but the essential nature of this reality is not to be distinguished from that of a center. In short, the background against which experience is supposed to come and go like the shadows on the wall of the cave in Plato's *Republic* is either purely fictitious or else no other than a vaster and more perdurable experience. And so the contrast falls away, and with it all reason for denying the substantiality of experience in its own right.

A somewhat more puzzling difficulty is offered by the supposed intermittence of experience. We see our friend during the day acting and talking and believe that the stream of his experience is running fast; then he lies down in his bed and goes to sleep, when, we say, he is unconscious; his experience has ceased to be. We watch the clock and observe that the hand that tells the minutes runs round the dial eight times, when lo! our friend begins to move. Then we say he awakes; the stream of experience which for eight hours, barring fitful dreams, had ceased to flow, now flows again. For the man himself and for his unphilosophical observers there is nothing in this situation to prejudice his identity; he knows and his friends believe that the same man that went to sleep is now awake again. But the skeptical philosopher says it cannot be, for sameness implies uninterruptedness of existence. The man that awakens is another man, and the original man when he went to sleep ceased to be. A thing that is, then ceased to be, can never be again the same. Such is the opinion which, I surmise, would be accepted by the great majority of philosophers at the present time. But let us examine the status of the fundamental proposition upon which it is based, that a thing which has been and then ceased to be can never be again the same, which is equivalent to the proposition that persistence through time, or continuity of existence, is indispensable for identity, and therefore for substantiality. Is this proposition an a priori truth, an empirical fact, or a mere assumption? For myself, when I try to examine it fairly I do not discover it to be at all self-evident—quite the contrary. And I place my reliance, first, upon intuition, which, in our consciousness of personal identity, offers at least one exception to its validity, and, secondly, upon the dictum of Kant that the predicates "existence" and "nonexistence" do not affect the nature of anything and are therefore no true predicates at all, in the sense of expressing properties.[1]   Consequently, a matrix self that was may be the same as a matrix self that is; it does not lose or gain any property from its lapse into or emergence from nonexistence, and would be the same, not only after a few hours of nonexistence during sleep, but also, if circumstances were right, as they were for Rip Van Winkle, after one hundred years. To be born again, to rise from the death of nonexistence are no miracles; they are everyday facts of common experience.

We can, I think, state the reason why philosophers have failed to recognize this. It is because, wittingly or unwittingly, they have accepted certain mistaken views of time. They have pictured time as a series of moments, unique and exclusive and existing independent of events or objects "at" those moments. Then when they consider the self as having been at a certain moment they picture that self as existing then, and when they consider the self as it exists at a later moment, after an interval during which it did not exist at all, they think they find two selves: the self of eight hours ago, say, and the self of the present; and, of course, *two things cannot be one and the same thing.*

[1] Immanuel Kant, *Kritik der reinen Vernunft*, Elementarl., II Th., II Abth., II Buch, III Haupts., IV Absch., in *Philosophische Bibliothek*, ed. by von Kirchman (Leipzig: Verlag der Dürr'schen Buchhandlung, 1901), Band 37, pp. 512–519.

They can, it might be admitted, be the same in nature, even as the imaginary and the real dollar are the same *in nature;* but they cannot be the same *in existence.* Time, like space, it is held, is a principle of individuation. But this whole way of viewing the situation is false. In the first place, there are no moments in and for themselves, independent of events; and if that is true moments are not intrinsically exclusive, but capable of overlapping when the things at the various moments are the same. Consequently it is false to suppose that you are a series of selves existing at as many moments in the past as you have lived through, as if, when you climb a ladder, you leave behind in your ascent a self poised on each rung you have surmounted. There is only one self, the self of the present; and this present self exists not only now, but then, for the then is definable solely in terms of what exists then; and since the present self existed then and is the same as the so-called past self, it is both now and then, and then is also, partly at least, now. Or, to put the matter in a way which we shall explain fully in our chapters on time, moments are not like parallel, but rather like intersecting, lines; a self can therefore be at several moments, being in fact their point of intersection, which, as we have seen, is the same as to say that the self is identical through these moments. Or, to express the matter in another way, we must avoid what Bergson would call the spatialization of time. In space selves that exist at different points are *ipso facto* different, for points are exclusive. But moments are not exclusive; therefore the essential matrix of the present self and all past selves is one and the same self.[1]

Since the conception of personal identity which I have been explaining and defending has much in common with the conceptions of James and Whitehead, it will not be out of place to compare the three views. According to Professor Whitehead [2] the existence of an individual consists of a discrete succession of "actual occasions" or droplets of experience, each as it arises totally replacing its predecessor as it perishes. Yet there is a sense in which no actual occasion vanishes utterly, for it achieves

[1] For further treatment of these points see the discussion of time, Chapters VII–VIII.

[2] A. N. Whitehead, *Process and Reality* (New York: The Macmillan Co., 1929), chap. iii and *passim.*

what Whitehead calls "objective immortality" by passing on to its successor a group of "eternal objects" which, as embodied in all the occasions of a given series, define its nature and personality. It is clear, I think, that Whitehead's actual occasions correspond to the phases of what I have called the focal self, and that his eternal objects correspond to what I have called the matrix self, his objective immortality being analogous to what I have described as the carrying over of the matrix from one phase of the focal self to another. But unless I misconceive Professor Whitehead's mode of expression, there is a fundamental difference between his view and mine. For his eternal objects are universals, believed to have a sort of Platonic existence independent of the stream of experience and ingressing there from above, for reasons which I find hard to understand. Conceivably, these same eternal objects might ingress in other series of actual occasions; they represent the first mode of conservation which I have distinguished—conservation through the generic aspects of experience. On the other hand, I should maintain that the matrix self has no existence independent of a stream of experience, and could not possibly be embodied in any other center; it is, therefore, not a universal, but a deeper stratum of individual existence within the ongoing pulse of experience, a true *res cogitans* which abides as the more superficial layers overlying it are sloughed off. It may, as in sleep, fall into nothingness, but is capable of a literal resurrection at later moments. My conception of the matrix self has, therefore, more in common with the notion of the "concrete universal" of Bradley and Bosanquet, for it is a universal in their sense by being able to exist at many moments and by providing a basis of unity for the different pulsations of experience, and it is concrete by being a unique, individual mode of existence.

James's theory of personal identity (see chap. x of *The Principles of Psychology,* especially pp. 339, 340) is a subtler version of Hume's, influenced perhaps by a suggestion of Kant,[1] and is closely similar to Whitehead's. For James, also, the life of the individual consists of a series of discrete pulses of experience, called by him "Thoughts," each perishing in turn before the advent of its successor. These Thoughts are similar to each other in a unique way, even as all members of a herd of cattle which

[1] *Op. cit.,* "Beilege II. aus der erst. Ausg. Dritter Paralogismus: der Personalitaet," p. 739.

have the same brand are uniquely similar; and by reason of this similarity each passing Thought feels toward its predecessor a certain "warmth and intimacy" which it does not feel toward the past of any other self, and therefore appropriates as its own the Thoughts which have this particular "Brand." Obviously the Thoughts correspond to the "actual occasions" of Whitehead and the Brand corresponds to the "eternal objects." The genuineness of personal identity is denied, and in its place is substituted a sort of fiction, not unlike a legal fiction: James uses the term "title." The theory suffers from the same defect as Whitehead's by conceiving of experience as a succession of discrete entities instead of as a process of accretion and attrition around a central core that remains relatively but literally invariant. Once this false step is made, the grossly inadequate concept of similarity takes the place of identity.

IV

Universals and Experience

CRITIQUE OF NOMINALISM

IN OUR discussion of the substantiality of experience we were led to distinguish between repeatable and nonrepeatable factors in experience, the repeatable corresponding to what have been called universals; and we asserted that if universals exist they contribute to the conservation of experience and justify us in regarding experience as substance. But we accepted repetition as a given fact, without discussing the problems involved. For how can anything be repeated and yet remain one and the same? Does it not become by repetition a class of many similar things, thus losing its singularity altogether? Is not the class the cash value of the universal? On the other hand, do we not actually find many things in some respects one and the same, possessed at once of unique and literally common factors? The problem is not only interesting in itself, as the subtlety of mind exercised in its study during the Middle Ages attests, but also of decisive metaphysical importance. We cannot well proceed further without making an attempt to solve it. The problem may be approached most simply by dividing all terms into two grand classes—the first including adjectives, relations, and common nouns, the second including proper names and demonstratives—and enquiring whether terms of the one class can be reduced to terms of the other class. As simple illustrations of terms of the former class we may cite "blue," "greater than," "circular"; of terms of the second class, "this man," "this table," "this blue patch," "Hitler," "Mussolini." It is to be noted that if I combine a demonstrative with a common name the combination is a demonstrative, as "this man," "this table." In traditional philosophy three types of solution to the problem of universals have been proposed: realism, nominalism, and an intermediate view, conceptualism; but since the meaning of these terms has been shifting and since they are not quite relevant to current discussions, except perhaps "nominalism," I shall use a somewhat different set of designations, as follows: by "nominalism" I shall mean the view that entities expressed by terms of the first class (commonly called "universals") can be reduced to entities expressed by terms of the second class (commonly called "particulars"); by "universalism" I shall mean the theory that particulars can be reduced to universals; by "Platonism" I shall mean the theory that universals and particulars are coördinate, but separate in reality; by "Aristotelian realism," that universals and particulars are coördinate, but yet merely distinguishable factors or aspects of a single reality, the individual. Because of its great importance in current discussions I shall begin with a study of nominalism and devote most of my attention to it.

That the reduction of universals to particulars is possible in the case of simple adjectives has been maintained by Russell.[1] Thus the term "red" may be defined as x's similar to *this*, that is to say, the class of things similar to *this*, where the demonstrative "this" points to a quale present in the mind of the person making the definition. Similarly, the universal "table" may be defined as the x's such that x is similar to *this*, where "this" points to or denotes a table present to or appearing in the experience of the one who makes the definition. This definition presupposes, first, that I can point to or single out a factor in a concrete situation within the given, such as the quale red or redness, or that I can single out a given object as a whole, such as the appearance of this man or this table, and through its appearance refer to whatever so appears or manifests itself. It is presupposed, secondly, that I am able, through the use of such a symbol as x, to refer to individuals or factors of individuals, such as qualia, other than the individual or factor of an individual at hand in my experience.

Against this definition there is the important objection to which Russell has called attention, namely, that I am able to define a simple universal such as "red" only by the use of another universal—a relational universal, "similar to." Hence even though it be possible to define all simple universals in the way suggested, there is at least one universal that cannot be so defined; from which one can perhaps infer that relations at least

---

[1] Bertrand Russell, *The Problems of Philosophy* (New York: Henry Holt and Co., 1912), pp. 150–157.

are irreducible universals. For suppose I try to apply the same method of reduction to the universal "likeness" or "similar to." Then I would proceed in this fashion. I would find a situation which contained the empirical or intuitive similarity of two individuals or factors in individuals—two reddings, such as the reddings of two roses, or the two roses themselves, to which, with their similarity, I could point—the similarity being, it is assumed, just as individual and just as empirical or given as the two reddings or the two roses. Then, pointing to the situation in question, I could define similarity as situations *x* such as, that is to say, similar to, this situation. The definition seems to be circular, since it employs the term "similar" in the definition of "similar"; yet the circularity is only apparent, for the similarity employed in the definition is not the same relation as the similarity to be defined, since it is a relation of higher type. The similarity to be defined is a similarity between individuals or qualia in a situation; the similarity used in the definition is a similarity between situations themselves—that is to say, between similarities. But granting that the definition be not circular, we find that it seems to suffer from the defect of involving an infinite regress. For while it is true that the similarity used in the definition is a different relation from the similarity to be defined, it is nevertheless a relational universal, and although our definition has reduced one type of similarity to terms of the individual, it has done so by the use of another type of similarity, which has not yet been reduced. I must therefore proceed to reduce this relation according to the scheme proposed. This, to be sure, can be done, but only by the use of a relation of similarity of the third order, which could itself be reduced only by the use of a relation of similarity of the fourth order, and so on. Thus we see that although each relation of any order can be reduced, any reducing definition will itself contain a relation of higher order not yet reduced.

The inferences to be drawn from this peculiar situation are not immediately obvious. For the fact that every relation can be reduced is evidence for the nominalistic view; while the fact that a relation not yet reduced must be used in the reducing definition seems to be evidence that universals cannot be defined away, which would tend to establish a realistic view. We might restate the issue in the form of a dialogue, as follows:

Realist: You cannot define the universal in terms of similarity, because there is always one type of similarity which you use in your definitions which you do not define.

Nominalist: Yet even this type can be defined.

Realist: But only by means of a similarity of higher order which you will not define.

Nominalist: Yet even this I might define; hence every relation, of whatever order, can be defined.

Realist: Still, many such relations never will, as a matter of fact, be defined; and there will always be an undefined relation of similarity of order "n plus 1" in any attempt you make to define similarity of order n.

Nominalist: What is important is not that this relation be actually defined, but that I see that it can be defined.   I may always use an undefined term and treat it as a logical fiction provided that I know that it can be defined in such a way as to eliminate it.

Realist: Granted.   But you no sooner eliminate your "logical fiction," as you now call similarity n, than it recurs, as similarity "n plus 1," to plague you; you never do finally get rid of the universal.

Now which of the two speakers has the last word?   Russell holds—or held—that a vicious infinite regress is involved, and that therefore the attempt to dispense with universals is a failure: one universal at least seems to be necessary, namely, the universal relation similarity; and if there can be one universal, why not many?

But the nominalist might still make the following rejoinder. He might admit that there is no way, by definition, to eliminate from thought all terms that function as universals, or at least that there is one term that he cannot eliminate; yet he might insist that the failure to do so is due rather to a defect in the general structure of our logical processes, exemplified and enshrined in the theory of types and in the proved impossibility completely to formalize any mathematical theory, than to the nature of things themselves.   The universal "similarity" would remain a mere logical fiction, useful, nay indispensable, in designating situations where *this* and *that* are concretely similar to each other; for the fact that we need a logical fiction does not prove

that there are in nature things literally corresponding to it.   We
need the fiction "acceleration at a point," but we do not know
that such a thing exists.   So in the real world there would exist
this and *that*, and situations where *this* and *that* are concretely
similar, but not a universal relation "similarity."   Just what this
concrete similarity might be we shall discuss later.   But before
we attempt to adjudicate the issue it will be well to see how the
nominalistic theory faces certain other tests.   Every good definition of the apparent universal must show itself capable of two
things: it must provide a satisfactory theory of the concept—
through which the universal is apprehended or employed by the
mind—and it must provide a satisfactory theory of communication.   Let us first see what the nominalistic theory can make of
each of these.   We shall find the same difficulties occurring,
alongside a seeming success.

With regard to the concept we find a variety of nominalistic
views: there is the theory that the concept is nothing more than
a word, or a type of behavior of which the word is only a part;
there is the view that it is nothing more than an image; and
finally there is the view that it is a unique mental structure, perhaps a mosaic pattern of related images, perhaps even an image-
less thought *sui generis*, but in any case nothing more than a collection of particular mental events—words, reactions, images, or
the like.   So far as the logic or metaphysics of the matter is concerned, it makes little or no difference which of these views is
held, since all are alike in reducing the concept to a class of
items.   There is thus a complete parallelism between the nominalistic theory of what the universal is, viewed objectively, as has
just been explained, and what it is viewed subjectively, as a mode
of knowledge or expression.   For just as the single essence or
universal is reduced to a class of similar objects or qualia, so the
single symbol or concept becomes a collection of words, images,
thoughts, or what else; and in the one case as in the other the
semblance of singularity is explained away by similarity.

For example, consider the word "blue."   I say *the* word
"blue"; but for the nominalist there is no such thing as *the*
word "blue"; there is only a class of printed or spoken word
sounds, each one of which resembles the others.   Or if we consider not the word "blue," but the meaning of the word, there is
again no such thing as *the* concept "blue," but only a class of

similar mental events. Or if we interpret a word as a "reaction," in behavioristic fashion, then once more there is no such thing as *the* reaction "blue," but only a class of similar reactions. If I see something and say, It is blue, and see something else and again say, It is blue, or if you see something and say, It is blue, neither one of us is saying anything that can literally be called the same; we are simply responding in similar ways. The word or the concept "similar" is itself but a class of similar words or ideas. If I see two roses and say, They are alike, or two pennies and again say, They are alike, I am responding to two situations with two words—or two meanings—which themselves, if I respond to them, I shall respond to with not the same word, but with a similar word—a word that will be similar to the word which I used when I saw the roses or the pennies.   It is to be noted that if one attempts a *definition* of a word or a concept according to the nominalistic point of view, one embarks upon the same infinite regress that we have already met with in defining the universal, objectively considered. For I have before me, let us suppose, two red things, and I say, This is red, and, That is red; then I use two words to which I may react by saying, They are similar (similar$_1$); but the word "similar$_1$" is itself a word, which, if I wish to define it, I shall have to define as a word similar (similar$_2$) to words which I have used when I have compared roses or other such things; but now, of course, if I wish to define "similar$_2$," I shall react to it verbally and say, It is a word that is similar (similar$_3$) to words that I use when I react to situations such as confront me when I see two roses, and so forth; and so, ad infinitum.   Thus the logical situation with regard to the concept is precisely parallel to the logical situation with regard to the nominalistic theory of the universal, objectively considered. It is to be noted that the nominalist may well prefer to define the universal, not as a class of similar things, but rather as a class of similar responses—as a word or a meaning—for the reason that there are apparent universals without instances.   However, if the universal is defined as a class of similar words or concepts rather than as a class of similar things to which similar words or concepts are applied, it would nevertheless be admitted that such words or concepts have their origin and justification in the class of similar objects. Because there are many things alike, a concept or word is formed—or rather a class of concepts or words is formed—each of which may be applied to any object of the thing class, or may serve to represent the class as some sort of whole or unity.

With the foregoing theory of the concept in mind, let us next ask how it can perform its functions in judgment. Little argument is needed, I think, to show that for the nominalist every judgment must be essentially a judgment of likeness or similarity. Thus if I judge, This is red, I must mean x is similar to *this*, where *this* is anything given, such as the red of a tie or a flag, or it might be some image of like color in my mind associated with the word "red." The function of the concept in judgment is to reveal the nature of the object in the sense of affirming its likeness to something that I already have given in mind. Of course it may happen sometimes that there is nothing at hand in my experience to serve as what I shall call the "base" of the concept, in which case the concept functions as a surrogate of the base, which may be exchanged for a base if a base appears at any time. The concept has then a purely symbolic and provisional function; it is like a check or note that I may eventually cash for the amount of its face value. In order to illustrate this theory of the judgment I have used the simplest example possible; but the theory would explain more complex cases in the same—or rather in a similar!—fashion. Relational concepts would cause no difficulty. Thus to offer a simple example: If I judge that a certain star is between two others, I am affirming that the situation among the stars is similar to some given situation, such as that which holds when one phenomenal book is between two other phenomenal books. If it be granted—as it must—that the factor of pattern or structure is as real an aspect of given experience as the elements of the experience, then the use of a relational concept in judgment is the affirmation of a likeness between the structure of the object judged and some given structure.

At this point it may be objected to this whole way of viewing the significance of the concept—or of the universal for that matter, if any distinction is drawn between them—that the theory makes the definition and functioning of the concept depend upon a transient element of the given, called by us the base of the concept, when it seems clear that the concept has a superior stability and fixity, even though one would deny it the eternity of the Platonic Idea. The answer to this objection would be that while any particular that may serve as the base of the concept is transient, there are always new particulars like any given particular which may serve as a base. It is an empirical fact that like elements do appear in experience. So we do not make the value of a check depend upon this gold in my purse, but upon any gold anywhere. We are even able to amend our definition of the universal to meet this objection: The universal (or concept) U is equivalent to the x's such that x is similar to T, or similar to anything which is similar to T, where T is a *this*, a given element of experience. In order to take care of the cases where there are no instances of the concept in any experience—a twenty-dimensional space, for example—the universal is defined as a class of concepts similar to this concept, *this concept* being a free construction formed on the basis of some primary experience, but going beyond the scope of any primary experience.

A more serious difficulty is offered by the problem as to what can be meant by the validity of a judgment according to the nominalistic theory. As we have seen, the nominalistic theory of judgment must hold that every judgment affirms the similarity of the object judged to some element or configuration of elements in the given. When the object judged is itself a portion of the given this similarity can be tested and validated; but when the object is transcendent it is obvious that this cannot be done. Let us take an illustration that does not involve over-complicated metaphysical assumptions, an illustration that retains its convenience despite its all too frequent citation by philosophers. Suppose that I make the judgment that a certain person is feeling pain; then what I mean is that his state of mind is similar to a state of mind of my own when I have, say, a toothache. There is, of course, no way of directly verifying this similarity: by no known process can I compare the state of mind of my friend with my own state of mind. But the difficulty is not so much one of verifying the judgment, for that is a difficulty that besets every theory of knowledge in its effort to deal with a case of this kind, but rather one of understanding the import of the theory—what it really means. The crux of the difficulty is obviously the asserted similarity. When the concept and its object both lie within the given the problem does not arise, for similarity is itself a factor in the given situation or configuration, namely, object–concept-applied-to-object. But when the object lies outside the given, what exactly *is* the similarity asserted? It should be noted that in any realistic theory of universals this difficulty does not occur, for in accordance with such theories there is a real identity between the base of the concept and what the concept describes, and this identity is precisely what is asserted to exist in the judgment and is the basis of the similarity. That is to say, I actually find in the concept, or in the base of the concept, something in my experience the same as exists in the object of judgment. With regard to a certain factor in the object, it is not transcendent at all, but actually present in my experience: something of another's pain is literally my pain. Even if I cannot verify intuitively that this is true, what would be true if it were true is intelligible. But for the nominalist there is nothing of the kind. The concept that discloses the object and the object are two numerically diverse entities; they have no literally common nature at all: a common nature is only a fiction. They are *asserted* to be similar. But what can be meant by this similarity? That, I repeat, is the crucial problem.

We might mean that in nature itself, somewhere *between* my concept of your pain and your pain, there is an objective relation of similarity, similar to the experienced similarity between two elements in the given. But the existence of such a relation is wholly problematical, and belief in it would not be in accordance with the general spirit of nominalism. It would certainly be difficult to give any physical interpretation of it. Such a view would, however, be consistent with the theory of Stout,[1] who denied that universals are entities, yet thought that classes, to which he believed universals can be reduced, have some sort of existence and unity in nature itself. There is, next, the suggestion of Professor Sellars,[2] which I shall try to restate as follows. Data, he says, "are similar if they are such that if they were compared they would be adjudged similar." In the light of the context of the passage—a context that is not entirely clear —I take similarity to be something that has no existence in

---

[1] G. F. Stout, *Studies in Philosophy and Psychology*, Henriette Hertz Lecture (London: Macmillan and Co., 1930).

[2] R. W. Sellars, *The Philosophy of Physical Realism* (New York: The Macmillan Co., 1932), pp. 171–175.

nature, but only in mind. It is an ultimate deliverance of the mind on comparing items, an effect of their presence together in consciousness. Therefore, to say that items of which both are not present to consciousness are similar—as is the case of your pain and my concept of it—is to say that if they could be, or were, both brought into the mind they would produce this effect. It is emphasized, moreover, that this effect, this sense of alikeness, is not something arbitrarily added by the mind, but is founded on the intrinsic natures of the things compared. That is to say, it would arise only in the presence of certain items, not in the presence of certain other items.

This last view deserves extended comment. An objection certain to arise in many minds would be that if knowledge depends upon a similarity between the concept or the base of the concept and the object, and if this similarity is nothing more than a subjective response, knowledge is made to depend upon an accidental circumstance. Suppose, it might be said, the things were together in the mind, yet the mind failed to make the requisite response. Or might it not make the wrong response? Might they not be in fact similar, yet be judged dissimilar, or not judged at all? I do not know how Professor Sellars would extricate himself from this difficulty, but the only issue out of it that I can see is to recognize that the similarity between two empirical contents or data is not, as he claims, a mere response of the judging faculty, depending for its existence upon the exercise of that faculty, but is itself as primary a factor in experience as the two items to be compared. This view of the matter rests, of course, upon the belief that the relational factors of experience are as primary as the other factors. In view of the foregoing discussion we must restate the similarity between the concept and the transcendent object described by the concept as follows: By the similarity between a concept or its base and the transcendent object described by the concept is meant that if the concept or its base were together with the object in a single whole of experience there would arise, as a causal effect of the natures of the concept or its base and the object acting jointly, the experience of similarity, what I am calling empirical similarity. Now this statement is, I think, unexceptionable and provides, if not a sufficient account of judgment, at least one that is noncontradictory and—so far—true.

A second crucial test that any theory of universals must face concerns its ability to provide for communication or mutual understanding. Can the nominalistic theory pass this test, also? To a realistic theory of universals communication offers no difficulty. For even though the sensory content of experience is, in its concrete fulness, unique, it is clear that, if universals be real, the generic properties, both simple and relational, of the sensory content would be common to many minds and would serve as a base for communication. To illustrate by means of a simple example: I see before me a row of phenomenal objects —books on a shelf. Of the three farthest to the left two have red bindings, but the third is bound in yellow, and the yellow book is between the red ones. Moreover, the yellow book is several inches taller than the red books, which are of much the same, or of similar (!) size. I take it that my reader, whoever he be, understands me. And on a realistic theory of universals it is easy to see how he can understand me. For although the exact size and shape and color of the books I see have never appeared the same in his experience, nevertheless the generic universals, "book," "size," "red," "yellow" (or at least, if he is color-blind, "color"), and "betweenness" have appeared there; and concepts corresponding to these universals are aroused in his mind which are the same as the generic meanings in my mind when I describe what I am seeing. If now I invite the reader to come and look at the books the concrete colors will not be the same in his mind as they are in mine, and the concrete shapes will not be the same; but there will be a factor of generic form that will be the same, for he, as well as I, will see books, shapes, colors, and an order of betweenness.

In terms of a nominalistic theory, on the other hand, there is no such simple account of communication possible, because there is nothing that is the same in your experience and mine—not even sameness of structure. The word "color" or the word "table" does not arouse the same meaning in your mind that it arouses in mine, and even the word "betweenness" has no meaning which is common to us both. In terms of this theory there can be no intersection or contact of minds on an ideal plane, as is supposed to be the case according to realism. The account of communication which nominalism must give has to be a more complicated one. The ground has already been prepared for this account in the definition we have given of the universal as U equals x such that x S t or x S y S' t: that is is to say, the universal is defined as things such that any one of them is similar to *this* or similar to anything that is similar to *this*. For when I say that the book is red it is at least consistent to hold that what I intend to do is to arouse in your mind, not a meaning that is the same as my meaning, but a similar meaning. I am saying to you that this is to be described by a description similar to my own description. I am hoping, or assuming, that the event of uttering the word "red" will cause an event in your mind—a similar sound event—that will cause there a similar concept event. If a similar concept event occurs in your mind you will get my meaning. To this it may, however, be objected that even so there will be no mutual understanding, since the base of my concept cannot be the same as the base of your concept. If by "red_1," I mean x's similar to T, where T is a quale in my mind, it is evident that T cannot be in your mind also, to serve as the base of your concept, "red_2." But, as already indicated, the definition of "red_1" is not x's similar to T, but x's similar to anything that is similar to T. If, therefore, there is anything in your consciousness similar to T, that will serve as a base for your concept. When I say that "red" means anything similar to T, and point to T, it is necessary and sufficient for mutual understanding that my pointing to T shall cause you to single out in your mind a quale similar to T. The situation is exactly the same with regard to structural or relational factors in experience. These are not, it would be claimed, identical in your experience and mine, but similar; and my understanding of any structural meaning that you suggest to me is in terms of a like structure within my experience. It is again necessary and sufficient for mutual understanding that when I point to T as a basis for my structural concept, you will be able to point to something, say T_2, similar to T, as a base for your structural concept.

We are now in a better position to make an appraisal of the nominalistic theory. We see that, could we overcome the difficulty in the way of reducing similarity, a perfectly consistent theory could be devised. But this difficulty is formidable, for if we try to obviate it in the way already suggested we may fairly be charged with committing what I think may be called epistemological malpractice. For if we accept the suggestion that we retain the universal similarity as an irreducible element in thought—as a necessary logical fiction—but refuse to admit the existence of anything literally corresponding to it in nature, we are proceeding on the assumption that a theory can be true which we cannot even state consistently, an assumption which would involve a disparity between thought and reality, permitting the attribution of full truth to all imaginable nonsense. Of course it is possible to have a conviction of the truth of a hypothesis even when there are difficulties as yet unresolved in the way of stating it; but such difficulties at least weigh heavily against its plausibility. It is true also that the kind of difficulty in this case is not peculiar to this situation, but is, as we have indicated, analogous to problems that beset the entire apparatus of thinking, and until the crucial puzzles connected with the theory of types, the axiom of reducibility, and Goedel's theorem are better understood we are perhaps not in a position to deny the possibility that some method may be devised for obviating this and kindred difficulties. But until—if at all—that can be done, to view the term "similarity" as a necessary logical fiction would be to give it an altogether privileged and, it would seem, unauthorized, status. If a concept is necessary it is true. Other logical fictions, like "acceleration at a point," however useful, are recognized not to be necessary and can be restated in such a way as to eliminate the element of fiction.

But the question of the truth of nominalism does not depend, in the end, on the possibility of consistent statement. For even if that could be made, universals might nevertheless be real. The nominalistic reduction of the universal is the definition of a class of things, and classes of things would have meaning, and this definition would hold of them without internal contradiction, since the universal similarity would be real if universals are real factors in experience. Whether they are real or not is to be decided, like all other metaphysical questions, by appeal to experience. If we can find them in experience they are real, and no logical ingenuity of definition could disestablish them. The reality of universals is a question, not of theory, but of fact. We must, therefore, by an examination of experience, see whether it is a fact or not. But before we look into this we shall find it worth while briefly to consider a view the opposite of nominalism, Ramsey's theory that particular terms can be reduced to universal terms.[1]

Ramsey's argument may be summarized as follows: Ever since the time of Aristotle it has been held that true particulars are absolute subjects, that is to say, subjects that can never function as predicates. Thus, Socrates, while he may himself have many attributes or predicates, such as "wise," "snub-nosed," "Athenian," "ugly," and the like, cannot himself be an attribute or predicate of anything; and therefore the term which stands for Socrates in a proposition can never function as predicate in any proposition, but only as subject. This would be the case with all genuine proper names. I may, of course, speak of any earnest seeker after truth as a Socrates, but I cannot say that he is Socrates. Even of Socrates I cannot meaningfully say that he is Socrates: the proposition Socrates is Socrates is nonsense. We may put the matter in another way, thus: A universal is a function that may take many terms as arguments; but a particular can never properly be a function, it can only serve as the argument of a function. But let us see whether this ancient theory is strictly true. We have, let us say, the predicate or universal "wise." "Wise" is then our function, and this function may take as arguments the individuals Plato, Socrates, Aristotle, and others:

$$(1) \quad \text{wise} \left\{ \begin{array}{l} \text{Plato} \\ \text{Socrates} \\ \text{Aristotle} \end{array} \right\} \quad (\text{wise}) \; x$$

But now consider any one of these particulars, say Socrates: then it is true that wisdom, Athenian citizenship, goodness, ugliness, and the like belong to Socrates:

$$(2) \quad \text{Socrates} \left\{ \begin{array}{l} \text{wisdom} \\ \text{Athenian citizenship} \\ \text{goodness} \\ \text{ugliness} \end{array} \right\} \quad (\text{Socrates}) \; x$$

In (2) Socrates appears as the function, and wisdom, Athenian citizenship, goodness, and ugliness are arguments which the function has. There is complete symmetry between (1) and

[1] F. P. Ramsey, *Foundations of Mathematics* (New York: Harcourt, Brace and Co., 1931), chap. iv.

(2); only so-called universals have changed places with so-called particulars. Socrates behaves exactly like a universal, while the so-called universals behave as particulars.

In effect what this argument comes to is that, for formal purposes, we may treat the individual as a class of predicates, or even as a predicate. Socrates, for example, becomes the class of predicates "wisdom," "Athenian citizenship," "goodness," "ugliness," and so on; Plato becomes the class of predicates "goodness," "wisdom," "beauty," "nobility," and the like; each individual is thus a different selection from among all predicates or universals. These classes of predicates will overlap, in as much as some predicates will belong to many different classes, but each class will presumably be unique since it consists of a unique selection of predicates. Each unique selection of predicates will itself constitute a predicate; hence to Socrates there will correspond the predicate "Socratic," to Plato, the predicate "Platonic," so that the two propositions, Wisdom belongs to Socrates, and, Wisdom is Socratic, will be equivalent. I would remark that from a metaphysical standpoint there is nothing new in this theory, for it is clearly the same as the well-known theory that the individual is a meeting point of universals. Now from a purely formal standpoint which ignores all questions of existence this view is, I think, impeccable. If existence is ignored we can always transform any proposition to the effect that the individual K has the predicate P into the proposition that P belongs to K or that P is $Kcal$ or $Kish$. But the question remains open as to which of these expressions is more in accord with the *facts;* in other words, which has in it more of mere symbolism or logical fiction? For the nominalist there is an element of fiction even in the expression K is P, since P is a mere *façon de parler,* the literal interpretation of the expression being, K is similar to Tk, or similar to anything that is similar to Tk; and the expression, P is $Kish$, is doubly fictitious, since $Kish$ is also fictitious. For an Aristotelian realist, also, who recognizes a fundamental distinction between universality and particularity that implies the impossibility without loss of meaning of reducing the individual to a complex of universals, and who believes that the universal has no existence apart from the individual, the proposition, P is $Kish$, is not permissible, since it fails to take into account either of these facts. For him, K is P, is a metaphysically more satisfactory expression. Only for the universalist is the expression, *P* is *Kish,* satisfactory.

CONSTRUCTIVE THEORY OF THE UNIVERSAL

Let us try to get at the facts through an examination of experience, and let us be as candid as possible. Suppose I listen to a simple melody, then hear *it* again. (Notice that I say "it," as if somehow what I hear now and what I heard then were one; but let us try not to be prejudiced by what I say for fear that I may be employing a mere logical fiction.) Frankly, I seem to hear something the same, and I mean this literally: something seems to *recur* as I hear the melody again. I do not mean at all that I am merely hearing something similar, for that would imply that I am hearing one thing and remembering another; I mean that there is some respect in which, when I hear the melody now that I heard before, I am hearing one thing. The matter is analogous to what I find when I view myself as existing in two situations, as we have explained it in our chapter "Experience as Substance" (Chap. III). I experience myself as one thing, not as two things; and yet the oneness of myself is not incompatible with differences between myself of yesterday and myself of today. Such also is the case with the melody: there is some sense in which there is only one melody, and yet I "hear it twice," as I say. And, accordingly, despite the sameness of the melody now with the melody that I heard then, it is evident upon examination that there are great differences between the two hearings. Even if the piece is played on the same piano and by the same pianist the individual sounds and their rhythmic relationships will be demonstrably different, and the concrete patterned wholes will be different since wholes of different elements are always different. There are thus two sets of tones, yet there is, nevertheless, something given as the same: in some sense, as I have said, there is only *one* composition—now how so? What is it that is the same?

First of all, the pitch of the sounds is the same, for on both hearings each tone is caused by the same number of vibrations of the sounding medium; moreover, the type of interval between the tones—whether a fourth, a fifth, a diminished seventh—and the general rhythmic type of both sets of tones—for example, three-fourths time, glissando, or accelerando—are the same. Let

me repeat: the concrete quale of each of the tones is unique, and
the concrete patterned whole that they form is unique; but the
generic character of the tones, and of the intervals, harmonic and
rhythmic, is one and the same.   What is one and the same is not
a concrete nature but a generic character.

Let us next consider the sameness of two things that coexist.
In the Persian rug on my floor there are two patches of color.
I *say* that the same patch is repeated in order to form the pattern, but let us pay no attention to what I say; let us try to get at
the facts.   If I examine the two patches I can see that as concrete
qualia they are different.   The blueing of the one is not the
same blueing, quite, as the other; and though I call them both
square it is evident on close examination that their shapings are
different.   The concrete natures of both, I repeat, are different.
And yet it remains true that something that I find in the one I
find in the other, and I embody this discovery in judgment: I
judge this to be blue and also that to be blue, I judge this to be
quadrilateral and that to be quadrilateral.   The sameness is
obviously not a concrete, but a generic character: not the blueing, but the blueness is the same; not the shaping, but the quad-
rilateralness is the same.   Thus the oneness of two things that
coexist is of the same sort as the oneness of things repeated in
time.

Suppose, however, that the two patches of coloring were just
alike in every particular: the blueings alike, the shapings alike;
what then?   In this situation would not something besides a
mere generic property be the same?   Would not the whole concrete nature be the same?   We shall find the discussion of this
hypothetical case fruitful.

It should be remarked in the first place that, of course, the
supposition is highly improbable: it is highly improbable that
two things should be exactly alike.   If we distinguish the intrinsic properties from their relational properties we may be sure
that with regard to the latter they cannot be all alike.   It has
been suggested that for at least one property—the identity of a
thing with itself—this is certainly true;[1] for if we call the one
patch *a* and the other patch *b*, then *a* may be identical with *a*

[1] J. M. McTaggart, *The Nature of Existence* (Cambridge: At the University Press, 1921), I, 96; also G. E. Moore, *Philosophical Studies* (New
York: Harcourt, Brace and Co., 1922), p. 262.

but cannot be identical with *b*, and *b* is identical with *b* but is not identical with *a*.   This supposed property of self-identity is nonsense, however; there is no such relation as simple identity, as we have shown.[1]   Yet, aside from this, it is clear that there are other relational properties with regard to which they cannot be the same: one patch, for example, is to the right of me, the other, to the left; or one more to the right, the other, more to the left.   Even if we were to suppose that the two shapes were so placed that one was above the other, and the two were contiguous, so that they became the halves of a single shape, the two would differ in at least one property, namely, that the one would be above the other.   To this it may be objected that the relation to a spectator is irrelevant, that if we abstract this relation there is no meaning in "above" and "below," "right" and "left": suppose the two shapes were the sole things in the universe.   The answer is, that if we do abstract, we are forfeiting the reality of the patches and are then arguing merely about abstracta, for a phenomenal object has existence only in relation to a spectator.[2]

Suppose, however, instead of two patches of color we consider two monads: might not they be exactly alike in their relational properties?   With regard to them, we can abstract from a spectator, since their *esse* does not depend upon *percipi*.   But consider what this would involve.   It needs no argument to show that the space relations of the two monads—and these, as we shall prove, involve the time–cause relations—could not all be the same unless each monad lived in a universe or a part of the one universe which was the exact duplicate or mirror image of the other, for without the hypothesis of complete symmetry in the disposition of the two monads all their relations would not be the same.   And not only these relations, but the pasts of the two halves of the universe would have to be the same, since the past determines and overlaps the present.   The histories, therefore, as well as the present state of the two monads would have to be exactly alike.   That such a duplication of parts of the

---

[1] DeWitt H. Parker, "Reflexive Relations," *Philosophical Review*, XLII (1933), No. 3 : 303–311.

[2] Here and in the following page I am arguing against the view expressed by Professor C. H. Langford in "Otherness and Dissimilarity," *Mind*, XXXIX, N. S., No. 156.

universe is enormously improbable would be granted, but the question may still be pressed, Would it be impossible? My answer is unhesitatingly yes, and for the following reasons. If there could be two things absolutely alike in intrinsic and extrinsic properties then we could distinguish between the nature or "form" of each—which would be identical—and something else, corresponding to Aristotle's "matter"—the "bare numerical difference" of modern writers—upon which the twoness of the things would rest. But in that case, it is clear, is it not, that the form and the matter would be indifferent to each other: they would be related in a purely external fashion; the difference in matter would have no effect upon the form. But, as we shall show, there are no purely external relations. Moreover, if, as we shall also prove, value is, as Plato held, a universal category, it is difficult to see how there could be two half universes exactly alike, for there would be no value in there being two. Repetition is, to be sure, one of the great principles of value in art—in music notably so, but also in the arts of spatial design, as any repeat attests—but in art repetition is never mere repetition, for something is always developed through it, some new emphasis or new illumination of theme. We want to hear the theme over again in order to wring from it its total value, which we do not achieve at first hearing; or we want the same in a new context for the sake of what the context does to it and it to the context; we want sameness in difference: mere sameness is boring. I conclude therefore that the two patches or the two monads cannot be exactly alike in all properties; and if they are not exactly alike, the total nature of each is unique. Since the total nature of each is unique, there is no need to base individuality upon some special principle like space or time or "matter" in the Aristotelian sense. Space and time cannot be principles of individuation, par excellence, for they are nothing but relations, and any type of relationship will individualize as well as they. As for matter, it has yet to be shown that, besides the complete concrete nature of anything, there is aught else. For myself, when I examine closely into the being of anything, whether monad, sensum, phenomenal object, or activity, I can find nothing there except the concrete nature of the thing. The *infima species* is the individual, and every universal is generic with relation to it.

If the universal is generic only, it follows that the thesis of universalism, to the effect that the individual can be resolved into a complex of universals, is false. Any set of universals, such as "wise," "snub-nosed," "ugly," "Athenian," and the like, might be applicable to another person besides Socrates, and could never be adequate to his full reality. Even so-called "definite descriptions," like the "husband of Xantippe" would not serve the purpose of completely covering the nature of Socrates, for in itself the definite description is also generic, since it is only by means of intuition that we can know that Xantippe is an individual, that there is only one of her. For all the mere concept "Xantippe" can tell us—a concept that can be explicated only in terms of genera—there might be two or more Xantippes, and therefore two or more husbands of Xantippe, or, in fact, no Xantippes at all, for no concept guarantees the existence of the corresponding universal. To put the matter in still another way: the proper name, unlike any other name, can never be defined; it can only be identified in an intuition. Yet the universalist theory of judgment, though inadequate, is true so far as it goes. If Socrates is wise, then wisdom belongs to Socrates and wisdom is Socratical, where by "Socratical" is meant a complex of universals which, not identical with Socrates, will hold of Socrates. And, in general, if the individual K has the predicate P, then the proposition, K is P, will imply the proposition, P is $Kish$, but will not be equivalent to it; for P is $Kish$ does not imply the existence of K, or the existedness of K, which is contained in K is P. The universalist theory of judgment is, therefore, like its theory of the individual, inadequate. Yet it contains its element of truth, for the individual always possesses universals, that is to say, generic aspects or factors: there is no absolutely individual thing.

To return to our attempt at a constructive view of universals: We have maintained that intuitively the universal is to be found as a generic character in many individuals—as red is to be found in a tie, a coat, an autumn leaf, or as a tonal pattern is to be found the same in many different renditions of a composition. In the way of this insight, however, the apparent spatial and temporal separation of individuals has seemed to interpose a screen. It seems as if we had two contrary intuitions: an intuition of generic sameness on the one hand, and of spatial and temporal separation of individuals on the other. With regard to temporal separation, however, as has already been indicated, the principle which we used in the discussion of personal identity provides a means of overcoming the difficulty. For I have shown that in comparing the present of an individual with its past we are not concerned with two individuals, since past individuals do not exist, but with a single individual, the present one, in which the matrix self of the past survives: the seeming evidence to the contrary is due, not to any intuitive separation of past and present, but to a false theory of the relation of past and present. So when I compare two renditions of a composition I am not comparing two separate musical structures, for the past and the present renderings overlap in the present, or if both belong to the past they are both present as remembered, and overlap in memory.

As for the difficulty due to the seeming spatial separation of individuals, that too can be eliminated I believe. We shall find it convenient to discuss the case of metaphysical space apart from phenomenal space. The problem with regard to the former is this: How can there be any identity between monads such as is implied by the reality of universals, when monads are distant from each other?—whether millions of miles apart or a centimeter makes no difference in principle. The answer is that distance does not involve any separation of the substance of monads, but merely, as we shall show, a time interval between events that occur in different monads. The difficulty is due to the persistent error, which cannot be sufficiently deplored, of transferring to nature the intuitive properties of phenomenal space. The fact that you and I are a thousand miles apart when we hear over the radio Schnabel's performance of the *C-Minor Sonata* does not imply any real separation of our experiences. These experiences may very well contain, despite the distance between us, an identical, overlapping factor, namely, the tonal structure of the sonata. When, indeed, events are simultaneous there is no distance between them except in a very Pickwickian sense.

Coming now to phenomenal space, we do seem to have an intuitive separation of items: the blue patch of color in the visual expanse of the rug is intuitively separated from the similar patch; there are, in fact, other patches between. It looks, therefore, as if we had a sort of antinomy of intuition: on the one hand we find the generic color of the two patches the same, but on the other hand the patches are undeniably two, and are seen to be separate. How can any part or factor of two such separated things be the same? We have already hinted at the answer to the question. It depends upon the theory of the unity of mind offered in our second chapter. It follows from this theory that two phenomenal items, like the two patches, while separated in the visual expanse, are not utterly separate in as much as both are items in a single monad. It has been shown that items phenomenally distant are, as items of a single mind, as closely connected as items phenomenally near. Now my claim is that the identity of the two patches is mediated through the fact that both are elements in a single monad: as items of the visual expanse they are separate, but as items in a single monad they are not separate. The mind constitutes another dimension within which they are connected. This connection through the monad is not artificial, for the reason that the phenomenally separated items have no existence except as elements of the monad. The following analogy may serve to clarify the situation. Consider two points on the outer surface of a ring: these points are obviously separate, and, if the surface of the ring were all, there would be no possibility of any connection between them. But grant a third dimension and draw the chord between the two points, and a connection is effected. Such is the case, I am claiming, with items phenomenally distant in space within a monad: they have identical factors *by way of* the interfusing dimension of consciousness.

Not only is the nominalistic theory intuitively false, but the theory of judgment that it proposes can, furthermore, be shown to be inadequate. This theory is to the effect that any simple judgment, such as, K is blue, really says, K is like *this*, where *this* is some element or factor in experience pointed to. Now I think no one can deny that the judgment, K is blue, implies that K is similar to something, such as T, which could serve as what I am calling the base of the judgment in question. There is nothing false in the theory: no contradiction between it and a more adequate theory. In fact, not only does the judgment, K is blue, imply the proposition, K is similar to T (or similar to something similar to T), but the two propositions are equiva-

lent, that is to say, both are true or both are false. But equivalence of judgment is not sameness of judgment. And what I
am actually asserting when I judge that K is blue is that K has
a certain property of the genus "blue"; that blueness is a factor
in K—is there in K. That I am not asserting that the concrete
blue is there is clear, because you understand the proposition
even though you are not seeing the blueing that I am seeing.
I am not even asserting what specific shade of blue is there,
but the bare genus only. This is the *sense* of what I am asserting. That this assertion is true when some other proposition
like, K is similar to T, or similar to something similar to T, is
true does not prove identity of sense with that proposition. The
propositions, K is blue, and, Two plus two are four, are also
equivalent, but they are not identical. Yet the consistency between an intuitively true theory of judgment and the nominalistic theory is an important fact: it explains the persistence of
nominalistic theories.

Equally inadequate, intuitively, is the nominalistic theory
of communication. Intuitively, communication is a meeting of
minds—a contact between a meaning expressed and a meaning
understood. To understand another is to mean what he means,
so that the mind of one is partly the mind of the other. Understanding is coming upon yourself in another mind. This constitutes the peculiar experience—and pleasure—of mutual understanding: the painful separation of the two minds is overcome
in an intellectual embrace. The unity of minds involved in
communication is, of course, only partial; if it were complete
there would not be communication but a mere dialogue with
self. The full concrete reality of the sensa in my mind is different from that in yours: the concrete reality of the patch which
I see is not the concrete blue that you see; the full reality of the
sound of my voice as I hear it is not the same with the full reality
of the sound as you hear it. Yet the generic blueness of each
patch is the same, so that when you say, "Look," and I look
and see, there is something the same in our two minds. In
seeing the patch in my mind I am looking into your mind, and
you are looking into mine. The situation is analogous with
regard to concepts. All that is in my mind when I say, "Rose," is
not in your mind; but there is a minimum of meaning—and this
is the logical meaning—that is common, and that common factor

is the basis of our mutual understanding. In a logically perfect language like mathematics the aim is to create concepts that are completely transferable from one mind to another. But, though false, the nominalistic theory retains its element of truth here also. For since the concrete nature of any sensum or any concept is always different in different minds there is never more than similarity between these totals.

When we come to enquire into the mode of existence of universals we are compelled to move again toward a recognition of the element of truth in the nominalistic view. For universals have no existence except as they are present in concreta, be these concreta sensa or concepts. They do not exist separate from particulars—as Plato thought and as Whitehead seems to think—and then ingress into particulars from some alien "realm of essence": their whole mode of being is as factors in concreta. Aristotle is right rather than Plato, and many of his arguments still remain valid. Even if we did not accept the principle of the denial of the existence of vacuous actualities, we should be certain that this is so. Universals, as genera, are essentially dependent existences. They seem to have an independent status only because it is possible to isolate them within the concreta in which they exist, and, by means of the concept, designate them as such. As thus abstracted, they have a quasi existence of their own, but only through the concepts that mean them. Moreover, because of the constructive power of the mind, it is possible to mean complex universals which have no existence—except the existence which they possess as meanings. But the fact that they are meant in the concept no more confers independent existence upon them than imagination confers independent existence upon fictions. The highly complex universals defined in the geometry of many-dimensional spaces have no more independent status outside the minds of geometers than has Shakespere's Hamlet.

The fact that universals have a quasi existence as meanings has led to the identification of universals with meanings. But this is a vast mistake. The concept is the mode of mental activity through which the universal is meant; it is not the universal itself. The concept "blue" is not the generic blueness that exists as a factor or property in any blue thing: I find the blueness in the thing, but I do not find the concept of blue there. The generic property is in the blue thing whether or not I abstract it through the concept or meaning. The concept bears the same relation to the universal that the proper name, the individual concept, bears to the individual that it means or names: as "blue" is to the given blueness in any blue thing, so is the name "Julius Caesar" to the historic individual meant by this name. The identification of the universal with the concept is a form of vicious subjectivism.

Although false, it is easy to see how this view has arisen. It has arisen because concepts, while not the universals which they mean, do nevertheless themselves embody universals. The concept "blue" is not my particular mental state, my transient mental process, an event appearing now and never reappearing, but the common denominator, the essence present in all my acts of conceiving blue, and present also in all your acts of conceiving blue. This presence of universals in meanings justifies us in speaking of *a* meaning or *a* word such as "*blau*" or "blue" instead of a class of words or meanings, as would be strictly proper if nominalism were true. For, as we have seen, according to that view there is no such thing as a word or a meaning; the word or the meaning which the word has is a fiction representing or symbolizing a whole class of mental acts. This class is, of course, a reality, but is not the word or the meaning. The word or the meaning is the essence present in all such acts: it is what they all have in common. We must accordingly distinguish (1) the universal meant by a concept, (2) the act of meaning or conception, as a unique mental process, (3) the essence of this mental process, *the* meaning or concept, which is itself a universal and is present as a single entity in all acts of meaning. It is clearly an easy thing to confuse this universal which is a meaning with the universal which is what the meaning means. The confusion is especially easy when the universal has no existence except as a meaning, as is the case with some of the highly complex concepts of mathematics. Here there is nothing that we can find by means of which we can contrast the universal as a meaning with the universal as a factor or a generic property of a concretum. Moreover, meanings have, as the development of mathematics shows, intrinsic relations among themselves that can be explored without reference to the presence of the universals meant in concreta, which alone would confer upon them existence. But that there is a difference between the universal as a meaning and the universal as a primary generic factor in a concretum is verified by contrasting, say, the meaning "blue," or the meaning "order," with the generic property which may be intuited as belonging to the blue sky or the row of books on a shelf. The universal as an existing, generic factor in a concretum is an object of intuition, whereas the universal as a mere meaning may never be intuited. We have no intuition or verification of the concept of a twenty-dimensional order; but we do mean such an order and operate very successfully with the concept of it. And yet, as the example of mathematical analysis proves, the fact that we cannot verify or intuit the universals meant explains the possibility of error when we operate with unverifiable meanings.

The existence of universals in meanings is the basis, as we have indicated, of all mutual understanding. It constitutes the intelligibility and the heritable essence of all discourse, scientific or poetic. When we read, "Now comes the pain of truth, to whom 'tis pain . . . ," an identical universal in meaning enters, through the vehicle of these words, into your mind and mine. This meaning is, moreover, the same—literally the same—with the universal in meaning that grew in the mind of the poet as he created this line. Hence—again literally, not fictitiously—a factor of his very mind lives anew, and has become immortal in the thought of his readers, resurrected from the dark womb of nonbeing.

V

Experience and Matter

OPPOSED to the philosophical conviction that experience is substance stands the belief of common sense that reality consists of "things": a collection of tables and chairs, roses and tulips, stars and atoms, and the like. And no matter how confused this belief 'may be, no philosopher can wisely treat it with contempt. For it contains, as every thinker admits in the end, a residuum of truth which no amount of sophisticated reflection can impugn. But this residuum is like the pure gold that the refiner comes at only after he has separated out of the crude ingot a mass of impurities. If we try to discover what, exactly, a thing is, we find it very illusive. We seem to hold it in our hands; we seem to see it face to face; but when examined it dissolves almost into nothingness.

What in fact is a thing? As a preliminary definition, we may try the following: A thing is an entity disclosed by sense perception—it is, therefore, something that can be seen, touched, smelled, tasted. All the familiar examples of things—the rose, the tulip, the chair, the table, the star—are of this character. To be a thing is perhaps not the same as to be perceived, but does at least imply the capacity to be perceived. What cannot be perceived is certainly not a thing: a state of mind is not a thing, for it cannot be tasted or smelled or heard or seen. There is, however, an objection that may be raised against this definition, to wit, that it defines a thing wholly in terms of our method of getting knowledge of it, whereas a good definition should express the essential nature of the object itself. Yet the definition does, I think, cover this point; for when I say that a thing is disclosed in sense perception I mean not only that my knowledge of it comes through the senses, but that it possesses properties analogous to—that is to say, of the same kind as—those given in sense perception; and analogy may be, in the limiting case, identity. Thus I not only know the rose by seeing and touching it, but I know it as possessing, if not the very size and shape that are given when I see and touch it, at least a size and shape closely similar.

With this definition established, we are, however, only at the beginning of our analysis. For it is clear that there are two very different kinds of things which people have accepted as substance: phenomenal or common-sense objects and scientific objects. The rose will serve to illustrate the one, the atom will illustrate the other. The first type is accepted by common sense as substance, the second by men of science. Of phenomenal objects it is characteristic that they *appear* in sense perception, whereas scientific objects do not *appear*. Thus, in the case of the rose, I can *see* it: its color, shape, and size are there yonder; but as for the atom, although I can *know*, for example, how large it is, I cannot *see* how large it is. It may be true that I have as much scientific information concerning an atom—and just as cogent reasons for believing in its existence—as I have concerning the rose or the goblet, but, I repeat, there is this crucial difference between them: in the one situation the object seems to be given, in the other it is not given. Or, reverting to our definition of a thing, we may put the difference thus: In the case of the phenomenal object, the analogy between the properties of the object and what is given in the sensuous intuition through which the object is disclosed is complete—the object has, for example, the size as you see it; in the case of the scientific object, the object has, to be sure, what we call size, but size only in the most abstract and general sense, and a size that can never be brought within sense perception.

The contrast between the scientific object and the phenomenal object cannot, therefore, be made entirely clear until we have studied the apparent givenness of the latter. We may well commence by asking the question whether its givenness is of the same order as the givenness of sense data. There are, it is true, some who question the given existence of what are variously called "sensa," "sense data," "sense elements," or the like, as separate, individual elements of experience—I am myself one of these, as will appear. None, however, would doubt, I believe, the existence and givenness as *factors* in experience of what whether separable or not I call the sound that I hear when I ring a bell, or what I call the taste of a cucumber when I eat a cucumber, or the perfume of a rose when I smell a rose. And in such cases it is clear that the givenness of these entities is the same as their existence as factors of mind. They are literally *given* or *present*. And because they are given it is always possible for a description which means one of them to pick it out and confront it face to face. If I am a student looking through a microscope and the professor says to me, "Do you see a moving shape of a certain size and contour in the field of vision?" then, if such a shape is present in my field, I can confront this description with the shape. The same mind that holds the description of the shape holds the shape also within itself. On the other hand, if the shape is not in my field—although it may perhaps exist in some sense—for me it is not given, and the description which I have of it cannot confront it.

Now, it is clear that phenomenal objects are not given in the manner in which sense data are given. For, in the first place, the whole of a sense datum is given: the sound that I hear is the whole sound, there is no more of it to be heard; the color that I see is the entire color; the perfume that I smell is the entire perfume. The sound, to be sure, may be regarded as a part of a melody the rest of which I do not hear, but the entire sound that I hear is heard: there is no part of that sound to be heard. Even with regard to the visual panorama facing my eyes it is true that the whole visual sense datum is seen; what is not seen is not a sensum, but a hypothetical physical object which might cause in me a visual sensum of such a kind that the sensum that I apprehend would be similar to a part of this new sensum. It is a law of sensa that they are given as total or not at all. But a phenomenal—or common-sense object—is never given as a whole in the manner in which sense data are given. A phenomenal object is a three-dimensional volume, with front and back, inside and outside. The other side of the goblet is not given, its finer parts are not given; no more than its "front surface" [1] is given. Moreover, when seen in perspective, there is a disparity between what is given and what is believed to be real. The familiar contrasts between so-called real size and shape and apparent size and shape illustrate this point. The phenomenal man— the so-called real man—is perhaps six feet tall, yet at a certain

[1] H. H. Price, *Perception* (London: Methuen and Co., 1932) , p. 142.

distance looks only about four feet tall. What is given is four feet tall, what appears is six feet. Or, to cite another familiar example, the coin is "really" circular—that is to say, the phenomenal object that appears is circular; but it may look like an ellipse when only the elliptical shape is given. Yet there are situations where the shape of the coin is given, as when I look at the coin in such a way as to see it as a circle.

In its entirety, therefore, the phenomenal object is given only as a meaning. Yet it is given in and through a sense datum which, in the majority of cases, acts as a symbol of it. If the phenomenal object were given as more than a meaning the whole of it would be present in full sensuous reality, but, as we have seen, this is never the case; at best only a part can be so given. It belongs to the nature of the phenomenal object that part of it, at least, may be given; its "surface" may be given. In that case the sense datum through which it appears is part of the thing that appears. And even when the sense datum is only a sign of the thing, and no part of it, it is a species of the same genus as the surface of the appearing thing. The four-foot appearance—sense datum—is a species of the same genus as the six-foot reality that appears through it. This is the circumstance that creates the illusion of the givenness of the phenomenal object in all cases and distinguishes the way in which a sense datum presents a phenomenal object from the way in which it may present other types of objects. When the sensuous shape, the figure 5, means the number five, there is a seeming presence of the number in the figure—the figure looks almost as if it were 5; but it is not a "real" presence of the number because of the disparity of the symbol, an arbitrary sensuous shape, and what the shape means; the number can be given only in a group, such as the Dionne "quints," which illustrates it.

If the phenomenal object be the sort of thing which I have indicated, then it cannot be substance, for at least two decisive reasons. The first reason is as follows. Since the surface of the phenomenal object may actually be given in sensuous intuition it must, as we have seen, coincide with the sense data that present it, and its metaphysical status must be bound up with them. If sense data are not substance, then the surface of the phenomenal object is not substance. And that sense data are not substance was demonstrated by Berkeley. For let us recall some of the qualifications which are possessed by anything that is substance: independence, which includes independence of the mind of the observer; causal efficacy; permanence despite change. But no one of these qualifications is satisfied by sensa, although, as for independence, it must be admitted that not all the arguments that have been used for disproof are cogent. For example, those who deny independence commonly argue from the seeming dependence of sensa upon the organs and apparatus of the central nervous system—of color upon the eye, sound upon the ear, and the like. Yet to this argument one may effectively make answer that dependence upon the brain and organs of sense is not dependence upon the mind, and that, besides, everything which exists has its conditions: no entity would qualify for substantiality on the basis of absolute independence. Or, again, one may argue, as does Samuel Alexander,[1] that the sense organs are not conditions for the existence of sensa, but rather, as it were, doors which open the mind to their presence. The conditions for the existence of sensa are physical, not physiological: not the ear, but the vibration of the air, not the eye, but the electromagnetic wave, are the conditions for the existence of sound and color. It is difficult to argue decisively one way or the other on the basis of such considerations; but the existence of alternative hypotheses shows at least that arguments for the dependence of sensa on the mind, drawn from the relation of sensa to the sense organs, are not conclusive.

The only conclusive argument with regard to the matter is that of Berkeley: The essence of a sensum is to be perceived; its *"esse est percipi."* That this famous phrase was interpreted as signifying that the essence of everything is to be perceived— with all the absurd consequences pointed out by the anti-idealists —was, of course, not Berkeley's fault, for what Berkeley said was that the essence of what he called "ideas" is to be perceived. And the beauty of this proposition is that it cannot be established or refuted on inductive, "scientific" grounds, but is strictly of a metaphysical character, that is to say, it depends upon the analysis of experience itself. A sound is the same as a sound heard; a perfume is the same as a perfume smelled; a color is

[1] Samuel Alexander, *Space, Time and Deity* (London: Macmillan and Co., 1920), II, 138.

the same as a color seen; the being heard, smelled, and seen are of the very nature of the sound, perfume, or color. The relation of the sensum to the perceiving self is not external but internal, so that to think this relation away is to think the sensum away. A world that consisted of mere sounds, colors, odors, and the like would not only be impossible on general empirical grounds, but intrinsically absurd. This is not a matter of mere "definition by initial predication"; [1] for we do not begin by defining a sound as a sound heard and then deduce, by mere analysis, that it is something heard; we observe the sound itself and discover that it contains, as part of its nature, being heard. Another way of stating the same fact would be this: Experience is an organic unity; hence neither one of its essential factors, the self or the sensa, can exist apart from the complex of the two. Mere sensa are abstractions.[2] Experience is like a triangle: there is a base composed of sensa and an apex, which is the self, and every element of the base exists in relation to, and only in relation to, the apex. If we make the *Gedankexperiment* of trying to think of a world of sensa without a self we find that we cannot do so, that the self inevitably obtrudes into such a world. We must fail, just as we should fail if we were to try to think of a triangle as a mere base without height. Existence is at least two-dimensional, "double-barreled"; it cannot be reduced to a one-dimensional sensuous line. As Professor Hoernlé has noticed, Berkeley's principle, *"esse est percipi,"* is the same as Whitehead's principle of the exclusion of "vacuous actualities." [3]

The failure of any one of the necessary prerequisites is enough to disqualify any proposed entity for the status of substance. It is, therefore, superfluous, in a way, to consider sense data with reference to the other qualifications, causal efficacy and permanence; yet our insight into the nature of sense data and the phenomenal objects presented through them will be increased if we do so, even briefly. To begin with causal efficacy: the passivity of sensa, as claimed by Berkeley, is a matter of

---

[1] R. B. Perry, *Present Philosophical Tendencies* (New York: Longmans, Green and Co., 1921), p. 128.

[2] George Berkeley, *The Principles of Human Knowledge* (1711), Sec. 5.

[3] R. F. A. Hoernlé, "The Revival of Idealism in the United States," in *Contemporary Idealism in America* (New York: Harcourt, Brace and Co., 1920), chap. xii.

direct inspection.[1]   A sensum may elicit action, as when I stop
my car on seeing the red color of the signal, but does not itself
act.   A sensum may be an occasional, but it cannot be an
efficient, cause.   It is something to which there may be reaction,
but it does not itself react.   The dancing flame that seems to
consume the wood on the hearth appears to do so only because
we take it as the index of the forces which we believe to lie
beneath.   But taken as a mere sensum, the flame is nothing but
a patch of light and color, changing against the wider visual
panorama of the wood, the hearth, and the room.

In the third place, it is equally clear that sensa are not permanent.   They come and go, arise and perish; there is nothing
of them that abides.   They are events, momentary existence.
We do speak of hearing the same sound and smelling the same
perfume:

> The voice I hear this passing night was heard
> In ancient days by emperor and clown:
> Perhaps the self-same song that found a path
>   Through the sad heart of Ruth, when, sick for home,
> She stood in tears amid the alien corn.

But the "self-same song" referred to in the poem was not the
same sound events, but the universal present in all such similar
events.   Even so we speak of hearing the same sonata or symphony when, obviously, what is the same is a universal, not an
event.   Likewise, to see the same rose or to sit in the same chair
or to wear the same suit of clothes or to come back into the same
room is not to undergo the same events but to experience the
same *type* of sensa.   In fact, viewed as a sensuous surface, the
same thing—the same room, chair, or rose—is nothing but a universal—a composition of odors, touches, or sights—strictly analogous, from this point of view, to a symphony which we may
hear again and again, tomorrow as well as today.   Our experience of sameness in the sense data is our awareness of the
invariance of the pattern and the generic quality.   The yellow
of the lamp shade is demonstrably a different concrete yellow
from what it was yesterday, and its shape a slightly different
shape, but it is still yellow and still shaped; we ignore the difference in the species, fixing our attention on the sameness of the
genus.

[1] Berkeley, *op. cit.*, Sec. 25.

We have, therefore, proved the unsubstantiality of sensa. There follows, as we have seen, the unsubstantiality of phenomenal objects. They are all of them, to use the language of Berkeley, "ideas." Perceptual experience is a panorama of ideas of objects, some of which are partly realized in sensa, as the rose is, others of which are merely signified by sensa of the same kind as the objects meant, even as the moon is, which looks round, but not as large and round as we think it to be. If we confine our attention, for the sake of simplicity, to visual phenomenal objects, the external world as it appears in perceptual experience is like a vast landscape painting. There are pure colors and lines and shapes, which, as in a painting, may engage our attention for their own sake and evoke vague emotional responses in us, and there are object meanings, comparable to the factor of representation in a picture, signified by the pure sensuous elements. Thus, in a picture, that bit of green color represents a leaf; and this pure red represents a rose; that graceful line, the curve of a girl's breast. But similar elements might be present in anyone's visual panorama; there too a pure red may appear and represent a rose; a bit of green, a leaf; a curve, a girl's breast. I would not imply that there is no difference between a landscape painting and the panorama of nature; but it is a difference in what lies behind—a difference in the attached field of countercontrol—not a difference in what appears to the eye. And the panorama of nature, as a panorama, is as unsubstantial as a landscape by Corot.

Another circumstance damaging to phenomenal objects is their replaceability by scientific objects. There is not one of them which, as a result of experimental research working hand in hand with the mathematical imagination, is not abandoned in favor of some system of molecules, atoms, or electrons. It is as if we had a room well and comfortably furnished for a time and then found that our old pieces would no longer do, and so put in their places articles of quite different style and make. For the scientific object is radically different, as we have seen, from the phenomenal object: it is given neither in the way sensa are given nor in the way phenomenal objects are given; no part of it is contained either as a whole or in its elements within sense experience; and no part of it can be so given. Even the atom as formerly conceived could not be so given: it was too small to be seen or touched, and it was without smell or taste or sensible heat or cold.   Science has not destroyed the phenomenal world, but it has destroyed its claim to substantiality, for in place of this world it has put another, unintuitable one.   Yet nothing of value has been lost in the process, for all the colors and warmth of perceptual experience are retained; the sun still rises in gorgeous display for any beholding eye, even though the mind has replaced it by a sea of electromagnetic waves.

There are two types of scientific objects, the picturable and the unpicturable.   The picturable type was characteristic of the history of science up to the end of the nineteenth century, and the great revolution of the science of our century may be summed up as the substitution of unpicturable for picturable objects.[1] But of course the picturable objects were not discarded all at once.   The earlier form of the Bohr atom is still picturable. If electromagnetic events are waves, they are to a certain extent picturable objects.   By a picturable scientific object is meant one which, while it cannot be given in human intuition, is nevertheless representable in imagination or diagram or model. Such an object is still a thing in the sense defined, for it has properties analogous to, that is, of the same kind as, those disclosed in perception.   If it moves, it moves like a wave, and can we not see the waves of the ocean move?   If there is distance between its elements, we can conceive of this as comparable to the spread between two articles of furniture in the room or the spread of the top of the table.   If it is here, it is here the way the typewriter is here; if it is between two other atoms, it is between as the typewriter is between the window and the door. The picturable scientific object, although the mere conceptual ghost of a thing, is still, perhaps, a thing.

But the unpicturable scientific object—is that a thing?   An object that is neither a particle nor a wave but somehow both, that is neither here nor there but is somehow both here and there, that does not rest or move in the way I rest in bed and my children move around me, that varies in size and shape according to its relative velocity, and even in mass according to circumstances—is that a thing?   Clearly such an object does not have properties analogous to those given in sense perception.   And

[1] Cf. Niels Bohr, *Atomic Theory and the Description of Nature* (Cambridge: At the University Press, 1934).

though it is true that I approach objects of this kind by way of sense perception, what I arrive at has no resemblance to what I started with. Scientific objects in their final phase are pure relational concepts, like the points of the geometer, and the entities that stand in these relations are pure x's, the concrete interpretations of which cannot be given by science. And so, when we have reached the goal of all possible knowledge of the thing, we have lost the thing entirely. We can, to be sure, express its nature in terms of a mathematical equation, but the character of the equation is such that nothing within the range of sensuous experience is compatible with it. What in the end we come to accept as the truth regarding the external world is utterly unlike what we had to begin with. The thing has disappeared in a mathematical equation, for the concepts there in use—space–time, mass, electric charge, action, energy—are so abstract that almost any type of entity will fit them except precisely that type of entity to which people had originally supposed them to apply, the thing of common sense.

With this conclusion we are, however, a long way from a statement of the metaphysical standing of things. Thus far our results have been predominantly of a negative character. To achieve a positive statement we must make use of propositions established in our second chapter. We have just proved that the sensuous surface of experience cannot exist apart from the total mind, and for this reason it may rightly be termed "subjective." On the other hand, since what we have in our second chapter called "countercontrol" pervades the entire sensuous surface, we are forced to the seemingly contradictory conclusion that sensa are objective. The paradox is, however, easily solved if we reflect that, like the countercontrol which is exercised over them, sensa are at the boundary of nature and mind, and that items at a boundary belong to both the bounded areas. Sensa belong at once to nature and to mind; they are passive in their mere sensuousness, but active in so far as they are under the control of forces streaming through them from within the mind and from the environment. This double status is in conformity with the intuitive ambiguity of sensa: their obvious subjectivity, which we have been stressing, and, despite this, their out-there-ness; their determination by the not-self and their recalcitrance to control by the ego.   Because of this ambiguity naïve thinking and common sense have never been able quite to come to a decision regarding the status of sensa.   On the one hand common sense is sure that it is in direct contact with things and that they possess the qualities appearing in them: the rose, it thinks, is as sweet smelling and as red for itself as it is for me; yet philosophy soon proves that red and sweet have no independent existence. Now the insight that sensa are at the boundary of the mind and nature establishes their status in a way to preserve the truth of both convictions.   For, as factors in mind, the red and the sweet are my sensations; yet, as belonging also to nature, they belong to the external world.   The external world is revealed as no "bloodless ballet" of primary qualities or mathematical formulae, but as an indefinitely rich and varied sensuous experience, with which each monad is in contact in perception.

How we come to distinguish a variety of things in the external world is to be explained as follows: The countercontrol exerted over sensa is found to be distributed and concentrated in certain centers, which we shall call foci.   For we learn that, in order to produce the sort of sensa that we desire or to eliminate undesirable sensa, the external control over them must be met by action at definite loci in our field of sensa, whereas other groups of sensa cannot be so controlled, but are controllable at other points in the field and by other actions.   For example, the various "views" of a candle can be altered or extinguished through action at the locus in the field where visual and tactile sensa fuse; while the sound of the electric fan can be controlled at a different locus and by a different action or series of actions.   What are called the "real" sizes and shapes—which are the sizes and shapes that coincide with the surfaces of phenomenal objects and especially the sizes and shapes evoked by the tactile sense—are those by way of which we gain control over groups of similar and interrelated items; such sizes and shapes are, of course, no more real than the rest, but, being more useful, are given a dignified status.   The size and shape of the man as the tailor measures him is of more consequence for the tailor's art, than the visual, perspective sizes and shapes, although they are of no more consequence for the painter's art, which aims at reproducing, not at controlling. Now the distinguishable foci of control over sensa are the metaphysical bases of things.

The connection of the panorama of sense with a field of distinguishable foci of control accounts for other peculiarities of our perceptual experience. Sensa are deployed and used as symbols in such fashion as to enable us to find our way about in this field. First, they are given rough distance meanings and are stretched out into a three-dimensional containing volume, corresponding to the three-dimensional system of forces acting upon them, in order to indicate how we must move to meet and control these forces. Sensa thus come to look as if they were at a distance from each other, when, as a matter of fact, they are all interpenetrating. This green patch looks farther off than that one, although they are both here together in my mind, because in order to control the one I have to move to the hill, but in order to control the other I need only walk into my garden. In the second place, and in intimate connection with the fact just mentioned, the visual and tactile sensa become signs of, and appear as if plastered over the surfaces of, complicated interior volumes set out in an enveloping volume. These volumes, embellished with the sensa that symbolize them, are the phenomenal objects or things of perceptual experience. It is notable that sounds, smells, and tastes do not acquire such definite spatial signatures and connections with phenomenal objects, and therefore represent an earlier and cruder type of sense perception. Phenomenal objects, although they are mental constructions having no independent existence, have nevertheless both theoretical and practical value. They have theoretical value in so far as they provide relief maps of concentrations of forces in control of sensa, and they have practical value in so far as they serve as guides to action in meeting this control. The advantage of scientific objects over phenomenal objects is not at all that they possess superior reality, for they are no more—and also no less—real than the latter, being also constructions of the mind; but they are superior in so far as they reveal subtler connections among sensa and provide more finely discriminated sketches of foci in control. The rigid, independent, statuesque little volumes of naïve perception now give place to the all-pervading field of interdependent electromagnetic activities. Yet, for many purposes, the phenomenal object is as good a guide to control as the scientific object. A carpenter can make a bed or a box guided wholly by such phenomenal objects as a saw, a plane, a hammer, board, and nails; he has no need of the atom or the electron. And a cook can make a pie guiding her hand by recipes involving only phenomenal objects, such as a pan, a stove, sugar, apples, knives, and the like. And, in general, we carry on the business of life in the phenomenal world of houses, tables, beds, knives, forks, spoons, and guns. There is no better example of harmonious adjustment—comparable to the adaptation of the pupil to the intensity of light—than naïve perceptual experience in relation to the environment of forces which control it—an adjustment difficult to understand on purely naturalistic principles, but easy to understand as the joint product of the coöperation of the human mind with a favoring, parent environment. Not esthetic perception alone, as Kant thought, but all perception may be taken as a hint of an underlying harmony between nature and man. For certain types of action, however, the brittle but cosy little volumes of ordinary perception are of little use: in the laboratory that subtler form of cooking which we call "chemistry" can accomplish its ends only through the use of the more elaborate recipes which we call formulae.

Within the total enveloping volume of our perceptual experience we find two types of sensuous shapes and two corresponding types of phenomenal objects: the shape which I call the seat of a chair will represent the one; the shape which I call that of a man and the sounds proceeding from its mouth will represent the other. The latter are of a type closely similar in all respects to the shape that I call my body, and behave in analogous ways. This shape that I call my body is unique because I know by intuition that it is under the direct control of myself. But in connection with the shapes similar to it there arise in my mind ideas of activities, of thoughts and volitions generically like my own yet individually unique, ideas which introduce me to a world of values and objectives otherwise unknown to me—not mine, but such as mine. The foci controlling the shapes now under consideration control coincidently these new ideas of activities, with the result that I am irresistibly lead to interpret the former in terms of the latter. That is to say, I believe that the focus animating the behavior of the shape is a self; and since this belief is determined by the environment itself, it is epistemologically sound.[1] We may, therefore, divide the foreign con-

_____

[1] See p. 14.

trol over sensa into two types: control the values of which we understand—control exerted from what I shall call "lucid" centers; and control the values of which we cannot understand—control exerted from what I shall call "opaque" centers. Thus the control exerted over our experience as the young violinist plays for us we can understand, but the foreign control exerted during a snowstorm we cannot understand. Yet the former is as much a part of the external world as the latter, and we are subject to it, as in the case of the latter, only through and by way of the sensuous surface of our experience. Whether in the end the distinction between the two types of foci is absolute is a question for our subsequent reflections.

It is interesting to notice at this point in our discussion that if we were to take the stand so often taken that nothing is given except sensa, and that the mind has no actual contact with its environment, there would be no argument from analogy for the existence of a fellow mind. For from the mere fact that the phenomenal object which I call my body is causally connected with my desires, I cannot infer that the phenomenal object which I call your body is animated by another self. Since both objects are parts of my own experience the proper inference would be that your phenomenal body is another habitation of my own self. If, to use an illustration which I believe is due to Professor G. E. Moore, a weight is falling on my phenomenal toe, and I expect a pain to occur in my mind, then, if a weight is falling on the phenomenal object which I call your toe, there is no reason, if we are shut up within our own sensations, to expect anything else than another pain of my own. Of course in the latter case the pain does not occur in my mind—a surprising circumstance; but this does not justify me in assuming that it does occur in another mind, for I have no reason in the premises for believing that there is anything at all outside my mind, not to say in another mind. If, however, as I have been claiming, we are directly aware of countercontrol in connection with all sensations, and hence in connection with all phenomenal objects, and therefore intuit an external world contiguous with ourselves, we have a perfect argument from analogy for the existence of other selves. For, finding that the phenomenal object I call my body is under the control of myself, and knowing that the phenomenal object I call your body is under some foreign control, it becomes all but certain that the character of the control is like that which I myself exert. Furthermore, when the contiguity of the mind with its environment is recognized we are able theoretically to account for and justify the overwhelming experience of the oneness of ourselves and our fellow men which we have on certain occasions. When we press the hand of one we love we have an experience of union, not with body alone, but with mind. For the materialist, or for the monadist of the Leibnizian type, such experiences are illusions, but for us they are intuitions of the unbroken contiguity of mind with mind, by way of the sensuous surfaces of both. When the lover clasps the hand of the beloved he experiences the countercontrol which she exerts upon his hand, through his tactile and kinesthetic sensations, and she experiences in her turn the countercontrol exercised by her lover, through her tactile and kinesthetic sensa; there is an unbroken circle of influence from one mind to the other.

Once the forces in control of a shape have been identified with the activities of another self it is easy to understand how the coincidence of the fields of countercontrol of two selves is established. The simplest points in the two fields to identify are the two lucid centers to which the fields belong. For the focus in control of the shape which I call you is the very focus that you call yourself and which you find in control of a corresponding shape in your field of shapes; and the focus in control of the shape which you call me is the same as the focus that I call myself and find in control of a shape analogous to the one which you call me. Or, to express the matter in terms of phenomenal objects rather than sensa, the volume in my field which I animate with the activities which I call you is identified with the volume in your field which you find to be animated with yourself. To illustrate, if I construct out of the relevant shapes a manlike volume sitting in a chairlike volume in my field, and call the former your body, that very volume coincides with the volume which you construct in your field and call your own body; just as the volume which you construct out of the relevant shapes in your field, lying on another volume which you have constructed and call a bed, calling the former me, is the same volume which I, in my turn, construct out of relevant and similar shapes in my field, and find to be animated by myself. Here now are two coincident foci in each field, animating identical volumes and

controlling corresponding similar shapes. The impulse to identify the foci in control of all similar shapes and volumes in the two
fields is irresistible, and this impulse is confirmed through the
fact that action in one field, at a given point in that field and
in relation to a certain determinate shape in the sensuous panorama of that field, is followed by changes in the field of another
self similar to the changes in one's own field: if I blow out the
candle in my field I blow it out in yours, also. It is only a small
step beyond the process of identifying foci in the two fields to
constructing a common "space" of foci, lucid or opaque, containing identical volumes, animate or inanimate. And the problem of identifying the fields of countercontrol of many monads
is only a more complicated problem, to be worked out on the
same principles as the problem of identifying the fields of foci of
two monads. For we soon learn that activity at a given focus
may be the ground of the occurrence of similar sensa in many
minds. When the violinist plays his violin there arise in the
minds of a thousand persons in the concert hall similar sounds
and similar visual sensations, as each may tell the others. By an
analogous process of thought all people ascribe the determination
of their similar roselike views to a single focus and locate them
in an identical volume in a common space, the focus being the
metaphysical rose, the one volume being the identical common-
sense object—the phenomenal object—that seems to appear in the
experience of each person through his sensa. All such sensa,
distributed though they be in different monads, change in close
temporal relations to each other and in lawfully similar fashion,
and are under countercontrol in each center, met by similar
actions having similar effects in the fields of each and all. We
shall call such similar sensa, under control from a single focus,
the periphery of a focus.

In its relation to peripheral sensa the focus represents the remote control of those sensa. Sensa are under double control—
the "near" control in the region of the body and the far or
"remote" control of the so-called stimulus. Remote control may
be more precisely defined as control through intermediaries, and
is, therefore, control which takes time to become effective. It
depends upon a coöperative causal chain, the last link of which,
in the case of perception, is the indispensable near control of the
body. We discover the existence of remote control when we

learn that we cannot meet the foreign control over sensa by acting at the loci of near control in the region of the body, but must move in such a way as to enlarge this region to include loci beyond it or send an emissary which will act directly at the remote focus. To control the sounds coming from my radio it will not do to act upon my ears—I must stretch out my hand and touch the indicator or induce someone else to do this; to meet the control over my experience exerted by my enemy I must either enter into hand-to-hand combat with him or I must shoot a gun. All communication from person to person is remote control. Communication permits confirmation of the intuitive evidence of remote control provided by the distance signs of sensa and the experimental evidence derived from movement, for the man who speaks to me can tell me that he has spoken to me, and by well-known means the time interval between his speaking and my hearing can be established.

As signs of the forces that control them, sensa become what Berkeley called a "natural language," and, since sensa are private, there are as many natural languages as there are monads. On the basis of these many natural languages the "artificial" common means of communication which we call language is founded. The possibility of a common language depends on the fact that, in general, the sensa determined by a focus are closely similar in different monads, and with regard to certain types of sense qualities—the so-called primary qualities—are indefinitely similar. It is a helpful circumstance that several types of sensa may denote the same control—which we express when we say that we can see and hear and touch, and even smell and taste, a bell. This circumstance permits those persons who are defective in one or more sensory fields to represent by means of whatever natural language they have the same forces that are signified by the sensa of normal persons. The symbols of the natural language are the given sensa; the symbols of the artificial language are artificially produced sensa—word sounds, written symbols, and the like—associated with similar groups of given sensa and standing for what is common to such groups—their universal, their generic, aspect. Since the generic aspect is common to the experience of many centers the symbols used in one center to denote the universal denote the literally same factor in the experience of other centers: the words "blue" or "between" that mean blueness or betweenness in my experience can mean blueness or betweenness in yours. By an analogous process the language of common sense arises to denote the constructs which we have been calling phenomenal objects—tree, house, moon, and the like—for similar monads, acting in coöperation, construct out of similar sensa similar phenomenal objects.   Finally, there arises the language of science, stripped of all elements of privacy and denuded of all symbolization of emotion, designed to serve the single purpose of social control of the environment.

VI

Space

IN PREVIOUS chapters I have offered reasons for accepting a spiritualistic conception of the universe. I shall now, adapting the general standpoint of Leibniz to modern knowledge, proceed to show how space can be interpreted in accordance with this view. We shall see that the facts of space offer no aid or comfort to the materialist, but that, on the contrary, as Leibniz saw, they lend themselves admirably to idealistic interpretation. I shall confine myself to a discussion of the most general facts, hoping that the mathematician, if any should read these pages, will pardon the absence from them of mathematical formulae. To each his special work: to the mathematician, analysis; to the metaphysician, interpretation. Of space St. Augustine said that we understand it only so long as we do not think about it; but one may claim on the contrary that no other large fact is so amenable to reflection as space, for with regard to it the mathematician has achieved a resplendent triumph, and to the metaphysician it is a very simple concept. There is a final mystery about space, but no different from the mystery of all things—the last mystery of fact.

I shall begin this study by setting down some very general propositions about space, which may at first seem rather too dogmatically stated but which will gain plausibility, I believe, as we proceed. First, space is no independent existence that could stand if all the things "in" space were removed. It is perhaps superfluous to state this proposition, for ever since the breakdown of the Newtonian conception of the world there has been practical unanimity in regard to it on the part of philosophers. Everyone recognizes that the conception of absolute space is unnecessary for physical theory and has no empirical foundation. We have no perception of space as such, no perception of mere volume, mere surface, mere point. Phenomenal volume is the volume of this room, this city square, the vault of the sky; perceptual surface is the surface of this wall, of this table, this floor, this picture; perceptual point is the point of this pencil, the corner where the three walls of the room meet, the intersection of rays of light.   Perceived distance is the distance of the tree from the house, of the lighthouse from the shore, the desk from the wall.   It is true that we speak of things as "moving in space," but phenomenologically they do not move in mere space: the ship moves on the sea; the airplane in the air; the fly buzzes in the bottle; the earth courses around the sun.   At best, the theory of space as a thing is a superfluous hypothesis, a mere luxury of thought; but, in addition, it is ruled out as a genuine entity on the ground of being a "vacuous actuality."

There is, however, a certain truth in Kant's assertion that one could think away everything from space, and space would still remain.   But what would remain would not be an existence, but a web of relations.   And that is what space is—a web of relations between monads.   It is no room in which monads—or whatever else be conceived to be the elements of reality—have their being, but an order or organization of them.   As such it is comparable to the organization of an army, or to the hierarchy of positions in a university, state, or business.   And as one may abstract the plan of organization from an army, a business, or a nation, so one may abstract the spatial order from the universe and make it an object of reflection for the philosopher or of fine analysis for the mathematician.   But even as the organization of an army cannot exist without soldiers or the constitution of a state be effective without public servants, so, it must be insisted, space cannot exist without monads.   There is a certain absoluteness about space, but it is the absoluteness of a form or order, not the absoluteness of a thing.

When, now, space is conceived as a system of relations many of the facts about space which might be thought to depend upon its being an existence remain valid and become intelligible. For example, the notion of empty space acquires meaning as a set of positions in the spatial order provided for in that order but not actually filled: just as when the captain of a company is killed in action his place remains, although empty for the time being (notice how language sanctions the analogy between space and social organization) , or when the president of a firm resigns his office continues, in the sense of being a possibility—although, of course, it does not become an actuality until the directors elect his successor. Abstractly considered, space is a system of possibilities of a certain kind, some of which may never be actualized; so far as this may be so, space is "empty." How much of space is empty is naturally an empirical question for the physicist.[1]

The so-called "impenetrability" of space is another fact that becomes intelligible when space is viewed as a plan or organization, for it may be understood as a law or rule of the organization. Two things cannot occupy the same place at the same time, even as there cannot be two presidents of the United States or two heads of the same firm. If this is true, space is not the principle of individuation, as it has often been thought to be; it is only one such principle. Any rule that confers uniqueness individualizes; for example, the rule that a husband shall have only one wife is a principle of individuation. The principle of the impenetrability of space is, of course, a more invariant and fundamental principle than the rule of monogamy, but it is not an a priori principle or necessarily universal.[2] The individuality of a monad depends partly on this rule, but also upon every other rule that confers uniqueness; and there is, as we have seen, a more basic individuality which is independent of space.

Another puzzling fact—if it be a fact—that becomes intelligible according to the view I am presenting is the "expansion" of the universe. The question whether or not the universe is expanding is a physical, not a philosophical, question; yet philosophy can, I believe, eliminate some of the strangeness that attaches to the idea at first thought. For the expansion of the universe does not require an absolute space into which it expands, as a gas expands in a chamber—as if the universe and space were two different entities, as the gas and the chamber are—but merely a flexible constitution to which the constituent elements of the universe conform. If space is a system of relations its parts may alter their relations to each other, as happens in any flexible scheme of social organization; space expands with the universe. And finally, even the idea of a variable, nonhomogeneous space

---

[1] Emptiness is clearly a relative concept. Thus a room is "empty" when there are no people in it, although it contains air. Even so, much of space may be empty of particles, yet all of space may be filled with waves.

[2] As contemporary physics has come to believe.

becomes intelligible. For if space is a sort of constitution of the universe there is no reason why it must be the same, except in its most general principles, everywhere, that is to say, among all groups of elements. It might well permit of local variations, as any adaptable social organization permits of changes in accordance with local conditions.

From these very general considerations let us now pass to matters of more detail. But first we must establish our answer to the question, What sort of entities are in space? This is the kind of question about space with regard to which the geometer does not give us the help that we need, for all that he ventures to say is that any collection of individuals of such a kind that the abstract relations assumed in the axioms of geometry may apply to them is "in space." As is well known, the points of geometry are mere x's such that . . . ; instead of "point," they might just as well be called "abracadabra." Nothing at all is assumed about the elements in calling them points, despite appearances to the contrary, except, as already said, that they stand in the specified relations. For all the geometer knows or cares the elements might be particles of matter or angels. Our answer to the question, as anticipated in the preceding chapter, is that any center of causal efficacy or focus is in space. The most obvious collection of such centers are the personalities that make up our social world. In citing these as examples I am aware that I am flouting the prejudices of some philosophers who think that minds cannot be in space; but, aside from all presuppositions, it seems clear that our friends are near or far from each other and from us, that we who live in Ann Arbor are between those who live in Detroit and Chicago, that when guests sit around a dinner table they are, as a collection, roughly circular in shape, that the teacher is at the apex of a triangle of which the pupils in the front benches form the base. If the universe consisted of nothing except members of the human social group, it would still be a perfect example of space relationships. Only those who believe that minds are mere ineffective epiphenomena can properly deny that they are in space. And, in addition to fellow minds, all centers of what we have called countercontrol, in any part of nature, are in space.

This view is in accordance with the more critical testimony of perceptual space experience. We can approach the problem through a consideration of the status of the image of a person who looks at himself in a mirror. From the point of view of pure phenomenology the image is at some distance behind the surface of the mirror; hence, if the mirror is in space, the image must be also. Yet while few people—one could say no people were it not for some eccentric philosophers—believe that the image is where it seems to be, they do believe that the mirror is where it seems to be. How can the difference between these two facts, which from a naïve visual standpoint are on an equal footing, be explained? The answer is that the image is not under control where it seems to be, but that the phenomenal mirror is under control in its place. The general rule of location of phenomenal objects in critical space perception is that we believe them to be where they are controlled. We therefore come to locate images where our minds are, since they are under control there, and take them out of the places where they appear. Or else, with equal consistency with the principle, we locate the image in the mirror, or in the water—for there as well as in the mind it is controlled. Interestingly enough, we come eventually to locate not only images in the mind but all phenomenal objects also, for we recognize that they too are partly controlled in the mind. Thus the whole sensuous content of perception acquires a double location—at the mind and at the stimulus or focus where it is controlled. This double location does not prove, as Whitehead and others have asserted, that there is no simple location; it proves that phenomenal objects abstractly considered are not properly in space at all. The foci from which they are controlled are in space, and so far as they are signs of such control they are given a pseudo location there, which, as we have seen, is ambiguous, being both at the stimulus or focus and at the mind. It is interesting to notice that we give to memory images the same double location—in the mind and where the phenomenal objects were from which they were derived. Thus my memory image of Castelfranco Veneto seems to be where Giorgione was born, but when I reflect that it is a member of the organism of my mind, I locate it there. We come, in the end, to the distinction between phenomenal space, which is the pseudo space of phenomenal objects, and "real" space, which is the space of foci, or centers of control. As contents of the mind, phenomenal objects belong to the subjective space of the mind, but as signs of control from other centers, they acquire a pseudo location where these other centers of control are. Thus the phenomenal moon as I see it is given an apparent location where the "real" moon is, but its actual location in space is where my mind is, which is where my body, or perhaps more definitely, where my brain is.

If the elements of real space are foci, or centers of control, then the various attempts, as, for example, that of J. Nicod in his *Foundations of Geometry and Induction*,[1] to construct a space world out of various sensa, such as sounds, smells, and the like, have no metaphysical, though they have much phenomenological, significance. Metaphysical geometry, as we may call it, must be constructed out of monads as materials. And whether this geometry is, mathematically considered, a geometry of points or of volumes or of some other pure conceptual element is not a question of formal simplicity or deductive clearness only, but of adequacy of application to the world of monads. There will be no attempt here to construct a metaphysical geometry in any detail. Complete physical knowledge would be necessary for this—a knowledge which I do not possess, and which is, in fact, not available. I shall attempt no more than an interpretation of the main concepts of such a geometry.

Centers of control are, then, the materials of our metaphysical geometry. These we discover whenever we experience counter-control. That there are many centers we know from such experiences as talking to two different persons, lifting a weight in each hand, responding to different perceptual objects, and the like. As many centers of countercontrol as are given to us, so many are the modes of response on our part, for the two are correlative. As our responses become more complex and fine, the number of centers of countercontrol revealed increases, until the limits of possible discrimination are reached by the microscopic methods of scientific investigation. The relative permanence of these centers of control is guaranteed in two ways: when the centers are lucid centers they can tell us of their permanence—a man may, for example, remind us that we met him and talked with him before; when they are opaque centers we infer permanence from the recurrence of the pattern of response and counterresponse. In the case of lucid centers both of these criteria are, of course, possible. The sameness of a person is known to us partly

[1] New York: Harcourt, Brace and Co., 1930.

through the sameness of the type of countercontrol that he exerts within our experience and partly through the sameness of his message or communicated meaning: he says the same sort of things to us. Invariably there is a general sameness of sensa accompanying the sameness of the type of control: our friends, our car, our house, and the like, look the same—but this similarity of "look" may be deceptive. Sameness of type of action and counteraction are essential; sensuous similarity is but a sign of this. There is, however, no sameness of pattern of control without some similarity of sensuous detail, for action is always by way of sensa, and sensa are a system of natural signs.

But though centers of control are the materials of metaphysical geometry, they are not the elements. For space is an abstract scheme of relations, a conceptual system or constitution, and the elements of a conceptual scheme are themselves concepts. The monads are the entities to which the conceptual elements apply, but they are not the elements themselves. That this is the case follows simply from the fact that at different times different monads may occupy the same position, when the conceptual element, the point or position, is the same, but the "things" to which this conceptual element applies are different. Moreover, if there is empty space, there are conceptual elements—positions—to which nothing in the real world corresponds at the moment. The elements of our geometry are, therefore, positions or points. I prefer the term "position," because "point" carries a connotation of thinghood, while "position" is obviously relational and conceptual. In addition to "position," we shall require two other basic concepts, "distance" and "betweenness." Whatever final and detailed form of metaphysical geometry will have to be accepted—whether, for example, Euclidean or non-Euclidean—as the result of physical investigation and metaphysical interpretation, these three space ideas—position, distance, and betweenness—or some formal equivalents of them, will survive as fundamental. Even if we were limited to the social world we should find that the members of that world were at distances from each other, that they have spatial position, and that they are ordered through relations of betweenness. We shall consider each of these concepts at some length.

First, position. As we have already seen, position is no thing which might exist if there were no monads "occupying" the position. Position, or point, is a relationship. This is true both of phenomenal space and real space. The phenomenal objects that appear in phenomenal space have no essential and independent "pointness" which might be supposed to be conferred upon them through occupation of absolute positions or to be an intrinsic quality, comparable to color or what not. The position of an item is its being above or below, to the right or to the left of, between or at a certain distance from, inside or outside, and the like, in relation to other things. If I am shut inside a room and cannot see out the window there are items which have what may be called superlative positions, as topmost or bottommost; but even so, their being topmost or bottommost is dependent upon the existence of certain other things which are relatively below or above them. It is a commonplace of physical theory that no position in the external world can be fixed except with relation to certain things which determine axes or *points de repère*. And it is not a question of the mere fixing of a position, but of the meaning and existence of the position. The position of the ship at sea *is* its distance from the land or from other ships; the position of the earth *is* its distance from the sun and moon, or its relation of betweenness to other bodies. The scheme of relationships may be abstracted from the items in its field; space is, in fact, such a scheme, but the abstract positions thus emerging are meaningless except as possibilities of distance and order. Positions in real space are an assemblage of possibilities of relationship. These possibilities may not all be realized—in which case there is "empty" space—but even such possibilities have no meaning except with relation to existing monads. A spatial position is thus an office comparable, in this abstract way as a meeting of relationships, to professional, military, or political positions. Kingship is a center of relations to subjects, and is meaningless except in connection with existing persons who are subjects; the presidency of the United States is meaningless except as a scheme of potential relationships to the citizens of our country. Even when the position is not actually filled this relativity is retained. The kingship of France is meaningless except with relation to Frenchmen who have been, or to those who, through a Royalist revolution, may become, subjects of a king. Even so, positions in empty space have no reality except as possibilities which may be actualized by existing monads.

If, as I have tried to show, position can be defined as a center of relations of distance and betweenness, we are thrown back upon these latter as the fundamental spatial concepts. Let us consider distance first. In phenomenal space distance is a given item. I can *see* the distance between my body and the wall of the room, or the distance between the ends of the table, just as clearly as I can see the table or my body and the wall. By means of tactile or kinesthetic experiences I can appreciate the distance between my finger and my thumb when I shut my eyes, or the distance between compass points placed on my skin. There is a phenomenal *spread* of items in one, two, or three dimensions—linear, areal, or volumetric. But this spread, be it observed, is never a mere spread: there is no blank phenomenal length, area, or volume. Our concern, however, is not with phenomenal spreadoutness, but with real distance, that is to say, the distance between monads; yet we had to consider the former in order to make the point that real distance cannot be identified with phenomenal distance. What, for example, is the distance between my friend in New York and myself? Am I to suppose that there is a spread existing in nature comparable to the intuited spread between my body and the wall of the room, within my experience? Or what is the distance between me and the sun? The astronomer answers, approximately 93,000,000 miles. Is, then, this distance the same as the visual spread to sun and sky when I look at the sun? The supposition is absurd, if for no other reason than because the visual spread, being essentially visual, is as subjective as all other visual elements of experience. It is a secondary quality, like color and sound, as Berkeley claimed. Can we think that this spread exists when no man looks up into the sky? Are there such spreads between all elements of the universe, between the atoms as well as between the stars in their courses? To answer yes would be tantamount to the assertion of the existence of a cosmic visual sensorium within which all monads are contained. But even if the possible existence of a visual sensorium be granted, it would be difficult to see how monads, which are not themselves visual elements, could be contained within it—you cannot see, any more than you can taste or smell, a mind, and a mind is our best example of a monad. When we look at a fellow man, as we phrase it, we perceive the visual spread between his body and ours, but this spread exists solely between his phenomenal body and mine, within my experience, or within his experience, if he looks at me; it cannot exist *between* his experience and mine.

What, then, is real distance? Real distance is the time required to communicate between one monad and another, in terms of a chosen method of communication. The time varies with the method of communication; it is one thing by telegraph, another by radio, another by speech, and so on; but in terms of any specified mode the distance and time are equivalent. Distance is thus a variable thing, as is recognized in the common saying that modern methods of communication have brought distant parts of the world nearer to each other; but it is not arbitrary, since it becomes determinate once the method of communication is fixed. We usually attribute the variation in distance to the variation in speed of communication, but only because we have inherited the assumption of the existence of an independent and invariable space; and to say that distance has decreased or to say that all methods of communication have increased in speed, is absolutely equivalent. To halve all distances or to double all speeds would be indistinguishable. Differences of speed of communication have meaning only with regard to comparative methods of communication, and whether we say that the speed is greater by one method as compared with another, or that the distance is less, is irrelevant. If it be objected that I can go faster or slower by the same method, for example, by driving my car at high speed or at low, at thirty or at sixty miles an hour, the answer is that in the broad sense of "method" the methods are different; for my gasoline consumption is different in the two cases, and the number of revolutions of the wheels of the car per minute is different, and so on, and these differences can all be determined independently of what I call the distance covered or the speed. It is interesting to remark that in some communities, as in Norway, distances are expressed in terms of hours of walking or driving—one town being so many hours away from another. And obviously this could be done universally. A distance, in the sense of a magnitude abstracted from a class of cases where the magnitude is found embodied, is a temporal magnitude in relation to an assigned method of communication—it is an interval, or time separation. It follows that there is no distance between centers when communication is impossible between them or, again, when communication is instantaneous. Between the angels, who are reputedly immaterial, there is distance if communication between them takes time.

In view of the fact that our concept of space presupposes the concept of communication, we must offer some explanation of our idea of the latter, leaving, however, its full analysis to our chapter on causality (Chap. XIV). It is plain, I think, that I am here using the term in a somewhat enlarged sense, so that it includes all causal relations between one center and another, and not merely those cases where one monad is able, as the result of this relation, to discern what was in the mind of the other (which is the usual interpretation). It includes, therefore, not only hearing and understanding what another person says, for example, but seeing him, or perceiving him through any other sense, since when I do perceive him there is a causal relation between him and me; it includes such physical phenomena as the radiation and absorption of light, the transmission of sound, heat, and electromagnetic waves, and any other manner in which events that happen in one center determine events in another center.

The definition of distance offered determines our definition of motion. By motion, in this connection, I mean physical motion interpreted metaphysically as a transaction between monads; I do not mean phenomenal motion, which is an event within a single monad. And motion, as a relation between centers, can no more be identified with the experience of motion, visual or kinesthetic, than distance as an experience can be identified with physical or metaphysical distance. Nevertheless, there is an analogy between the two. For phenomenologically, motion is at least change of distance. The car that moves on the road as I look out the window changes its distance from the trees and houses; the fly that moves on the window pane changes its distance from the northwest corner along a given axis, and so forth. Analogically, in nature, the motion of a center is a change in its distances from certain other centers to which the motion is referred. A center moves toward another center when the time of communication between them is lessened; it moves away when this time is increased. From a purely kinematic standpoint it does not matter which center is said to move; it is only when we take other centers into consideration, and view the motions of each of the first two with reference to them, that it becomes meaningful to say that the one rather than the other moves; then, if one changes its distance from the centers taken as *points de repère* but the other does not, the former will be said to move and the latter to remain at rest. If, however, we view motion not from the outside, as is done in kinematics, but from the inside, we may then distinguish the center that moves, in contradistinction to the center that is moved toward, as the one within which the change of distance is initiated. So, if I walk up to a man, it is I who move, because I am a member of a system—my body—from which the initiation of motion starts. In human beings the initiation of change of distance manifests itself in kinesthetic sensations.

For some purposes it is useful to define motion as change of neighborhood. So, to move from San Francisco to Detroit is to change one's neighbors; and, in general, whenever we think of motion as change of *place,* this conception is natural, for there is no such thing really as a place: a place is a collection of neighbors. We shall find the conception of neighborhood extremely significant when we come to the study of problems of causality, but closer analysis shows that the definition of motion in terms of neighborhood is the same as the definition in terms of distance. For, from a purely spatial point of view, a neighborhood consists of foci between which the distances are small; hence, change of neighborhood involves shortening the distance to certain foci and lengthening the distance to certain others, which, if our definition be correct, means altering the time of communication between the relevant centers accordingly.

We may now define velocity as the time taken to make a change in neighborhood. Thus the velocity of an automobile may be defined as the time taken to go from Ann Arbor to Detroit, or from any neighborhood to any other when the distance or time separation of communication between the two places or neighborhoods is well known and constant; that is to say, the velocity is the time required to reduce the distance or time separation of the car to either place to zero, beginning at the other place. Of course this definition gives only average velocity, but a precise definition of actual velocity at a moment can easily be constructed, in accordance with the theory of limits. Velocity is a rate of change of neighborhood; and since this rate may itself change, acceleration may be defined in the usual way as the rate of change of velocity.

The third fundamental spatial concept is order.   Geometers
have shown that spatial order can be defined in terms of the relation of betweenness,[1] and we shall accept this relation as basic.
In perceptual space, order, defined in terms of betweenness, is a
phenomenal fact: for example, the perceived order of the books
on my shelf, of the trees along the avenue, of the stories of a
building, of the typewriter and the wall of the room and the tree
seen out of the window.   In phenomenal space one thing is as
clearly seen as being between two others as the things themselves
are seen: the wall is seen between the typewriter and the tree,
one book between two others, the middle story between the lowest and the topmost.   Order is an aspect of the given visual
Gestalt.   It would, however, be as grave a mistake to suppose
that an exact reproduction of this given relationship exists in
what is called the external world, which we have identified as the
world of monads, as it would be to suppose that perceptual distance exists there.   It is impossible to transfer to the world of
the monads what is true of items within single monads.   One
monad cannot be between two others in the way a seen book is
between two other books, because monads are not visual elements: they do not and cannot form a visual *Gestalt*.   But although the concrete relationship given in visual intuition cannot
exist between monads, there may exist a relation between them
which has all the formal, abstract properties of the visual relationship, and, following the law that perceptual relations are
analogous to metaphysical relations, the visual may be a symbol
of the metaphysical.   This analogy may be illustrated thus: the
situation in nature expressed by the proposition that Detroit is
between Buffalo and Chicago is formally analogous to the situation seen on a railway map when one observes the name and symbol of Detroit between the names and symbols of Chicago and
Buffalo; or the situation in nature which I express by saying that
the wall of the room is between me and yonder tree is formally
analogous to the visual relationship between the seen wall, the
tree, and the body.   The relationships cannot be the same, but the
formal properties of the relationships are the same.   Identical
relationships cannot exist between different types of things, but,

[1] Bertrand Russell, *Introduction to Mathematical Philosophy* (New York:
The Macmillan Co., [1919]), p. 39.

once more, the formal properties of such relations can be the same. Between women there can be no relation of "brother of," but the formal properties of the relation "brother of" are the same as the formal properties of the relation "sister of." It is hardly necessary to add that in pure geometry no concrete relationship is connoted by the relation "betweenness": "betweenness" means merely the relationship "x having certain formal properties," even as "point" does not mean anything concrete but merely "x standing in such and such relations."

Having rejected the visual, phenomenal interpretation of the relationship "between," we must find some concrete interpretation that shall hold between monads, a metaphysical interpretation which shall not only embody the results of the formal analysis of the geometer but go beyond them. The interpretation which I suggest is as follows: In terms of any specified method of communication, or in terms of any specified method of moving from one neighborhood to another, a monad B is between monads A and C, or a collection of monads B is between two other collections A and C, when, in order to communicate from A to C, or in order to move from the neighborhood A to the neighborhood C, the message must pass through B, or motion must take place by way of B. For example, by means of travel over the Michigan Central Railroad Detroit is between Chicago and Buffalo; by means of telephonic communication with my friend in Detroit the telephone exchange here is between me and my friend. There is no further meaning to "between." It has no significance except with regard to communication. Three entities which could not in any way communicate with each other could not have this relation to each other. No material or other special ontological character is presupposed, but only the possibility of communication. As it stands, however, the definition is incomplete, for it presupposes rigid means of communication. Now if I wish to walk from Ann Arbor to Ypsilanti I may, of course, go by the road, when the relation between will be unique because the road is a rigid route of communication; but if I choose to wander over the fields away from the road many different sets of stations are between here and Ypsilanti. Hence, in order that the relation between may be unique, the definition must be emended, and the emendation follows traditional meth-

ods by prescribing that communication be by the shortest route.
"Between" means, therefore, "by way of by the shortest route."
It is understood in this discussion that A, B, and C stand for distinct stations, and that if B is between A and C, then C cannot
be between B and A. We may then define a line as the collection of stations including A and C and all stations x such that
either C is between A and x, or x is between A and C, or A is between x and C. A straight line is thus a collection of stations
between any two of which it is the shortest route of communication. Lines which intersect are shortest routes with a common
station; parallel lines are shortest routes that have no intersection. If the Euclidean postulate be true, there is only a single
line parallel to any given line which includes a given station not
included in the given line. Shortest routes have a single station
in common with other such routes. Space is a vast, three-dimensional network of such routes.

Our discussion of space thus far has left the question of its
continuity or its discreteness open, and we cannot give any final
answer to this question until we have solved the corresponding
problem in regard to time; for, since distance is defined in terms
of duration, if duration should turn out to be discrete, distance
would have to be discrete. On the other hand, time might be
continuous and yet space discrete if there were minimal time intervals in the process of communication, that is to say, if we could
not get nearer to a given monad than a finite distance. It would
follow that there are a finite number of positions or stations between any two, and no station between two that are at a minimal
distance. In this case the total distance between stations would
be equal to the number of the minimal distances between stations. There could, of course, be no next points, for the very
fact of space depends upon there being some time interval between points. We shall find, as a result of our later discussions,
that actual distances, as opposed to possible distances, are always
finite in number, or, what comes to the same thing, that the number of actual positions, and hence the number of actual monads,
is finite.

Although, if space is discrete, there can be no next points, it
does not follow, as one might suppose, that there are no next
monads. That there must be contiguity in the Aristotelian sense

of nextness we have already found to be true in our discussion of the relation of the mind to its environment; and we shall find new reasons for this when we come to the discussion of causality. That discreteness of space may be compatible with contiguity between monads may be explained as follows. Suppose two monads, A and C, between which, in the spatial sense defined, there is a monad B packed as closely as possible, in other words, so placed that the distance between A and C is as small as possible. Now suppose that between A and B and between B and C there is a medium with which all are contiguous. Then there would be no distance between the monads and the medium, since they are contiguous; but, since next-to-next relations are not transitive, the pairs A and B, B and C, would not be contiguous, and there would be distance between them. Whereas, for example, there would be no time lapse in communication between A and the medium, there would be a time lapse of two minima between A and C. We shall find this suggestion very fruitful in our discussion of causality. The adoption of some such scheme as this makes possible another interesting interpretation. If we understand by a line a set of stations and we suppose that there are minimal distances between stations between which there are no stations, the distance along a line between two stations would be equivalent to the number of stations on the line, minus one. The distance between A and B would be the stretch between A and B. Equal stretches, defining a distance conceived as an abstract quantity that may be present in any number of different stretches, would therefore be a number, and distances along a line would have the order of the stations or positions on the line, the greater distances following the lesser, beginning at any point.

In our discussion of space it has been insisted that one cannot carry over to real space the elements of perceptual space, in any literal fashion. Real space, in fact, is something that cannot be perceived at all. Real space is a system of possible routes of communication with reference to time of communication (distance) and order of communication (betweenness); and possibilities are not perceptual things. You can no more perceive space than you can perceive the constitution of the United States or of the British Empire. The literal elements of perceptual space are, as Berkeley divined, secondary qualities, as secondary as color or sound: the spreadoutness of an area, the bigness of a volume, the stretchiness between things in a given dimension, their visual betweenness, their being above or below, to the right or to the left, their perceptual roundness, squareness, triangularity, and the like.   There is, nevertheless, as all philosophers have recognized, a certain correspondence between perceptual space and real space.   This correspondence is, however, not peculiar to space, for there is a correspondence between the sensuous elements of space and metaphysical elements: the motion that I see the violinist make corresponds to his action as he appreciates it; and, in general, we may accept as a valid metaphysical principle the aphorism of Herbart: *"So viel Schein, so viel Hindeutung auf Sein."*   In other words, to every element in the perceptual field of a given monad there correspond activities of other monads. To perceptual things there correspond monads or systems of monads; to changes in such things, changes in the experience of these monads.   So the experienced distance between phenomenal things corresponds roughly to the time required to communicate between the monads controlling such things, and the perceptual spatial order corresponds to the order of communication.   To shapes, there correspond the time and order of communication of bounding underlying monads.   Thus in the case of the perceptual circle the elements of the circumference are equidistant from the inner element which we call the center, and in the corresponding real world there is a station so related to a group of stations that the times of communication between it and them are equal, and such that any route of communication that passes through it and one of them must pass through another also.

In concluding this chapter I would refer to a subsequent one, "Some Cosmical Aspects of Time," for a discussion of the problems of space raised by the relativity theory.   We shall find that everything established here will hold there.   This chapter may, in fact, be regarded as preliminary to that one.[1]

----

[1] I am happy to find general confirmation of the theory of space expressed in this chapter in the work of E. A. Milne, *Relativity, Gravitation and World Structure* (Oxford: At the Clarendon Press, 1935), chap. i.

VII

The Temporal Experience

I N NO field of philosophic speculation has there been more of
the two chief intellectual vices—conventionality and extravagance—than in the discussion of time. Conventionality is illustrated there by the persistent survival of fragments of the substance theory of Newton; extravagance, by such beliefs as that in the
existence of past events (Broad), or, what is worse, the existence
of both past and future in a *totum simul* (Royce), or by the denial
of the reality of time (McTaggart).[1] The cure for both vices is
a more candid and careful examination of experience. For
since, as Kant held, time is the characteristic form of the inner
life, its nature cannot fail to be revealed there. We shall, accordingly, begin with an analysis of the temporal aspect of experience, and only afterward consider its cosmical significance.

The temporal aspect of experience shows itself to be a complex of related aspects. Perhaps the most striking aspect is *passing away*. The sound that I hear disappears; the colors fade on
the hills; the twinge of pain is eased; the sharpness of sorrow, the
loveliness of youth and beauty are no more. This is the aspect
of time that has impressed the poets of all ages and countries.

> Eheu fugaces, Postume, Postume.

> Mignonne, allons voir si la rose
> Qui, ce matin, avoit desclose
> Sa robe de pourpre au soleil,
> A point perdu, cette vesprée,
> Les plis de sa robe pourprée
> Et son teint au vostre pareil.

> Nothing gold can stay.

---

[1] C. D. Broad, *The Mind and Its Place in Nature* (New York: Harcourt,
Brace and Co., 1929), p. 252; Josiah Royce, *The World and the Individual*,
Second Series (New York: The Macmillan Co., 1904), Vol. II, Lecture III;
J. M. McTaggart, *The Nature of Existence* (Cambridge: At the University
Press, 1921), Vol. II, chap. xxxiii.

Or in the telling, if inelegant, language in which Plato sought to laugh away the fact: "Existence has a leak in it, and is as a man with a running at the nose." [1]

Equally important, however, is the complementary and contrasting aspect of *coming to be* (genesis). The sound that I just heard has disappeared, but a new one has emerged; tick-tock follows upon tick-tock; day was swallowed by night, but lo! here is the dawn again; a man has passed away, but at the same moment a child is being born into the world. Experience is an unremitting spawning of novelties: new colors, new sounds, new touches, new scents, new tastes, new thoughts, new passions crowding in on the heels of similar things going out. Much of this novelty appears to come into existence unwilled by myself, but much of it, also, is my own work. The endeavor of all art and manufacture is to create—to bring into being something that was not in being before. To deny the aspect of coming to be is to give the lie to the whole creative life of man; every venture of the artist or the humblest workman, turning his lathe, is evidence to the contrary.

But coming to be and passing away are not absolute. For coming to be is always coming into, and passing away is always passing out from, a region of experience that endures. The gray rings that rise into my visual field as I smoke my cigarette form against the relatively stable background of the yellow expanse of the phenomenal wall of my room; the shadows of momentary fancies fall across abiding affections; the new work of art takes a place alongside classic works of old in the museum. And behind the flux and reflux of phenomenal objects and transient feelings the matrix self persists, observing, controlling, and commenting upon the scene that shifts before it. It is impossible, therefore, to construe time as a mere replacement of events, like this: *a, b, c, d, e, f, g*, where it is understood that as *b* appears, *a* disappears, and as *c* appears, *b* disappears, and so on; it should, rather, be construed like this:

$$M$$
$$a\ b\ c\ d\ e\ f\ g$$
$$l\quad m\quad n$$

where *M* represents the matrix self that remains constant through

---

[1] Plato *Cratylus* 440.

the entire flux of experience, the first line of small letters represents the most evanescent items of experience, and the second line, items that are by comparison relatively stable.

Even so, however, the picture is not complete, for as items pass out from experience they leave behind traces or echoes of themselves through which it is known that they were. The poet has expressed this fact:

> Music when soft voices die
> Vibrates in the memory;
> Odors when sweet violets sicken
> Live within the sense they quicken.

These traces provide that steady enrichment of experience, that snowball growth, of which Bergson wrote. Hence our complete diagram of time would have to be something like the following, where the letters a', b', etc., represent echoes or traces.

$$M \quad \begin{matrix} a \\ b \\ c \\ d \\ e \\ f \end{matrix} \quad \begin{matrix} l \quad a' \\ \\ m \quad a' \ b' \ l' \\ \\ n \quad a' \ b' \ c' \ d' \ e' \ m' \end{matrix}$$

All these aspects of the streamlike character of experience are illustrated by a melody as we listen to it or play it. First, there is the series of sounds, each dying as its successor appears; then, the continual enrichment of the musical experience by the memories of the tones as each passes, without which, as a contrasting background to the new tones as they arise, their musical significance for harmony or discord, as passing tones or as leading ones, and the like, would be impossible; finally, persistent throughout, there is the plan and intention to play the notes, which is fulfilled as each note comes, or the plan merely to listen, if someone else is performing. Thus for the full description of the temporal aspect of experience three types of existence are required: primary events, perishable and irrevocable existences, such as the musical tones; traces or echoes, derivatives of the former, which mediate knowledge that the events were; and, finally, continuants or substances—plans, purposes, knowledge—items of the matrix self, through which the flux of events is recorded and partly controlled.

The coming to be and passing away of events has usually been accepted as a one-way affair, forward, never backward. Yet there have not been wanting other views of the matter, as witness the Greeks with their theories of ˙returning cycles and Nietzsche with his notion of "eternal recurrence." Today it is fashionable to deduce the univocal "go" of time from the second law of thermodynamics, according to which energy flows from higher to lower levels, but never contrariwise. Now I do not doubt that this law has great significance, but to deduce time's vectorial flow from it is to go very far afield in order to explain something that is grounded on the immediate, and to base an a priori truth, which results directly from the analysis of experience, upon a hypothetical, empirical generalization. The asymmetry of time has a twofold metaphysical ground: first, the direction of the will from plan to realization or disappointment. It is manifestly impossible to go the other way, to begin with disillusion or success and go back to the plan, to hope and expectation. After disillusion there could not be hope, nor after failure, a plan. Secondly, time's flow is unique because historical truth is cumulative and piles up like a snowball. In order to make this manifest let us suppose that experience could retrace its steps, and that after the successive phases a, b, c, d, it began to go backwards, c, b, a. Even so, however, it would be true that a had been, and that b had been, and that c had been, and to every truth there corresponds a trace or echo; so that when c came again it would come loaded with traces of all past events, hence would not be the same c that it was before; and so for b and for a. The second cycle of the world would therefore not be the same as the first cycle, and all subsequent cycles would be different. Time could flow backward only in an echoless existence, where each event perished utterly, leaving no trace behind. But existence is none such.

With the foregoing review of the temporal aspects of experience as a background, we are prepared for a study of the more difficult and subtle problems connected with time. First, there is the problem of the relation to each other of coming to be and of passing away. Is an event completely over and done with when its successor appears? If it is, how can one account for the definite temporal *Gestalt* of transition, where it seems as if the earlier were somehow present alongside the later, as when we *see* the second hand of a watch move or hear two tones played legato? If it is not, and the earlier event is actually present with the later, how can the one be earlier and the other later, the one be past and the other present? For to be past is to be nonexistent, and to be present is to be existent; and how can we unite the nonexistent with the existent in one whole?

In order to make the problem concrete, let us consider motion, and fix our attention upon what happens when a fly moves without stopping over the surface of a mosaic window or floor. Let the path of the fly be vertical through the middle of the squares *a*, *b*, *c*, placed one above the other, each block being just large enough to contain the body of the fly. Now it is clear that when the fly is in block *b* its being in that block is entirely subsequent to its being in block *a*, and that when it will be in block *c* its being there will be subsequent to its having been in block *a* and in block *b*. But what is the case when the fly is crossing the boundary between blocks *a* and *b*, or *b* and *c*? As the front end of the animal is pushing over the line into *b*, or as its rear end is just leaving *a*, can we say that it is in *a* or in *b*, or that its having been in *b* is subsequent to its having been in *a*, or that its having been in *a* has preceded its having been in *b*? Of course, when the animal is partly in one and partly in the other we can say that it is in both, but what I am asking is this, What happens when the least part of the fly is crossing the line—its front end just entering *b*, or its rear end just leaving *a*?

Two opposed types of answer have been proposed, both of which, in my opinion, lead away from the fact as presented in experience. One is the answer dictated by orthodox mathematics wedded to associationist psychology. According to this view the body of the fly is made up of punctual elements, each capable of occupying a single element of space, these elements themselves forming a Cantorean continuum of points. The movement of the fly would therefore consist of the successive occupying of points of the spatial continuum by punctual elements of the fly's body. Each of these occupations would come after all the preceding occupations; and since, according to Dedekind's postulate, which is satisfied by the Cantorean continuum, the boundary between *a* and *b* may be counted as belonging to *b*, we should an-

swer the question asked above by saying, that when the last part
of the animal is crossing the line between *a* and *b*, its position is
absolutely subsequent to every preceding position, and the fly is
definitely in *b* rather than in *a*.   The appearance to the contrary,
as evidenced by our "seeing it cross the line," would be explained
as due to memory; the preceding positions would not in any sense
coexist with the present, actual position, but their images would.
The *Gestalt* of transition would be explained as a complex of a
single actual position plus the memories of preceding positions.
Such is one theory: it has several dubious aspects, to which we
shall have to return when in a subsequent chapter we discuss the
problem of continuity, the continuity of time as well as of space;
but I wish to center attention for the moment on a single matter,
namely, that there is not a shred of evidence that the experience
of transition, of movement, of passage, is due to image or echo
elements.   Transition is a primary experience, just as original,
unique, and unitary as color or sound.   The explanation
through imagery is a hypothesis, not necessitated by the facts but
devised in order to support another hypothesis—the Cantorean
structure of space and time.   In the sequel we shall give reasons
for doubting the validity of this hypothesis.

The other answer to the question is essentially that of Bergson,[1] which leads, as we shall see, straight to the *totum simul* of
Royce.   According to this explanation a movement or process is
a simple, indivisible whole, and any attempt to break it up into
sharply separate or distinct events, supposedly successive to each
other, is a falsification of the facts.   The movement of the fly
over the pane is a single fact; hence the question whether the occupation of *b* comes after the occupation of *a* is misleading.   A
like answer would be given in the case of the melody: the melody
is a single whole, not a mere succession of tones.

The theory must, however, face the following embarrassing
question, How extensive is this movement—whole?   If it embraces
the motion of the fly over the window pane, why should it not
embrace the entire life of the fly?   If the melody is a single indivisible whole, why not the symphony?   And if the symphony,

---

[1] H. Bergson, *Introduction to Metaphysics* (New York and London:
Macmillan and Co., 1912) , pp. 48–65; and *Essai sur les données immédiates
de la conscience* (Paris: Félix Alcan, 1912) , chap. ii.

why not the life of the listener? Or, for that matter, the history of the universe? That we are confronted with the *totum simul* of Royce is evident. But if the *totum simul* is real, there is no passing away. If the melody is a *totum simul,* no single note can be lost; if motion is a *totum simul,* no earlier occupation of position can disappear when a later one is actual—all must be real, when any one is real; if the process of the universe is a *totum simul,* nothing at all passes away. Passage becomes an illusion. But we know that passage is a fact, and hence, because the theory implies a conclusion that is false, the theory itself is false. The early sounds of the melody have disappeared when the last note is heard; the previous occupations of position by the fly are no more when it has moved definitely into a new section; the baby has ceased to be when the man has come to be; and all the past generations of human culture have perished that we might play out our peculiar parts. It is true, to be sure, that the traces of the early sounds, of the preceding occupations of position, of the past phases of human culture persist; but these traces are not the events themselves. The events are gone, lost, irretrievably vanished. The Bergson–Royce theory commits the mistake of confusing events with the truth about events. The truths are indeed eternal, but the events are perpetually perishing.

The solution of the problem that I am going to propose depends upon the frank recognition of the essential truth for which Bergson contended, that becoming is an irreducible category of reality and cannot be analyzed into a succession of states of being. It differs from Bergson's position, however, in contracting the application of the concept of becoming to the present, in its double phase of the coming to be of one event on the heels of the passing away of another. All other events are unreal, past events as well as those that are yet to be born. There is, therefore, an ultimate distinction between an event that has not occurred and one that is coming to be, or between an event that is passing and one that has passed. Only the coming to be and the passing away, I am insisting, are real events; the others are merely traces or hopes. For Bergson, on the contrary, if I understand him, a whole string of events may be a single act of becoming, and transition is the double phase of this whole. But this is false: a string of events is a construction within the present rising or perishing event. To revert to our illustrations: not the whole journey of the fly along the pane is real, but only a single pulse of movement, such as the crossing of the line between the two sections—the moving, the going, the taking up of a new and the abandoning of an old position. All other positions are unreal, those definitely abandoned and those definitely not yet occupied. Or consider the melody: only the rising of the new note on the heels of the one that is perishing is real; the notes that came before are nonexistent, equally with the notes that have not been played. The oncoming of the new and the passing of its predecessor is the minimum, but also the maximum, of the reality of events; all else is echo or expectation. This minimum-maximum is grasped in our experiences of moving, growing, changing, developing, passing, crossing, doing—in all the –ing types of experience. And behind this we cannot go in analysis. If it is the defect of the Bergson–Royce theory that it expands this minimum-maximum of events to include a whole string of events, it is equally the defect of the mathematical theory that it contracts it to a static, dead point of being. Just how large it may be we shall consider shortly when we come to the study of the problem of duration. But this much at least we may regard as settled: the minimum-maximum can never include more of any single strand of events than the transition between two events, although, as we shall see, this transition may be broader in one string and narrower in another. That the view I am proposing requires the abandonment of the orthodox, Cantorean theory of continuity, both in space and in time, I am not unaware; but that is a matter of so special and intricate a character, being bound up with the general theory of infinite classes, that I must postpone its study for consideration in a separate chapter.

But let us remember that this minimum-maximum of events is not all there is of reality; for, in addition, there is the matrix self which, running through events, survives their successive disappearance, and there are the traces of the events, through which they achieve a vicarious immortality. Now our second problem in regard to the general character of time will concern itself precisely with these traces, and, in particular, with their relation to the primary events of which they are echoes, on the one hand, and their relation to the self, on the other.

Bergson [1] has made the valuable distinction between two kinds of memory—memory in the sense of the persistence of habits, and what he calls pure memory, or remembering. Thus, in the first sense, I remember how to swim each returning summer when the warm days permit ocean bathing; in the second sense, I remember that a big wave engulfed me and nearly drowned me six summers ago at Nantucket. Since the second sense of memory is more complex, and an adequate theory of it will provide for the first, I shall confine my analysis to the latter. We may state the problem in the form of a paradox: The act of remembering is an event in the present, yet offers itself as attending upon as well as knowing a past event. When I remember the engulfing wave I not only have knowledge of the event, but it is as if I were actually present at the event. Yet how can I be present there, since the event, like all past events, is no more? It will not do to say that this seeming presence is mere seeming, a case of the "as if," on all fours with every other act of knowledge where the idea offers itself instead of the object; for memory is a form of intuitive knowledge, the differentia of which is the co-presence in the mind of the act of knowledge and its object. Intuitive knowledge is epistemological consubstantiation between idea and object, the real presence of the one in the other. Something of the past event must, therefore, have survived into the present, and must be directly apprehended in memory. The question becomes then, What has survived? The whole event cannot have survived; to believe that it has would involve falling into the error, which we have just scotched, of supposing that events are eternally actual—a supposition in contradiction with the essential character of an event, namely, *passage*. Moreover, it is evident that memory and the event remembered are not completely identical. The disparity between the memory of being almost drowned and the event itself is obvious. If one asks how we can know this, when our only avenue to knowledge of the event is memory itself, which we cannot compare with the event since the event is no more, the answer is that we can at least compare this memory with any event that is now passing, observe the general disparity between the two, and then carry this general difference over to the specific case. We can be cer-

[1] Bergson, *Matière et mémoire* (Paris: Félix Alcan, 1906), pp. 75–89.

tain, therefore, that the image of an event is not the event. But if not, where can the identity between the knowledge of the past event and the event itself lie?

In order to give a final answer to the question we must establish a certain lemma: that what one remembers is not a simple event, but one's experience of the event. A scrutiny of any example of memory will, I believe, serve to establish the truth of this proposition. It is true that I *say* that I remember the event itself—my first birthday party as a child, my college Commencement, and the like—or that the veteran says that he remembers the battle of Bull Run, but an attentive examination reveals that what memory recaptures of the birthday party or the Commencement is the event as envisaged from the point of view of myself, and no one can doubt, I should suppose, that what the veteran remembers is his own part in the battle—his experience of the battle. There is a fundamental difference in this regard between memory and perception, for in perception there is always reference beyond the perceptual experience to the focus of external control over the experience. The thrust to react immediately and exert control counter to the external control compels this extraversion in perception. But memory is not directly controlled from beyond the mind, but only, if at all, indirectly. In free association there is almost pure, internal direction of memory; when, on the other hand, one remembers something that is of use in solving a present practical problem there is obvious indirect control by the environment, but only by way of the intracortical processes of association. And now we have the answer to our question: The element of identity between the remembered event and memory is the self that remembers. Every event that we remember is an event that happens to us, and leaves a trace in the matrix self; on the occasion of a certain association the trace develops into an image of the event. Although the image is not, as we have seen, identical with the event which it echoes, the total remembering experience is partly identical with the total past experience because the latter included the self, which, although modified by the event, reappears in the new experience. This identity accounts for the intuitive character of memory.

This insight into the nature of memory leads to certain notable changes in the conventional view of time. Most important of all is the result that past and present cease to be regarded as mutually exclusive. For the traces begotten on the matrix self by events endure throughout its life; therefore something of all its past moments abides into the present. This implies that the elements of the present or actual self are of different date and age: some go back to its beginning; others are a few years or only one year old; some are of yesterday. Time is not properly to be represented, as it used to be, by a series of points on a line each of such a character that if it has location at a point it cannot have location at any other point, but, rather, as was suggested in an earlier publication,[1] by a series of overlapping areas, most simply perhaps by a series of concentric circles: the outermost representing the present, and the successive inner circles representing preceding moments of the past, the innermost going back to its beginning. This diagram of the nature of time brings out the fact I am referring to, that the present literally contains, and so overlaps with, portions of all the past of the individual.

The paradoxical character of this result vanishes when two facts are borne in mind, (1) that time as such does not exist, and (2) that all that does exist is present. If the older view were true, that time is an existence made up of mutually exclusive moments, then it would be impossible for past and present to overlap; but since time is nothing in itself, but a mere abstraction from existence, it follows that if anything once *was and still is,* as is the case with residua or traces, past and present must overlap. If the past has any existence at all it must be present, for to be and to be present are identical. The merely past is precisely what has ceased to be: it is nonexistent. On the other hand, the past that is not merely past is both past and present: it is part of the present. It is true, however, that there are no past *events.* The very concept "past event" is internally contradictory. For by "event" we mean a happening, and a happening is something going on, and what is going on is *ipso facto* present. There are, therefore, only present events. Nevertheless, events are intrinsically transitory; passing away belongs to their essence. They are; they are present; and lo! they are gone. We do, to be sure, speak of past events—the signing of the Treaty

[1] DeWitt H. Parker, *The Metaphysics of Historical Knowledge,* University of California Publications in Philosophy, Vol. II, No. 5 (Berkeley: University of California Press, 1913).

of Versailles, the invasion of the Ruhr, the accession of Hitler to power, and the like.   But what we are really referring to when we so speak are not events—for the signing of the Treaty, the invasion of the Ruhr, and so forth, are not going on—but certain historical *truths:* that there were events called by us the "signing of the Treaty," "the invasion of the Ruhr," and the like.   The echoes that are the bases of these truths exist, but not the events themselves.

The question immediately presents itself as to how, if at all, there can be a temporal series if there are no past events.   A series cannot be composed of null elements.   And the question is as pertinent with regard to personal, as it is with regard to cosmical, time.   We can approach the problem at its most simple and critical point by asking another question: What is the relation between any event and the event that immediately replaces it? In putting the question thus I am aware that I lay myself open to the objection that there are no next events, no immediate successors, if the temporal series be, as it is assumed to be in mathematical physics, a Cantorean continuum.   In order to meet this objection I would be willing to rephrase the question as follows: What is the relation between any event and any succeeding event that follows as close as you please?   I prefer to put the question in the first form, however, because within experience there are next events, and for the present we are limiting ourselves to an analysis of experience: as we hear them two tones played legato are next events.   But the way the question is put is open to another objection which brings out the problem perfectly: How can there be a relation between two events, of which one is called the successor of the other, when the earlier, the one that is past, does not exist?   When the successor arrives the first is not at all, for it is a so-called past event, and we have just shown that there are no past events.   There cannot be a relation between a thing which exists and nothing.   In this particular case, however, there is a genuine relation, for, in accordance with a result which we have established, when the coming to be of the one note follows on the heels of the passing of the other, this following-on-the-heels-of is an experienced, hence a real relation.   This shows that the earlier note is not quite over and done with when the later note arrives.   But now, let us shift our question to the relation between the note that we are hearing and the predecessor of its predecessor. In this case there can be no doubt that the earlier note is utterly past when the present one arrives, and that there is no experienced relation, no empirical succession between them. The sole possible answer to the question in this case is, therefore, that there is no relation at all. There may be a relation between the living event and a trace of the past one, and there may be relations between traces; but there are no relations between events, except between this present event and its contiguous events. There is, I conclude, no such thing as a temporal series of events. The final questions that emerge are, then, What is the structure of the traces begotten on the matrix self by the events that fertilize it? and the corollary, What is the structure of historical truth?

The theory that I am going to propose can best be disclosed by means of an analogy with the dating of physical objects. Consider a few groups of such objects: a set of archaeological remains or geological formations—such as vases or rock strata—or the tissues of an organism. In the first place, it is to be remarked that all these objects are present objects, yet they are given a date in the past: this rock, we say, belongs to the Silurian period, so many hundreds of thousands of years ago; this vase to the Mycenaean age, 1500 years B.C.; this arterial tissue is old tissue, seventy years old, perhaps—but, in comparison, this epidermal tissue is new, not more than a few weeks old. This double dating shows the fallacy of "simple location" in the matter of time. Moreover, the dating is made on the basis of certain definite characters of the objects, characters that we shall call "temporal" signs, on the analogy of the theory of the local signs of sensations. Now in the matrix self, also, the residua are present, yet they too have their temporal signs, which establish their relative pastness. These temporal signs give to the matrix self a two-dimensional structure of an interesting sort: for all traces, as present, are on a single level, while, in so far as they are traces, they belong to different moments. Our illustration of the concentric circles may again be helpful. All such circles, as members of the same plane, have the same index, but as forming a series through the relation of inclusion, they have different indices.

What precisely are the temporal signs of residua? Every memory, as we have seen, offers us objects and events as if they were passing before us; but that these memories are not the objects and events themselves is proved by comparison of the memory of an event or object with a genuine event or object. The presentation, therefore, is a matter rather of the intent of memory than of the real presence of the object or event. The memory is a picture or description of the character that the event or the object had, but is not a reinstatement of either. And, as thus pictured, objects and events have absolutely no temporal signs; like all works of the imagination, of which memory is a species, they are essentially timeless, dateless. In itself, the breaking of the doll as it is remembered has no more location in the life of a woman than an event in a drama; and the broken doll itself as limned in memory is as timeless as a statue or painting. But if the temporal sign is not to be found in the memory image, where can it be found? There is only one possibility open: it belongs to the self of the memory, to its relation to affection and the life plan. Whereas it is true that as mere image the broken doll has no intrinsic place in the life of the woman and might occur when she was a grandmother as well as when she was a child, the emotion that recurs throughout her life, on the contrary, belongs only to childhood, and could not belong to any other period. Taken with this emotional freight, the image comes as a residuum of her remote past; from the point of view of her present life it is archaic. Or to consider other examples: the memory of the broken troth that returns with such pain and despair would not fit into the disillusioned life of the man past middle age; despite the freshness and vividness of the relived emotion it is marked with the sign of the past. Or the dark wonder that colors all events of childhood puts them back into the past, far from the sophistication and learning of maturity. Or the fulfilment of a project must come after its inception, and the ways and means must come in between. From these illustrations it is clear—and they might be multiplied indefinitely—that the temporal sign of a memory is relational; it is derived from the way it fits into the plan of the whole life of the person. The traces of the past fit themselves together into a series like the pieces of a puzzle. But the whole series is present.

Very important for the determination of temporal signature is remembered empirical sequence. Just as there is an immediate experience of one event following on the heels of another, so there is a memory of such a sequence. Even as the minimum-maximum of reality is a rising sequent upon a perishing, so the traces of reality have a similar doubleness. My memory is therefore not of a and of b, but of b on the heels of a, and of c on the heels of b, and of d on the heels of c, and so forth. Wherever there are remembered sequences of this kind we reconstruct the whole out of such parts, in accordance with the principle of the transitivity of the sequences, ab, bc. Since no life consists of a single sequence, but of many that go abreast, there is the problem of fitting an item that belongs to one in relation to an item that belongs to another. This is done in accordance with the principle of empirical togetherness. There are items that are experienced as being together and are therefore remembered as having been together; all such items will belong together in what we shall call an empirical moment. Items that precede any item in such a moment will, with a reservation to be explained presently, be before all items in that moment. The series of empirical moments is therefore a two-dimensional series, if viewed with regard to the strands of empirical sequence which it contains. For example, the sequence of motions of the dancer is a sequence parallel with the sequence of tones of the accompanying music.

A final problem is that of duration. Duration is a supposedly quantitative property as opposed to the purely ordinal properties of time. A string of events, like a lecture, appears to last a long or a short time, or longer or shorter than another string of events; strings of events may have a comparable temporal order yet be very different in the matter of duration, just as the order of points on two lines is the same but their lengths may be unequal. The spokes of a wheel follow each other now slowly, now swiftly; the musician plays the notes of a melody first at one speed, then at another. Just what is duration? Is it an intrinsic property, perhaps the essence of time, as Bergson has declared, a purely subjective addition, or possibly a relational property?

That the experience of duration depends upon many apparently subjective factors is a commonplace of observation. The lecture seems long if it bores me, short if I am interested; if experience is relatively unvaried, as in semisleep, time passes quickly, slowly if there are slight variations, rapidly again, if the variations are many. In childhood the whole apparent pace of experience is relatively slow; in maturity it is fast. Yet to dismiss duration as purely subjective is impossible in view of its exact measurement. The two lectures, one of which seemed long and the other short, are proved to be of equal duration by turning to the clock: both lasted exactly one hour. The child's or the countryman's slow year are proved to be of equal duration with the city man's swift year by reference to the revolution of the earth about the sun. Since, nevertheless, there can be no denying that the felt slow tempo of the child's experience, or of the adult's when life is monotonous, is a genuine property, it cannot be discarded as mere error, but must be recognized as a different sort of thing from duration in the so-called objective sense. Not much is gained, in my opinion, in calling one subjective and the other objective, for the former is just as real as the latter.

Indeed, when the supposedly objective sort of duration is closely examined it shows itself to be both puzzling and elusive. For myself, I cannot find any intrinsic character in events identifiable with it. An event is what it is, it has such and such characters: it is a sound event, a thought event, a kinesthetic event, or what not; but aside from its seeming fast or slow in the fashion called subjective, there is nothing intrinsic to the event, no plus character, which could be distinguished as duration. Over and above the order of events in a string of events, they may seem to have a stretchiness that is relatively long or short, dilating or contracting, but this is indistinguishable, I repeat, from so-called subjective duration. An objectively short duration may have an exceedingly long *protensity*, and vice versa. These considerations lead irresistibly, I believe, to the conclusion that objective duration is not an intrinsic but a relational property of events; that is to say, *only through relation to other events has an event duration.*[1] I do not mean that it merely appears to have duration through relation; I mean that it actually has duration through relation; duration is a relational, but nonetheless real, property of events, or (more guardedly stated, for reasons that will transpire presently) of what are called events. The duration of a so-called event, such as a lecture, is a property that corresponds to the fact that it exists alongside the rise and fall of many other

[1] My view of objective duration, since it, too, depends upon correlation, is like Bergson's except for the fact that I view duration as a real—albeit relational—property of substances.

events, such as the succession of tick-tocks made by the clock or the revolutions of the minute hand around the dial. To have a long duration is to exist alongside the rise and fall of many other events; to last a short time is to exist alongside fewer events. The measure of the duration of an event is never anything else than the number of some parallel series of events. To last a year—to have a duration of a year—is to exist parallel with the rise and fall of 365 revolutions of the earth around its axis, and of one revolution of the earth about the sun; to last an hour is to exist parallel with the coming to be and passing away of sixty revolutions of the minute hand about the clock. A rapid process is one that begins and ends parallel with the rise and fall of few of the events taken as standard; a slow process is one that is parallel with many such events. Objectively, the duration is the fact of existence parallel with other events; slowness or swiftness depends upon our expectations or desires in regard to these matters. A man is slow at changing a tire if the process is parallel with thirty minute-hand revolutions, because we expect, and so desire, that it should be parallel with only fifteen.

If this view is correct the surprising result follows that if there were only a single line of events, they would have no physical duration at all. And the objection is sure to be raised, that the single series of events might move fast or slow, and hence endure a longer or a shorter time. But if it is true that duration is relational the supposition is meaningless. The events of the single series would rise and fall, but they could not have any objective duration or pace at all. They could have subjective pace—if the self that lived through them were bored, the pace would be slow, if interested, the pace might be very fast—that is all. Lurking in the background of this supposition there is, I fear, a subconscious lingering belief in an absolute Newtonian time, independent of events and with its own equable, imperturbable flow, with reference to which the stream of events is compared. The same remnant of Newtonism lies behind the similar argument that we might speed up all clocks and so double the measured duration of any other process yet leave the "real" duration of the process the same. The reply is, of course, that you could speed up your clocks only by creating a new parallelism between them and some new, standard series of events, with relation to which all events would not only be measured as being

swifter, but would actually be swifter. These and kindred difficulties vanish if it is held steadily in mind that there is no
intrinsic duration of the objective sort—that this kind of duration
exists only through relation to parallel events; and that fast and
slow are comparative, not absolute, terms.

The problem of duration is, however, far from being solved
by the recognition of its relational character. When we think
of events as having duration through relation to parallel events
we usually have in mind what have been felicitously called
strings of events, rather than elementary events. A lecture, for
example, is not a single event, but, strictly speaking, a string
of events. This is true whether by the lecture be meant the
series of spoken sounds, heard sounds, thoughts expressed, or
thoughts understood. Or if I am measuring the duration of a
walk I am clearly not measuring a single event, but a string of
steps or other lesser, elementary events. By a string of events
should be meant a series of events all of which are connected
by some underlying purpose, significance, or cause. The ticks
of a clock are a string of events as being all due to a single cause;
the steps of a walk, as having the same cause and also as expressing the same purpose; the notes of a melody as having the same
cause, expressing the same purpose of the player, and embodying
a single musical significance. I do not stop here to enquire
whether, in the end, cause, significance, and purpose may not
be identical; their relations to one another, as well as to the
events they govern, will engage our attention in the chapters on
causality. I shall not, moreover, debate the question whether or
not a string of events should be called an event, for that, like
the question whether or not a "past" event should be called an
event, is a terminological issue which usage has decided in the
affirmative. On the other hand, it is clear from what we have
established in regard to past events that a string of events is not
an event, whatever it be called. For a string of events, no more
than a past event, is a happening, an occurrence. Only the
events that are presently rising and falling—the one on the heels
of the other—are happening; the other members of the string
either have happened, hence are not, or else are going to happen,
hence again are not. A string of events is, therefore, largely an
ideal construction within what we have called the minimum-
maximum of events, which alone is real. I shall assume, further-

more—pending the discussion of infinite classes in the chapter "Finite or Infinite" devoted to that topic—that there must be elementary events.   For otherwise either reality would be infinitely complex, each event being itself a string, and the events of that string being themselves strings, and the events of these strings being again also strings, and so on—which, as I shall try to show, is impossible—or else, since strings of events are not events, there would be no events at all.   The question that confronts us, then, is whether *elementary* events—which are the only true events —can have duration, whether such an event can coexist with the rise and fall of other elementary events.

If we answer in the negative, it is hard to see how even strings of events, since they are composed of elementary events, could have duration either.   What would have duration would be not the string of events, but the string of the events—the underlying continuant or substance, the purpose, cause, or significance that unites them and persists throughout their rise and fall.   The duration of the continuant would be measured by the events of which it is the string, or by any other parallel series of events, but the events themselves would simply rise and fall; they would not have duration.   It would, of course, be a pardonable manner of speaking to attribute duration to events, but false none the less.

If, on the other hand, we answer that elementary events may have duration, we are faced with a well-known difficulty.   In order to present this difficulty in as simple a fashion as possible, let us suppose that the event E that has the duration, has duration in relation to two other events, x and y, with the rise and fall of which it is coexistent, and let x be the earlier of the two. Then it would seem as if the parallel event E, whose duration we are studying, must be divisible into two parts, an earlier part parallel with x and a later part parallel with y.   And since the earlier part is parallel with x, it would seem as if it must disappear with the disappearance of x, from which the inference would be inevitable that event E, instead of being a single, elementary event, would be a string of two events.   We should then come out with the same result as before: elementary events, the only true events, would have no duration; only continuants would have duration.

This argument would be unanswerable if it were true that

existence and nonexistence were the sole categories of being, but fails in view of the primacy of coming to be and passing away. For when E, an elementary or true event, not a string of events, comes to be, it comes to be as a whole, and no part of it is passing away or has passed away; likewise, when it is passing away, it passes as a whole, and no part of it has passed away until the whole has passed away; otherwise, the event would not be an event and would forfeit the dynamic, quivering, moving character intrinsic to an event, and the distinctive quality of becoming would be lost in a mere succession of static states of being. Only strings of events come to be in part and pass away in part. Thus the life of a man, which is a string of events, may be said to come to be and to pass away in stages—first the baby, then the child, then the adolescent, and so forth, each coming to be and passing away in turn; but the elementary events of which that life is composed flash into being and pass out of being as atomic wholes.[1]   Hence the coming to be of an elementary event such as E may be parallel with the rise and passage of many events without dividing E; for when the parallel event x is passing E is still coming to be as a whole; no part of it has come to be, therefore no part of it could perish with the perishing of x. Any event whose rise and fall coincides with the rise and fall of many other events will be called a slow event or will be said to have a slow pace; when an event is parallel with few events it will be called a fast event or will be said to have a fast pace.   As we have noted, a string of events does not properly have duration, but its continuant does; yet it may be said to have the duration of its continuant.   The measure of the duration of an elementary event or of a continuant is the number of the parallel events.

---

[1] Cf. A. N. Whitehead, "Time," Section VI in *Proceedings of the Sixth International Congress of Philosophy* (New York: Longmans, Green and Co., 1927), pp. 63–64.

VIII

Some Cosmical Aspects of Time; Time and Relativity

WHEN the restriction of the concept of time to personal experience is removed certain special problems arise, of which some have been made more acute by the contemporary theory of physical relativity. In this chapter I wish to consider these problems.

Our first problem will be the definition of the concept "moment," and especially "present moment." When its application is restricted to a single monad, "present moment" means the existing phase in the life of the monad and consists of the matrix of the monad together with the parallel events that are going on within it. That there are parallel events there needs no proof, for such events are the objects of direct intuition: for me the dancer sings and smiles and dances "at once." The parallelism of events in the life of the monad is an aspect of the empirical complexity or togetherness of the items of experience. The concept "present" is, to be sure, a term of variable application: it applies to this event, to that parallel event, and to that other parallel event; but on the passage of these events, it does not apply to them, but applies to new events. There is, however, no difficulty in this, for the application of the concept is never in doubt; its extension is the range of whatever events there are, and lo! they are these and these, as we point to them. When, on the other hand, we seek to apply the concept "present moment" to the cosmos the matter is not so simple. The temptation would be to define it as the class of simultaneous events, the term "simultaneous" functioning as the analogue of the empirical togetherness or parallelism of events within a given monad. But this definition contains two difficulties. First, there is no empirical relation of simultaneity between events in noncontiguous monads. The only observable relation of simultaneity is the empirical togetherness of events in a single phase of the life of contiguous monads—no monad experiences the parallelism of events distributed in separate monads; but apart from some such experience of togetherness, it is hard to see what the relation could be.　The special aspect of this difficulty brought to light by the physical theory of relativity I shall consider at the close of the present chapter.　Aside from this special difficulty there is, nevertheless, a fortunate way out of the general difficulty.　We can drop the term "simultaneous" altogether and define the present moment simply as the class of existing events.　We do not even need to say *existing* events, for, as we know, a non-existing event is no event—it is a truth or a trace.　"Event" and "existing event" have the same meaning.　The present moment, therefore, would be nothing else than the class of whatever events there are.　And even within the single monad, it is clear, the concept "parallel" or "simultaneous" is unnecessary in defining the present, for from the mere existence of two or more events there it follows that they are parallel; the existence of the one and the existence of the others is a primary fact.

But even this simplified definition of "present moment" as the class of existing events holds a real, if subtle, difficulty when applied outside the given monad.　The difficulty lurks in the concept "class."　For except in the case where we can point directly to its membership (definition *per enumerationem*), a class is determined by a common property or relation; but with regard to the class of existing events, what is the determining property or relation?　When the scope of the definition is limited to the given monad—that is, to ourselves—there is no difficulty, because we can determine the class as the events that are happening to ourselves, to which we can, at least theoretically, point directly.　But obviously we cannot point to the events that happen to separate monads.　We must, therefore, find some common property which they all possess or some relation either to a given thing or to each other.　It might be suggested that the common property required is eventness, or being an event, which all events obviously have in common.　But there are two difficulties in using being an event as the defining property: in the first place, we do not wish to exclude substances, for surely substances as well as events belong to the present moment; in the second place, if we avoid this difficulty by enlarging our common property in such a way as to include substances—"being a substance or being an event"—or by reducing substances to events (as some contemporary philosophers try to do), our property becomes so broad as to be equivalent to being or existence, and, as Kant showed, existence is not a property. This is the same difficulty we should run into if, in defining the present as the class of existing events, we were to take existence as the common property.

Happily, there are two ways out of this difficulty. One is to make use, in our definition, of some relation which any given event bears to events in other monads, through which all are bound together. Then the present moment would consist of *this event* and such events as bear the relation in question to this event. By "this event" we mean, as we have seen, any event to which we can point, that is to say, any event in our own mind. The problem now becomes that of finding some such relation. And there is a relation that will serve: the relation of overlapping or contact between monads. If monads overlap then *this event* is parallel with some event that belongs to some other monad, and hence is parallel with the other events in that other monad; some one of these events is either common to another monad or else is parallel with one that is common, which in turn is parallel with the other events in that monad; and so on, until every event is included in the class "present moment." We may call the resulting relation between events "indirect parallelism."

There is, however, a simpler, and wholly compatible way of defining the present moment. It is obtained by reconstructing the rejected definition of the present as the class of existents. We rejected this definition because of our difficulty in finding a common predicate distinctive of the class, the only predicate at hand being the pseudo predicate "existence." But now contemporary logicians have shown how existence can be defined; we can use this definition in order to define the class in question, and in such a way as to avoid the use of any pseudo concept. The assertion of existence, we are told, is a statement about a concept, to the effect, namely, that the concept is realized or has application. Thus, if I say, God exists, I am not predicating "existence" of God—there is, as Kant showed, no such predicate— I am asserting that the concept of God is realized; the concept of God, not God, is the subject of the proposition. The notion of the realization of a concept is, moreover, a thoroughly empirical one. For example, if I say, There are men, or, Men exist, I can *see* that the concept "man" has application or is realized in this or that individual man whom I can point to: the concept fuses with, or, as it were, fits on to, the intuited object, as a cap fits the head. So, if I say, God exists, I mean that the concept "God" has application of this kind; I cannot, to be sure, verify it, as I can verify the existence of men, but at least I can give a perfectly intelligible meaning to the assertion that God exists. *In principle* it is verifiable, for God himself, if he exists, can verify it. Similarly, the assertion that another monad of a certain definite description exists means that that description is realized, and can, in principle, be verified by the monad itself if it is self-conscious, or by another monad that could get into immediate contact with it, as multiple personalities are in contact with each other. Accordingly, the realm of existence, which is the same as the present moment or the "now," can be defined as the range of application of first-order concepts; in the symbolism of *Principia Mathematica,* it is equivalent to x such that $F(x)$, where both x and F are variables, and where F denotes any first-order concept. F must be restricted to first-order concepts because a second-order concept is realized, not by individuals, but by species of a genus. Thus the concept "color" is a second-order concept, which is realized through green, blue, violet, and so on. On the other hand, a determinate shade of green, blue, or violet is a first-order concept, because it is realized only in some intuitable individual. That "the present moment" is not an empty class we know because we can directly verify, in our own experience, the application there of many first-order concepts. But it is to be observed that the definition of this class in no wise restricts it to the given. Moreover, the class is a variable class, for a concept that has application, such as "leader of the Fascist State of Italy," did not have application jointly with the application of the concept "Mazzini," and would not have application jointly with the concept "Soviet State of Italy."

The discussion of the variable nature of the class defined as the present moment leads inevitably to the problem of the definition of "past moment." Since moments do not exist apart from events, our definition must proceed on the same principle as that employed in the definition of the present. If we grant, as I have held, that there is a unique relation—the relation of indirect parallelism—between existent events ("existent," let me say again, is a redundancy used in deference to popular usage, for the sake of ready communication of meaning), the definition that suggests itself by analogy with the definition of the present would be: A particular past moment is this remembered event (or this event otherwise known to have existed), together with such events as are correlated with it. Or, using the term "class" as a convenient logical fiction, and using as an adjective the term "coexisted," defined to mean "did exist and was uniquely correlated with," in the sense already indicated, we may tersely define the general concept "past moment" as a class of events such that any one of them coexisted with any other one, or, still more briefly, as a class of coexisted events. In defining a past moment it is impossible to dispense with some relation between past events, for the reason that whereas "exist"—as the field of realization of first-order concepts—though variable, is always unique, since what I point to is always unique and therefore defines a unique class, yet the corresponding term "existed"—defined analogously as the field of first-order concepts that *were* realized—would not define a unique class or "moment" of events, since all events, except such events as are present, did exist; hence, all moments of the past, rather than a single moment, would be thus defined.

The definition of the past as the field of first-order concepts that were realized is, however, open to the obvious objection that it is circular, in that the phrase "were realized" already implies pastness. In order to remedy this defect it is necessary and sufficient to find some empirical meaning for "was realized." And, fortunately, this can easily be found. For "was realized" is precisely equivalent to the state of affairs when, first, a concept is at once not realized—that is to say, when the event in question does not exist—and when, secondly, some trace of the event, like a memory or a document, does exist—in other words, if the concept of the trace is realized, in the strictly empirical sense of "is realized" which we have already defined. Thus the birth of Christ belongs to the past because, in the first place, my concept of the birth of Christ cannot be realized—as the concept of the birth of some infant now being born into the world can be realized by attending the accouchement—and because, in the second place, traces of the birth of Christ, such as the manuscripts of the Four Gospels, exist. With regard to events in our own experience, the empirical character of the definitions of present and past is evident. For having a concept of an object we can observe that it applies; we can observe that it does not apply, as we watch its object disappear; and we can observe the emergence into experience of a trace of the object—memory. When the concept applies the object is present; if the concept does not apply, but its trace exists, the object is past. From these definitions it becomes abundantly clear, as we have already insisted, that an event that did exist (or, popularly, a past event) is really nothing at all; that what is meant is *truth*. The past event that we call the birth of Christ is really the truth that our concept does not have application, together with the truth that a trace does exist; in brief, the past event is the *truth* that Christ was born, and the moment of the birth of Christ is the class of truths which includes that truth together with all truths of the form "such and such an event coexisted (in the sense defined above) with the birth of Christ." And such truths, like all truths, are present. As we have shown, the past is part of the present; the contents of the past have double temporal signature.

The definition of the past which we have been offering discloses a new difference between time as a purely personal and time as a cosmical concept. For the basis of the truths that make up the past of a single monad consists, as we have seen, of the traces that are immediately generated in the matrix self by the events that befall it. Out of these traces are formed the memories in which the history of the individual is apprehended. But when the matrix self dissolves at death, where is the basis of the truths about its life? Where, for example, is the trace of the birth of Christ? The manuscripts of the Four Gospels, we have suggested, are the trace, but clearly these are secondary or derivative traces; they are not primary traces, like the memories of his past that each living monad treasures. The Sacred Person himself has disappeared, and all those who assisted at his birth —the Divine Mother, Joseph, the lowly shepherds, the Wise Men from the East, and the dumb beasts that gathered round—are no more. And yet, if historical truth is eternal, as we shall argue in our chapter entitled "The Eternal," there must exist somewhere traces of all events. In the substance or matrix self of the universe they must be preserved. Let us remind ourselves that

while the human monad perishes there is something closely related to it, namely, the physical system, on which its body and
its mind depend, that is eternal.   There, if we could find them,
are the traces of all events.   It is inconceivable that what happens to the mind and the body should not leave its impress on
the physical world.   The physical system, as we shall try to show,
is a vast recording mechanism; but it is clear that to us many of
these traces are inaccessible.   In the case of such an event as the
birth of Christ we are fortunate in having ready to our hand for
interpretation such traces as the manuscripts of the New Testa-
ment and the works of other writers of the early Christian epoch,
together with architectural and similar monuments.   These
traces, though they are for us mere phenomenal objects, reveal,
nevertheless—let us not forget it—relatively permanent elements
in the structure of the physical world.   My thesis is that there are
elements of the physical world corresponding to every event, so
that every event echoes eternally.   A trace may be relatively transitory, but there is always an echo of that echo.   The manuscripts of the Four Gospels may disappear, but the truth that they
record cannot disappear, which means that some echo of the
events they record will endure throughout all time.   Even if all
men should perish these echoes would endure and would provide
a basis for the apprehension of the corresponding truths to any
mind that could recover and interpret them.

In order to define the order of the moments of time it would
be natural to try to imitate our procedure in defining the order
of the past events in the life of the single living monad.   But
once more we find that we cannot simply carry over the procedure from the field of the single, living monad to the field of
the cosmos.   In the case of the single monad we could define the
order of past events in terms of the traces left by the events in
the matrix self, but in the case of the cosmos we cannot do this
for the reason that not only the events, but also, as we have
just observed, the primary traces of the events have disappeared
(they have disappeared in the case of all events that have happened in the lives of finite, perishable monads) , and only secondary traces remain, the time order of which does not correspond to
the order of the primary traces.   For example, the date of the
Four Gospels is different from the date of the birth of Christ which
they record.   The order of the moments of time must, therefore,

be defined in terms of truths rather than of traces. It is identical with what in the broadest sense may be called history. The definition of this order will then proceed most simply in this wise. We must view the historical process as composed of strands of historical truth, each strand consisting of truths of the following type: event *B* followed on the heels of event *A*; event *C* followed on the heels of (or, more simply expressed, followed) *B*, and so on. Proceeding in this way, we shall get all past events (more accurately, the truths about all past events) arranged in series, it being understood that if *B* follows *A*, and if *C* follows *B*, then *C* follows *A*; and, of course, conversely, if *A* precedes *B* and *B* precedes *C*, then *A* will precede *C*. Having thus established these strands or series of truths, we must next proceed to correlate them. It might seem as if this could easily be done on the basis of the coexistedness (defined above) between past events; that is to say, truths about events that coexisted would be correlated to form a single level of truths, or moment of time. The order of these moments would then be determined by the order of the so-called past events that compose them. And if all events were minimum events, this would be a satisfactory procedure. But the difficulty is that some events are long and some are short; hence long events, being contemporary with several successive short events, would belong to many different moments, and, even when contemporary among themselves, would not define a unique moment. A line or level of events does not, therefore, satisfy the usual definition of a straight line: it is not true that any two points—here read "events"—on a line determine a line. Our procedure must be more complicated: in any class of coexisted events we must pick out the minimum event (or events) as what we shall call an indicator event; then this event, together with whatever events coexisted with it, defines a moment. Now of other classes of coexisted events, some will be such that none of their member events will belong to the given class defined; others will be such that some of their members do belong, and other members do not belong. The former classes are easily seen to be either before or after the given class; the relative position of the other classes can be defined by the indicator event or events in those classes. If the indicator event in a class precedes any event in the given class, its class defines a moment that precedes; if, however, the indicator event follows any event, the class follows.[1]   In this way we can establish an order of moments that will include all so-called past events.   The problem remains to define "precedes" and "follows."   This can readily be done: Any class of past events will precede any other class if some member, say the indicator event, of the former class determines in any way the existence or character of any member of the latter class; if on the other hand, any member of the former class is determined by some member of the latter, it follows the latter.   Since long events may belong to many moments and since some events in a preceding moment may belong to monads so distant from monads to which succeeding events occur that the former could not possibly influence the latter, even through communication by light ray, we could not define the order of moments in terms of just any events in two different moments.   Here, therefore, is another difference between our view of time and the orthodox view: for whereas according to the latter each level of events—or moment—could be represented as a line parallel to all other lines, according to our view the lines are not parallel, but constantly intersect; and if there is an eternal substance, all moments intersect in that substance.   That is to say, it is not true that if a point on a line (an event at a moment) is lower down than (belongs to a moment preceding) a point on a line above it, all points on the former line (all events at the former moment) are lower down than (precede) the points (events) on the latter.

In our account of time scant attention has been given to the problem of the nature of the future.   Yet this has been no oversight.   For what we call the future does not have reality on a level with that of the past and the present.   The reality of the present is all-inclusive, and, distinctively, that of events; the reality of the past consists, as we have shown, of echoes and truths.   What holds the future to match this?   We speak of future events as if such things were, but it is evident that the very concept of a future event, like the concept of a past event, is nonsensical; for an event is a happening, and what happens is

[1] My procedure here is obviously similar to that of Bertrand Russell, as expounded in *Our Knowledge of the External World* (New York: W. W. Norton and Co., 1929), pp. 125, 126; only, since I am assuming that there are minimum events, and that any class of coexisted events is finite, it is much simpler.

ipso facto present. Or, to put the matter the other way round, a future event, if it exists, is not future—for the future is, presumably, the realm not of things that are but of things that will be, and an event that will be is not an event, since to be an event implies being, and being implies being present. If the future does not have the reality of the event, neither does it have the reality of the trace. The past as it disappears leaves a deposit, an inalienable, eternal part of the structure of reality; the future, never having been, contributes nothing. This difference between past and future is strikingly revealed when we compare the mental process by means of which we claim to know the future with that by means of which we claim to know the past. Memory is a species of intuition through which we are admitted to the very presence of the reality of the past; but—barring the dubious claims of clairvoyance—we have no intuitive knowledge of the future; prophecy is inference, not intuition. Even the knowledge of the future claimed by ancient and modern soothsayers, gotten from dreams, the flight of birds, the entrails of animals, the conjunctions of the planets, or the like, is inference, no less than the knowledge claimed by the astronomer of the rise of tomorrow's sun or the return of a comet or a solar eclipse. In the case of the past there is a determinate part of reality eternally there to be intuited; this is not so in the case of the future.

It might seem, however, that we could claim for the future at least the status of truth; that on this plane the future is level with the past. The astronomer, it may be said, knows the truth that a comet will return no less than the historian knows the truth that a comet was sighted by Halley. Barring the matter of memory, our knowledge of the past, also, is largely through inference; and inference forward can give us truth just as genuine as can inference backward. The future would be, therefore, a selected part of the total realm of truth; it would consist of such truths as that the sun will rise, that the comet will return, that the man will die, or, more generally expressed, that such and such an event will exist, which, accurately stated, means that such and such a concept will be realized. We could then define the future, following the analogy of our definitions of past and present, as the totality of truths of the form "such and such a concept will be realized."

But with regard to this definition there is much that should be said. In the first place, it is never simply true that a concept will be realized, or, in common terms, that an event will happen; it is only probable that it will happen. Even with regard to the concept of the sunrise or the return of the comet, it is only probable that they will have application; it is not true that they will. We cannot, therefore, know the future as we can know the past, for the thing that is only probably so may not be so, no matter how highly probable it is. Our inferences from the documentary evidence that Halley sighted a comet may be only very highly probable, but at least there is a truth that he sighted a comet or a truth that he did not sight one; and if he sighted one there is somewhere in the world a trace of that fact, and this truth is potentially knowable by means of some determinate avenue of investigation; but of the return of the comet there is no truth—no truth that it will return and no truth that it will not return, and no determinate avenue of investigation by means of which such a truth could be ascertained. In the strict sense of truth there is, as Aristotle claimed, no truth about the future. When men of science or the people talk of future events, or the truth about the future, they either do not know what they are saying, or they mean probabilities. And probabilities are not truths, not even of a lesser sort; a merely probable truth is a nonsense. It is impossible therefore that the future should be, as was suggested, the totality of truths that such and such concepts shall have application, for there are no such truths. Yet there are probabilities; hence we could venture the definition that the future consists of the totality of probabilities that such and such concepts will have application. And then it becomes our problem to determine what, exactly, this can mean. And since, in order to do this, we shall have to assume the truth of results to be established in the sequel, I shall do no more than state the matter categorically. The probability that concept C will be realized means that C is not realized and that there exist tendencies in the direction that, or intentions that, C shall be realized. Just as the basis for the truth that a concept *was* realized is the existence of a trace, so the basis for the probability that it *will be* realized is the existence of a tendency toward its being realized, or a desire that it should be realized. These tendencies are, of course, like all existences, present. The reality of the future,

like the reality of the past, is present.   Such is the full—and only
—reality of the future: probabilities and tendencies.   There is no
more.   But that is much.   The rest is—nothing at all.   And we
shall leave to the reader the easy but fascinating problem of
working out definitions of future moments and their order on the
analogy of past moments and their order, only in terms not of
truth but of probabilities, in accordance with our basic definition.

Thus far in our discussion of the metaphysics of time no account has been taken of the revolutionary changes supposed to
have been effected by the physical theory of relativity.   Our
neglect has, however, been strictly in accordance with our fundamental methodological assumption that beliefs founded on ordinary experience are the primary and the sufficient materials for
metaphysical construction.   We are prepared, nevertheless, to
accept the further principle that no metaphysical concept can be
in opposition to science.   It is incumbent on us, therefore, to
show that the metaphysics of time as we have developed it is
consistent with the essential notions of physical relativity.   In
particular, we must reconcile our reduction of space to time and
our theory of duration, which make time the central concept,
with the conception of "interval" basic in the relativity theory,
which is a blend of space and time.   We must show that interval
can be expressed wholly in terms of temporal concepts.   We
must, furthermore, find a way to escape the difficulties raised by
the relativization of simultaneity and temporal sequence with
regard to different observers and moving systems.
        It will assist us in the solution of these problems if we have
in mind the distinction drawn in relativity theory between
spacelike and timelike intervals.   A timelike interval is defined
as an interval between events such that it is physically possible for
a body to be present at both events.   (The term "interval" has,
of course, its technical meaning, which we do not need to discuss
at this point.)   An equivalent definition is as follows: An interval is timelike when the time between the events is longer than
would be required by any mode of travel—in particular by that
of light—to go from the one event to meet the other event.   Thus
the interval between the event of my leaving Ann Arbor at 7 P.M.
in order to attend the theatre in Detroit and my arrival at the
rising of the curtain is timelike because I can be present at both

events, and I can be present at both events because the time between them is longer than is required for travel by train or auto from the one event to the other. And, of course, if I could travel on a ray of light, I should have time to spare. All events that belong to a single biography or monad are timelike, because the matrix self may be said to go from one to the other. It is obvious, furthermore, that timelike intervals are such that it is possible to send a message from the one event between which the interval holds and the other event, by means of which the one event may influence or in some way determine the character of the other.

Now, so far as timelike intervals are concerned, there are no important difficulties. In the first place, the temporal order of events between which they hold is the same for all observers, that is to say, if A is before B for one observer, it is before B for any other observer also. Hence the order may be held to be objective. In the second place, the timelike interval can be expressed, without remainder, in terms of time, and therefore need not be accepted as a concept more objective than time. It is in fact equivalent to the duration which an observer traveling on the body which moves from one event to the other would judge the duration to be. The duration may be regarded as made up of two components: the time required by the moving body to get into the neighborhood of the expected event, and the time of waiting, after arrival in the neighborhood, for the event to occur. We shall call the first "distance time"; the second "waiting time." When the expected event is an event that occurs to us following a given event, independently of any motion on our part, there is no distance time, only waiting time; when, on the other hand, the interval between the events is so short in relation to the means of locomotion from one to the other that the whole time is required to get from the first event into the neighborhood of the expected event, there is no waiting time, only distance time. If, for example, I meet the rising of the curtain at the theatre in Detroit by leaving Ann Arbor just in time to get there, there is no waiting time after my arrival; the entire time is distance time, as would be the case if I were to travel by light ray to meet an event a second hence and 300,000 kilometers away. By taking the longest possible path from the given event in order to get into the neighborhood of the expected event just when it arrives, it is always possible to move in such a way that the entire time will be distance time; the time of this motion is equivalent to the interval.

When, however, the physical interval between two events is spacelike, the difficulties are not so easily overcome. An interval is spacelike when it is not possible to move in such a way that a person on the moving body can be present at both events between which the interval holds. This is the case when the distance between the events is so great or (and) when the events happen so close together that no means of travel is fast enough for presence at both events. If, for example, two events occur within a second and at a distance of 300,000 kilometers, or within half a second at an interval of 150,000 kilometers, the interval is spacelike, for not even travel by light ray would enable one to be present at both. Obviously, if there be simultaneous events they are spacelike, unless they be events happening to the same monad—in other words, happening in the same place. In the case of events between which the interval is spacelike it is clear that no message can be sent from one to the other; consequently, no influence upon the character or existence of the one can be exerted by the other. Such events are causally independent. Now, when the interval is spacelike the time order of the events is held to be ambiguous, for it is always possible to move in such a way as to make them appear now simultaneous, now one before the other, now the other before the one. And there is no way of deciding between observers whether the appearance to the one or the other is right. For example, separated events, that is to say, events that occur to different monads, which appear to an observer as simultaneous cannot so appear to any other observer in relative motion to the first observer. Einstein's famous example of the train moving in relation to the railway platform proves this.[1] To an observer O, midway on the railway platform, lightning flashes at A and at B, the light rays from which arrive to him with empirical simultaneity, will appear to be simultaneous, and he will inevitably judge them to be simultaneous by the sole test available; but to the observer O', midway on a train moving relatively to the platform in the direction from A to B, the flashes will be judged to be in the order B before A,

---

[1] Albert Einstein, *Relativity* (New York: Henry Holt and Co., 1920), chap. ix.

because the flash from B will appear before the flash from A. And they cannot be judged otherwise, for O' has no other test by which to judge them. And since motion is relative, and relativity is symmetrical, the station being regarded as moving relatively to the train with as much justification as the train is regarded as moving relatively to the platform, there is no way of deciding which is right and which is wrong.

This is not all, for not only are events simultaneous in one system not simultaneous in another, but the relation of simultaneity is not transitive. Suppose events A and B to occur 300,000 kilometers apart, and event C to follow B in the same monad as B, within one second after B, and at an equal distance from A. Let us suppose, furthermore, that for some observer A and B are simultaneous. Then, not only will A and B be simultaneous for some observer, but A and C also; for the interval between A and C will be spacelike, since even by travel by means of a light ray it would be impossible to be present at both events, A and C. But one would expect that if A is simultaneous with B, and A is simultaneous with C, then B would be simultaneous with C. But, on the contrary, C is subsequent to B, and since the interval between B and C is timelike (being occurrences in the life of one monad), this will be true for all observers. It would follow that, objectively speaking, there are no simultaneous events; therefore there is no way of defining moments in such a fashion as to catch all events; some events would remain homeless, and their order, whether before or after, would be indeterminate. This would obviously play havoc with the order of events as we have constructed it.

Nevertheless, those who take relativity theory seriously as philosophy are not perturbed, for they hold that the very question whether there is absolute simultaneity or not is meaningless on the ground that a question has meaning only when there is some way of answering it by yes or no, whereas by no method known to man is it possible to determine whether or not two events "really" are simultaneous or not. The question has at least no *physical* significance.

From the point of view of a strictly operational interpretation of physics this is undoubtedly correct, but it cannot suffice for metaphysics.[1] For the question whether any other events or

[1] For the operational point of view see P. W. Bridgman, *The Logic of Modern Physics* (New York: The Macmillan Co., 1928), chap. i.

substances exist besides *this* event or substance (*this* event being, as we know, one that is happening to ourselves) is a perfectly intelligible question. The concept of coexistence is one that is directly illustrated and verified in our immediate experience; it is, therefore, a thoroughly empirical concept. And we could hardly answer the question we are asking in the negative. For we could conceivably ask it with reference to every event in our lives, as it occurred, and we could not suppose, unless we were prepared to accept solipsism, that the string of events that make up our own biography is all there is. Neither the events that occur within a monad, nor the monad itself, are self-sufficient; they depend for their being upon other substances and other events, in the body, in the environment, and in the Omega system. They cannot be unless these others also are. There must be, therefore, coexistent events or substances, and it is impossible to distinguish between items that are coexistent and items that are simultaneous. The notion of simultaneity, as we have shown, is, in fact, a derivative of coexistence.

What then is the issue from this impasse? To some the issue that I am going to propose will, I fear, seem drastic; but it is, so far as I can see, the only one possible, namely, to limit the significance of relativity theory to the purely phenomenal realm. Men for whom science is metaphysics have accepted as fact the relativization of simultaneity and the substitution of the interval for space and time. The interval became for them the objective reality; space and time, mere secondary qualities. Against this view, I must insist on the primacy of time. I have shown how space can be expressed in terms of time; and it is generally admitted that timelike intervals can be expressed in terms of the time required for a body to be present at both events between which the interval holds, or, more precisely, a timelike interval is equal to the number of standard events spanned by a body's motion when it takes the longest way round in getting from one of these events to the other.[1] When the interval is spacelike it can also be expressed in terms of time, as follows.[2] Let S and T be two events belonging to different monads, M and N, between which the interval is spacelike. Let Q be an event which

[1] Bertrand Russell, *The Analysis of Matter* (New York: Harcourt, Brace and Co., 1927), p. 52.
[2] *Ibid.*, p. 370.

follows S in the life of monad M, and let this event be a message sent immediately after T to M, and by the most direct route; then the timelike interval SQ measures the spacelike interval between S and T.   It is obvious that this, according to our conception of space, is exactly the same as the distance between M and N, for it is the same as the time required to make the trip from M to the neighborhood of N, or to send a message from M to N. Thus, even the interval, the foundation stone of relativity theory, can be expressed in terms of time; there is, therefore, no reason within the theory itself for assuming that the complex notion of interval, with which nothing in our experience is known to coincide, has metaphysical significance. It is, on the contrary, best interpreted as a convenient, yet merely symbolic, mathematical construct.

But we must go further in rejecting relativity theory as metaphysically valid. The failure of relativity theory to give a satisfactory account of simultaneity or coexistence is sufficient, I believe, to relegate it to a purely phenomenal status.   That is to say, far from its being true, as has been assumed, that common sense presents us with mere appearance, while relativity theory offers us the objective facts, the situation is the other way round: the common-sense view of the facts is correct, while relativity theory is a theory merely of phenomenal objects or appearances. We have seen that a distinction must be made between an event which is an occurrence in the life of a monad and the appearances of this event, which are phenomenal objects in the lives of other monads—signs of the existence of the primary event, or, as we may say, echoes of it or messages from it. The experienced activity of the violinist in drawing his bow over the strings is a primary event; the sounds heard by members of his audience are its appearances—echoes or messages in their minds. Every primary event has its echoes in the lives of other monads, and these echoes, as we know, constitute a natural language through which the existence and formal properties of the primary event are expressed. Now it is my conviction that relativity theory is a theory of messages only, especially visual messages, and that, owing to the seeming constancy of the velocity of light, there is a slight disparity between the primary events and the appearances of the events with regard to the time order of the primary events, when the interval between them is spacelike, as the appearances are reported to observers belonging to systems in relative motion to each other. Consider the Einstein train and platform, and events on the earth compared with events on Neptune. First, the train and platform. It is clear that there is no physical means, granting the apparent constancy of the velocity of light, for determining whether the primary events A and B are simultaneous or not. For O, they are simultaneous, because O receives messages from the events at once—the only test for simultaneity in the given case; while for O' in relative motion, they are not, since O' does not receive the messages from the events at once, but in succession. And relativity theory gives an absolutely correct picture of the situation *with regard to the messages*. Since the messages from, or echoes of, the primary events are always different in the lives of different monads, there is no contradiction in their being for one monad simultaneous, for another successive; but the events themselves, that is to say, the primary events, being unique indivisible existences, either are or are not coexistent. Yet it must be admitted that, since all our knowledge of the events comes through their echoes, we have no way of telling whether they are or are not coexistent.

Or consider the case of an event on the earth, E_1, and an event on Neptune, E_2, between which the interval is spacelike. Since the light distance between the earth and Neptune is eight hours, there are an indefinite number of events on Neptune, including E_2 within this period, the interval between any one of which and the given event on the earth, E_1, is spacelike. Now, I say, some one of these events is simultaneous with the event on the earth, but it is physically impossible to discover which one. Eddington has offered a striking illustration of this fact.[1] Suppose that a lover on the earth has a sweetheart on Neptune, and that they agree to say "I love you" at the same time, say, at twelve noon. Then it will not do to say "I love you" when the clock strikes twelve for each on his respective planet; they must say it for eight hours on end, in order to be sure that each has said it when the other has said it; for during the period of eight hours the interval between all the events on each planet will be spacelike with reference to the given event on either planet. There

---

[1] A. S. Eddington, *The Nature of the Physical World* (Cambridge: At the University Press, 1928), p. 49.

will be groups of two utterances of this tender thought, one on each planet, which will be simultaneous, but no one will be able to determine which they were; wherefore, if, during this period, the lover and his beloved had breathed " I love you" a single time only, they could not be sure that it would have been at the same time. But of one thing at least they could be certain, so I am insisting, and this might be of interest to them provided they happened to be philosophers as well as lovers—that their utterances would be unequivocally either coexistent or not co-existent, despite the fact that they could not discover which.

To this solution of the problem the objection will doubtless be made that it depends upon assuming the existence of some-thing, namely, absolute simultaneity, which in no case can be verified. But two types of unknowability must be distinguished, intrinsic and extrinsic: the "things-in-themselves" of Kant, the "stuff" of certain critical realists, are intrinsically unknowable, but God or the coexistence of events in separated monads is only extrinsically unknowable. God is not intrinsically un-knowable, for he is unknowable only to the finite mind, but is known, therefore knowable, to himself; the coexistence of sepa-rated events is at present unknowable to man, but the fact that the coexistence of events within contiguous monads is knowable to such monads shows that the coexistence of events in different monads is not per se unknowable, since this would be known if there were a monad such as God contiguous with every monad.

As a further illustration of the type of difficulty presented by the theory of relativity from a metaphysical standpoint, let us consider the following simple case. Suppose that A and B are two events between which the interval is timelike, and let B be an event that is now happening in my life and A some event, like my birth, that precedes it. Then, while the time order of these two events, namely, that A precedes B, will be the same for all observers, nevertheless I know that there is a possible stand-point for which A is a present event and B a future event. In other words, for that observer, I am just being born, and this event that is actually occurring in my life is a future event, and for that reason nonexistent. And it must be admitted that there is no known way by means of which I could convince the hypo-thetical observer that I am right and he is wrong, convince him, namely, that my birth is in the past and the writing of this sentence in the present. Have I therefore no right to believe the testimony of intuition to the existence of the present happening and the pastness of my own birth?—or, let us say, the pastness of some event of my childhood that I remember, like a sleigh ride in Saranac, New York, A.D. 1889? Here is a clear case of the metaphysical ineptitude of relativity theory. No one would hesitate to claim that he is in a favored position for the determination of the facts in a case of this kind. Intuition and memory rightly claim precedence over scientific hypotheses. Or consider an analogous case. There is a standpoint for which Caesar is now crossing the Rubicon and Washington's winter at Valley Forge or Mussolini's march on Rome is a future event. But we cannot help asserting the truth of our own standpoint and the falsity of the other. And this is no mere prejudice on our part, but the result of what may with entire accuracy be called "inside information." We know that all three events are no more, and we know this because we know that our own ongoing phase of culture exists and that it could not exist and have the peculiar quality it possesses if these events had not existed and died.

Such considerations as these point to a genuine distortion of the facts through what we may call the relativity situation. They give evidence to the theory which I am proposing, that relativity theory is concerned not with the facts as they are in themselves—not with events, happenings, or occurrences—but with the messages from, or appearances of, these events. The message does not quite report the event; and, in general, the further an observer is from the fact, the greater the opportunity for disparity between the fact and its appearance. On the other hand, the closer we are to the facts, the more intimate is our knowledge of their time relations. For example, with regard to events on Neptune in correspondence with events on the earth there is a range of eight hours during which simultaneity is unknowable; whereas on the surface of the earth, at the most widely separated points, the range is only one tenth of a second. Within our own experience we can immediately verify the coexistence of two events: we can hear the bell ring as we strike the key of the typewriter and as we see the black mark appear on the paper. Inevitably, and consistently with our general presuppositions, we are led to an interpretation of the so-called Fitzgerald contraction opposed to the original view of Lorentz [1] that it represents a real deformation of the object. That the contraction is symmetrical as between two moving systems is an indication that his cannot be the correct view. [2] The real time, and so the real distances and shapes—for these, as we have seen, are expressible in terms of time—are such as they are reported by an observer closest to the events and bodies in question and at rest in relation to them. [3] Only an observer standing within the body itself and so participating directly in the events can report them with complete accuracy. Any observer in motion relatively to them is bound to report them incorrectly. If we could communicate with people on Neptune we should take their word for the time order, sizes, and shapes that are close to them, not the report of our own light messages; we should prefer their account of the facts even to our own.

We return therefore to an absolutistic view of time. But note that our view is profoundly different from the older type of absolutism, for to us time is still not a substance, but an order, and an order past our finding out but not past all finding out. That there are other reasons for believing in an absolute order we shall show in later chapters.

[1] "Electromagnetic Phenomena in a System Moving with Any Velocity Less than That of Light," in *The Principle of Relativity*, by H. A. Lorentz, A. Einstein, H. Minkowski, and H. Weyl (London: Methuen and Co., 1923), pp. 11–34.

[2] This point was admirably made by Bergson in his *Durée et simultanéité* (Paris: Félix Alcan, 1926), chap. iv.

[3] The "proper time" and "proper mass" are the time and mass as given by one who has what we are calling "inside information."

IX

Finite or Infinite?

IN OUR chapters on space and time we made the tentative assumption that the elements of both were finite, but reserved the proof of this for a closer scrutiny of the general problem of the mathematical infinite, in its philosophical aspects and implications. The problem as to the type of order of points and moments—whether it be, for example, discrete, dense, or continuous—could, again, be solved only in connection with a more general discussion. To this discussion we shall now apply ourselves.

The definition of infinite number that we shall use is the current one: A class has infinite cardinal number when there is a subclass such that its members can be put into one–one correlation with the members of the given class. Since classes are similar, or have the same cardinal number, when their members can be so correlated, an infinite class is such that a part or subclass is equal to, that is to say, has the same number of members as, the whole class. It is easily seen that this subclass is itself an infinite class, hence possesses a part which is infinite, which in turn possesses an infinite part, and so on—infinite classes within infinite classes, an infinitely complex Chinese box. It can readily be proved that an infinite class cannot be exhausted by the subtraction from it of a finite or an infinite number of elements.

$$\infty - n = \infty \qquad \infty - \infty = \infty$$

Different types or orders of infinity have been distinguished,[1] but we can leave the consideration of them to a later phase of our enquiry.

Two sorts of proof have been offered for the existence of

[1] Bertrand Russell, *The Principles of Mathematics* (Cambridge: At the University Press, 1903) , chap. xii; A. Fraenkel, *Einleitung in die Mengenlehre* (Berlin: Julius Springer, 1928) , p. 24.

infinite collections: a priori proofs and proofs derived from an examination of the structure of reality, especially its space and time structure. It is now generally recognized that the a priori proofs are fallacious, and it can be shown, I think, that a single fallacy taints them all. For consider the following examples of such proofs. First, that of Dedekind.[1] Assume, as we surely may, that there exists a thought, t, then there is a thought of this thought, t_1, and a thought of that thought, t_2, and a thought of this last thought, t_3, and so on. Now, it is claimed, the collection of all such thoughts is an infinite collection because, if you take as your subclass the total collection minus t, the members of that collection can be put into one–one correlation with the members of the original collection, as follows: t_1 with t, t_2 with t_1, t_3 with t_2, and so on. Similar to this proof is that of Royce. A map of a country is part of that country; therefore in order completely to map the country there must be a map of the map, and a map of the map of the map, and so forth. Or a picture of an object on that object (such as the picture of a tomato can on the can) is itself not pictured; yet as a part of the object it must be pictured if the whole object is to be pictured; hence a picture of the picture is required on the picture, and so a picture of the picture on the picture, and so on—with the result that an infinite number of maps or pictures are required for complete mapping or picturing. Royce has another proof, derived from Bradley. Let there be two things in the world; then these things will be related; but the relation will also be a thing, hence the relation will itself be related to each thing, and that relation will in turn be related, and so on—with the result that the totality of things involved in this situation will be infinite in number.[2] Finally, consider the proof once offered by Russell, which, however, he now rejects.[3] I introduce it here as an excellent example of the fallacies involved in all these alleged proofs. Granted that there are a finite number of things, n, then

---

[1] R. Dedekind, *Was sind und was sollen die Zahlen?* (Braunschweig: F. Vieweg und Sohn, 1893) , Sec. 66.

[2] J. Royce, *The World and the Individual*, First Series (New York: The Macmillan Co., 1904) , Vol. I, Supplementary Essay, pp. 494–512.

[3] Russell, *op. cit.*, Sec. 339; also *Introduction to Mathematical Philosophy* (New York: The Macmillan Co., [1919]) , pp. 78, 81, 134, 135.

there are 2 raised to the nth power classes of such things; and 2 raised to the $2n$th power of classes of classes of these, and so on—with the result that the totality of all such things is infinite in number:

$$n + 2^n + 2^{2n} + 2^{2^{2n}} + \ldots = \infty$$

The mistake common to all such "proofs" is the assumption that the totality indicated—totality of thoughts, of maps, of pictures, of relations, of classes—exists. In certain of the examples it is almost obvious that the totality does not exist. In no mind does self-consciousness go beyond the third order at most: a thought of a thought of a thought; nowhere does there exist a more complicated system of mapping than a map of a map of a map, or of picturing than a picture of a picture of a picture; and a relation that relates the terms of a relation to the relation can be shown to be nonexistent, for the original relation relates the terms, but is itself no term that requires relation to the terms. (See pp. 204–205 for full discussion.) With regard to the last "proof," it is clear that while there are surely n things, and possibly 2 raised to the $2n$th power of classes of those things—if anyone has a mind to classify them—and possibly again 2 raised to the $2n$th power classes of those classes, or even more—under the same condition—yet there will never be more than a finite number of classes, for classes do not exist apart from a mind that classifies, and no matter how far any mind should go in classifying classes of things, then classes of classes, and so on, it would never get further than a finite number of classes of n given things There is a special difficulty inherent in this last alleged proof which has caused Russell to reject it, namely, that the hypothetical totality of all classes formed out of a given class is an illegitimate totality because it is made up of classes of different order: classes, classes of classes, classes of classes of classes, and so forth. Because of the paradoxes that arise out of the formation of such totalities they are today regarded as invalid by most logicians. But the reason which I have offered for the rejection of this proof is more fundamental, since it affects all proofs of this type.

To this argument it may be objected that, while there are not an infinite number of actual thoughts, maps, pictures, classes, there are at least an infinite number of *possible* thoughts, maps, pictures, classes. But the very manner of expressing this counterobjection reveals its fallacy. For it is said that there are an infinite number of possible classes; but to say that a possible class *is*, is to talk nonsense, for the possible is precisely something that is not, that does not exist. If now it is said that a possible class is "real" or "subsistent," even if not existent, one is simply taking refuge in a word, "subsistent" or "real," to hide an inability to think straight. The sole reality of a possible class is a certain law or rule in regard to a special type of activity. Thus if I say that the number of possible classes that may be made out of n things is 2 to the nth power, what I mean is that, given n things and a mind interested in classifying them, then, if they are classified, there will be 2 raised to the nth power classes. And if now I say that there are 2 raised to the $2n$th power classes of classes of such things, what again I am really meaning is that, granted that some mind has constructed the 2 raised to the $2n$th power classes which he can make out of the n things, then, if he classifies those classes, there will arise 2 raised to the $2n$th power classes of classes. But such classes are not, either existent or subsistent, until they are formed. And it is clear that, granted that some mind keeps on classifying—forming classes, classes of classes, classes of classes of classes—there will never arise more than a finite number of classes. In the same way, and in the same manner and sense, there will never be more than a finite number of thoughts of thoughts of thoughts, or maps of maps of maps, and the like. And I cannot emphasize too strongly that the phrase "the totality of possible x's" is really nonsensical, whatever the x's be, and however convenient, for certain purposes, the phrase may be. And, of course, if there is no such totality, it cannot have a number, either finite or infinite.

Having established the failure of a priori proofs for the existence of infinite collections, we turn to the evidence offered by an examination of the structure of reality. The space–time structure has always seemed to offer such evidence. Let us consider space. In any set of axioms for geometry we find an axiom (or an equivalent axiom) to the effect that there is a point between any two points, from which it is usually inferred that there *is* an infinite number between any two; and another axiom (or an equivalent axiom) to the effect that beyond any point there is a point, from which it is inferred that the totality of points con tained in any half ray is infinite in number.[1]   Or, if such assumptions or their equivalents are granted, there are simple proofs designed to show that a one–one correlation can be set up between the points on any part of a segment of a line and that segment—in other words, that the part is equal in cardinal number to the whole, hence is of infinite number; and similar proofs have been devised to show that there are as many points in a square inch as in the area of a room, in a cube, as in all space, and so on.[2]

Such considerations are, it must be admitted, impressive, but they are subject to two important reflections.   In the first place, it is now universally recognized by philosophers that the axioms of geometry are not intuitive truths in regard to the structure of the real world, but hypotheses or postulates, which may or may not be applicable.   And when we look for the evidence for their literal applicability it is found to be wanting.   Phenomenal space certainly does not contain an infinity of points between any two points; there is unbrokenness and contiguity, as we shall see, but the number of discriminable elements is finite.   And it cannot be claimed that experimental physics has demonstrated the existence of more than a very large number of points.   The most that one could say in favor of the literal application of geometry to physics would be that it has *worked,* and so seems to be an account of the real world.   When an engineer builds a bridge or a physicist makes a prediction, in accordance with a result obtained from a differential equation, he seems to be giving confirmation to mathematical concepts which, until very recently, were believed to presuppose the existence of infinite classes.   Yet even on the "classical" interpretation of mathematics such evidence is hardly conclusive, for the verification of mathematical concepts is never more than approximate, and while it may be simpler for the purposes of calculation to assume that there are an infinite number of points between any two on a line, by no experimental method could one detect a difference in result if there were only an extremely large number of points.   There is, moreover, as we shall see, another interpretation of these same

[1] D. Hilbert, *Grundlagen der Geometrie* (Leipzig: B. G. Teubner, 1903), chap. i, Secs. 3–4.

[2] For a good summary of such proofs see E. V. Huntington, *The Continuum* (Cambridge: Harvard University Press, 1917), p. 71.

axioms of geometry which leaves their applicability untouched and at the same time eliminates the infinite class. I would add that recent cosmological theories based on the notion of a finite universe show that there is no intuitive necessity in the hitherto assumed infinity of extent of real space.

Parallel considerations apply in the study of the temporal structure of reality. It is assumed in the usual formulations of kinematics and dynamics that there is a moment between any two moments, from which it is inferred that there are an infinite number of moments between any two, the structure of time being regarded as a one-dimensional continuum comparable to the points on a line. But, as we found to be the case in geometry, we must hold in mind that the mathematical theory of mechanics and dynamics is a theory, that its axioms are hypotheses or postulates, not intuitive truths regarding the structure of the real world. And when we come to examine the evidence for the applicability of these theories we find a situation parallel to what we found to be true of space: phenomenal time is made up of events following one on the heels of another, distinguishable, yet at the same time contiguous, and, since contiguous, of a nature precisely to forbid the possibility of there being an event between any two events. When, moreover, the array of parallel events is set up in the fashion described in the last chapter we find no evidence from direct experience to show that the array is comparable to a geometric line in the complexity of its elements. Similarly, the fact that the mathematical theory of mechanics works would be evidence in favor of the reality of an infinitely complex series of moments only if the axioms of mechanics could be stated exclusively in such a way as to presuppose the existence of an infinite class—but this is no longer true. And even if this were true, the fact that mechanics works would not be conclusive evidence, since there is no experimental proof that it works with absolute accuracy.

The most potent argument for the application of the concept of infinity to reality arises, however, from the consideration of past events. It may be that there is not an event between any two events, but was there not an event before any event? As we let the mind proceed backward from *this* event to its predecessor, then to the predecessor of that, to the predecessor of this last, and so on (or, rather, since past events do not exist, from historical truth to historical truth preceding), is it conceivable that there should be a first historical truth? And, if there is no such truth, is not the totality of truths infinite in number, even as the totality of negative numbers is infinite? Indeed, the comparison between the moments of time and the negative numbers is a very apt one. Zero will represent *this event*, or the present; and the series of negative numbers $-1, -2, -3, -4, -5, -6,$ and so on, will represent the series of past events; and both series will be "open," that is to say, neither will have a first element.[1] Moreover, if, as we have claimed, every event leaves its trace, must there not exist an infinite number of such traces; must not present reality, which contains all traces, be infinitely complex? The only alternative would seem to be the admission of a finite number of past events, which would imply a first event.

However offensive this alternative may at first appear to be, the usual argument offered for its rejection, restated by Kant, is not cogent. Kant's statement of the argument is as follows:

> For let us assume that it [the world] has a beginning. Then, as beginning is an existence which is preceded by a time in which the thing is not, it would follow that antecedently there was a time in which the world was not; that is, an empty time. In an empty time, however, it is impossible that anything should take its beginning, because of such a time no part possesses any condition as to existence rather than non-existence, which condition could distinguish that part from any other (whether produced by itself or through another cause). Hence, though many a series of things may take its beginning in the world, the world itself can have no beginning, and in reference to time past is infinite.[2]

The first mistake in this argument is the assertion that if there were a beginning of the world, there would be empty time preceding the beginning; but contrariwise, as we have seen, since time does not exist apart from events, it would come into existence along with the first event. The mistake is like the mistake made in arguing that the world cannot be finite in extension, because if it were, there would be empty space outside it; but since the world includes all, there could not be anything—

[1] For the conception of the infinite class or series as "open" see H. Weyl, *The Open World* (New Haven: Yale University Press, 1932), especially chap. iii.

[2] Immanuel Kant, "First Conflict of the Transcendental Ideas, Proof," in *Critique of Pure Reason*, tr. by F. Max Mueller (London: Macmillan and Co., 1881), p. 345. Compare the similar proof in Aristotle *Physics* VIII. 1.

not even empty space—beyond; hence the world must be infinite in extent. But, contrariwise once more, since, as has been established, empty space is precisely nothing at all, there would be nothing at all outside it if the world were finite. So likewise, before the first event—if there were one—there would not be empty time, there would be nothing. Therefore the question why the world should begin at one or at another moment could not arise.

Other difficulties in the way of conceiving of a first event may also, I believe, be met by clear thinking. One such difficulty is the following. Every event comes to us as emerging, not spontaneously out of nothing, out of the void, but from a matrix already existing; moreover, every event appears on the heels of one that is perishing—it has an edge that fits it on to an event just gone. If, therefore, we follow the stream of past events backward and reach a first event, would not the matrix out of which it arose have to be static, for otherwise would not the matrix itself consist of a string of events, compelling us to begin our search for a first event anew? But how could there be a static reality, if reality is experience and its core volition? To this difficulty I would answer, first, by concurring in the necessity for a matrix from which the first event would spring—a matrix for which one could not assign a beginning of existence, since outside it there would be no time or existence, no time before it or existence from which it could come. But that this matrix must be static or else consist of a string of events I would emphatically deny, because it might be a single flash or quiver of activity, yet longer than any long event that we could imagine contemporary with it. Out of this now would come the first event—theologically speaking, the created world—and therewith the birth of time.

If this hypothesis be correct, as I believe, the infinite is excluded even from time. For, although from the first moment the universe has been growing in complexity as each new event leaves its echo, the complexity will always be finite. We can see that this is so if we compare the series of events, and consequently the series of traces, with the series of whole numbers. There will be a zero element, the original matrix; a first member, the first event or echo of that, corresponding to the number one; and an increasing but denumerable set of following events and echoes, corresponding to successive numbers, the total number of which, no matter how large it becomes as time passes, is always finite, precisely as the number of numbers we can count, however many, is finite. Each new event that occurs will add one to the number, but even though the series continues open and endless, the number will remain finite. The present structure of the universe also—this present and all subsequent presents—with all the echoes it contains in its bosom, is, therefore, magnificently complex no doubt, yet finite.

Thus far I have tried to show that there is no evidence for the existence of an infinite collection. But it is possible to go further and to show that an infinite collection is impossible—for the reason that the concept is self-contradictory. Of course the phrase "self-contradictory concept" is nonsensical, for a concept cannot contradict itself; yet the phrase does stand for something, namely, the abortive attempt to think together into a single concept incompatible and more elementary concepts. A self-contradictory concept is a failure in conception, therefore is really no concept at all. To say that reality cannot exemplify a self-contradictory concept is simply to say that it cannot exemplify nothing at all! Or, to put the matter somewhat differently, a concept denotes a form; a self-contradictory concept is an effort to denote a complex form, but fails because it attempts to unite incompatible elements of form and hence does not denote any form; therefore, to assert that reality exemplifies a self-contradictory concept is to assert that it has a particular form when there is no such form, which is tantamount to asserting nothing, that is to say, to talking nonsense. And it is clear that the usual method of showing that a concept is not self-contradictory, by exemplifying it, is unexceptionable, for if there exists something that has a form, the concept of that form is a genuine concept. Yet even though an exemplification of a concept cannot be found, the concept is not proved to be self-contradictory, for the mind can think forms that have not been exemplified.

In order to prove that the concept of an infinite collection is self-contradictory, we shall begin by showing that the attempt to prove that it is noncontradictory by exemplification through the series of cardinal numbers is no more cogent than the attempts through exemplification already examined. This attempt differs from the others, however, by appealing not to empirical existences but to other concepts. It is exemplification of a concept through other concepts rather than through individuals. We have the series of numbers

$$A \quad 1, 2, 3, 4, 5, 6, 7, 8 \ldots$$

Now let us take the double of each of these numbers,

$$B \quad 2, 4, 6, 8, 10, 12, 14, 16 \ldots$$

Then we have set up a one–one correlation between all the numbers A, and a subclass of the numbers B. It follows by definition that the collection A is infinite. And, it is said, such a correlation can be set up in an infinite number of ways. But the *petitio* of this argument is fairly obvious. For it assumes the existence of such a collection as A is supposed to be. As a matter of fact there are only eight elements in A. Putting a row of dots after 8 or writing "etc." or "and so on" does not magically create more than a finite number of numbers. Such signs merely indicate that I may subjoin another number, or as many as I have time and patience for, in accordance with the law for the generation of cardinal numbers. In B, also, I have only eight numbers. Obviously I may get more, following the law for the generation of these numbers, but I shall never have more than a finite number of them. Against this, the orthodox Cantorean will insist that A stands for *all* the numbers, not merely for those which are counted or set down on paper. But the *petitio* is exactly there: A is intended to stand for something, namely, all the numbers, when the existence of such a collection, if A stands for more than the eight set down or some other finite class of numbers set down, is the matter in dispute. In what sense are there more than are set down? In the sense that someone has thought of more? But no one has ever thought of more than a finite number of numbers. In the sense that there are collections of more than eight members? Well and good; but we have shown that there is no reason for believing in the existence of collections of more than a finite number of numbers. If someone counters that A represents not actual numbers but possible numbers, the answer is that the possible is exactly that which is not, that by a possible number I can mean only a number that may exist under certain conditions—say by an increase in the number of empirical things in the world, or through somebody's thinking of another number—but in no case will more than a finite number of such numbers exist. It is therefore not true to say that in B we have a correlation between some of the numbers and all of the numbers, but rather a correlation between such numbers as are there set down and their doubles, *together with* the statement of a law by means of which we "see" that it is always possible to create a number which shall be the correlative of any number we have by the simple process of doubling the number. Both *A* and *B* are open series, that is to say, series to which members may be added in accordance with a simple law—in the case of *A*, the law of adding one, in the case of *B*, the law of adding two. But in no case and under no circumstances are there more than a finite number of numbers.

The fact that there is no positive evidence, from exemplification either in nature or in the conceptual field, that the concept of an actual infinite class is consistent, leaves the possibility open that it is internally contradictory. And that such is the case is easily seen, despite all attempts to darken counsel. The essence of the matter is contained in the supreme paradox of the infinite, now become its classical definition, that the part is equal to the whole.[1] Just how paradoxical this is can be exemplified as follows: Given the line *ac*, and *b*, a point between *a* and *c*, then, following the ordinary assumption that there are an infinite number of points between *a* and *c*, the class *ab* equals the class *ac*, although all the points between *b* and *c* are not included in *ab*. There are just as many points between *a* and *b* as there are between *a* and *c*, despite the fact that there are other points between *b* and *c*, which do not belong to *ab*. *ac* includes all the points in *ab*, and all in *bc*; yet is no larger in cardinal number than the points in *ab*.

Or, if we assume that there is a collection *A* of *all* the numbers, and that *B* is a collection of the even numbers, then *A* equals *B*, despite the fact that *A* includes all of *B* and the odd numbers, *C*, besides. Or, *B* equals *A*, despite the fact that *A* includes the odd numbers that are not contained in *B*.

1 See B. Bolzano, *Paradoxien des Unendlichen* (1851, reissued in *Philosophische Bibliothek* [Leipzig: Dürrsche Buchhandlung, 1920], Bd. 99), Sec. 13.

A   1, 2, 3, 4, 5, 6, 7, 8, 9...
B   2, 4, 6, 8, 10, 12, 14, 16, 18...
C   3, 5, 7, 9, 11, 13, 15...

The sole reason why the absurdity of this is not recognized is the apparent success of setting up a one–one relation between the elements of the part class and the elements of the whole class: for example, each number with its double, and the points of *ab* with the points of *ac*, in accordance with such a simple geometrical construction as is shown in the accompanying figure, where, seemingly, for every point in *a'b'* there is a point in *ac*, and vice versa, and where it is clear that the points in *ab* are only some of points in *ac*, since *a'b'* is equal to *ab*. But I have already shown that this process of one–one correlation

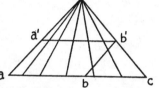

does not prove what it is supposed to prove. In the case of the numbers, one never has more than a finite number of numbers either in class *A* or in class *B*. One can, to be sure, always find the double of every number that one sets down, in accordance with a simple rule; but the doubles of *all* the numbers never are a totality, because there is no such class as *all* the numbers, in the unrestricted sense of "all," but only all such numbers as are counted or set down. Since both classes are open it is possible, of course, to add to either class: simple numbers to the one, doubles to the other; but there never *are* more than two equal finite classes. The situation is the same with the correlation of points. For every point on *a'b'*, a point can be made between *a* and *c*, according to the geometric rule that a point can be made between any two points; likewise, for any point that is made between *a* and *c*, a point can be made between *a'* and *b'*; but there is no totality of such points between *a'* and *b'*, or between *a* and *c*, except the points that are made.[1] Possible points are not genuine entities, any more than possible numbers are, as explained above. And under no circumstances are there more than a finite number of points in *a'b'*, or in *ac*.

---

[1] The apparent cogency of the argument is due to the assumption that points exist before they are made or "occupied"; but this is true neither of phenomenal nor of physical space.

Hence the absurdity of the proposition that the part equals the whole, stands.   Since, therefore, the concept of infinite number is absurd, that is to say, indicates no genuine form, reality cannot realize it; reality cannot have a form that is no form.

The inferences from the above argument are of the utmost importance for metaphysics.   First of all, it follows that there are only a finite number of individuals in the universe—a finite number of monads, of events, of elements of monads, of systems of monads, of moments of time, and points of space.   It follows also, negatively, that the order of monads, of events and traces of events cannot be dense or continuous in the sense of classical mathematics; that is to say, there cannot exist an event between any two, or an occupied point between any two, because, as is easy to show, if that were the case their number would be infinite. From every part and aspect of the world—even from its past strongholds, space and time—the infinite, both cardinal and ordinal, is excluded.   It is, moreover, of some importance to us to observe that mathematicians themselves have found ways of expressing all the indubitable propositions of geometry and analysis without the use of the infinite.   I would refer, for example, to the notable work of Felix Kauffmann, *Das Unendliche in der Mathematik und seine Ausschaltung*.[1]   The possibility of excluding the infinite depends essentially upon conceiving infinite series—whether discrete, dense, or continuous—not as collections of existing elements, but rather as rules for the construction of open series.   Thus, in the case of a simple progression, we need to postulate the existence of a single element only, the first element, and a rule, which should be stated, not as is done in the classical manner, existentially and statically—that there *is* an element following each element or that each element *has* a successor, which leads directly to the absurdity of the infinite—but rather, as I should say, permissively and dynamically —that following any element an element *may be* constructed. When thus restated the series remains open, for given a series of any finite number of elements, it is possible to add one; yet the series never becomes infinite, because the members actually constructed always remain finite.   The natural numbers are the simplest example: given a first number, zero or one, and define

---

[1] Leipzig und Wien: Franz Deuticke, 1930.   See especially chap. iv.

the follower of any number as n plus one, the series of natural numbers results, not as an infinite series but as an open series, always finite yet always capable of being extended according to the rule, by adding one to the last number constructed. Or consider an example of a dense series—the rational fractions, defined as pairs of natural numbers, p, q. Then instead of saying, in orthodox fashion, that there *is* a fraction between any two fractions, we say that between any two fractions there may be

constructed   fraction according to the rule that if $\dfrac{p}{q}$ and $\dfrac{r}{s}$

are fractions, and $\dfrac{p}{q} > \dfrac{r}{s}$, then $\dfrac{p+r}{q+s}$ will be a fraction $< \dfrac{p}{q}$ and

$> \dfrac{r}{s}$. In this way, again, the series is left open, for ever new fractions between any two given fractions can be constructed; but there never is more than a finite number of them.

Like the progression or the dense series, the continuous series is subject to the seeming difficulty of involving an infinite class, and has besides certain difficulties of its own, well known to students of the philosophy of mathematics. Now although it is far from my purpose to enter upon a thorough discussion of the mathematical continuum, it will yet be useful to us to have in mind how it is possible, following Kauffmann, to treat the problem of the real numbers—the most important example of continuity— without the concept of the infinite class. In the first place, it is recognized that a "real" number is no number at all, but a symbol for a rather complex set of relationships between the so-called rationals. These relationships arise in this way. Let us consider any well-defined ascending open (not *infinite!*) series of rationals, say those whose square is less than two, and the correlative descending open (again not infinite) series of rationals whose square is greater than two. These series are open but not infinite because there are never more than a finite number of constructed rationals in either series, yet it always remains possible to construct another member of the series. Neither one of the series has a limit since, as we say, there is no number whose square is 2; we can construct numbers whose square is just a little less than 2, increasingly less—the ascending series—and numbers whose square is only a very little greater than 2—the descending series—but, with regard to the ascending series there is no rational such that between it and a member of that series there is a member of the series and a member of that series only, and such that, moreover, it lies after any members of the series that may be constructed; for the only rational that lies after any member of the ascending series that may be constructed is a member of the descending series; and between that element and any member of the ascending series there may be constructed members not only of the ascending series, but of the descending series as well. The situation is similar in the case of the descending series—there is no rational such that it stands before every member of the descending series that may be constructed, and such that there are members and only members of the descending series that stand between it and members of the descending series; for the only rationals that stand before all members of the descending series are members of the ascending series, and between such elements and members of the descending series there are members not only of the descending series, but of the ascending series as well. Yet—and this is of fundamental importance—the difference between any member of the ascending series and the corresponding member of the descending series may be made as small as we please; for we can always construct a member of the ascending series greater than the member that we have constructed, and a corresponding member of the descending series smaller than the one we have constructed. Now by an irrational number we mean precisely this situation: the absence of limits in the two series, and the fact that if we consider segments "across" corresponding members of the two series, they may be made as small as we please. In the case of the rational real numbers, of course, both the ascending and the descending series have a common limit. Thus $\frac{1}{1}$ is the common limit of the open series of ascending fractions less than $\frac{1}{1}$ and of the open series of descending fractions greater than 1.

Thus far we have attempted to show (1) that there is no empirical evidence for the existence of an infinite collection, and (2) that there cannot be an infinite collection, since the concept of the infinite collection is self-contradictory. These are purely negative results and leave unsolved the problem that gives importance to the whole discussion, namely, the ordinal structure of space and time. Since it was the problem of this structure in the field of motion and spatial measurement that first suggested the theory of the infinite class, the suspicion would seem to be not unfounded that there is some aspect of the structure not to be accounted for in the ordinary theory of the finite class. This we shall find to be the case. The metaphysically significant fact obliquely sighted through the pseudo concept of the infinite class or series is the truth that certain classes are not complete or closed.

Let us consider the matter with regard to time first. The number of echoes, as we have seen, is finite, and the corresponding number of historical truths, also, is finite; yet the number of echoes and truths is always being enlarged because new events are constantly occurring. Since moments of time are classes of truths, the fact will be the same with regard to them, also: they are finite, but always increasing. We may compare the series of moments to the series of whole numbers 0, 1, 2, 3, 4, 5, 6, 7 . . . . There is a first number, and the number of actual numbers, no matter how many we set down, is finite, but the class of numbers is never closed, for we can always get another by adding one to the last. Similarly, the time series, even though it has a first moment, as I believe, is an open series.

Or, if we view time, not as something spreading out in one direction, but as the organization of events within the limits of a fixed duration, we find a comparable situation. Every fixed duration—that is to say, every string of events parallel with a given event—consists of a finite number of minimal, indivisible, atomic events following one on the heels of another; but we are aware, nevertheless, that it is possible, under certain conditions, for this series to be replaced by a series with a larger number of events. Thus, in a given time, that is to say, parallel with some standard event like the swing of the pendulum or a metronome, I may play, not three notes, but six, or, if I have played six, perhaps twelve—always a finite number, but always possibly more.

The situation is similar with regard to space. The actual number of points, as we have already shown—that is to say, the number of occupied points—is finite. And the distance between any two such points is a finite distance; in other words, the measure of the time required to communicate between any two monads is always a finite number of standard events. (Of course it might be twice that number of events, or n times that number, in case some series of events parallel with the first is used as a standard, where there are two—or n—events to one). There is no such thing as an infinite distance between points, because there cannot be an infinite number of events with which to measure it, and because, as we have seen, distance implies communication, and there could not be communication at an infinite interval of time. Nevertheless, whatever be the distance between two points, we are aware that the distance might be half as great, and if it were half as great that it might be half of that, and so on. We cannot say, therefore, that between any two points there is a point, but that, given any two points, there might be one between, in the sense of "between" defined. Since points do not exist unless occupied, there is never more than a finite number of them; but there might be one more than there are, and if there were one more, then one more than that, and so forth. Since the number is just what it is, a finite number, and since possible points are as meaningless as possible classes—a possible point being only a law that under certain conditions there might be another point—there never are an infinite number. There is, therefore, not a point between any two, but only the possibility that there might be one between the two that are. As we have seen, distances and points themselves do not exist until they are occupied—except as rules for the creation of new distances and points. Again, if space be not finite, it does not follow that it is infinite in the older sense of infinite; it follows only that it is open, that no matter how far apart two monads are, they might be farther apart. In other words, it does not follow that there are points beyond any point, but only that a monad may be at a greater distance from some fixed monad than any distance realized.

Thus far the main interest of our discussion has been the cardinal infinite; but the ordinal infinite is of equal significance. The orthodox interpretation assumes that space and time have the structure of the continuum, permitting, therefore, the correlation of points and moments with the real numbers. Our primary question is: To what extent is this assumption justified—to what extent is the continuum a valid picture of reality? That phenomenal space and time have some sort of continuity, called "sensible" continuity—as evidenced by the spread of visual extension and the flow of the stream of consciousness—is generally recognized. The sensible continuity of visual extension remains a fact despite the diversification through patches of different shape and color, as illustrated, say, by the surface of an oriental rug; and the sensible continuity of time remains equally a fact despite all differences in shape and rhythm of events, as shown, for example, by a moving picture, or by such a process as uninterrupted walking.

Sensible continuity of extension in two dimensions may be described by the following definitions and axioms: [1]

1. Shapes are either contiguous or separated; when separated, there is a shape between them: therefore there are no holes in an extension, it is unbroken.

2. By contiguous shapes are meant shapes such that there is no shape between, and such that together they form a new shape. On the other hand, separated shapes do not form a new shape.

3. A given shape may be divided into included contiguous shapes, these latter into included contiguous shapes, and so on until minimal shapes are reached—that is to say, shapes that cannot be further divided. These shapes do not preëxist to the process of forming them, but are merely possible, that is, they are shapes which might be so constructed as to take the place of the original shapes, their sum having the same size and outline as the original shape: they could fit into the original shape.

These axioms must be supplemented by ones regarding lines and distance.

1. Any two contiguous shapes form a line.

2. Lines are either straight or not straight, equal or unequal. Equal lines are said to have the same length.

3. A line may be divided into included lines, these into included lines, and so on until minimal lines are reached. a is an included line within c when there exists a line contiguous with a, such as b and such that a and b make up c. Note that it is not said that these included lines exist, but only that they may exist.

---

[1] These axioms and definitions—or equivalents—are necessary, but not sufficient for the adequate description of sensible continuity in two dimensions. I believe, however, that they suffice for the purpose in hand.

4. An included line is shorter than any line that includes it.

5. A straight line is the shortest line between minimal shapes.

6. A straight line may be divided into equal lines, any one of which may be the unit of measure of the original line, which is then equal to so many of the measure. The line expressed in terms of the number of its measure is its distance; that is, "distance" is the measure of a line.

Sensible continuity in time may be described through the following axioms:

1. Events are either contiguous or separated; when separated there is an event between them: therefore there are no holes in time, time is unbroken. This is true despite sleep and swooning, which are holes not for the person affected—therefore not for sensible time—but for an observer, who nevertheless fills these holes with events in his own life.

2. By contiguous events are meant events such that there are no events between them. Of two such events, one may be said to follow on the heels of the other.

3. An event may be divided into included contiguous events, and these latter into included contiguous events, and so on until minimal events are reached—that is to say, events that cannot be further divided. Minimal events are the only true events; larger, including events are really strings of events.[1]

4. A minimal event may be parallel [2] with a string of many other events, all of the same type. Any one of these latter may serve as a unit of measure of the original event, which is then said to have a duration equal to so many of the measure. "Duration" is the measure of an event.

A comparison between empirical continuity—as characterized by the axioms above—and mathematical continuity [3] reveals the following important differences: (1) In the mathematical continuum there are an infinite number of elements; in the phenomenal continuum, a finite number; (2) The elements of the phenomenal continuum may be divided, but the divisions do not preëxist to the process of division, and they reach a limit in the

---

[1] The nature of strings of events has been discussed on p. 148.

[2] For the meaning of "parallel" in this connection see pp. 151–152.

[3] For a description of the mathematical continuum see E. V. Huntington, *op. cit.*, chap. v.

minimal elements of the phenomenal continuum; while in the mathematical continuum division is unlimited, and the results of divisions exist; (3) In the phenomenal continuum two elements may be next to next, that is to say, there may be no elements between them; but in the mathematical continuum there are always elements between—contiguous elements do not exist; the empirical continuum is unbroken, the mathematical, broken; (4) In the empirical continuum bounding elements are next to next or contiguous with the elements which they separate; whereas in the mathematical continuum the bounding elements (Dedekindian "cuts") are not contiguous with elements which they separate—but although there are no contiguous elements, it is possible to get as near as you please to the bounding elements from either side, or, what comes to the same, the distance between elements, one on each side of the boundary, across the boundary, may be made as small as you please.

These differences suffice to condemn the mathematical continuum as a description of reality. In order to rehabilitate the mathematical continuum it will not do to argue, as Russell once did, that the "real" events in nature conform to its pattern, and that the unbrokenness of the phenomenal continuum is mere illusion, for any such bifurcation is nonsense; conscious events are as real as any, and have the character which they are intuited to possess. Facts cannot be eliminated by calling them bad names. And, on the contrary, our fundamental metaphysical principle, which we have called speculative empiricism—empiricism extended through the imagination—demands that we interpret the whole of reality in accordance with the part that we best know—the given. It follows that cosmic space and time must be construed as empirical continua, which implies the acceptance, in the sphere of time, of the relation of empirical succession between events—coming to be and passing away, on-the-heels-of—as a reality; in the sphere of space it implies the acceptance of the contiguity of monads, to be explained more fully in our chapter on the mechanism of causality (Chap. XIV). It implies also the rejection of the view of real space and time as composed of discrete elements: time as composed of droplets of experience, space as composed of Leibnizian windowless monads.

Nevertheless, as has already been indicated, there are certain elements of truth in the mathematical concept of continuity when the concept of the infinite series is reinterpreted as an open series, rather than as a collection of existing elements, infinite in number. Natural science has demonstrated the existence of a far greater complexity in the physical world than in the given phenomenal world: the magnifying glass shows more than the naked eye, the microscope more than the magnifying glass, and refined methods of physicochemical analysis a multiplicity un-intuitable in human experience. Corresponding to each minimal element of phenomenal extension are multitudes of physical elements, and corresponding to each minimal phenomenal line, multitudes of positions in physical space. The suggestion is then inevitable, as we have explained, that more positions are possible, that although there are never more than a finite number of points between any two points, in the sense that there are never more than a finite number of monads which have positions be-tween, there might, however, be more between; and, similarly, the distance between two monads might always be less: it is always possible for them to move closer to each other. Thus the series of points in space is not a dense series in the sense that there *is* a point between any two, but in the sense that it is pos-sible that there should be a point between: whatever be the actual number of points between, it is not a closed number but an open number. The facts with regard to time are analogous. Parallel with minimal phenomenal events are multitudes of events in na-ture: parallel to every color event, for example, trillions of vibra-tions. The suggestion is then inevitable that within any duration, that is to say, parallel with any event, there might be more events than there are: the number of events between any two, while always finite, is not a closed series but an open series—under certain conditions there might be more members in the series than there are. Thus both in space and in time there is a truth corresponding to the postulate of density in continuous series. And, interestingly enough, there is also a truth corresponding to Dedekind's postulate. For, with regard to space, the open series of diminishing distances between any two points always has a limit—the zero distance of monads that are in contact with each other. So, with regard to time, there is a limit to any decrease in the interval between events—the zero interval of events that fol-low one on the heels of the other. Yet, for all these significant applications of the concept of continuity to space and time, it cannot be too strongly emphasized that there are also significant respects in which space and time are discrete: the number of monads between any two monads is always finite, and the distances of monads separated along a straight line from a given monad are a discrete series; the intervals between separated events are always measured by a finite number of parallel events, hence all events between two given events, excluding those in contact with either, form a discrete series in terms of their intervals from either event.

X

The Theory of Relations. I*

IN MANY of the studies which we have made thus far we have
employed the concept of relation—in our chapters on space,
on time, on the analysis of experience—but we did not stop to
consider what, in fact, a relation is. We have, however, reached
a point in our investigations where we cannot well go on without
enquiring into the special significance of this type of concept.
Each relational concept has, of course, its unique meaning: the
relation "father of" has a different meaning from the relation
"above"; yet there are certain general facts about reality which
are implied by the use of any and every relational concept.
These are the facts which we shall investigate in the present chapter.

We shall find it profitable to begin with certain well-known
definitions of relation. A relation, or relational adjective, is
defined by W. E. Johnson as "a type of adjective whose meaning
when analyzed exhibits a reference to some substantive other
than that which it characterizes," or, again, "a relation is properly defined as a transitive adjective," [1] the ordinary adjective
being distinguished as intransitive. As Charles Peirce expressed
it, a relation is winged and seeks a perch. If I say that A is
father of, my thought is incomplete and in motion, and comes
to rest only when I adduce another substantive—A is father of B.
The definition given by Whitehead and Russell is the following:
"A relation as we shall use the term will be understood in extension: it may be regarded as a class of couples (x, y) for which
some given function $\Psi(x, y)$ is true." [2] In order to provide for

* In writing this and the following chapter I have borrowed freely from
my book, *The Self and Nature* (Cambridge: Harvard University Press, 1917),
chap. ix, although the treatment is new.

[1] W. E. Johnson, *Logic* (Cambridge: At the University Press, 1921),
Part I, p. 203.

[2] A. N. Whitehead and Bertrand Russell, *Principia Mathematica*, Second
Edition (Cambridge: At the University Press, 1925), *21, p. 200.

the asymmetry of certain relations, this definition is qualified in a note to the effect that the couples in question have a "sense." [1] The Whitehead–Russell definition may be criticized on the ground that it covers only dyadic relations, but it is easily modified so as to give it complete generality, to wit: A relation is a class of individuals to which some function $F(x, y, z \ldots)$ applies. The unmodified definition would be sufficient only if polyadic relations could be reduced to dyadic, but this is easily shown not to be the case. For example, we might try to reduce, A gives B to C, to the logical product of the propositions, A gives B, and, B is given to C; but this will not do, for this logical product might be true when it was not true that A gives B to C, in the case where A gives B to D and D gives B to C. From the point of view of intention, the Whitehead–Russell definition says in effect that a relation is a function with many variables. A relation is a many-valued function in contrast with a simple concept, which is a one-valued function, $F(x)$, x is red, x is a house. The two definitions, the one given by Whitehead and Russell and the other given by Johnson, are different in an important respect—as we shall see—but agree in so far as both assert that a relation applies to more than one individual.[2]

Among traditional discussions of relation there have been two dominant theories, both claiming that a relational concept can be reduced to the type of the simple concept. According to the one theory, the monadistic, a relational concept can be analyzed into simple concepts each characterizing one of the individuals between which the relation is said to hold; according to the other, the monistic theory, a relation is a predicate that applies to the whole composed of the individuals concerned. Let us consider first the monadistic, of which Leibniz was the great protagonist.

The monadistic theory may be formally stated as follows: Every proposition asserting a relation, aRb, can be analyzed into two propositions, $r_1(a)$ and $r_2(b)$, where r_1 and r_2 are simple, nonrelational predicates, such as "blue" or "square." Thus if a

[1] *Ibid.*, p. 26 n.

[2] On the pseudo concept of a relation "between" a thing and itself see my paper already referred to, "Reflexive Relations," *Philosophical Review*, XLII (1933), No. 3. It is there shown that even identity is not a one-term relation.

is father of *b*, this fact would be strictly equivalent to the two facts, the possession by *a* of a certain property, let us call it paternity, and the possession by *b* of another quality, let us call it sonship. This would be the entire meaning of the proposition. But the defect of this analysis is that it loses the unity between *a* and *b* which is essential to the meaning of being a father or being a son. The adjective that belongs to a substantive by reason of relationship, the relational adjective, is of such a kind that you can deduce the existence of another substantive in addition to the substantive to which it applies. Thus from the possession by *a* of the quality paternity, you can deduce that a *b* exists; from *b*, possessed of sonship, you can deduce that an *a* exists. But the possibility of the deduction depends upon the existence of some unity between *a* and *b*.

The necessity for unity in relationship can be clearly seen from a study of relations between elements of the given. If two visual shapes are given and I find that one is greater than the other, it is evident that the situation is not equivalent to the two simple facts that *a* has size *x* and *b* has size *y*, for the whole meaning of one being greater than the other implies the relevance of the one to the other. This is perhaps even more obviously true if we consider the situation where *a* is inside of *b;* the mere being of *a* and the being of *b* do not account for the situation of the two with reference to each other. We may now try to take account of all the facts by following some such procedure as that of Johnson and ascribing to each of the shapes *a* and *b* a new relational adjective: to *a*, "greater than *b*," to *b*, "less than *a*"; or to *a*, "inside of *b*," to *b*, "outside of *a*." But it is, I think, abundantly clear that the adjectives in question, in their very statement, express and imply a unity between *a* and *b*. For the shape *a* is not merely greater than or inside of, but greater than *b* or inside of *b*. One might think that a plausible case for monadism could be made with regard to a relation such as likeness, where one might suppose that the situation could be analyzed into the two propositions, *a* is blue, say, and, *b* is blue, say; but once again an essential factor in the situation would be lost, to wit, the co-presence of *a* and *b* in the mind through which they are experienced as alike.

This defect of the monadistic theory is far more serious than the flaw alleged by Russell, namely, the inability of the theory to convey the sense or direction characteristic of an asymmetrical relation. When a relation is symmetrical, he suggests, you might be able to carry out the analysis of $a\mathrm{R}b$ into $r_1(a)$, $r_2(b)$ without loss of meaning; for there is no difference of sense or direction in such relations: r_1 and r_2 would be on an equal footing. This would be the case with such relations as "sister of" or "equals." When, however, the relation is asymmetrical, r_1 and r_2 would not be on an equal footing, and there would be no way, from an inspection of these adjectives, to determine the direction of the relationship, whether from a to b or from b to a, in the case, say, of such relations as "greater than" or "father of." [1]

I confess that I am unable to see how this argument would hold against an intelligently expressed monadistic theory. In order to see this we must make a distinction, in the case of any asymmetrical relation, between what may be called the active and the passive elements of the relationship. Thus in, a precedes b, a is active, and b passive; in, a is father of b, a is greater than b, a is husband of b, the a's are active and the b's are passive. In the case of symmetric relations there is no distinction between active and passive. Now then, as we have seen, in reducing any relation, the monadist must ascribe different predicates to the individuals related, and it might very well be true that a certain type of predicate would correspond to the active, and another type of predicate to the passive, element of the relationship, in which case the distinction of sense would be entirely taken care of. The distinction in sense can be reduced to a distinction between two types of predicates. In the case of symmetric relations the predicates would, of course, be the same in type. Thus, on Johnson's analysis of such a relation as "father of" into, a is father-of-b, and, b is son-of-a, the two predicates "father-of-b" and "son-of-a" clearly show which is the active and which is the passive member of the relationship. In this way, the objection of Russell may be shown to lose all its force when applied to the monadistic theory, although, as we shall show, it retains its force when applied to the monistic theory.

Against the insistence on unity as a factor in relationship, it may, however, be claimed that unity is purely subjective, a mere addition of the mind to the elements with their relational

[1] Bertrand Russell, *The Principles of Mathematics* (Cambridge: At the University Press, 1903), Sec. 214.

characters. And, at first sight, it does look as if something could be said for this theory with regard to many relations between elements of the given. The relations "above" and "below," "right of" and "left of," "similar to," "greater than," imply a unity that is hard to conceive of apart from a mind that compares the elements concerned. It is important to note, nevertheless, that this does not imply that the unity is something irrelevant to the relations in question, for it seems certain that the relational characters of elements that are above or below, to the right or to the left of would not exist apart from the unity conferred upon them by the subject. The truth of the matter is that the unity is essential to the entire relationship, even though it be conferred by the mind. It is difficult on reflection to see how the monadistic theory can take any aid or comfort from the fact that there are certain relations that cannot exist apart from the mind— for a subjective unity is still unity. It might be asserted, however, that there is no unity in the case of relations between centers or monads. The most fundamental relations of this kind are causal and cognitive ones, upon which all social relations are built. If, therefore, the monadist could show that these relations do not imply unity, his case would be a good one. But with regard to just these it can be demonstrated, I think, that unity is essential, and therefore a monadistic interpretation impossible.

For let us consider causal relations, first. Suppose I speak and you hear, or I walk and you see me walk—then your auditory and visual sensations are causally connected with my intention to speak or to walk. Now since, on a monadistic theory, each of these events exists within a different mind, and minds are separate, the relation of causation can be nothing more than the fact that each event has some quality as it occurs. But what can this quality be? For there is nothing besides the events: there is event a in one mind and event b in another mind—that is all. It is indeed true that b follows a, and follows regularly. But mere sequence is not causation, even when sequence is habitual; there must be, in addition, necessity, by means of which the existence of a future event can be predicted from a given past or present event. To this the monadist may reply, in Humean fashion: Fact is the sole necessity, or, rather, necessity is the subjective side of fact. The habitual sequence of a upon b constrains the mind to infer from the proposition, a exists, the proposition, *b* will exist soon after. The purely logical tie of implication between the propositions which state the facts—a tie that exists only for a mind—is the only unity there is; and the constraint felt by the mind in passing from one proposition to the other is all the necessity there is. But, as we shall show in detail in Chapter XIII, in order that there may be some justification for the confidence that we place in such implications there must be an objective unity among the facts themselves. The logical tie is valid only because of some real tie. Monadism involves, in effect, a denial of causality, for which a mere correlation of past events is substituted; but from a mere correlation of the past, as we shall see, prediction in regard to the future, whether prediction with certainty or with mere probability, is impossible.

Is monadism more successful in its interpretation of the cognitive relations between monads? If one is willing to renounce prediction, it is perhaps possible to deny causal relations between monads. The conception of the universe as a multitude of separate lives, each running its course unaffected by the lives of others, while wholly unreal, is perhaps not utterly unthinkable. One might conceive of the apparent interactions of minds as due wholly to chance conjunctions of events resulting from the internal development of each. If you seem to influence my life by your thought or example, the change in me may really be due to some spontaneous growth within, which just happens to coincide with the expression of your thought in teaching or action. Such an accidental harmony of events is, at least, a statable doctrine. But it is not possible to deny cognitive relations between monads. For even if your life is without any other influence upon mine, if I can affirm your existence, I must have knowledge of you. How can monadism interpret this knowledge which one mind has of another?

Monadism is committed to a representative theory of the knowledge of other minds. Since monads are existentially separate, the knowledge which one has of another cannot imply that the mind which knows possesses the life of the mind known, but only ideas which mean or represent that life. Now whenever an idea knows an object there is presumably some relation between the two, by reason of which the idea knows this object rather than that; the idea and the object are not on the same level with reference to each other that they are with reference to the rest of the universe. I may interpret this relation variously as resemblance or as causation. Suppose I interpret it as some resemblance between the two, by reason of which the idea may take the place of the object and reveal its nature to me. How then would monadism interpret this resemblance? In accordance with the scheme to which it is committed the relation must be reduced, as we have seen, to qualities of the terms related. Suppose the idea is of you laughing formed by me through the interpretation of sensations of my own which I refer to your body, and the object which my idea knows and resembles is you laughing; each would then have the quality of laughter. The "alikeness" or unity of the two would be a mere reaction of the mind to the object as represented in the idea and the idea itself reflectively considered, as both are present in consciousness. But, as Royce pointed out, the mere fact that one thing resembles another does not make the one a knowing of the other. There are always many things alike; what then makes the idea a knowing of this rather than of some other like thing—of you laughing rather than of somebody else laughing? How does the idea pick out its object from the whole class of similar things? There is no way open for the monadist to explain this selection in terms of causation; he cannot say that an idea means an object when the latter controls it or otherwise determines its character or existence, for he has denied the existence of causal relations. Once more the monadist can get no further than the preëstablished harmony of Leibniz. He offers us correspondences, but does not give us what we require—linkages. An idea becomes a mere state of mind undetermined by the world which it seeks to know. Subjectivism or skepticism is the logical outcome. The possibility that our boasted knowledge be only a vagrant dream becomes more than a vain suggestion.

My conclusion is that since monadism cannot explain away the unity that is an essential aspect of relationship, it has failed as a theory of relations, and that we must seek elsewhere for a satisfactory interpretation. The alternative traditional theory is the monistic. According to this theory, any relational proposition is to be interpreted as a subject–predicate proposition, the subject, however, being the whole formed by the individuals related, and the relation so-called being a predicate of that whole. If the situation is aRb, then this should be rewritten $R\,(ab)$, where R now stands for a predicate. Thus the monistic theory is like the monadistic in reducing relations to adjectives, only instead of breaking up and distributing the relation among the individuals, it ascribes the relation as a single adjective to the whole which the individuals form. A relation is a predicate of a situation, not of an individual. It follows that individuals have no independent status, but exist only as members of a whole; and, since all things are related, an unconditional monistic theory of the universe is deduced. It is clear that whereas the monadistic theory is more in accord with Johnson's definition of relation, the monistic view is more in accord with the Whitehead–Russell definition.

We may illustrate the theory by means of certain simple examples already cited. Thus, if a is greater than b, a and b being two shapes, the relation is not a predicate of either shape; if I say that a is greater and b less, these are verbal forms of expression that do not correspond with the facts, for the fact is that neither a nor b has, by itself, any predicate corresponding to the relation "greater than"; the relation pertains not to them taken severally but to the total situation of which they are elements; the relation "greater than" qualifies the whole ab, and a or b only as they are members of this whole. We might express the matter in this way: the whole ab contains greater-lessness or is a greater-less situation. Or if I say that a is father of b, I do not mean merely that a has a relational property and b another relational property; I mean rather that a and b constitute a whole or situation qualified by, let us say, paternity.

Now against this theory of relations Russell has directed the same type of criticism that he directed against the monadistic view, but—in my opinion—with greater success. That is to say, he claims that this theory also is unable to give an account of the sense or direction of an asymmetrical relationship. Thus if I reëxpress the proposition, a is greater than b, as, ab contains inequality of magnitude, I am unable to tell whether a or b is what I have called the active or the passive member of the situation. So, if I reëxpress the proposition, a is father of b, as ab contains fatherhood, I am again unable to make this distinction. The monistic theory of the relationship, since it loses some of the significance of the original proposition, is an inadequate interpretation of it. It is notable, on the other hand, that no loss of meaning occurs when the monistic theory is applied to symmetrical relations. If a is equal to b, or if a is sister to b, and I reëxpress these propositions as, ab contains equality of magnitude, or, ab contains sisterhood, the criticism in question is inapplicable; for there is no distinction in these cases between the active and the passive elements.

Russell's own statement of his objection is as follows:

> The monistic theory holds that every relational proposition, aRb, is to be resolved into a proposition concerning the whole which a and b compose—a proposition which we may denote by $(ab) r \ldots$
>
> The proposition "a is greater than b," we are told, does not really say anything about either a or b, but about the two together. Denoting the whole which they compose by (ab), it says, we will suppose, "(ab) contains diversity of magnitude." Now to this statement . . . there is a special objection in the case of asymmetry. (ab) is symmetrical with regard to a and b, and thus the property of the whole will be exactly the same in the case where a is greater than b as in the case where b is greater than a . . . in the whole (ab) as such, there is neither antecedent nor consequent. In order to distinguish a whole (ab) from a whole (ba), as we must do if we are to explain asymmetry, we shall be forced back from the whole to the parts and their relation. For (ab) and (ba) consist of precisely the same parts, and differ in no respect whatever save the sense of the relation between a and b. "a is greater than b" and "b is greater than a" are propositions containing precisely the same constituents, and giving rise therefore to precisely the same whole; their difference lies solely in the fact that *greater* is, in the first case, a relation of a to b, in the second, a relation of b to a. Thus the distinction of sense, *i.e.*, the distinction between an asymmetrical relation and its converse, is one which the monistic theory of relations is wholly unable to explain." [1]

So far as I know, there are only two possible replies to this objection. One is the suggestion of Royce that asymmetrical relations can be reduced to symmetrical relations of a higher order. For example, the proposition, a implies b, where the relation of implication is asymmetrical, can be restated as, Not $(a$ and not-$b)$, or as, Either not-a or b, where all the relations— "not," "and," "or"—are symmetric. But, as a matter of fact, asymmetry is not removed in this restatement, because in either expression the distribution of the negative, as between a and b, is not symmetric. There would be symmetry only if, a and not-b, were equivalent to, Not-a and b, and, Either not-a or b, were equivalent to, Either a or not-b, which is not the case. Such

---

[1] Russell, *The Principles of Mathematics*, Sec. 215.

asymmetry will always be found to be true of every reformulation of asymmetrical relations in terms of symmetrical relations. The other suggestion is that the distinction between active and passive is purely subjective. There are, as has been admitted, certain situations where this seems to be the case. Below or above and before and after in space, before and after in time—where "in time" includes only events that are definitely past—are relations in which the distinction between the active and the passive appears to depend upon the point of view of the subject. Let me change my position, and what was above becomes below; or let me look at *a* and *b* from the *b* end rather than from the *a* end, and then *b* precedes *a*, whether *a* and *b* be two items in phenomenal space or whether they be two historical facts. If I am surveying the past and I start from now, then, as I look back, yesterday is before day before yesterday; on the other hand, if I start from the birth of Christ, day before yesterday is before yesterday. Now may it not be the case that, from the absolute viewpoint, all such particularistic interpretations, which depend upon an arbitrary *point de repère* or base, would disappear when every relational situation, no matter how seemingly asymmetrical, would turn out to be symmetrical?

The answer is twofold. In the first place, even where asymmetry depends upon a choice of base which is clearly subjective, as in the case of the relationships "above" and "below," "right" and "left," the asymmetry is real as a fact of experience. The contrast between the active and the passive elements of the given cannot be destroyed by any rearrangement from an absolute standpoint. Of course, it might be true that the contrast exists only within the given, and that all relations between monads, such as spatial and causal relations, are symmetrical. But—and this is the second point—such relations are not in fact symmetrical. For, whereas it is possible to think of, or consider, certain events, *a* and *b*, either way—*a* before *b* or *b* before *a*—after they have happened, they do not happen either way; absorption does not occur before radiation; death does not occur before birth; impregnation before conjugation; the boiling of water before the lighting of a fire. These simple illustrations, which might be multiplied indefinitely, prove that the difference between the active and the passive is a fact that cannot be ignored by any satisfactory theory of relations.

Both the traditional theories of relation are thus shown to be inadequate. An alternative theory, which recognizes the equal reality of both individuals and relations and gives up the attempt to reduce the latter either to individuals or to the wholes which they form, has been offered by Russell. A pluralism, not of individuals, but of individuals and relations, is accepted as ultimate. The individuals are either simple, corresponding to the atoms of monadism, or complex, when they are capable of being reduced to individuals in relation. It is not pretended that we know what the absolutely simple individuals and relations are, but it is thought that science must assume their existence as an ultimate goal for research. By means of these as elementary constituents, things of any order of complexity, even of infinite order, can be built up. Space can be constructed out of simple elements called points and simple relations such as betweenness; matter can be built up out of elements such as electrons and relations such as action or electric charge; the self can be understood as consisting of sensations as elements, with laws of association and "mnemic" causality as relations, and so on.

In my opinion, the most conclusive argument against a theory of this kind is the critique which Bradley levelled against all relations, but which, as a matter of fact, applies solely to this specific theory of relations. For consider any relational situation, symbolized by aRb. Then, according to the theory in question, a is one thing, R is another, and b still another, each just what it is, distinct from the others. But if this is so, then not only will there be, as premised, the given relation between a and b, but, unless the whole situation is to fall apart, there must also be a relation between a and R, and b and R. And since relations and individuals are distinct entities, there must be relations between the new relations and the given relation and the given individuals, and so on ad infinitum. But, argued Bradley, an infinity of relations between a and b is equivalent to no relations at all; the theory of relations results in the destruction of all relations; it is therefore self-contradictory—hence false.[1]

Both Russell and Royce seek to evade this difficulty by maintaining that the infinite regress is harmless, and does not undermine the relationship: R, it would be claimed, relates a and b

[1] F. H Bradley, *Appearance and Reality* (Oxford: At the Clarendon Press, [1930]), chap. iii.

in the first instance, and the new relations implied by the original one do not destroy its integrity. But even if the infinite regress were harmless—which, because of the fundamental objection to all infinites, I should deny—the force of Bradley's argument is not met. The point that is not met is this: If you take individuals and relations as distinct and ultimate, you get a complexity in your analysis of the situation which does not correspond with the facts. If *a* is father of *b*, no such infinitely complex situation can be observed; in so far as relations can be directly observed they bind individuals quite simply. This was the contention of James, although he failed to see that it is no objection to Bradley's philosophy, but rather a confirmation of it, since it shows the futility of the analysis of reality into simple terms and relations.[1] To restate the argument: Even if the infinite regress of relations is not vicious, it is false, for it is inconsistent with the nature of reality as we find it in experience.

The root of the difficulty lies, as is indicated, in treating a relation as if it were itself an individual. If so treated, it must, of course, be brought into relation again with the original individuals related. The infinity of relations pointed out by Bradley is the inevitable consequence. To defend this is to persist in the original error. The relation is not one thing, and the two terms, two others. A relation is a mode of union of individuals, not a new individual which must itself be related. When, as the result of some triumph, pride and exultation color all a man's thought, there is surely a relation between his thoughts and his emotions; they are permeated with each other, and we recognize immediately the union that is present and directly experienced. What we observe, however, is a union of thought and emotion, but not a union of the union and the emotion. It is not assumed, I suppose, that there is any infinite complexity in immediate experience, but only in experience reflectively considered. But the point of interest is whether the account is a description of any actual situation; and we have seen that it is not. And we can see how the infinite regress arises. In the description of the relational situation, we use a word to

1 William James, "The Thing and Its Relations," reprinted in *Essays in Radical Empiricism* (New York: Longmans, Green and Co., 1922), pp. 106–109. See also G. F. Stout, "Alleged Self-Contradictions in the Concept of Relation," *Proceedings of the Aristotelian Society*, 1901–2 : 1–14.

designate the relation, which, being a word, is an individual thing; we can therefore enquire into its relation to the words used to designate the individuals related. This relation will now itself be designated by a word, which in turn will be another individual thing, whose relations to the other words we have been using can be sought and designated by a word, and so on. Thus, substituting letters for words, if we designate a relational situation by three letters, a, r, and b, these letters are related, a to r, and r to b; we must then designate these new relations by new letters, s and t. But these letters are themselves related to the other letters; hence, if we wish to symbolize these new relations, we must use other new words, and so on; it is clear that we are developing an infinite series. But notice that the series is a series of words or letters used as symbols which we ourselves create by our own choice, and that the series does not stand in one–one correspondence to the facts in the original relational situation which we are trying to symbolize. For in the original situation there are not even three things corresponding to three words or letters used to designate it, but only two—not things denoted by a and r and b, but only things denoted by a and b, since the relation is itself not an individual at all. Notice, moreover, that the series of words or letters is not an actual infinite—no series, as we have seen, is such—but only an open series, the number of whose terms depends upon how far one chooses to go in the process of finding words to designate relations between symbols. Finally, if we take the three letters, a, r, and b, as our original situation, there are only three elements in that situation, for the relations between these letters are not themselves individuals—only the words we shall use to designate *them* will be such. This process is extremely interesting, but it is of interest for the logic of symbols—it has no metaphysical significance for the theory of relations.

The argument of the preceding paragraph shows, I think, that the customary expression, aRb, is a bad symbol for relationship, since it places R on the same plane with a and b. $R(ab)$ or $F(ab)$ is better, because it clearly indicates the difference in status between a and b, on the one hand, and R. But even these expressions are defective in that they symbolize a relation by a thing, R or F, which may easily lead to the misunderstanding in question. Only by symbolizing relationship by a **relation** can this misunderstanding be entirely avoided; for example we could write simply *ab*, where the relationship of juxtaposition of the two letters would serve as the symbol for relation in general.

But stronger than any purely dialectical difficulties of the theory of the independent existence of individuals and relations stands the plain fact of their dependence on each other. No object with which we are acquainted remains unaffected after it has acquired a new relation, or possesses whatever total nature it has apart from its actual relations. No man is wholly the same after he has undertaken new duties, accepted a new office, joined a club, got himself married, or begotten a child. In the case of social relations, the theory that relations are *external* is palpably false. But it is no less false in the case of physical or psychical relations. The weight, the energy, indeed—as we now know—the apparent size and shape of physical things, are dependent upon relation to each other; it is even impossible to define such properties apart from relations. In the realm of the mind all the new facts and new light upon old facts introduced by the so-called *Gestalt* psychology have shown the dependence of psychical elements upon relations. The mutual dependence of elements and relations is shown, furthermore, from the fact that not all individuals can stand in all relations, and not all relations can obtain between all kinds of individuals. One thought cannot be heavier than another, or one color larger than another; one proposition may imply another, but it cannot surround another.

We may sum up the arguments against Russell's view as follows: (1) You cannot treat relations as independent facts, because if you do you fail to explain how they can unite individuals, and so you make them incapable of performing their proper function; (2) Individuals are not independent of relationships, but are at least partly made what they are through relation; (3) Relations are not independent of individuals, for particular relations can exist only between particular individuals.

The preceding critique of theories of relations leads us to a positive theory which we are now in a position to develop. But before we go on to construct this theory there are certain general considerations regarding relations which we shall find useful to advance. And first I wish to take a stand regarding the peculiar view of Russell, expressed in his *Principles of Mathematics* (Sec. 55), that all relations are universals and have no instances, not because the theory has intrinsic worth, but because the study of it will lead to matters that are important.   Before examining Russell's argument for this view I will state certain reasons which lie close at hand to render it, to say the least, unplausible.   In the first place, the very notion of there being a universal without instances is so strange that it immediately excites suspicion— why should relations have no instances, when qualities do have instances?   In the second place, it seems to be a plain matter of fact that relationships are just as individualized as qualities. If the concrete greening of one leaf is not the same as the concrete greening of another leaf, so the relation of ruler to subject is not the same in England as in Germany—it is not even the same for all Germans, not the same for Jews as for "Aryans."   Every relationship is as concrete, unique, and instantial as the individuals between which it holds, which does not, of course, imply that there is no generic sameness between such relationships of the kind discussed in our chapter on universals.

And now for Russell's argument.   The argument is based on an analysis of the relation "difference," where the relation does not denote difference of quality but "bare numerical difference," in virtue of which individuals are two—a relation which would presumably hold between precisely similar things.   The detailed argument is as follows:

> . . . even if differences did differ, they would still have to have something in common.   But the most general way in which two terms can have something in common, is by both having a given relation to a given term.   Hence, if no two pairs of terms can have the same relation, it follows that no two terms can have anything in common, and hence different differences will not be in any definable sense *instances* of difference.   I conclude, then, that the relation affirmed between *A* and *B* in the proposition "*A* differs from *B*," is the general relation of difference, and is precisely and numerically the same as the relation affirmed between *C* and *D*, in "*C* differs from *D*." And this doctrine must be held, for the same reasons, to be true of all other relations; relations do not have instances, but are strictly the same in all propositions in which they occur.[1]

In a note Russell indicates the real point of this argument: "The relation of an instance to its universal, at any rate, must be

---

[1] Russell, *The Principles of Mathematics*, Sec. 55.

actually and numerically the same in all cases in which it occurs." [1]

In attempting to assess the worth of this argument we may note the highly dubious character of the relation "bare numerical difference" which Russell uses as a touchstone for his general thesis. If we are correct in our theory of universals, there is no such thing, since no two individuals can be exactly alike in all properties, intrinsic and relational. In fact, the relation "difference," like the relation "identity," is not a simple, unanalyzable relation, but a symbol for a situation of the form, x has F, and y does not have F, or xRb, and $\sim (y$R$b)$. That is to say, things may be said to differ when one has a property that the other has not, or when one has a relation to a given term that another has not. This is the full and sufficient meaning of difference. This defect in the argument does not seriously affect its force, however, for, as indicated, its nerve lies in the assertion that the most general way for two items to have something in common is for both to have the same relation to a common term, which would be impossible if relations are individualized by the terms between which they hold, for each of the two items would have to have a different, unique relation to the common term. Two similar terms could not even have the same relation—whatever the relation of particular to universal be called—to the universal with respect to which they are similar, for even the relation of particular to universal would be individualized by each individual to which it applied. If a is red and b is red, then the relation expressed by "is" would be a different relation in each case. But, if so, how could a and b be similar, or how could they form a class?

This difficulty reveals the importance of a true theory of universals, for it stems entirely from the false Platonic notion of the universal as having existence independent of the particular, in which case there would have to be a relation between the universal and its particulars. But if universals do not exist independent of particulars, there is no relation between them and their corresponding particulars. a and b, if both red, do have something in common, but not because they have the same relation to a third thing, the universal redness, but because they have a common factor, the generic quality redness. If a and b

[1] *Ibid.*, p. 52 n.

are red, they are not other than redness; for redness belongs to the nature of each, and a thing and its nature are not separate. It must be admitted that language seems to sanction the existence of a relation between universal and particulars, but we must beware of interpreting reality in terms of the defects of language. As we have tried to show in our chapter on universals (Chap. IV), the universal viewed as something separate from the corresponding particulars is but a fiction. Moreover, the sameness of relation which many individuals may bear to a given term is never more than generic sameness; it is not absolute or individual sameness. For example, the relation of children to their father is, as a plain matter of fact, never the same absolutely—not the same for the daughters as for the sons, or for each son or daughter —yet it is generically the same; and the children have something in common by reason of the fact, not that each possesses the same concrete relational character, but that each possesses the same generic relational character as the others. To put the whole matter in a nutshell: the only sameness which many things may have is generic sameness; and this does not depend upon the fact that the many things have relation to a common universal, but upon the fact that the universal is present as a factor in the nature of each of the things in question; whereby these things are, to that extent, not many things, but one thing.

It follows that there is no relation between subject and predicate. This may seem to be a surprising, even a preposterous, notion, but it is easy to prove that we fall into an infinite regress unless we are prepared to accept it. For if a, let us say, characterized b, then if characterizing is a relation—we shall call it "characterizing$_1$"—we have the relational adjective "characterizing b" as an adjective of a. But now, "characterizing b" must itself characterize a, hence we have the relation between a and the adjective "characterizing b," which would be the relation "characterizing$_2$." But corresponding to this relation we should have the adjective "characterizing b, characterizing," which would itself characterize a, and so we should have the new relation, which we may call "characterizing$_3$"; and so on to infinity. To put the same matter in another way: if in $F(a)$ there is a relation between F and a, we must have $F'(F, a)$, and so $F''(F', F, a)$, and so forth, exactly as Bradley supposed.

It follows also that there is no relation between genus and

species.[1] This too may appear to be a hard saying, and to have
a suspicious air of paradox, but the strangeness disappears as
soon is it is remembered that universals do not exist apart from
particulars.   I can perhaps state the matter best through an
analysis of a concrete case.   Suppose it is true that *this* is red;
and, of course, we know that red is a color.   We have already
seen that there is no relation between *this* and redness—from
which it clearly follows that there could· not be a relation between *this* and color, for color is as much a factor in the nature
of *this* as red is, hence could no more be distinguished as something separate from *this*.   But how then could I distinguish red
as something separate from color?   What would red be as a
moment in *this* that was not color?   In the two propositions,
This is red, and, *This* is a color, I am simply calling attention to
two layers of generality in the existence of *this;* but these layers
of generality are not separate, even though I use separate words
in order to designate them.   They cannot, therefore, be related.
The proposition, Red is a color, does not presuppose the existence of red or color independent of some individual any more
than it presupposes the separate existence of red and color; what
it means is, If anything is red, it is colored.   The a priori certainty of such propositions as, Red is a color, or, Two is a
number, is derived from the fact that subject and predicate are
immediately seen not to differ.   In such propositions as, Man
is an animal, on the other hand, it is not immediately evident
that they do not differ; only on further information does it become evident that this is so.

---

[1] But there is, of course, a relation between genus word and species word,
even as there is a relation between subject word and predicate word; and the
existence of these relations has misled people into belief in the supposititious
relations discussed.

XI

The Theory of Relations. II

THE foregoing critique of theories of relations implies, as we have said, a positive theory which we may now present. The dependence of this theory on all the views we have rejected will be evident—in fact we shall do little more than put together into a consistent whole fragments of truth in these views. But this can be nothing against our view, for it would be strange if traditional and recent theories did not each contain an element of truth, since they have been framed by men with a vast experience in the problems at issue and with no other motive than the love of truth.

The conclusion that we can draw from our previous reflections is that the fact of relation is not simple, but complex. We may therefore distinguish various aspects. First, whenever there is a relationship between individuals a specific character is conferred on each by reason of the relationship—or, more accurately, part of the fact which we designate by the phrase "being related" consists of the possession by the individuals concerned of certain characters, which may be called "relative," or, generalizing a term from biology, "acquired," characters. Thus if A is father of B, A will possess certain sentiments in regard to B and B will possess certain other sentiments in regard to A which would not exist in either A or B except for the relationship. If A is greater in size than B, then, as the two exist in one unity of consciousness, A will have a character which we may call "superiority to B" and B will have a character which we may call "inferiority to A," characters which are not possessed by A and B apart from the relationship. The very form of the relational proposition suggests this analysis, as Johnson and Russell have pointed out, for the entire latter part of the proposition may be regarded as a predicate of the earlier term of the proposition, as subject. So, A is father of B, can be restated as, A is (father of B), and, inverting, as, B is (son of A). This aspect of the fact of relationship is rightly insisted on by the monadists; but they go astray, as we have seen, because they seek to reduce the whole meaning of relationship to it.

The question arises whether all the characters of an individual are relative characters. That this is so was the thesis of Leibniz. It would be admitted that when we examine an individual we do not immediately find that all its characters are determined by known relationships; but it is maintained that all its characters would be found to be due to relationships if we knew all the relationships—with the result that no characters would be left as genuinely "native" or "original," as we may call characters un-determined by relationship. If one thing is predecessor of an-other, its nature is clearly richer than this relationship; you can destroy the relationship or give to the thing the converse rela-tionship—make it successor—and it will still be in part what it was before; but if we could abstract from all relations, would the thing have any nature left? My considered opinion is that there is only one type of individual that is wholly made by its relations, namely, the mathematical entity, which, however, is a fictitious entity, made by definition to have those characters, and those only, which are expressive of the relationships in question. In the case of all real individuals, their entire natures cannot be equated to the totality of their relative characters; some non-relational characters render them in part independent of their relations to other individuals. Into the making of every indi-dividual its relations to other individuals have entered as a creative factor; but in every case the individual started with a nature not made by the relationship. Go back as far as you will into the process of the making of anything you know, you will always find, alongside the acquired and relative, the native and original.

There is, therefore, to put the matter in another way, some truth in the view of relations as "external." A consideration of the various sense qualities proves this most clearly. Take colors for example: the nature of each color is certainly not unaffected by its juxtaposition with other colors, upon which its significance for feeling depends, as every student of pictorial art knows; yet if, without ever having seen color before, one were to open one's eyes upon the blue of the sky, a distinct and specific quale would enter into experience. And if you put a color and a tone together in experience, you modify the nature of each; yet in so far as one item is color and the other is tone, there remains an aboriginal essence not affected by the relationship. And while our perception of size is the result of numberless comparisons, as is well known, there is, nevertheless, a purely qualitative aspect of spreadoutness or voluminousness irreducible to relation. Causally, existentially, sense qualities are dependent upon stimulus and receptive organism; but no one has ever been able to deduce the quality from the relationship. We find a multitude of related elements, each with a nature of its own; when we study that nature we find that it is for the most part relative, and the more we study it the more relativity we discover; yet we never discover complete relativity—an unacquired residuum remains.

The existence of acquired or relative characters is thus an essential aspect of the fact of relationship. That it is not the whole of this fact was proved by our criticism of monadism. There is at least the further item of unity, which, as we have seen, monadism denies. Now the necessity for unity emerges from all those considerations which we adduced in demonstrating the insufficiency of that doctrine, and which we do not need to repeat. That unity cannot be eliminated on the ground of subjectivity was also shown. Unity is as objective as the existence of the individual and its relative characters. Because of the unity which these characters imply, we cannot reduce a relation to qualities of the related individuals. Yet we should not treat relation as something over and above the relative characters of individuals and their unity. As soon as we do this we are beginning to treat relation as itself an individual, and then we fall into the difficulties recounted in our critique of the theory of relations as self-subsistent realities. Russell falls into this error when he raises the question, What serves to unite a and R and b in the proposition aRb? [1] and answers by postulating an indefinable and irreducible unity which distinguishes aRb from a and R and b. But this statement of the situation is clearly redundant. Relation and unity are not different facts; unity is one aspect of the complex fact, relation. There is no reason for asking what unites a and b in the proposition aRb, for R itself

[1] Bertrand Russell, *The Principles of Mathematics* (Cambridge: At the University Press, 1903), Sec. 54.

does this. The unity of *a* and *b* is given in the fact of their being related. You cannot demand the unity of *a* and R and *b*, because R is not another individual besides *a* and *b*, but just the unity between them which you are seeking. Relations are modes of unification of elements, not further elements requiring unification. Despite the countenance which linguistic usage may give, relations have not, to employ the language of Leibniz, one foot in one individual and another foot in the other, with a part stretching between. Relations are not thus suspended in the air; they are supported throughout their whole length; there is no part of them that does not belong somewhere. They are neither divided up among the terms as Leibniz thought, nor suspended between them as Russell seems to picture them, but are characters of terms when united. We should not think of the unity which relation involves as a link or a tie or as glue, as a thing which affixes itself externally to elements and thus unites them. We should picture relations rather as running through elements, as embedded in them, or as threads upon which they are strung; or if we cannot help picturing them as bonds, we should picture them as so tight that they cut into the flesh and leave no space between.

A couple of illustrations will illumine this discussion immediately. Suppose some impulse or passion contends with a principle in the mind of a man. The struggle of the two is what we should call their relation. Yet if we examine the concrete reality before us, we shall not find that this relation has any existence alongside the two forces; it is rather a character of each in its connection with the other; it is that which makes each a contending rather than a coöperating force. Again, if *a* is greater than *b*, "greater than" does not exist alongside *a* and *b;* it is a character which *a* possesses in its togetherness with *b*, when we compare them. You cannot find it anywhere between them; its whole self is distributed among them—as "greater than," a character of *a*, and as "less than," a character of *b*—in their union. The "feeling of relation," of which James wrote, is not an independent something alongside the elements related. Relations have a peculiar instability of status. They are certainly not individuals; like adjectives, they are secondary to individuals, and so are unsubstantial. Yet they are, with equal certainty, not mere adjectives of individuals. They are something more than the individuals taken singly, for they unite them and give a specific coloring to each.

In so far, however, as we recognize unity as a fundamental category we are denying the sufficiency of the concepts "individual" and "quality" for the description of reality. Yet this does not imply that we regard the concept of relation as unanalyzable. Unity is irreducible, but not relation. Relation is a complex concept, susceptible of just the analysis we are trying to give it. The reality of unity is unmistakable for two reasons: the failure to dispense with it in any attempt to describe reality— a failure which I hope has been abundantly proved—and the immediate evidence which experience offers of its presence. I find, for example, the unity of hue and intensity in a color, or the unity of various extents of space in a whole of space, just as surely as I find the extents and the qualities themselves.

A final phase of the fact of relationship is the existence of a system formed through the unity of the individuals related. Consider aRb. The situation not only involves the possession by a and b of relative properties, and the unity of a and b, but also the existence of (ab), the whole, or ordered couple, formed through the unity of its members. This whole possesses properties which neither of its members can claim as its own. Take, for example, a phenomenal line. The elements of the line have relations of distance and order, and through their contact constitute a whole, the line, with properties not possessed by any element of the line: the line is continuous and of such and such a length, while the elements, taken singly, are not continuous and do not have length. An army has a strength and array not possessed by any single soldier. A color scheme has a unity and an emotional significance not to be predicated of any individual color. The converse of this is also true: the elements have severally properties not possessed by the whole. The single colors have hue, but the picture has none; the soldiers are conscious, but not the army; the side of a triangle has length, the triangle only area.

The existence of a whole, of which the elements related are members, is the modicum of truth in the monistic theory. The conclusions which are usually drawn from this truth as to the status of the individual in the whole, are, however, wrong. It is assumed, namely, that the whole completely determines the nature of the elements. This view of the situation rests on the supposition that the individual is completely made by the relations into which it enters. But, as we know, the making of the individual through relations is only partial, it applies only to the acquired properties of the individual. And far from its being true that the whole completely determines the nature of the individual members, it is true, conversely, that the elements determine the nature of the wholes which they form. As we have seen, you cannot impose all relations upon all individuals; the sort of relation which one thing bears to another, and so the sort of whole which they compose, flows from the nature of the things themselves. An appeal to concrete illustrations is convincing. Social relations have their basis in the instincts and mental faculties of individuals. Of course it is true that relationships once established modify instinct and mental faculty. I do not mean to argue that individuals are ever isolated, ever free from allegiance to some whole. What I am contending for is this: when we watch the genesis of new systems we perceive that they are established from below in the first instance, that they grow out of the nature of the elements which are to compose them. To be sure, as the relation becomes established the individuals undergo modification, and they have owed part of their natures to the wholes of which they are already members, for every new whole grows out of the bosom of some old, existing whole; moreover, the new whole is usually modelled after some extant whole, as our American universities were copied from Oxford and Cambridge, or as the fertilized ovum grows to be like a man or a woman. Nevertheless, the new whole does not preëxist to its members, determining them; rather they, with the spirit of adventure upon them, go forth to create it, which only then comes into being. A study of the more abstract relations confirms this view. Equality of size changes to inequality through the expansion or contraction of either of the quanta so related. Even so, likeness may become unlikeness, and vice versa. The influence of whole and element is not one-way, but mutual. Colonists establish a new society, then find themselves changed by the order they have founded.

That the whole cannot tyrannize over the parts Russell has conclusively proved from the nature of asymmetrical relations.[1]

---

[1] *Op. cit.,* Sec. 215.

Suppose we consider the simplest case of asymmetry, when the relation is dyadic, as for example, *a* precedes *b*. Then, in accordance with our interpretation, there must exist a whole formed of the related elements, a whole which will possess a nature of its own. This whole, to use the language of Frege, will be a "couple with sense." But how can you determine its sense or direction? Not by a mere survey of the whole, (ab); for this whole, as whole, is perfectly symmetrical with reference to *a* and *b*; whether it be aRb or bRa is entirely indeterminate. Only when you take some one element in the whole as base or starting point, and regard both from its point of view, going from the one to the other, can the asymmetry be determined. The sense of the couple, therefore, its nature so far at least as this character is concerned, is dependent on the parts. And that the choice of a base is not arbitrary, and so not without clear metaphysical significance, is proved by cases of irreversible asymmetry. Temporal and teleological relations—among the most significant of all relations—are striking instances. As we have already noted, you may survey the time sequence forward or backward, but you cannot grow either way. You may look back from the goal to the plan, but you cannot act by beginning with the goal and then going back to the plan. Even if the choice of a base were always arbitrary, the matter for which I am arguing would still hold.

Moreover, from the point of view of the limited monadism of this book it would seem that, as between the ultimate individuals or monads and the wholes into which they enter through relation, the metaphysical primacy must belong to the former, since there is no inclusive experience corresponding to the latter. On the other hand, it should not be forgotten that all monads are united with each other directly, through contact, or indirectly; and therefore the wholes which they form, including the final whole, the universe, are not fictions to which nothing real is relevant. Thus the members of a human society, a nation or an army, for example, are united with each other through the contact of each with its body and of all with the geographical landscape of light and air, water and soil which they occupy. Moreover, the special way in which the experience of any center is determined by other related centers depends upon its position in the whole, as will be explained in the following chapters. Nevertheless, since a whole such as an army or nation is not itself an experience, it is not a metaphysical entity, but has the status of a logical schema with properties corresponding to the activities of monads which have effects on related monads.   The strength of an army corresponds to certain experienced effects of the actions of officers and men on each other and the enemy; the constitution of a nation consists of the interest of the citizens in certain kinds of coöperation, together with appropriate sentiments toward their leaders.   In the case of phenomenal objects, however, in contrast with metaphysical entities, wholes are of the same type as their elements, and are therefore equally real: a phenomenal triangle or square is as real as its sides, the composition of a painting as real as its constituent colors or lines.   But such wholes derive their existence from the centers of experience within which they "appear"; they, also, have no independent reality of their own.

An important difficulty which the theory of relations as we have been developing it must face arises from the distinction between the original and the relative characters of the individual. Every individual, we saw, owes some of its qualities to its union with other individuals, yet not all its qualities, for there are in addition some which are native to the thing itself.   But now, when we consider the qualities of individuals, are we not confronted with the same situation over again?   For every time that an individual entered into a new relationship it would acquire a new quality, which would therefore enter into relation with those already possessed by the thing.   The problem of relation would be shifted from between individuals to between qualities within each individual, where, seemingly, the same distinction would have to be drawn over again between an original and an acquired aspect of the qualities in question; for, according to theory, the qualities should undergo mutual modification by being brought into relation with each other.   Since everything exists both on account of itself and on account of other things, there would be a part of the quality that would remain the same before entrance into the new relationship, and another part that would be different.   Call the one a and the other b.   These two parts would be in relation; hence they would modify each other, and, as in the case of the individual, we could distinguish in each one part as the same and another part as different—in a, for example, parts c and d.   But clearly this would involve once more the problem of the relation between the original and the acquired, only this time within a quality of the individual. Again the problem is shifted—from between individuals to between qualities, then within single qualities. Obviously an infinite regress is commencing, and our individual, which seemed simple enough at first, is becoming infinitely complex.

Royce here, as in a previous case, accepts the infinite regress as harmless and the infinite complexity of each individual and each quality as no more than just the truth about the constitution of everything.[1] The regress arises, he says, in the attempt to determine the self-identity or uniqueness of a thing in contradistinction to those aspects of its nature which it owes to its relations. The purely original is a limit in the mathematical sense, to which we may approach indefinitely by an endless process of making distinctions between what a thing is as related and what it is in its native character—a limit which, however, we can never reach. But this solution of the difficulty, although it contains a certain truth, which will be pointed out directly, is nevertheless subject to the same defect as that which marred Russell's dealing with the problem of the infinity of relations between an individual and its relations to other things—it accepts as real in the individual a complexity far beyond anything given in our experience.

The solution of the problem is, however, within our reach. The difficulty arises, as Royce pointed out, from the effort to separate out the original from the acquired properties of related things, or, what comes to the same, to mark off the identity from the difference in things which change and acquire new relationships. But this separation cannot be made, for the two interpenetrate, and the give and take between them is not of something which exists alongside each, but is just the very nature of each. The infinite regress which arises when you try to separate the identity from the difference is a proof—and this is where I would differ from Royce—that the whole attempt at separation is fallacious and futile.

For example, consider a situation which we have already presented. Through some new relation to the public a man's thought of himself becomes tinged with pride. His thought of

[1] Josiah Royce, *The World and the Individual*, First Series (New York: The Macmillan Co., 1904), Vol. I, Supplementary Essay, pp. 538–588.

himself becomes a proud thought. We can now distinguish, if we will, the two factors in his new state of mind—the pride and the thought; and it is true that the pride and the thought are united with one another, and that there is a mutual influence of one on the other. But this union does not involve a new complexity and a new problem of relation. The thought in union with pride takes on a new quality; but what it takes on is not something other than itself and other than pride: it becomes a *proud thought;* and the pride does not acquire something different from thought: it becomes simply *pride of this thought.* Here—and generally—whenever the qualities of things are modified by union with other qualities the mutual modification consists in each taking on the quality of the other; no new complexity of relationship is developed in each, but a simple fusion of the two into a total quality. The infinite regress of which Royce and Bradley make so much develops through the supposition that when an individual is modified through relationship you can find *one part* that remains the same despite the relationship and *another part* which is the increment of difference created through the relationship. The man is the same as he was before the new relationship, and, of course, he is also different, so you want to separate the sameness from the difference. You want to find the thought as it was originally, and then, alongside it, the difference which was made to it through its union with pride. But I say the thought is the same in being thought, and different in being proud thought. And if you persist and ask, Is there not in the thought itself some part which is just thought and some other part which is the ingredient of pride? I answer, There is none; there is not the slightest part of the thought which is not permeated with pride; there is no part which is not at once the same and different. It is impossible to separate the sameness from the difference, to get the sameness pure and the difference pure.

The principle just employed to solve the problem of the relation between the qualities of related individuals serves to solve the similar problem of the relation of the qualities of the whole formed by these individuals. For there too the qualities come into relation with and modify one another. But the interrelation of qualities of a whole involves the same type of unity as the interrelation of qualities of an individual in the whole.

There also the qualities modify one another, but through participation, not through the creation of new qualities, so that no further complexity is involved, least of all an infinite regress.

The recognition of interpenetration as a special type of unity throws much light upon the definition of the individual and its distinction from quality. An individual is usually defined as something that can exist by itself. But since it is impossible wholly to isolate anything, we should never know, if this definition were true, whether anything were an individual or not. Moreover, since individuals derive their relative characters from other individuals, the statement cannot be exact. We cannot take the individual out of the universe, and so we cannot define it as if we could. However, starting from the given whole in which the individual lies, we may define the individual as something that can be *found* separate from the rest of the whole. This does not mean that the individual could exist out of the whole, but that one does not find other parts of the whole—although one does find what is universal and common to all parts—when one finds a given individual part. I can find John without finding Mary, although both belong to the one universe, social and physical. It might, however, seem as if there were a limit even to this, in as much as the relative characters of an individual cannot be known without a knowledge of other individuals with which the given individual stands in relation. I cannot know that a is in relation to b unless I know b as well as a. Yet this objection fails because the knowledge of b is not a finding of b in a, but an inference from the relative characters of a to the existence of b with its correlative characters. An individual, then, is not something that could exist by itself apart from the whole, but something which can be found without finding other elements in the whole and which does not derive all its characters from such other elements.

Next, what is the definition of "quality" in distinction from "individual"? The Aristotelian tradition has it that an individual is something besides its qualities, their subject or bearer; but this entity is certainly not empirical, therefore not real. The qualities in their unity are the empirical thing, which owns any one of them and to which any one of them may be attributed. The notion of subject served two purposes: it accounted for the identity or persistence of the individual despite change, and it served to distinguish the individual from the universal. How identity and difference, permanence and transiency can be conceived to coexist in a changing thing without the notion of a substrate is clear from the foregoing discussion: the permanent is an invariant quality of the individual; the transient consists of other, variable qualities, relatively short-lived, succeeding each other and in turn united with the invariant quality. The paradoxes of this situation are the now familiar paradoxes of the thing and its relations, to be solved in the fashion suggested. We have already illustrated the matter sufficiently I believe in our chapters on the self and time (Chaps. II, VII). The need for a subject or substrate to provide for the uniqueness of the individual sprang from a misconception of qualities, rooted in the Platonic philosophy. Qualities were thought to be universals; hence, since the individual is a unity of qualities, it, too, without something to guarantee its particularity, would have become a universal, an Idea. But in our chapter on universals (Chap. IV) we have shown that qualities should not be confounded with universals—qualities are *infimae species,* universals are generic aspects of qualities. The blue that I see in the sky is a concrete quale, of which blueness is a mere generic factor. Qualities do not have to be made unique through attachment to a "subject"; they are given unique.

If this is true, does it not follow that the distinction between individual and quality disappears? For in the same fashion that individuals unite into systems, qualities seem to unite and form individuals, what we call an individual being really a complex quality composed of lesser individuals—elementary qualia. The matter is, however, not so simple as this. For, in the first place, while, as we have noted, individuals can be found separate from each other and in many cases can exist separate from each other, elementary qualia cannot be found in isolation, and have no separate existence. Thus the concrete blue of the patch of sky that I see cannot be found or exist separate from its shape or spreadoutness, and even the whole complex of qualities which constitutes the patch cannot be found or exist separate from the self of which it is a factor; but two selves can be found separate and each can exist on the disappearance of the other. Mere shape, mere blue, mere extensity are not viable existences. It follows that a certain complexity of qualities must be achieved in order for separately discoverable existence—individuality—to become possible. The individual is a complex of qualities, but not every quality is an individual. And when qualities have reached the complexity of individual existence their mode of unity with other such existences is different from the mode of unity of simple qualities. When simple qualities unite they are intertwined, involved, fused with one another; when individuals unite they retain a certain aloofness from each other, both as to existence and knowledge.

The distinction between quality and individual depends in the last analysis, therefore, upon the distinction between two types of unity: the first, one in which the items are fused in one another, the second, one in which the items retain a separable mode of existence. The one is the type of union of qualities, the other is the type of union of individuals. Qualities in their union constitute individuals and interpenetrate one another; individuals unite and form wholes and are alongside one another. A quality in its union with another quality in a thing takes on the other quality as its own; but an individual in its union with another individual, although modified by that other, does not assimilate its characteristics. When a man and a woman marry, each is modified by the relationship, but this does not involve the feminizing of the man or the virilizing of the woman; the modification may consist, rather, in making the one more masculine and the other more feminine. It entails adjustment to one another, not fusion in one another. Within the individual, however, the union of qualities involves a taking on by the one of the other: the blue becomes extended, the extensity becomes a blue extensity.

Failure to distinguish these two types of unity, or, what comes to the same, failure to distinguish qualities from individuals, is characteristic of all mystical types of monism. For, according to the monistic scheme, individuals are reduced to qualities of the whole which they form through relation; whence it follows that they must participate in one another, as the qualities of an individual do. Since all things are related to all things, the result is the doctrine of universal compenetration— each in all and all in each. The clearest evidence against this view is afforded, as we have seen, by asymmetrical relations. For in the case of such relations, the adjustment that is implied in the relation of the elements to one another is specifically not the elimination of difference and distinction, but the reverse: one element becomes a predecessor, the other a successor, one a father, the other a son, and the like. There is a greater differentiation between father and son than between a man and a boy to whom he does not bear the paternal relation. Or a man in relation to his wife is a far more highly differentiated person than he is in relation to other women. Relation is not so much a source of identity as of difference, of richness. A clear case of union without interfusion is that of elements of space into wholes of space. Here the whole is indubitable; yet the elements are not fused in one another, for each can be found separate. Moreover, the sort of relation and wholeness that they possess demands this very separation. Even contiguous elements do not have toward each other the type of unity possessed by qualities of an individual—such as have the color and shape of a visual form. If they had, since all elements are mediately in contact with any one of them, they would all flow together into one; they would reduce to a single point. In this case the union, along with the distinctness of the individuals united, is a plain fact of observation.

Another important distinction among relations is that between the static and the dynamic. In general, dynamic relations are denoted by verbs, such as "causes," "hates," "loves," "gives," and the like, while static relations are denoted by adverbs, such as "above," "below," "between," and the like. Relations denoted by a noun and a preposition, such as "father of," "king of," "son of," form an interesting group between the first two. Characteristic of dynamic relations is the mobility of the elements related and their activity as parties to the relationship. Thus in the relationship denoted by the term "loves," the state of mind of both lover and beloved is constantly changing, and their feelings toward one another are active—that is to say, they involve a readiness for action and are causally effective. On the other hand, it is characteristic of the static relations that, although they may disappear, they seem to be changeless while they last, and the elements related have no causal efficacy. The relation between the center and the points on the circumference of a mathematical circle is changeless, and the points themselves are inactive. The same also appears to be true of the elements of a disk in the field of vision, or of the shapes of books in a row—

the shapes seem to be immobile and not to have any causal efficacy in relation to one another, so far as betweenness is concerned. With regard to static relations, however, it is significant that they hold between abstractions only. Mathematical relations are obviously of this kind, and, if our theory of sensa is correct, so also are the relations of colored and other sensuous objects in the field of experience, for these, too, are abstractions. In its concrete reality, on the other hand, sensuous experience is penetrated by activities, so that the elements of the living experience, from which the sensuous shape is abstracted, are anything but immobile or passive. In fact, there are no truly passive real relations. Even the visual shape, so seemingly static, expresses an unstable equilibrium of forces acting within experience. Nevertheless, there is a relatively static aspect of most dynamic relations, well expressed in the difference between such locutions as "loves," on the one hand, and "is lover of," on the other hand. This appears to be the case with all relations denoted by a noun and a preposition. The relation "king of" is certainly dynamic, but the phrase denoting it places the emphasis on the relative constancy of the relation between the king and his subjects. All relations defined by a constitution are of this intermediary character, as are, for example, the relations implied in the offices of president and vice-president of the United States. The spatial relations of the physical world, since they hold between elements that are essentially dynamic, are themselves dynamic relations; yet, in so far as they are factors in the eternal constitution of nature, they are static.

Despite the help that language may give in the analysis of relations, it is often misleading, here as elsewhere. We have already noticed that we cannot take at their face value the relations "before" and "between," when asserted to hold of elements of the physical world. The relations that obtain there are only generically the same as the relations that hold between items of given experience, despite the use of the same words to designate them. This kind of ambiguity is the basis of the metaphorical character of language. An even greater pitfall is laid for analysis by the simplicity of the words often used to designate relations which, on careful consideration, turn out to be highly complex. Thus, as Professor Sellars has well explained, there is no simple "knowledge relation"; what passes for this is a richly complex situation, the basic underlying relation being causality, when knowledge of the physical world is in view.   A similar case of a pseudo relation is the so-called interest relation, supposed by certain theorists to be the foundation of value.   The fact that we use a simple verb form like "knows" or "loves" does not prove that there is a simple relation uniquely denoted by it.[1]   Social relations, also, such as "father of," or "husband of," are obviously not so simple as are the words that mean them; and the basic underlying relations are not indicated by language at all.

[1] Cf. below, pp. 302–304.

XII

Causality: Nature of Causality; Phenomenological Critique

B Y THE process of abstraction it is easy to create the illusion of a causeless world. Imagine an experience consisting solely of watching the sequence of pictures on a screen; forget the events in the external world with which we believe them to be connected and allow no interference on the part of the spectator. Or substitute for the pictures the visual phenomenal objects that occur in the mind as one watches a drama, and think away the actors that control them and the attentive interest of the spectator that keeps them in mind. Either experience would contain sequences, an orderly procession of events, but no causes. Or let us change again the object of our contemplation. Let us imagine a world consisting wholly of physical events happening in complete independence of each other yet exhibiting certain uniformities expressible in terms of statistical laws. Such a world, also, as recent philosophers of science are proud to affirm, is a causeless world. But neither the world of pure esthetic objects nor the world of pure science is an actual world. For no real experience of art, be it of moving or static pictures or of drama, is a passive panorama of phenomenal objects, for both its existence and its character are determined by the creative interest of artist and spectator, actor and producer. The world of independent causeless events as pictured by "science" is equally unreal. For the mere event is itself an abstraction— there are no mere events, but only experience events—and as a human enterprise, science is concerned, not with the mere statement of statistical uniformities among past events, but with their use in the prediction and transformation of future experience into more valuable forms. The "mere" or "pure" scientist is an abstraction from the actual man, who is no passive observer of a given, independent world, but one who purposefully interferes with its course every time he sets up a piece of apparatus in his laboratory, makes the record of an observation, or performs the ordinary activities of a human being.

A causeless world is not only an unreal world—it is not even a possible world. The fact that one can construct a set of propositions internally consistent among themselves, affirming the existence of a certain kind of world, does not prove that such a world is a possible world. If this world is constructed of abstractions, it is not a possible world, for only the concrete is a possible existence. Of course, if what is meant by a possible world be simply one which is internally consistent, then, to say that such a world is possible is to utter a tautology and to say nothing as to the possibility of its being a fact. To show this, and to show that the concrete, actual world is a world of causes, will be the main result of the following chapters devoted to the investigation and critique of the causal concept. A candid scrutiny of experience and of contemporary scientific thought leads, we shall prove, to the rehabilitation of the concept of cause.

First, however, we must get before us the essential facts covered by the causal concept. I shall set these facts out very briefly, as follows:

1. It is recognized by all philosophers that causality presupposes change, and, in particular, to use the language of contemporary philosophical analysis, a succession of events. I do not say that causality is concerned exclusively with events or can be understood merely in terms of events—I shall, indeed, show that this is not true—but I am saying, as all philosophers would say, that in a static world there would be no causality, and with whatever else causality is concerned, it is concerned with events. Causal enquiry is always concerned with happenings: with what caused this earthquake, this illness, this Italo-Ethiopian war, or with what are the effects of this illness, this depression, this war. The practical interest in causality is with events: how to cure this illness, stop this war, alleviate this depression, build this house, or mend this road. The illustrations cited are obviously of systems or complexes of events; and, as we shall note, we are inevitably brought, in any causal enquiry, to a consideration of systems, even though we may seem to be concerned with single events—the murder of an archduke, the fall of this stone, the pumping of this water—for these, on further analysis, turn out to be whole strings of events. It is doubtful whether we ever have

to do with a true minimal event in the causal enquiries either of science or of practical life. Nevertheless, the strings of events with which we are usually concerned have a unity which impels us to select them from the vast background of all events. They are, for the most part, though not always, confined to a restricted region of space, they have a distinctive qualitative pattern, and they belong to a limited span of time. Since all events are unique, those that we call causes and those that we call effects are unique: this event causes that event.

2. Despite the uniqueness of the events among which the causal relation holds, such events are always instances of classes of events, and the causal relation can be stated—and usually is stated—as holding between classes. Thus, we not only say that the European war, together with an expansion of credit, together with a fall of prices, together with similar events caused the depression of 1929—, but we also say that any background of recent general war, together with an expansion of credit, together with a fall of prices, and so on, is always followed by a depression; or, again, we not only say that Socrates' drinking of the hemlock caused his death, but also that whenever people drink hemlock, they die; we not only say that this stream of water quenched that fire, but that water quenches fire. The possibility of asserting causality between classes of events is equivalent to what we call the lawfulness of nature. A recent writer [1] has, however, insisted that causality between unique events is primary, and that cause in the sense of causal law is secondary; but this is a mistake, for the unique happening is always capable of generalization and the possibility of generalization is, as we shall see, essential to causality. Even such a unique occurrence as that Brutus killed Caesar can be generalized, as, first, that Brutus would kill any tyrant, generalizing Caesar, and, secondly that any brave patriot would kill any tyrant, generalizing Brutus. The possibility of this type of generalization is obviously necessary to the practical value of causality. Moreover, apart from causal laws we do not, in general, know what is the cause or the effect of an event. From the mere fact that the boiling of this water is the sequent of the heating of this water, I do not know that the heating is the cause of the boiling, for it might be true, for all that I could know from the single

[1] C. J. Ducasse, *Causation and Types of Necessity* (Seattle: University of Washington Press, 1924).

case, that the boiling was caused by something else in close connection with the heating. Only after repeated trials of heating water and finding that boiling follows, under the most diverse circumstances, can I have a well-founded suspicion that the one is the cause of the other.

3. The regularity of the sequence of events of the kind *b* following on events of the kind *a* is not a mere matter of history, for there is some sort of "necessary" or internal connection, direct or indirect, between such events which justifies an inference from a sequence of the kind *a* that has occurred to the probable occurrence of a sequence of the kind *b*. That is to say, prediction is possible. It used to be thought that the inference was certain, but we now know that it is probable only. Yet, as we shall show at length in our next chapter, the fact that the prediction is only probable does not eliminate the need for an underlying connection in causal sequences of the kind *a, b* that have occurred; the existence of such a connection in the past is our sole reason for belief in the probability of a future sequence of the kind. Only so are we justified in using our knowledge of the past for guidance in creating new states of affairs in accordance with a plan—memory of the past being transformed into expectation regarding the future. Only so again do statements contrary to fact have validity, as when we say, for example, that if the United States had not entered the War on the side of the Allies there would have been a peace without victory. Such statements are interesting for the reason that they are not concerned with the coming to be of a new sequence of a kind that has already occurred, but with a hypothetical sequence that has never occurred and will never occur, although, to be sure, they are made on the basis of repeated sequences of a related kind. Equally significant are statements asserting the probability of the occurrence of sequences of a kind that have not yet occurred, on the basis, nevertheless, as in the preceding case, of similar sequences that have occurred. All creative work depends upon the possibility of making such predictions, as when an artist expects to get a certain result from a combination of pigments not tried before, or as when a chemist who has invented the formula for a new dye predicts its properties before it is manufactured. An adequate theory of causation must, then, take account not only of what we may call routine predictions, but also of con-

trary-to-fact predictions and what we may, I think, call creative predictions.

4. The next moment in the analysis of causation I shall call origination. By this I mean that if we consider a series of events and enquire into their cause we come inevitably to some center or complex of centers as a source or starting point. We see a series of concentric waves on the surface of a pond; we pass from the later waves to the earlier, then to the dropping of a pebble into the water, from this, finally, to some small boy's act, which we recognize as the *fons et origo* of all the wavelike events. Or we find certain novelties springing up in the life of a people, and we notice that we can trace them all to the deed of some single man whom we call a reformer. Events of great moment are happening in Europe, some in Asia, and eventually some in America, and we know that they all spread out from the act of the assassin who killed the Archduke Franz Ferdinand, in Sarajevo. We observe rays of light streaming out into the most distant parts of space, and we can trace them back to a certain locus which we call a candle. Using this last illustration as typical, we might call this principle the principle of radiation. For from every focus we find series of events spreading out in wavelike form in space and in time, like light radiated from innumerable sources. And in human affairs, on the basis of this principle, we hold some one individual responsible for—to blame for—what may happen.

5. Equally important, however, is a principle that operates in a sense opposed to this one; I shall call it the principle of convergence or absorption. We trace the series of waves on the surface of the pond to the small boy's deed, but, on further enquiry, we find that this very deed was itself determined by thoughts and acts in the minds of a whole gang of boys; the crime which, originating in the mind of the Serbian assassin, caused all Europe to break into flames, was inspired by the sentiments of a group of conspirators. In the end, it is never a single focus that is responsible, or to blame, but a neighborhood, a system of foci. A deeper enquiry shows that we cannot stop even with the gang in our search for the causes of the boy's deed, but must go on and trace it to his parents and associates, in short, to that whole neighborhood which we call his environment. Similarly, with regard to the origins of the Great War, we discover

that the causes lie further than the band of patriots, that a wide
network of economic and political systems is involved. Every
focus is a point of absorption of influences that converge upon it;
and from it, in turn, influences diverge, to be absorbed by neighboring foci. It might seem as if this principle were contradictory to the preceding one; for did not the principle of radiation
imply that each series of events had a single cause? Here, in
truth, we have a problem, but it is clear that, somehow, the opposing principles are both valid; for the facts show that origination is at once single—that a series of events starts from one
focus—and multiple, issuing from a neighborhood, for the focus
from which the series of events springs has been determined to be
what it is by its neighborhood. It is interesting to notice, furthermore, that sometimes a focus seems to be a mere point of
transmission of influences from its neighborhood, like a trans-
parent medium through which light passes, and that at other
times there is some reconstruction of influences, even as in an
opaque medium there is refraction of light, so that what is received is not merely passed on but given a new direction. And
I should suppose that the latter, on deeper enquiry, is always
found to be the case, which points the way to the solution of the
problem just posed and provides a partial answer to the old
question of freedom versus determinism. For, although the
series of events is determined by the whole neighborhood—and,
in the end, by the universe—nevertheless it is determined in a
preëminent way by the single focus which we ordinarily call its
cause or source, inasmuch as there the manifold influences from
the environment are given a unique form, from which subsequent
events take their distinctive coloring. There are, moreover, as
we shall show in our chapter on levels of causality (Chap. XIV),
relations of dominance and subordination among the determining factors of an event or a series of events, relations which justify the common practice in the human social world of holding
one person more responsible than others among those who are
responsible, as when we hold the ringleader more accountable
than his subordinates in a conspiracy, or the ruler more liable
than his subjects, or when we praise the general more than the
private for a victory. So important is this principle of relative
dominance and subordination of causal factors that we might
well have made it a separate point in our analysis.

6. The last principle, conservation, is much the same as what Russell, following Semon, has called "mnemic causality." I shall begin my explanation by citing an illustration which I heard Morton Prince give in California, in 1909. It is a common occurrence in domestic life for the wife to get angry with her husband for what he regards as a very trivial and inadequate provocation. The absent-minded man has perhaps put the baby's rattle in the ice chest instead of the bureau drawer. This single act is indeed trivial and no just ground for anger, but the fact is that such things have happened for the last ten years, for as long as the couple have been married. And when the wife becomes angry she is reacting, not to the husband's single stupid deed, but to a whole set of such deeds, and, as a protest against the class of deeds, her anger has some justification. The principle involved in this banal and bourgeois illustration is indispensable for the explanation of personal change and social development. It explains the transformations in the attachments of friends and lovers, the resentment of the lower against the upper classes when the latter are overbearing and forgetful of their responsibilities, for these changes are seldom the result of single acts, which can be forgiven and forgotten, but of many acts in the past. Since in all such cases the events to be explained happen as the result of past—and therefore nonexistent—occurrences, the problem arises as to how the latter, although past and nonexistent, can be effective nevertheless; and the answer is, as the name of the principle we are invoking indicates, that they or their surrogates must somehow be conserved in the present situation out of which the new event springs. An adequate theory of causality must provide for this conservation.

We have now before us the main elements of the concept of causality, with the exception of one very important phase—the fact of levels of causality—which I am neglecting at this moment because of its difficult and controversial character; but, aside from this matter, the account above represents, I believe, a fair summary of the principles which, because of their interconnection, may properly be brought together under one concept, "causality." Although there may be divergent views as to the interpretation of any one of them, all have, I believe, gone essentially unchallenged except the third—the existence of an internal relation or "necessary connection" among the events in a causal series. This factor has been attacked from two points of view: (1) from the phenomenological side, on the ground that we have no experience of necessity and, therefore, in accordance with what we have called the empirical principle, no valid concept of necessity, and (2) from the point of view of the philosophy of scientific method, that we have no need for it in the work of science. We shall devote the remainder of this chapter to a consideration of the first of these attacks, leaving the second to a chapter by itself.

The attack on causal necessity from the phenomenological aspect received its classic statement from David Hume, and since little or no advance has been made over his argument as set forth in the *Treatise of Human Nature* I shall use it as a text for my discussion. The essence of Hume's thought is distilled in the following sentences from "On the Idea of Necessary Connexion":

> The idea of necessity arises from some impression. There is no impression convey'd by our senses which can give rise to that idea. It must, therefore, be derived from some internal impression, or impression of reflection. There is no internal impression that has any relation to the present business, but that propensity, which custom produces, to pass from an object to the idea of its usual attendant. This therefore is the essence of necessity. Upon the whole, necessity is something that exists in the mind, not in objects; nor is it possible for us to form the most distant idea of it, considered as a quality in bodies. Either we have no idea of necessity, or necessity is that determination of the thought to pass from causes to effects, and from effects to causes, according to their experienc'd union.[1]

Such are Hume's own words. We shall not attempt to enter upon the fascinating problems of interpretation that arise as soon as one tries to explicate Hume's words in terms of the general drift of his philosophy, or dwell upon possible inconsistencies lurking within them, but shall rather interpret them in terms of our own categories and distinctions, in a fashion which is nevertheless true to the general Humean spirit. We shall find that, so interpreted, there is much truth in them—but not all truth, and the small remainder is of crucial metaphysical importance.

In the first place, I take Hume to be saying that in the world of what we have been calling phenomenal objects there is no

[1] David Hume, *Treatise of Human Nature*, Part III, Sec. 14; ed. by T. H. Green and T. H. Grose (London: Longmans, Green and Co., 1898), I, 460.

observable necessary connection among the events in which such objects participate. If I watch one billiard ball roll on the table, strike another, and displace it, what I observe is a mere succession of event A, ball striking ball, followed by event B, second ball moving in a certain direction and at a certain speed. That is all. Absolutely no connection between the events which would enable me to understand why the second ball should move when struck, or move at the speed and in the direction in which it does move, is observable. And just as nothing of the kind is observable in the single case, so nothing of the kind is observable if I watch many, a thousand, a million, an indefinite number of occurrences of the kind. Of course, as a result of observing many such incidents, I may get into the habit of expecting event B to follow upon event A, but whatever other warrant there may be for this habit, there is nothing that I can observe in the succession of these events to justify me in trusting it in any new case, when, observing A, I am tempted to predict the approaching existence of B. And it will not do to object, on Bergsonian grounds, that I have no right to separate event A from event B, maintaining that there is really only a single event AB with its own indiscerptible unity, and that Hume's difficulty arises solely from trying to break this event up into two parts, ignoring the internal unity within the single, whole event. For the succession *breaks itself:* now A exists, when B does not yet exist; then B exists, when A no longer exists—this is especially obvious in cases where, A having existed, I have to wait for B. And when I observe the existence of A, B not yet existing, I cannot find anything in A which requires that it should be followed by B rather than by C, say; and no scrutiny of my memory or of any record of the succession A-followed-by-B, or of any smaller parts of this succession, within A or within B, after it has occurred, will reveal a reason why, starting anywhere, the subsequent parts of the succession were whatever they were. If, I repeat, I look anywhere in the world of pure phenomenal objects, the succession shows itself to be a brute fact, nothing more.

The fact that, in making predictions from causal laws, we deduce our result from premises has led to the supposition that there is a relation between events analogous to, or identical with, the relation of implication. This supposition is, however, false, for the reason that the relations expressed in the premises are not themselves internal or "necessary." The formulation of the premises is an induction from past events among which the relations have held; but since there is no necessity that these and only these relations should hold among such events, the supposition that they will continue to hold in the future is, so far as anything can be observed among the events themselves, groundless. Hence, although the deductions from the premises are logically necessary, their applicability to the expected events is problematic, and no logical relation between the events is proved. The necessity that exists in the relation of implication is a necessity that obtains among propositions; to suppose that the same relation exists among events is an unwarranted introjection.

As an example of the fallacy under consideration, let us take the case of a billiard ball struck by two other balls simultaneously, each of the latter impinging in a different direction and with a different velocity; then, in accordance with the law of the parallelogram of forces, we can deduce the direction and the velocity of the resulting motion of the first ball; but it is overlooked that this law does not itself express any necessary relations, because, for all that we can see from an examination of events of the kind, they might very well have been otherwise; hence there is no reason to think that the law will hold of like events in the future. Or consider the Newtonian law of gravitation, $G = \dfrac{mM}{D^2} K.$ If we substitute constants for the variables in this equation, we can deduce—and the deduction will have logical necessity—the gravitational forces between given masses m_1 and m_2 at a given distance, d_1; but the fact that the deduction is necessary does not prove that the gravitational relations between the given masses at the given distance is one that must obtain for all time, for we cannot discern in the nature of the elements of the situation any "necessity" that the relations should be as they are expressed in the law; in particular, we cannot see why gravitational force should vary as the square rather than as the cube of the distance, or as the product rather than, let us say, the sum of the masses involved; or why the gravitational constant should be K rather than L. And if the premises—or "law"—may be different, the conclusion may be different also. Once again we find ourselves confronted with blind fact, not logical lucidity.

What is true of phenomenal objects is true also of the sensa that function as signs of them: no internal relation or necessary connection is observable. If I watch the changing visual shapes that mean to me the clouds, there is no ground discernible among them why this shape should follow that, rather than a different, shape; or if I watch the succession of colors of a sunset as they fade, I can find no connection among the color events that would account for their succession. It is true, to be sure, that I can explain the succession of shapes or of colors in terms of the laws of reflection and refraction of light and the precipitation of liquids; but in so doing I have passed beyond the sphere of mere sensa to that of phenomenal or scientific objects, among which, also, as we have just seen, there are no internal connections. The laws of light and of liquids are mere statements of relations that have been found to hold for a time; they do not express necessary connections. There is, moreover, a further element of the inexplicable in the relation of these laws to sensa: the correlation between so many electromagnetic vibrations and red, for example, or of a different number of vibrations per second and blue is just a brute fact; we cannot see why the colors should not be interchanged, or why, given such a correlation in the past, it should persist in the future.

It is clear, therefore, that in the realms of sensa, of common-sense phenomenal objects and of scientific law, Hume's thesis is established: in these realms there is no observable necessary connection or internal relation between events, nothing which could serve as an "impression," or, as we should say, an experience, from which the concept of such a connection could be derived.

It is noticeable, however, that all these realms are abstract and so have no existence by themselves. Neither sensa nor phenomenal or scientific objects have any metaphysical standing of their own. Only as factors in the concrete experience of a monad have they substance. May it not then be true that if we turn from them to concrete experience, and especially if we look to its basis, the life of volition, we shall find the internal relations or necessary connections that we seek? This, the central thesis of every voluntaristic metaphysic, is, I shall show, the case. And we shall discover that even in those abstract realms where internal connections are not to be found, they are yet to be found when taken in that living unity with volition without which they have no existence.

I can best express what is meant through some examples of concrete experience, analogous to examples already employed in another context. It is, let us say, a sunless winter's day full of hard work, one of a succession of such days; there comes a pause in the day's activities, when suddenly into the mind flock a train of images—a boat and a stream, and bright warm sunlight, banks with green verdure and protecting branches of trees, the sound of the dipping of oars and the singing of birds. If, now, we consider the sequence of these images just by themselves, we discover no connection among them that would explain why these and just these images should arise in the mind rather than some other set of images, or why they should have the order that they do have. Nor could we see why such a train of images should ever arise again, as it does when similar circumstances of wintry sunless days recur. But, on the other hand, if we study the images, not by themselves, but in connection with the desires which they obviously express, we come to understand two things: first, that—in conjunction, of course, with the total situation in which they occur—desire has brought these images into existence, and, secondly, why it has brought just such images as these and in just such an order as this. We become witnesses of a creative act—our own act—and behold an example of a necessary connection or internal relation between events which explains why one image is linked to another in the train. Taken by themselves in abstraction, they are an incomprehensible series of events, but viewed as satisfying a desire, they are tied one to another through the desire that creates and interpenetrates them all.

Or look within yourself when, in accordance with a plan, you are walking home: you will find a succession of kinesthetic sensations, as step follows step. If now you consider this train of sensations in abstraction, all by themselves, you will find no internal relation among its members—no necessary connection between one step experience and another—but, on the other hand, if you view it, as it should be viewed, in relation to your plan, you can see that each step experience is necessary, and necessary in relation to the others, as fulfilling the plan. Or if you sit at the piano and play a musical phrase, sound after sound will arise in your mind; and if you view the sounds as mere sounds, you will never perceive why, given the succession of tones

you will hear the following tones

But if, on the other hand, you consider the tones in connection with the intention to play the piece, which you enjoy, then you understand immediately what brought the tones into existence and why, given the first series of tones, the second set should follow, and in the order in which they do follow. In similar fashion, if you are listening to someone else play that choral, and hear the first few tones, there is nothing you can find in those tones taken by themselves which should require that they be followed by the other tones that do follow. Of course, if you have heard the piece played before, or if you play it yourself, you will expect the other tones that belong in the piece, but, as Hume showed, this expectation has no basis in the mere tones themselves. It is only when, as in the other cases cited, you take the tones in connection with the purpose of the player and the value they have for him, that you know that, given the earlier tones, the others must follow; you know that there exists in the player something that will create those tones, and just those tones, and in the order in which they occur. And generally, when within yourself, or in your social environment, you can find events connected with value—with purpose, plan, desire, intention—you have discovered not mere succession, but necessary connection, and a basis for the repetition of the succession.

In the course of the history of philosophy objections have been raised again and again to this account of causal necessity; but I think they have all been summarized in a single passage of Hume's *Treatise of Human Nature*. Before citing this passage, however, I wish to recall our answer to an objection not stated by Hume in exactly the form in which it constantly recurs in more recent literature; for, having met this obstacle, we can, I believe, meet all the others that have been thrown in our path. The difficulty we encountered (see p. 59) was the fact that from a mere desire or intention known to ourselves we can never predict with certainty any event or train of events, because they depend upon so many other conditions. In a daydream no image events would occur without intact cerebral connections; and if one is stricken with paralysis, the intention to walk or to play the piano will not enable one to do either. Our reply to this objection was that no one ever thought that a known intention was the sole ground of any event or series of events, but only that it is *a* ground, and, in the cases cited, an example of internal relation or necessary connection among the events which it penetrates. It is a necessary, not a sufficient, condition of their occurrence. In view of the multiple determination of every event, to deny that a factor is a determinant of an event because there are other determinants would be tantamount to destroying all determination. What we claimed was that, among the coöperating causes of events, desire is one. We are now claiming further that it provides the impression or experience from which the concept of causal necessity is derived, and hence, on any empirical or Humean basis, provides a justification for it. In the sequel we shall make the final claim that the tendency to read into nature intentions generically similar to our own, characteristic of the aboriginal animistic view, is, under definite limitations, justifiable *as philosophy*, and that we can understand why, nevertheless, science has led to the abandonment of this tendency as an element in the common-sense practical picture of the world.

We are now ready to consider the objections of Hume. For convenience I shall quote the entire relevant passage as it stands in the *Treatise*:

Some have asserted that we feel an energy or power, in our own minds; and that having in this manner acquired the idea of power, we transfer that quality to matter, where we are not able immediately to discover it. The motions of our body, and the thoughts and sentiments of our mind, (say they) obey the will; nor do we seek any farther to acquire a just notion of force or power. But to convince us how fallacious this reasoning is, we need only consider that the will being here considered as a cause, has no more a discoverable connexion with its effects, than any material cause has with its proper effects. So far from perceiving a connexion between an act of volition and a motion of the body, 'tis allowed that no effect is more inexplicable from the powers and essence of thought and motion. Nor is the empire of the will over our mind more intelligible. The effect is there distinguishable and separable from the cause, and could not be foreseen without the experience of their constant conjunction. We have command over our mind to a certain degree, but beyond that lose all empire over it. And 'tis evidently impossible to fix any precise boundaries to our authority, where we consult our experience. In short, the actions of the mind are, in this respect, the same with those of matter. We perceive only constant conjunction; nor can we ever reason beyond it. No internal impression has an apparent energy more than external objects have. Since, therefore, matter is confessed by philosophers to operate by an unknown force, we should in vain attempt to obtain an idea of force by consulting our own minds.[1]

In this passage Hume makes three points: (1) that the connection between an act of volition and a motion of the body is inexplicable; (2) that the "empire of the will" over the mind is equally unintelligible, because all we perceive there is a "constant conjunction," not an "apparent energy" or necessary connection between the will as hypothetical cause and its supposed effects, such as new feelings or ideas; the effect there, as in the case of external impressions, being "distinguishable and separable" from the cause, hence incapable of being foreseen without their constant conjunction; and, (3) that even if, as seems to be admitted, we do have "command over our mind to a certain degree," beyond that we "lose all empire over it."

The last point—to begin with the easiest—we have already met by calling attention to the obvious truth that a divided authority is still authority; there are, indeed, external controls over our ideas (we shall ourselves make much of this fact in a later chapter, and we have already taken note of it, from a different point of view, in our theory of countercontrol), yet the existence of these controls, while it limits, in no way invalidates the intuited control exerted within experience by the will. And it makes no difference to the reality of this control that we are unaware of the

[1] Hume, *op. cit.*, Part III, Sec. 4; Green and Grose, I, 455.

complexity of countercontrol, which may be as great as the complexity of the electromagnetic field of the brain.

The second point is the most important and is met by showing that Hume has misread the facts. For it is said that the will as cause is distinguishable and separable from its effects, whereas, although distinguishable, it is not separable: it is not separable in time, since it persists alongside its effects; and it is not separable in existence, because, as we have seen, it penetrates effects, and they have no being apart from it. Thus, as I hum a tune, my intention to hum does not cease as the tones arise, but persists throughout their rise and fall, and when it ceases they cease; the intention and the sounds are not two facts, but two aspects of a single fact. It is equally untrue that we perceive no more than a constant conjunction between these aspects, for the connection between an event *as fulfilling a plan* and that plan is something more. And, because of this connection, we are able to expect the occurrence of an event within experience from the intention to produce the event, even when the observation of constant conjunction is impossible, as it is impossible whenever we do something that we have never done before—whenever, for example, we play a new composition or utter a novel thought. All creative action involves the confident expectation that deed shall follow upon intention. And our confidence is not based, as one might perhaps interpose, upon the general conjunction of plans and purposed events—which, as Hume himself showed, would not provide a reliable basis—but upon the intuition of what he called "energy" in plans themselves. Naturally, the success of our expectation depends upon the coöperation of a system of causes external to the plan, in the body and in nature —all causation depends upon coöperation—but the significant fact is that we do intuit what Hume called "necessary connection" between any intention and any event that fulfils it.

The first point offers problems somewhat different from those involved in the other two, because it takes us explicitly out of personal experience into the external world. And until we have come to some definite conclusions regarding the relation between mind and body we are not in a position to do the matter full justice. There is, however, one consideration that may be advanced at this step in the development of our argument, namely, that in this passage, despite his original and revolutionary ideas, Hume is still, as so often, under the influence of the Cartesian dualism of mind and matter, volition and motion, a dualism that is meaningless for those of us who do not admit the existence of "vacuous actualities" such as matter and motion, in the physical sense; and once this dualism is overcome, the objection loses most of its force. It does, nevertheless, as we have allowed, retain some of its power—until a satisfactory theory of the coöperation of causes within the mind, volitions, and causes without the mind has been developed. Later we shall offer a theory which we believe will eliminate some of the mystery from the relationship.

In our discussion of causality we have freely used the terms "necessary" and "necessity" in the phrases "necessary connection" and "causal necessity," and have sought to show that we have an experience from which the concept meant by these terms is derived—in other words, that the concept is not a factitious or empty one. We have not, however, given any precise definition of the concept. We shall now attempt to remedy this omission.

It would, I think, be admitted on all hands that the status of the concept of necessity remains at the present time very obscure and equivocal. According to the older tradition in philosophy, the concept applied to certain "truths," called "necessary" or "a priori" truths, such as the principles of logic and arithmetic, certain laws in mechanics like the conservation of mass and energy, certain propositions in geometry like the parallel-line axiom, and even certain principles in ethics such as the "greatest happiness for the greatest number" and "justice." This class of truths contrasted with another class called "empirical" or "a posteriori." Contemporary philosophy would, on the other hand, exclude all the propositions in geometry and mechanics, is hopelessly divided with regard to the necessity of any ethical propositions, and is far from clear with regard to those propositions which have always seemed most indubitably "necessary"— the principles of logic and arithmetic. It is very striking that, while the concept "necessary" and its opposite "impossible" are freely used with reference to these last propositions, little attempt is made clearly to define them. My own view is that the concept has no meaning when applied to a single proposition of any sort taken by itself, and applies only to the relation of one proposition to another. In order to show that this is true I shall examine some typical discussions, meager as they are, in contemporary literature. I shall begin with Russell.

In Russell's *Introduction to Mathematical Philosophy* we read:

> . . . The traditional view was that among true propositions, some were necessary, while others were merely contingent or assertoric; while among false propositions some were impossible, namely, those whose contradictories were necessary, while others merely happened not to be true. In fact, however, there was never any clear account of what was added to truth by the concept of necessity. In the case of propositional functions, the threefold division is obvious. If "ϕ_x" is an undetermined value of a certain propositional function, it will be *necessary* if the proposition is always true, *possible* if it is sometimes true, and *impossible* if it is never true.[1]

To this definition of "necessary" as applied to propositional functions, we may add the definition of "necessity" as applied to a proposition in the essay "On the Nature of Cause" in *Mysticism and Logic:* "A proposition is necessary with respect to a given constituent when it is the value, with that constituent as argument, of a necessary propositional function. In other words, when it remains true however that constituent may be varied." [2] For example, the propositional function, If x is a man, x is mortal, would be a necessary propositional function because it is true for all values of x; while the proposition, If Socrates is a man, Socrates is mortal, would be a necessary proposition. But if these definitions were adequate, there would be no essential difference between a necessary propositional function and a contingent propositional function, provided all the values of the former happened to be true; and, a fortiori, there would be no essential difference between a necessary proposition and a contingent proposition except that the former was one of the values of a propositional function whose values happened all to be true, that is to say, were all as a matter of fact true, while the latter was a value of a propositional function, of which all the values were not, as a matter of fact, true. The illustrations offered of propositional function and proposition bring this out. And if this were the full meaning of "necessary" as applied to propositions, it is obvious that we could dispense with it altogether.

Moreover, it may be objected to Russell's interpretation of the meaning of necessity as applied to propositions that it fails to cover the difference between propositions such as (1) If x is red, x is colored, or (2) p or not-p is true, where p denotes any proposition, or (3) Two plus two equals four, on the one hand,

[1] Bertrand Russell, *Introduction to Mathematical Philosophy* (New York: The Macmillan Co., 1919), p. 165.

[2] *Idem, Mysticism and Logic* (New York: W. W. Norton and Co., 1929), p. 207.

and such a proposition as, If *x* is a man, *x* is mortal for all values of *x*, on the other hand.   Propositions of both types are, of course, regarded as being always true; but the latter are considered so because as a matter of fact men are mortal, or because some other such state of affairs exists, while the former are thought to be true independent of any empirical situation whatever.   We can know that the latter are true, it is claimed, only as a result of empirical observation, but we can know that the former are true by the mere inspection of propositions themselves.   Yet this account of the matter, also, is unsatisfactory, because a great deal that is unexplained is assumed in the supposition that propositions of the former type are true at all. For these propositions are not true in the sense that through them, taken by themselves, we can know anything about the world of matters of fact.   From (1) we cannot know that the red things of the world are colored, for we do not know, from this proposition alone, that there are any red things; from (2) we cannot know that judgments about existing things are either true or false, for we do not know either that there are any judgments or that there are any things to judge; from (3) we cannot know that a class of two existing things taken together with another separate class of two existing things are four things, for, again, we do not know, from the proposition taken by itself, that there are any things at all.   As Wittgenstein has said, we know nothing about the weather when we know that it is either raining or not raining: we do not know that it is raining and we do not know that it is not raining.   We must combine a so-called necessary proposition with some empirical proposition before we can get a "picture of fact": to the proposition, If *x* is red, *x* is colored, I must add the proposition, There are red things, when I can know that there are colored things; and so on for the others and for those like them.   But if necessary propositions are not pictures of fact, how can they be true at all?   And that they really are not true—and perhaps not even propositions, for a proposition would seem to be something that is either true or false— appears to follow from a point which Professor C. H. Langford makes,[1] namely, that necessary propositions have, strictly considered, no contradictories.   The contradictory of, Two plus two equals four, is not, as one might suppose, Two plus two is not

[1] C. I. Lewis and C. H. Langford, *Symbolic Logic* (New York and London: The Century Co., 1932), pp. 477, 478, 484.

equal to four, for the latter statement is not a false proposition, but nonsense; and, similarly, to say, If *x* is red, it is not colored, is not to utter a proposition, but to gibber; and so with the rest. But a genuine proposition always has a contradictory. So-called necessary truths are therefore not truths, and therefore not propositions, but "analytic expressions," for it is clear that what one is doing when one says, If *x* is red, *x* is colored, is analyzing the nature of redness; so, to say, Two plus two equals four, is to analyze the nature of four; and to say that a proposition is either true or false is to analyze what we mean by "proposition"; in other words, what we are doing in all these so-called necessary propositions is *defining* "color," "four," "proposition." And clearly all strict implications between analytic expressions are themselves analytic expressions, for if *a* and *b* are analytic expressions, and *a* strictly implies *b*, then the logical product of *a* and not-*b* is not, as Lewis has claimed, an "impossible" proposition, but no proposition at all, in other words, nonsense. And, by the way, to define the strict implication between *a* and *b* as "the logical product of *a* and not-*b* is impossible," is to define *ignotum per ignotius*, for what is meant by "impossible"?

Are there, then, no necessarily true propositions? And is there no logical necessity? The answer to both questions is yes: necessary propositions are all propositions that are inferences: a proposition is necessarily true if it follows from a true proposition. If *a* entails *b*, and *a* is true, then *b* is necessarily true. But notice, necessity is relative, never absolute; a proposition is necessary only in relation to another proposition that is true. To say that a single proposition is necessarily true is either not to say anything more than just that it is true or to say that we can know that it is true because it follows from another proposition which we know to be true; we do not need, therefore, to discover whether it is true by intuition or observation. In other words, logical necessity is simply that relation between propositions which makes inference possible.[1]

If this be the meaning of logical necessity, the question before us is whether, and on what ground, causal propositions are necessary, a question which we now see to be equivalent to the query: Is it possible, and if so how, from propositions expressing past or present states of affairs to infer propositions expressing

[1] Cf. F. H. Bradley, *Principles of Logic*, Second Edition (London: Oxford University Press, 1922), Book I, chap. vii, pp. 199–203.

future states of affairs?   And the view which I am maintaining
is the contradictory of the view expressed in a famous book by
Wittgenstein as follows:

> 5.135   In no way can an inference be made from the existence of one state
> of affairs to the existence of another entirely different from it. . . .[1]
> 5.1361   The events of the future cannot be inferred from those of the present.[1]

I have been asserting on the contrary that from propositions
stating that certain events are happening or have happened, I
can infer other propositions asserting that certain other events
will happen; and this inference is no less genuine albeit only
probable.   And, if I am right, the reason that we can make this
inference is not that there is some direct necessary connection
between one event and another—how could there be any such
connection between a present event and a future event, when
future events do not exist?—but because there is a creative will
which, having brought forth the one event needs the other to
complete its intention.   If we know the intention, we can infer
from the given event to the future event.   As we have seen, the
sound events of a melody, taken abstractly, have no necessary
connection among themselves, but each is connected with the will
that creates them; hence, indirectly, they are connected among
themselves, and the earlier may be said to be the causes of the
later, and from the earlier the later may be inferred.   This connection with the creative will is the "causal necessity" about
which there has been so much controversy among philosophers.
This necessity is not, however, the "logical necessity" that obtains
between causal *propositions* in relation to each other, when we
deduce one from another in prediction, but it is the basis of
that.   That is a relation between propositions, whereas this is
a relation between an intention and the events that fulfil it, a
necessity which, as Plato said, is not logical,[2] but which all lovers
know and understand when, out of their love, deeds spring.   If,
indeed, the world were independent of the will and everything
we wished happened as a mere favor of fate, there would be no
causal necessity.   But everyone who has ever willed anything and
found that what he willed leaped into existence knows that this
is not so.

[1] L. Wittgenstein, *Tractatus Logico-philosophicus* (New York: Harcourt,
Brace and Co., 1922) .
[2] *Republic* 458, d 5.

XIII

Causality: Methodological Critique; Causality and Probability

IN OUR last chapter we studied the critique of causality proceeding from the analysis of experience offered by Hume. We shall now study the critique of causality advanced by contemporary students of the method of science, and apply the emerging insight to the problems of induction and natural law. If the first critique belongs characteristically to the eighteenth century, the second is typically the contribution of our own time. Between lie the efforts of Kant and others, at the dawn and during the course of the nineteenth century, to defend causality against Hume. These efforts forge a link between the two critiques, for the twentieth century has sought to prove the negative of what the nineteenth century was bent on demonstrating: the one tried to prove that science cannot do its work without assuming the validity of causality; the other tries to show that science has no need of causality. In its study of the matter the twentieth century has gone far beyond the nineteenth in scope and depth, for whereas the latter based its reflections on the physical sciences only, as Kant did, the former, besides effecting a fertile union of mathematics, logic, and methodology, has brought the social sciences into the picture. Even to draw the outline of this magnificent synthesis is beyond the scope of the present book; our task is the simpler, but no less difficult, one of appraising the validity of the underlying assumptions.

The most important result claimed for the newer critique of causality is the substitution of probability for the old concept of necessity. From this the inference is drawn, not that causality is disproved, but that it is rendered superfluous, and, in the long run, a superfluous concept is equivalent, for scientific purposes, to a false one. The relation of probability to causality will be, therefore, the center of our reflections.

Leaving the sciences out of consideration for the moment,

we can show that within the circle of ordinary human affairs—
so the argument would begin—probability is not only all that we
have, but all that we need. In our intimate relations with our
friends and associates it is not indispensable that we should be
able to make infallible predictions regarding their behavior, for
our confidence in them does not depend upon invariable regularity, but only upon constancy and fidelity for the most part.
The wise man expects and is prepared for disappointment and
disillusion as being all part of life. Indeed, a certain measure of
unpredictability and waywardness adds spice and zest to social
relations. On its more mechanical side, also, life goes forward
very well on the same basis of reliability tempered with surprise.
That the trains should always run on time, that the bus should
be at the corner every day and at the very minute that we expect
it, is not essential; it is only essential that in a very large proportion of cases this should be true, justifying us in the belief that
the train or bus will probably be there when we want it. Just
so, instruction can proceed if students can expect the professor
to be at class most of the time, and if he can expect them to be
on hand with fair regularity; but it is not necessary that it should
be known with certainty that the class will be held every day.
In the realms of business and politics certainty is out of the
question, yet business and political activity proceed. No one
can predict with certainty the course of the market, the fluctua-
tions of public opinion, or the alignments of states. "You cannot sometimes always tell," it is said on the "Street." The pru-
dent statesman or man of affairs will be right in the long run,
yet will be ready for surprises. The French statesman could count
on the general coöperation of England, but could not have predicted the separate naval treaty with Germany, nor foretold Hitler's
ten years' peace with Poland. In the arts and professions the situation is no different. Juries cannot be absolutely certain of the
guilt or innocence of the accused, yet can render verdicts that
have a very high degree of probability; physicians cannot be
sure of the effect of a drug on all patients, for there are idiosyn-
crasies, yet they can prescribe correctly most of the time; and this
is enough for the peace and health of the community. And even
when scientific method is applied to social affairs no more than
statistical probability is achieved. The classical examples are
the vital statistics concerning births, deaths, marriages, suicides,

murders, anatomical and physiological measurements, and the like, upon which the various types of insurance, and, more recently, certain forms of administrative policy are based. But mere statistical probability implies the renunciation of certainty in the prediction of individual events, although it offers by way of compensation considerable accuracy in predicting the general character of a group or class.

Now according to the new theory of the methodology of science, no more than statistical probability—although a much higher degree of probability—is obtainable there. The statistical methods first applied with such success in thermodynamics are given universal scope. As a result the centuries-old belief in the exactness and perfect determinability, in accordance with mathematical law, of physical processes is discarded, and the supposed difference in kind between the logic of the physical and the social sciences disappears. The admitted difference in the degree of probability of prediction between the two classes of sciences has no philosophical importance, and with increase in experimental data the analogy between them is becoming closer. Molar phenomena are interpreted as being essentially group phenomena, with regard to the behavior of which, as groups, there may be a very large amount of regularity, and hence the possibility of prediction with a high degree of probability; whereas electronic phenomena are interpreted after the analogy of the social unit, whose conduct is unpredictable, or predictable only so far as the individual is a member of a group.

No doubt it is possible to admit all the facts just cited, as well as many of the interpretations put upon them, and yet find an easy way to rescue the validity of causal necessity in the old-fashioned sense. The way I have in mind is to fall back upon the older subjective theory of probability. According to this way of looking at nature all connections there are necessary, but our judgments in regard to them have no more than probable validity owing to the limitations of our knowledge. Probable judgments are held to express a ratio between data available to us, namely evidence, and all possible data, a ratio that would be transformed into unity—in other language, into certainty—if our knowledge were complete. This way of defending the orthodox theory of causality is, however, all too easy, for it fails to meet the newer theory of probability on its own ground, doing no more than to adhere to the older theory as an alternative dogma. But philosophy is not a choice between dogmatisms. The contemporary frequency theory of probability, which is part and parcel of the newer view of science, conceives of probability not as a dilution of truth with ignorance, but as a type of judgment in conformity with an objectively indeterminate state of affairs. In other words, the fact that scientific judgments are only probable, is not due to our ignorance, but, it is asserted, to the lack of necessary connections in nature herself. A convincing critique of the new philosophy of nature must at least try to remain on the same ground that it occupies, and then show the insufficiency of the concepts which it offers. When this is attempted two lines of criticism emerge, one with regard to the sufficiency of the theory of induction proposed as a basis for probable judgments, the other with regard to the applicability to nature of some of the most fundamental concepts of the new theory of probability itself. The former will occupy our attention first.

Whether potentially certain or unavoidably only probable, scientific judgments are based on the inductive process. An adequate theory of induction is, therefore, presupposed even by a probabilist theory of scientific method. If causality in the old sense is to be discarded, what, then, on this theory, can take the place of the necessary connections between events hitherto conceived to be the sole possible ground of validity of induction? Though recent theories of what might be called "causeless induction" are at variance in detail, they do not differ essentially from that proposed by Charles Peirce, which I shall therefore present for study, as being typical of all.

The theory may be briefly restated as follows. Let us suppose that there exists a collection of objects—beans in a bag, wheat in a hold, or what not. Let us suppose further that we are interested in some predesignated character of the elements of the collection. If now we can obtain a fair sample of the collection (a fair sample being a part sufficiently large, but smaller than the whole, the members of which are selected at random from different subclasses of the whole) and make observations with reference to this character, we shall be able to infer the probable frequency of the character in the whole from its frequency in the sample. Thus if our sample of beans in a bag gives three white to one nonwhite, we can infer that in the whole collection there are probably three times as many white as non-white beans; from which it follows that the chances that any bean in the bag that we select at random shall be white will be as three to one.[1]

We are now invited to conceive of nature as a vast grab bag or pie and of the investigator as like one Jack Horner, who puts in his thumb and pulls out a plum, or sample, from which he is able to infer the frequency among the contents of the bag or pie of any character in which he happens to be interested. He finds, as Galileo found, that all the samples of falling bodies he has investigated illustrate certain functions between abstract relations which we designate by s, t, g, v, a, and the like; he therefore infers that the probability that any new case of a falling body will illustrate such functions between similar abstract relations will be practically one. Or with regard to the tossing of pennies, having found that among his samples about as many heads as tails turn up, he infers that the probability of heads or tails in any toss will be one half.

Admirably ingenious as this theory is, it nevertheless presents great difficulties as a general theory of induction. We may admit the validity of the theory for the sort of example that Peirce employs—collections of "things," like beans in a bag or grains of wheat—and if nature consisted of entities of this sort, the theory might have general validity. But things are only phenomenal objects, apparitions or pictures, having no existence outside the mind. Nature consists not of things, but of events. The physical or "real" black or white ball is a system of events that come and go; so is the fall of a stone, the toss of a penny, the expansion of a bar of steel. The actual situation in induction is a sampling of events that are occurring or have occurred, from which the character of events that will occur, but which, of course, have not happened, is inferred—a very different matter from inferring the character of an existing collection of objects from an existing part or sample. The Peirce theory makes the covert assumption that future events exist as a part of a collection of all events of the kind, and that one can sample this collection and then apply the result of this sampling to any event, future or past; but this whole way of viewing the matter is false, since future events are

[1] Charles Peirce, "The Doctrine of Necessity Examined," in *Chance, Love and Logic* (New York: Harcourt, Brace and Co., 1923), p. 129.

precisely events that do not exist.   The problem of induction is
not that of inferring the whole from the part (for in nature
there is no whole of events), but of inferring the character of
events when they shall exist from the character of events that
have existed; and the question always is, why should events that
are to come have the character—even the merely probable character—the frequency—that events have had in the past?   And
to this question the Peirce theory offers no answer.   Its underlying assumptions are essentially childish and materialistic, without application as soon as nature is conceived of in terms of
events.

The more recent theories of induction, based on newer developments of the theory of probability, as represented by such
men as von Mises [1] and Reichenbach [2] are open to similar and
even graver objections.   For these thinkers induction presupposes the existence in nature of "probability series" of a type
defined by Reichenbach as follows: (1) The frequency of a character among the members of the series (that is to say, the ratio
of the members having the character to all members of the series)
approaches a limit.   This implies, of course, that the series is an
infinite series.   This limiting frequency defines the probability
of the character in the series.   (2) Given a finite section of a
probability series with the length n and the frequency h, then
there exists a probability u that the observed frequency h represents within a limit of exactness $\pm \delta$ the probability within the
whole series, on further prolongation of the series.   This second
characteristic of a probability series is clearly needed in view
of the fact that only a finite section of a series is ever given.   And
finally (3) the greater n is, so much greater is the probability u
that the observed frequency h represents the probability in question, within the limits of accuracy $\pm \delta$; that is to say, this probability increases with n toward one.

With regard to these assumptions I would make the following comments.   First, in nature there are no series of events, for
only the passing event is real.   Second, while it is true that there
are series of *traces* of past events (records made by observers,

[1] R. von Mises, *Wahrscheinlichkeit, Statistik, und Wahrheit* (Wien:
Julius Springer, 1936).

[2] K. Reichenbach, *Wahrscheinlichkeitslehre* (Leiden: A. W. Sijthoff, 1935);
see especially Abschnitt 10, pp. 365–423.

memories, and the like), these traces are not infinite. The infinite probability series is therefore a mathematical fiction. Actually, there exist only finite series, as in the case of the tossing of a penny, where only the ongoing toss, together with the record of the tosses already made, exists. From such finite series we are, as a matter of fact, able to predict that in the long run—and the long run is incapable of exact definition—the frequency of a very large number of records of events will approximate a certain number, and approximate it more closely as the number of recorded events increases. But no matter how far we prolong the series, the series is finite. And the fact that we can construct mathematical series of the type postulated by Reichenbach and the school to which he belongs says nothing as to the existence of such series in nature. On the other hand, the utility of such series for the solution of statistical problems of physical or actuarial science is not to be denied. But in metaphysics useful approximate relevance is not enough; a picture of the actual state of affairs is mandatory.

So the theory of induction offered by those who would substitute probable connections for necessary connections is a failure. We must now raise the question whether this failure requires a return to the older type of theory. In order to answer this question we must look more narrowly into the nature of probability itself. What exactly do we mean by a "probable" proposition, or by saying that a proposition is "probable"?

We shall for the time being rule out of consideration all subjectivistic theories, that is to say, all theories that would base the probable judgment on ignorance. This implies finding an interpretation of probability in terms of fact. But to do this is, prima facie, not easy. A proposition is true if it corresponds to (is a picture of), or expresses, fact and hence may be verified by fact; a proposition is false if it does not express, or correspond to, fact. We may also add that a proposition is true if it is entailed by a proposition that is true, and is false if its contradictory is entailed by a proposition that is true. In this sense it is true that there are eleven large numbers on the dial of my watch, and that Napoleon was crowned emperor by the pope. But what of a proposition that is probable? What is its relation to fact? If it corresponds, it is true; if it fails to correspond, it is false; yet as merely probable, it does not appear to do or to fail to do either. Probability seems thus to be neither fish nor fowl nor good red herring.

The clue to the solution of the puzzle is to be found, I believe, in the nature of certain propositions which, while they have the appearance of being either true or false, are, as a matter of fact, not either true or false. The propositions that I have in mind are propositions—as we say—about the future, such propositions as: It will rain tomorrow; President Roosevelt will be reelected; This heat will melt this piece of iron. For if I say, It will rain tomorrow, the proposition is not true, because there is no fact of which it is the picture, since tomorrow's rain does not exist; nor is it false, for, again, there is no fact with which it could fail to correspond. On a deterministic hypothesis, the proposition might be entailed by certain other propositions known to be true, and on this basis we could say that it was true; but we cannot assume the truth of the deterministic hypothesis, which begs most of the questions we are raising. If not true or false, what then is the status of the proposition? The answer is, I think, clear; the proposition is precisely a probable proposition. When I say, It will rain, I mean, it will probably rain. Or if I say that Roosevelt will be reëlected, all I can possibly mean is that he will probably be reëlected. I cannot say that either proposition is true, or even that either will be true: for what is the state of affairs that corresponds to the truth, if it be truth, that it will be true? But I can say that the proposition will probably be true, which is the same thing as to say that it is probable. To say, It will rain tomorrow is probably true, is precisely the same as to say, It will rain tomorrow is probable. "Will probably be true" is redundant for "probable." Now it will be found, I think, that all propositions about the future are probable propositions.

It can also be shown, I believe that all probable propositions are about the future, from which it follows that propositions about the future and probable propositions are, extensionally at least, the same. On the surface, this may appear to be preposterous, for there seem to be probable propositions about the past. The proposition, Homer wrote the *Iliad*, would seem to be such a proposition. Yet consider this proposition as typical of the whole group of its kind and ask this question concerning it: Is the proposition, Homer wrote the *Iliad*, a true proposition or a false one? Surely it is one or the other! It must be either the case or not the case that Homer wrote the *Iliad*. And if you believe that he wrote it, what can you mean by adding that he probably wrote it? Here is perhaps an instance where a subjectivistic theory of probability might seem to work, for one might claim that by "probably true" is meant that there is more evidence for than against the view that Homer wrote the poem. And I grant that this is what some people may mean when they say that Homer probably wrote the *Iliad;* yet when people use the term "probable" they do not usually mean anything of the kind, for they are not discussing evidence at all. Thus, when I say that a man of eighty will probably die within the next ten years or that a loaded penny will probably fall heads, I am not making any assertion regarding the evidence for either event. Even when I say that it will probably rain, I do not mean that there is much evidence for rain or an overbalance of evidence for rain, although, to be sure, I could not know that it would probably rain unless there were evidence to that effect. I am not talking about the evidence that it will rain, any more than when I say that a proposition is true I am talking about the evidence that it is true. An objective theory of probability cannot admit such confusions. And with regard to the original proposition under discussion and all propositions of its kind, examination will show that there are really two propositions expressed in one sentence—a matter-of-fact or truth proposition to the effect that Homer wrote the *Iliad*, which is either true or false, as the case may be, and another proposition, a probability proposition, to the effect that people will discover that Homer wrote the poem. This second proposition is not true and not false, because there is yet no fact—people discovering that it is true—to make it true. But, like all propositions about the future, it is a probability proposition. When I say that people will discover that Homer wrote the *Iliad,* I am saying the same thing as if I said that Homer probably wrote the *Iliad.* And this proposition is typical of all probability propositions supposed to be about the past; they are really about the future, and they state that someone will discover that such and such a proposition is true. These propositions are therefore concerned with *knowledge* of fact, not with mere fact apart from knowledge; and this is the element of truth in the subjectivistic interpretation.

In support of the view that probable propositions are about the future I would point to the common use of such propositions. They are of use in games of chance, where we are always interested in *expected* events; and they are of use in the various forms of insurance, where again we are interested in various forms of expectation—expectation of life or death, of fire, of shipwreck, and the like. The realm of the future is the realm of the probable. Only in the field of historical research is this not obviously the case; and yet there, also, as I have tried to show, probable propositions are still about the future—the future of knowledge.

The mind is, however, extremely reluctant to admit probable propositions as being *sui generis,* set apart from propositions that are either true or false. A good example of such reluctance is Russell's definition of a probable proposition as a propositional function of which some values are true. This is in line with the tendency among contemporary students of probability to shift the locus of probability away from the individual event to the class or "*Kollectiv*." If their interpretation were correct, to say, It will probably rain, would be equivalent to saying, It sometimes rains, or, more explicitly, There will be some rainy days. We now seem to have a proposition that is either true or false. The insurance man does not know when this man will die, but he does know that a certain number of his group will die within the year; we do not know how this penny will fall, but we do know that half of a large group will fall heads. To say that the proposition, This penny will fall heads, has a probability of one half would be equivalent to saying, Half of a large throw of pennies will fall heads. But this shift from the individual to the class does not avail to transform probable propositions into matter-of-fact propositions, that is to say, true or false propositions. If the future were already in being, this transformation might be possible; but the classes of future events required by the theory no more exist than do individual future events—the class of tosses of events cannot exist if the single toss does not exist; hence propositions regarding classes of future events cannot be either true or false, but only probable. The death rate in a given population group, or even the ratio of heads to tails in the tossing of pennies, is itself only probable, albeit the probability is exceedingly high. All propositions about the future are probable only, as we have shown.

We must therefore admit the probable proposition as *sui generis*. This is, of course, freely admitted by many students of the matter today. But where these thinkers are often in error is in the static character of the theory of probability developed by them, based as it is on the assumption of actual series, which, while they may exist by the postulational fiat of the mathematician, do not exist in nature. Now in place of a static theory of probability and induction I wish to offer a sketch of a dynamic view—a sketch is all that the limits of this volume permit—which I hope will be free from the difficulties of the former, yet provide room for the important insights contained in it. I shall state this dynamic view through a set of numbered propositions, each of which I shall try to illustrate and illumine. The theory I am offering is frankly a metaphysical theory, and is constructed in terms of the general philosophical outlook of this book. That it owes much to contemporary thought concerning probability needs hardly be said.

1. An observed frequency of events is the sign of the existence of a force for, or interest in, that *kind* of event. Even as we take repeated human behavior of a certain kind in our social world to indicate an interest in behavior of that kind—repeated attendance at motion-picture theatres as indicative of an interest in motion pictures—and when we have observed part behavior of the kind believe ourselves justified in expecting the remainder behavior to make up the behavior whole, so when we observe in nature repeated series of a type, we infer an interest in events of that type and believe ourselves justified in expecting the later members to follow upon the earlier members. The existence of interests in *types* of events is here the Ariadne thread, and, be it noted, most interests that we know are of this sort—even hunger seeks primarily food, not this or that individual dish. The interest provides the creative link between the earlier and the later members of the series in the way already explained and justifies us in "extending the description" [1] from the past to the future. What we call a "law of nature" is a relatively permanent interest in a type of event, revealed through an observed frequency. A continuing interest in a type of event is, then, the *basis in fact* of induction. In place of the static classes of things of the

---

[1] Cf. R. H. Nisbet, "The Foundations of Probability," *Mind*, XXXV (1926) : 1–27.

Peirce theory, or the series of events of the contemporary theory, we propose a dynamic, generative principle. The procedure here is parallel to that employed in our discussion of the infinite, where, also, instead of a collection, we offered a principle. It remains true, however, that even though the interest is the basis of induction and the *ratio essendi* of the observed class of events, the class of events is the *ratio cognoscendi* of the existence of an interest of a particular kind, and, as we shall see, the ground for assigning a definite number to the probability of an event. The proposed theory of induction is a simple application to a special problem of the interpretation of nature after the analogy of the social world suggested in an earlier chapter. The full defense of this interpretation belongs to a later stage of our enquiry; it is offered now as a hypothesis designed to render intelligible an otherwise opaque region of fact. I would add that the success of the hypothesis in this application is one good reason among others for accepting it.

2. While the observation of a frequency gives ground for believing in the existence of an interest in a kind of event only, and so, as it were, sets the stage for probability and prediction, probability proper pertains not to the type of event but to the individual event. For an interest in a type of event can be satisfied only if there are individual events; the interest is, therefore, centered in this event that is about to happen. And, in general, to say of an expected event that it is probable is to say that there exists a force tending (i.e., an interest) to bring it into existence. The statement that it will probably rain means that there is a tendency toward rain in the neighborhood. Or, again, to say that it is probable that the sick man will recover is to assert that there are forces acting in his organism making for health. Hence, although probability judgments are not matter-of-fact judgments, they have a matter-of-fact basis; only the basic fact is not an event or a class of events, but a force or interest. When probability is low we use the term "possible" instead of "probable"—as when we say that it is possible that the man will recover. Sometimes we even say that it is possible but not probable that so and so will happen; but this is an inaccurate use of terms, for possibility does not stand in contrast with probability, being simply a low degree of it. If we use terms accurately, whatever is probable is also possible, and whatever is possible is

probable; even what we call "improbable," if it is possible, is probable to a degree. An event is impossible, on the other hand, when there is no force acting in such a way as to bring it about; its probability is zero. Ordinary unscientific usage, however, designates all events that have a probability greater than one half as probable; those that have a probability less than about one half are called improbable, though possible.

The view I have been defending, to the effect that possibility is a low degree of probability, is opposed to that of Stout and others, who hold, as Leibniz did, that possibility and probability are concepts on two different planes. According to Stout,[1] any concept defines a possibility, or rather, is a possibility. The concept "man" means, It is possible that there should be men. Even of fairies or of ten-dimensional space we could say that they were possible, although, of course, improbable. Only self-contradictory concepts, such as the famous "round-square," would be impossible. Formerly, two types of impossibles were recognized, the ideal or conceptual impossible, and the real or physical impossible. The former would be absolutely impossible, the latter only relatively impossible, and the two are not logically equivalent. On this view, fairies would be ideally possible, but physically impossible. Nowadays, however, one would maintain that even fairies were not physically impossible, but only very highly improbable. But how can it be true, I would ask, that any defined state of affairs, entity, or event, is possible unless there is some force or tendency operating in the universe in favor of its existence? If there is no such force, what is added to a concept by saying that it is possible? Is possible fairy more than just fairy? If perhaps "possible" means consistent or not self-contradictory, why not say so? why use the term "possible"? On the other hand, a very low degree of probability would attach to every concept if every concept has what Whitehead calls its "lure"; but if so, the concept is possible not as such, but because of its lure. If we are right, even a self-contradictory concept, so-called, is not as such impossible, but is impossible because, being properly no concept at all but only an abortive effort to form a concept by seeking to unite incompatible elementary concepts, there cannot exist in nature a tendency toward nothing.

[1] G. F. Stout, "Truth and Falsity," *Mind*, XLI (1932): 297.

3. Our next problem is to define quantity of probability or the measure of probability. What are the metaphysical implications of a probability of one half, say, or two thirds? We can best come at the answer to this question if we first ask the meaning of a probability equal to one or equal to zero. Probability zero means, as we have indicated, that there is no force operating in favor of the type of event in question, and so none in favor of any expected event of the type. The probability of figs growing from this thistle is zero, means, There is no force in the universe tending toward getting figs from thistles. On the other hand, a probability equal to one means that there is an interest acting in favor of the expected event and either that there are no competing forces or that this force has completely dominated all such other forces. Thus the probability that this water will boil under standard pressure when I have heated it to one hundred degrees centigrade is, let us say, one, which means that all tendencies that would prevent it from boiling have been overcome. Let us remind ourselves, however, that probability one is not truth, and probability zero is not falsity, because the proposition to the effect that the water will boil has yet no object (boiling water) that could confirm it, since the water has not yet boiled; and in the same sense the proposition which asserts that figs will grow from this thistle has as yet no object, for the future is still unborn. Truth and falsity have to do with existence—with the present and the traces out of the past which the present contains—whereas probability pertains to the nisus toward, or the preparation for, existence; and even the event that is certain—whose probability is one—is not yet born.

4. Granted the definition of probabilities zero and one, it follows that a fractional probability presupposes the existence of competing forces, some favoring the type of this event and some favoring its contrary type or types. If I toss a penny, since the probability for heads is one half, there must be a force for heads, but also a force for tails, since its probability is one half, too. If I throw dice, and the probability is only one sixth for a one spot, there must be an approximately equal force for each of the other faces of the die. Since, moreover, by the general conditions of the situation, the two faces of the coin or the six faces of the die cannot occur together, it must be the case that now one and now another of the forces or interests gains the ascendency during the

toss; otherwise there would be perfect equilibrium and nothing would happen. But since the forces are equal, the number of times each is in the ascendency will in the long run be equal to that for any other; and there must exist relatively permanent conditions to insure the maintenance of the proportion; otherwise, no matter how often the proportion had obtained in the past, there would be no reason to expect it to continue into the future. The maintenance of the proportion can best be understood as a compensatory phenomenon. It is well known that in any probability series there may be runs of luck—for example, in tossing pennies, a succession of all heads or all tails—yet, as gamblers say, the luck always changes, and changes in such a way as to keep the proportion equal—or the ratio constant—in the long run. What happens then, as I conceive it, is a compensatory strengthening of the opposing force or interest, such as occurs, for instance, in the case of a balance of power among states, where if one coalition becomes notably stronger than the other, as manifested by a series of diplomatic or military victories, the opposing coalition is induced to strengthen its armed forces and win new allies, until equilibrium is restored. Or all these points can be illustrated from the sphere of well-known human interests, as follows. Let us think of a man equally interested in his work and his amusements. Then, over a long period, the time he spends on activities of each type will be approximately equal. But from this law no one can deduce on a given occasion of choice whether he will devote his attention to an amusement or a matter of business. On the other hand, one can know that if he is found engaged for some time in the pursuit of amusement, his professional ambition will soon intervene to put a stop to it and a compensatory period of intense work will follow.

It will be noticed that we do not use the "principle of indifference" to explain the equality of probability of the faces of the die or the sides of the coin, but, rather, following the contemporary theory, look upon this equality as expressing a simple law of nature, empirically discovered, in each case, by the experiment of tossing the coin or the die. If we load the dice we get a different law and different probabilities, but there is no essential difference between the situation where the dice are fair and the situation where they are loaded. Equality is due to an unstable, but automatically reëstablished equilibrium of forces, not to "indifference," which nowhere exists in nature. When the statistical phenomena are not a single series of events, but many coexisting parallel series, a similar interpretation in terms of a conflict of forces or interests is suggested. For example, consider the death rate, ten in a thousand, of the population of a certain community. We should think of each thousand organisms as subject to competing forces, which we may roughly classify as those favoring the death and those favoring the life of the organism. In each case, the issue of life or death will be decided by the resistance of the organism; and in each year ten out of a thousand will not have the resistance necessary to combat the forces favoring death. Granting then that resistance is hereditary and the forces favoring death relatively constant—be they within or without the organism—the frequency of deaths in the population will remain relatively invariant, and will provide a basis for prediction over a long period. If, moreover, through some years the forces favoring life become unusually strong because of better hygiene, better food, and so on, and if the ratio is maintained in the long run, there will develop a compensatory increase in the forces favoring death, by means of wars or through overcrowding in large cities. Every fractional probability is, therefore, the sign of a conflict of forces or interests, and of an unstable but continually reëstablished balance of interests tending to maintain the frequency among competing classes of events.

In our account of probability we have run counter to the contemporary theory in making probability an affair of the individual event and not solely of the class or "*Kollectiv.*" For us, to be sure, a frequency is the sign of an interest in a kind of event, and such interests are what we call laws of nature; we do, therefore, recognize the element of truth in the contemporary theory. We have claimed, however, that since a class or type has no existence except through individuals—an interest in a kind can be fulfilled only through individuals of that kind—the ultimate topic of probability must be an expected, individual event. Contemporary probability theory, on the other hand, denies the very propriety of speaking of the probability of an individual event. Nevertheless, everyone would admit that we do in some sense apply theory to the individual event. The gambler is interested in this throw of the dice or in this turn of the roulette wheel, and he does do something about it, and what he does is guided by the theory of probability. A closer study of this matter will bring us nearer to the goal of our argument—a final appraisal of the bearing of the theory of probability upon the causal concept.

Perhaps the most interesting suggestion as to how to deal with the individual event within the framework of the contemporary theory is that of Reichenbach, who holds that any statement that we may make about the individual event is not of the nature of a predictive proposition but of the nature of a wager.[1] If the probability of a certain kind of event is, say, three to one, even so I do not predict that this event rather than its contrary will happen—for although the chances favor it, it may not happen—but I do *bet* on it, and will lay my money on it, because, if I can make many such bets, I shall win in the long run. I know nothing about this individual event, but I do know something about the class of events to which it belongs, and, using this information, if I lay a class of wagers, I shall come out on top. All of life, in its concern for the future, is, as sportsmen call it, a gamble. But that this interpretation, however ingenious, is inadequate, can be shown by the examination of the pathetic case. Suppose my child is ill, what can I know and what can I do about his recovery? The physician tells me that the statistical frequency for recovery from his disease is as three to one. But does it comfort me to know this, if all that is meant be that three out of four children recover, when mine may be the fourth, that will not recover? If I could divest myself of my special love of my child, retaining only my love for children in general, it would comfort me; but since I must remain the anxious father of this beloved child, how can it, if the probability tells me nothing about this individual case, but only about a class of cases? Suppose now the physician informs me that if he were to give the child a serum, its chances of getting well would be increased to ten to one. What then should I do? Should I cause the child discomfort and let him take it, although taking the serum will give me no ground for hope that my child will recover, but only serve to reclassify him by putting him in the class of children who have taken the serum, where nine out of ten recover? According to theory, even as a member of this new class, nothing is known about him as an individual. The doctor, on the other

[1] *Op. cit.*, Secs. 75–76, pp. 387–398; see also Sec. 80, pp. 410–420.

hand, although no more interested in this child than in a hundred others, will wish nevertheless to give him the serum because he will want to make up a class of a hundred children, of whom ninety will recover instead of seventy-five, to the furtherance of his general humanitarian and professional aims. He will lay his Reichenbach class of wagers on recovery in the serum group as against the nonserum group, and come out ahead professionally, in the long run. But I as a father passionately interested in this one child, cannot lay a class of wagers on recovery, for I have only this one child, who, if he recovers, will never again be attacked by the disease. And if the theory is carried out consistently, to the bitter end, it implies that nothing the physician or the nurse can do will affect my child's case; they can only put it into ever new groups, where, indeed, the frequency will be increasingly favorable for the group, but not at all more favorable for the individual.

But how unreal this whole way of thinking is! For every practical man, including every practicing physician, knows that he does affect the issue in the individual case. And I venture the suggestion that this difficulty of the frequency theory of probability would have won more respect if the theory had not been devised by mathematicians and statisticians, mere observers of phenomena, but by practical men and experimenters, who not only observe but intervene and guide phenomena; or if it had not been devised with especial reference to games of chance, where again men are mere observers and are expected not to cheat, that is to say, not to intervene. But what the practical man knows that he does—whether he be an experimenter in a laboratory or a farmer planting and irrigating his fields or a physician treating his patients—is precisely to intervene, to add a force to the forces struggling for mastery in the individual case, and this added force may well turn the issue into victory.

The question still remains, however, whether we can foretell the future in the individual case or whether the best we can do is to get a high degree of probability. And here it is most important to distinguish between the two possibilities when there is failure to attain certainty—whether the failure is due to ignorance, which may conceivably be remedied, or to the intrinsic nature of the situation, when no increase of knowledge at the moment would offer a remedy. Now everyone recognizes that in a very large number of cases we do not as a matter of fact know how to predict the individual event. In all games of chance it is obvious that we do not. Statistical laws acquaint us with the existence of a conflict of forces, each favoring different kinds of events, and they tell us how the conflict will come out in the long run, with reference to a class of cases, in view of the prevalence of compensatory law, but they do not enable us to determine the issue of the conflict in the individual case. If a doctor simply diagnoses the disease of his patient but does not make a careful study of his constitution, he can know no more than the chances of his recovery, for he has done no more than put him into a statistical class. In many branches of the physical and biological sciences this is the only sort of information we have, and for some purposes, for insurance calculations, for example, that is all we are interested in having. In regard to sciences of this type it is clear to me that our inability to predict the individual event is partly—but not wholly, as used to be thought—due to the limitations of our knowledge. For the statistical sciences do not acquaint us with the whole field of forces operating in the concrete, individual situation; it is no wonder then if they cannot foretell what event will emerge out of such a situation. And if all science is statistical, it must be conceded that we can never predict the individual event. But recent philosophers of nature have been hasty in asserting that this is so. For geography, descriptive geology and biology, history, biography, and individual psychology provide us with knowledge of individuals. In these sciences the investigator is not interested merely in a type as it expresses itself in a group of phenomena, but in a determinate, limited, individual field of forces. And there he may be able to discover which of opposing forces has the upper hand, and what events will therefore ensue. Of course he may overlook some factor in the situation, when his prediction will be false, but theoretically, if the field of forces is open to inspection, he will be able to discover which force has prevailed; then the probability of the ensuing event becomes one to one, and is predictable. So the physician can detect the waning character of a disease and predict recovery, providing he can isolate the patient from intervening infections. Once a force is in control, the outcome is no longer in doubt.

This conclusion is in harmony with what we know of ourselves intuitively: we know that once a purpose has dominated our minds we must go on—the deed must be done, provided always that outward circumstances are favorable and nothing supervenes to deflect our purpose. If something does supervene, then a new conflict of forces occurs, and the issue becomes once more unpredictable, until the superiority of one or another force is again revealed. Any expected sequence of events may thus be broken if a new force inrupts. The threat of interference imparts an element of uncertainty to all predictions, except where isolation of the field of forces is possible long enough for a dominant force to express itself in the anticipated series of events. And with regard to this matter, also, we have the testimony of our inner experience: we cannot be sure that we shall carry out our intention fully if a new intention crosses—we shall probably not finish playing that piece of music, as we planned, if some friend calls to see us before we are through. We shall not be able to predict an individual event, therefore, either, because, as in games of chance, we do not know the field of forces operating in a given case, or because, even when we know the forces, either we cannot isolate them, or they are in conflict, so that we do not know which will prevail. The existence of forces in conflict sets an intrinsic limit to the power of prediction. What the practical man does is to weight one of the balanced forces in a conflict, adding force to its force, so that it will prevail and the event that he desires will emerge. When the physician treats his patient he does not merely reclassify him, but gives a new direction to the forces that are battling in his organism. Until one of the forces dominates the situation he will not be able to predict the outcome, but he may at least know that, without his intervention, the event could not have happened as it did. So the farmer may not know that if he plants and fertilizes his field he will get a crop, for he cannot take into account all the forces that may interfere to prevent this result, but he does know that, without his action, he will have no crop. He can at least provide necessary, if not sufficient, conditions for the event.

We may summarize the results of this chapter in their bearing on causality briefly, as follows: The contemporary critique of causality has failed in so far as it has sought to prove that science has no need of causality, for even probable inference presupposes the stability of frequencies, which is understandable only through *verae causae*—forces or interests—capable of generating events. An event or series of events is probable if there exists a force tending toward its realization. The existence of a necessary connection between events—not between the events as such, but between the events through the forces that generate them—remains then unassailed. Even the uncertainty of the individual events can be explained through a conflict of causes. A probability less than one is the expression of such a conflict. And when the individual event or series of events happens it is not causeless, since it occurs as a result of the eventual dominance of one of the contending forces. The older determinism, such as that of Laplace, which conceived of every future event as predictable at any time, must, however, be abandoned, for although we can be certain of individual events or series of events when the conflict is ended, we can know only probabilities when the conflict is going on; prediction must often wait until a later moment. But there is no incompatibility between causality and this streak of indeterminism in the universe. The status of causality emerges unimpaired, therefore, out of this newer critique: probability itself rests on causality.

XIV

Causality: Mechanism of Causality and Levels of Causality

IN OUR last two chapters we have been concerned to defend the concept of causality against attack, first from the empirical side, under the leadership of Hume, and secondly from the point of view of contemporary philosophy of science. In accordance with our radically empirical standpoint we have been led to identify the efficacy of the cause with the observed control which the will exercises upon items within experience, thus falling back upon an ancient tradition in philosophy; but at the same time, under pressure of the facts and reflections adduced in recent discussion of probability, we have abandoned the deterministic implications of the older conception of causality. One might perhaps characterize our view as "causality without determinism." We are now prepared to discuss some of the problems which arise in connection with the other aspects of causality distinguished by us at the outset, problems which I am grouping together under the label "mechanism of causality"—only the mechanism of which I am writing is not mechanical.

It will be convenient to begin by using a distinction often made between "immanent" and "transeunt" causality. By immanent causality I shall mean the control which is exerted over items of experience within the field of a single monad by the activities or self of that monad. We have already had occasion to illustrate this control by means of the daydream and the voluntary action such as walking or playing the piano. Experience is reconstructed, as we may say, from within. But the most superficial examination of experience shows that alongside this reconstruction from within there occurs a process of reconstruction from without. The birds' songs that I hear are obviously not determined by the self of the monad; neither are the changes in the brightness of the colors of the visual field as daylight fades into afternoon and evening. Reconstruction from without covers the entire range of what we have called the countercontrol of experience. Moreover, the immanent causality or control from within does not occur in independence of control from without, for even in the daydream, as in the night dream, hardly noticed sensa play a part, and these are under countercontrol; action is always reaction, construction is always reconstruction of data determined from outside. The determination of data from without is transeunt causality; it is causality from one center to another.

For any monadism of the Leibnizian type, transeunt causality proffers an insoluble problem, the only recourse being to explain away interaction between monads as mere correspondence between items in different monads; for us, on the other hand, who conceive of the mind as contiguous with its environment, the difficulties involved, although genuine, are not grave. Two types of transeunt causality should be distinguished: that between a monad and its contiguous environment and that between a monad and its remoter environment. The former is simply illustrated by the countercontrol exerted in the case of given sensa—expressed in the psychophysical language, any example of direct stimulation of a sense organ; the latter is illustrated by any case of communication between persons, as when you speak and I hear, or you sing and I clap. The problem of interaction in the former type of case is solved through the conception, already proposed, of the overlapping of contiguous monads through common sensa, when countercontrol is exerted directly upon these sensa, as directly from the outside, therefore, as from the inside. The forces that exert the control from the outside are, to be sure, not disclosed to us in their full reality, as our own activities are; they remain opaque to our perception, that is to say, their goals are not disclosed; but, unless we are utterly wrong in our earlier reflections, the forces, as bare activities, are disclosed. And while we can have no direct knowledge of the fact, we may infer that the forces that we ourselves exert— or are—in our own field of experience are intuited, in their turn, in the contiguous fields.

When, however, interaction occurs between a monad and remoter monads the situation is more complex. For if I speak and you hear, there is in fact a determination of the sounds that you hear from my center, but there is no overlapping of sensa, for the sounds that you hear, while they are produced by me, are not heard by me; they are not the same, but only similar to, the sounds that I both produce and hear. And the counter-control that you experience in connection with the sounds which you hear is not the indirect control that I exercise over these same sounds. My control over the sounds occurs by way of other monads. I no more directly control the sounds which you hear than I control directly the words which you see when the telegraph boy brings you a telegram with a message from me. The problem that confronts us is, therefore, the problem of mediated, or, as we have called it, remote, control. It is essentially the same as the traditional problem of action at a distance. And while admitting that we do not know exactly how remote control is exerted, we are justified in offering a hypothesis, as follows.

It was suggested earlier that when, for example, I speak, sounds are produced both in my center and in nature, which is contiguous with me. I wish now to make the further suggestion that the sound heard in nature evokes a response, the production of a new sensum—whether similar or not to the first we cannot say—which is experienced in its turn by other monads contiguous with nature though not contiguous with me, but which is not sensed by me, who am deaf to it. This then evokes a new response when perceived, the production of a new sensum, the intensity of successive sensa diminishing all the while until finally, at the end of a chain, each link of which is forged in the general way indicated, there appears in your center a sound similar to the original sound that I produced in my center, only less loud— a sound obviously controlled by me, but indirectly, through the coöperation of many other centers. If this hypothesis is correct, there are numberless sensa experienced in nature but unperceived by man. The situation as I conceive it is analogous to the method of communication used in the Alps, where one man yodels to another within hearing, who then takes up the call and yodels to another within his hearing, and so on, thus communicating with the last man in the series, at a great distance. These chains I propose to call communication, or radiation, chains. A graph of a communication chain follows:

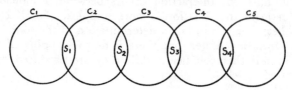

Here the circles marked c_1, c_3, c_5 represent noncontiguous centers; c_2 and c_4, the medium with which they are contiguous; and s_1, s_2, s_3, and s_4, the successive sensa in the process of communication from c_1 to c_5. Notice that each center overlaps with its immediate neighborhood, and that the overlapping part contains a common sensum. As explained in an earlier discussion, there is a time interval between the successive sensa, although no interval of time exists in the appearance of a sensum in contiguous monads.

What we are calling "absorption" or "concentration" is the reverse of radiation. Each monad is the terminus of many diverse radiation chains, via which sensa arrive; these sensa form patterns, to which the self of the monad in which they appear reacts, either in their wholeness or by picking out one or another single element in the whole. The reaction may be such as to produce a sensum of a new type, or one of the same type, mirrorwise. The violinist who, reading his score, produces sounds that interpret it, illustrates the former type of reaction; the man who, hearing a song, begins to sing that song, illustrates the latter. From each center chains of radiation proceed, and to each center chains of radiation converge. There is reason to believe that these chains proceed from the remotest parts of the universe, and to these parts return.

But the reaction of a monad is never merely to the instantaneous pattern of its sensa, but to the echoes of past sensa as well. These echoes account for what Russell has called "mnemic causation." [1] In the example given in an earlier chapter the anger of the wife is determined not solely by the new pattern of sensa produced by the thoughtless act of her husband, but by "memories" of similar astonishing and disturbing patterns in the past. Through such memories the entire past of the individual is effective in any act. Three theories have been offered with regard to the metaphysical status of memories: that they are conscious, present in the mind at all times and ready to play their part in determining action when occasion arises; that they are true mental states but unconscious; or, finally, that they are mere physiological structures, engrams, developing into conscious memories under appropriate conditions. The first of these alternatives is clearly wrong, because no one possesses the con-

[1] Bertrand Russell, *The Analysis of Mind* (London: George Allen and Unwin, 1921), Lecture IV, pp. 77–92.

scious memories of all events of his past, although echoes of all events exist; the second, if literally meant, is nonsense, for to speak of unconscious mental states is like speaking of nonmental mental states. The third alternative remains. Yet, in accordance with our interpretation of the brain as being itself an experience contiguous with personality, the other views have a certain truth if properly interpreted; for to say that echoes are engrams is equivalent to saying that they are conscious states, only not states of myself, therefore "unconscious," not intrinsically, but to me.

Other interesting points regarding the determination of conduct through echoes may be illustrated by a further example. Suppose an officer issues a command to his orderly at 8 A.M., and the orderly executes the command at 10 o'clock. We naturally assume that the command is the cause of the execution of the order; yet how can it be, when it is over and done with long before its supposed effect occurs? This puzzle is solved by making a distinction between what *was* a cause and what *is* a cause of an event. An item *was* a cause of an event if it belonged to a causal chain of which the event was or is a sequent in the chain; but only a true event, that is to say, a present event, can *be* a cause. In the illustration given, the command of the officer *was* a cause of the event, but *is* not the cause; the cause is the echo of the command, preserved in the brain of the orderly and producing a memory of the command when the clock strikes, the two together, the sound and the memory, touching off the execution of the command. It must not be forgotten, however, that apart from the permanent action tendencies or wishes of the orderly neither the echo nor the striking of the clock, singly or in conjunction, would suffice to produce the action in question. A fellow officer may have heard the command and may even remember it at the time when he, too, hears the bell, but he will not execute the command. In this example of causation, as in all, there are the two factors, the one which, following traditional terminology, we may call the efficient cause, and the other the occasional cause or causes—the efficient cause being the habits or intentions of the monad, the occasional cause being the pattern of sensa and the memories that provide the stimulus for the reaction. A noncontiguous monad can cause action in another monad only by providing occasional causes for its activities; it cannot affect directly those activities themselves and so become an efficient cause of the other monad's conduct. It might perhaps be thought that intentions as changed by events, in connection with occasional causes, are sufficient to explain action, without the use of memories: the orderly in our illustration may, in fact, respond to the sound of the bell without explicit memory of the command of the officer, impelled solely by his habit of obedience, which has been given specific direction by the command; and the offended wife may "explode" without definite recollection of the stupidities of her husband. It would, however, be as grave a mistake to isolate intentions from echoes as it would be to isolate them from sensory stimuli both within and without the organism. All activities, as we have observed, are intertwined with sensations and images. That intentions are not separable from echoes is proved by the fact that, if asked to explain his conduct, a man will always refer to past events: the orderly will say, "The officer commanded me to do it"; the wife will recount the complete list of her husband's stupidities, the memories of which will all come flocking in upon her.

The great importance of mnemic causality may, however, easily lead to an exaggeration of its explanatory power, in the direction of a deterministic view of conduct. But its power is definitely limited by the following two factors in the determination of conduct. First, memories are effective, as we have noted, only in relation to activities; but the activities may be in conflict, and no certain prediction is possible when there is conflict. Secondly, the matrix self, as a striving for unity and equilibrium expressed in the life plan, tends to inhibit stereotyped modes of action attached to memories of the past if they are harmful, replacing them by novel modes which creatively combine mnemic modes (imagination). So, to continue one of our examples, the wife may control her anger for the sake of good relations with her husband, or may devise a new method of living with him that will enable him to avoid the actions she finds distasteful. The freedom of the monad consists in this inner spontaneity of the matrix self, together with the fact that, however much it yields to the pressure of the environment, it modifies the environment in its turn; thus, although it is true that the world has made me what I am, it is also true that I have made the world that makes me.

In our account of causality so far we have presupposed that

all causality is through chains of events, each monad determining occurrences in other monads through neighboring, intervening monads.[1] But there are reasons for believing that this is not a sufficient account of the matter, for it seems to overlook two important aspects of causality: causality through "wholes" (organization) and what we shall call "depth" or "underneath" causality. I shall consider the former first, although we shall find that the two are interrelated. Some illustrations may call attention to the point under discussion.

An ophthalmologist, examining the eyes of a patient, informs him that he has a disease of the kidneys; an internist, observing the gigantic height of a youth, makes a diagnosis of overactivity of the pituitary; or, if the height is normal, the clinician infers that another gland is active in such a way as to depress the activity of the pituitary and preserve a normal or healthy stature. In such cases—and they are legion—we seem to have evidence for (1) direct action of remote parts of the organism upon each other, and (2) action of a kind to preserve a certain plan or wholeness of the organism; from which we are led to infer that the plan or whole is active in determining what occurs in the part.[2] It used to be held that this seeming action of the whole on the parts was peculiar to living things, but certain facts recently brought to light through research into the structure of the atom suggest a similar situation there. It appears to be the case, namely, that an electron takes account of other electrons in its neighborhood, and in its passage from one stable state to another is determined by the whole atomic configuration of the moment. In fine, physical units are themselves organisms, at least to this extent. Another fact (3) that appears to prove action by the whole is the dominance of certain parts over others, owing to their "position" or office in the whole. The control exerted by the glands of special secretion, or by the central nervous system, is an example from the organic realm.

---

[1] The theory that all causality is through next-to-next relations has been called "concatenism" in a recent article by William Savery: "Concatenism," *The Journal of Philosophy*, XXXIV (1937), No. 13 : 337–354. The origins of the theory are there traced to Charles Peirce and William James.

[2] See the impressive array of facts making for such "homeostasis" cited by Walter B. Cannon in his *The Wisdom of the Body* (New York: W. W. Norton and Co., 1932) .

In the social world similar facts are to be observed.   The most obvious is the dominance of certain individuals over others. The opinions of members of the American Supreme Court in regard to the constitutionality of a law have an effect upon conduct which the opinions of mere laymen do not have.   The general and the private may say the same words; but in the one case all will listen and action will follow, while in the other case no one will pay attention and the words will be without effect. Or consider the influence of the words of a Mussolini or a Hitler, or even a Roosevelt, in comparison with that of the words of an ordinary citizen.   Obviously, the difference is due to the position of the one in comparison with that of the other; but position is a matter of the configuration of elements in a whole.   It is the "constitution" of a group, whether written or unwritten, which gives the one an influence that the other cannot have.   Although compensatory social phenomena tending to the preservation of the group as a whole are not so obvious as similar phenomena in the organism, they appear nevertheless to be real.   To cite a timely example: in the event of a strike public opinion will begin by favoring the strikers, but if the latter push their cause too far, opinion will shift to the other side in order that the essential needs of the community may be served and total disorganization avoided.   Or consider the almost universal rise of dictatorship, serving this same end, when the conflict of parties becomes so intense that stability of government is jeopardized.   Or, in order to illustrate social wholes through differential uniqueness of behavior, compare the effect of the speeches of Hitler upon the German people with their effect upon the French!   And in the control which a legislator's constituency "back home" exerts upon his actions at Washington we may clearly see how the social unit takes account of other remote units.

Such facts as these are impressive, but it is too easily taken for granted that they can be explained only through the conception of causality by the whole.   At all events, let us try to see whether we cannot explain them without this conception, in terms of causation through neighborhood and next-to-next relations.   Beginning with social phenomena, because they are most intimately known to us, and taking the last of our points first, it seems clear that the fact that the individual takes account of remote individuals in a social whole does not necessarily depend upon any direct causal influence from them, but only upon *knowledge* of what *they* would do if he does certain things himself—a knowledge of their present opinions and intentions, therefore, gained in the first instance through neighborhood relations. Such is the case with the politician who takes account of the wishes of the folks back home, and such is the case generally with all social accommodation. No action by the whole is required, but only knowledge by a given monad of the relatively permanent intentions of other monads—a knowledge gained originally in their neighborhood. And, having in mind the rapid methods of communication by radio and telegraph, we can see how such knowledge may be quickly imparted *from* a distance, but not *at* a distance, when these intentions change. When we discuss corresponding biological facts we shall have occasion to note the importance of other circulatory media for an alternative explanation of the claimed causality by the whole in that realm also. The existence of rapid causal chains, through next-to-next relations together with the possibility of knowledge by one monad of the permanent intentions of other monads, renders unnecessary the supposition of the unmediated causality of the whole.

The fact of causal dominance can also be explained without the assumption of action through wholes. All that is needed is the existence of a tradition in the minds of the several members of a group inculcated through neighborhood relations in the family and the school by proximate teachers and parents. The term "tradition" translated into the metaphysical language which we have been using means the opinions and the habits of action of some monads with regard to the opinions and the wishes of certain other monads—the boss, the commanding officer, the judges of the Supreme Court, the president, in short, the constituted authorities. The constitution of a country is, in effect, just the existence of such opinions and habits of action. When they change in notable fashion the constitution changes. If the boss's, the commander's, the judge's, the president's, the emperor's word no longer receives the respect of other members of the society and provokes no appropriate response in action, a revolution has occurred. This was the case in France when Louis XVI became Hugh Capet, or in Russia when in 1917 soldiers paid no heed to the commands of their officers. Compensatory social phenomena can be explained in the same way if we include love, that is to say, regard for the welfare of other members of one's group as a factor in determining the behavior of monads. If some of the members of a group find that the interests of their friends or children or neighbors are put in jeopardy by any course of action on the part of others of the group, they are bound to withdraw their sympathy from that minority, and will accept almost any measures of reorganization that will bring security. Compensatory action is not action by the group as a whole but by individual members of the group who are interested in the preservation of a kind of life in the group. Love—a passion of the individual for the welfare of other individuals of the same group—can perform all the functions attributed to the whole.

If we are allowed to interpret biological facts by analogy from social facts, we can explain away much of the evidence advanced for causation by the whole in that realm also. The seeming immediate influence of one part of the organism upon another, remote, part can be explained through the functioning of a very rapid circulatory system carrying messages from the one to the other. The blood stream is in fact a circulatory system of this kind. Through the blood stream disease in one organ is carried to other organs, so that its presence in one can be used as an index of its presence in the other. Compensatory phenomena can be explained if we may assume, as in the case of analogous social phenomena, that certain elements in the organism—such as the white corpuscles or the various antibodies in the blood—have an interest in the perpetuation and welfare of the other elements of the system. They would play the part of the government and the police, and of all patriots, in the social system. The dominance of an organ, of the brain for example, would be explained as due to the "constitution" of the system, which itself would be a matter of "tradition"—of stabilized habits of action in the ordinary run of cells with regard to stimuli coming to them from certain other, preëminent, cells or organs. Therefore, if certain lemmas are admitted, monadism is as effective as holism in accounting for the facts.[1] But our discussion must be regarded as provisional until we have examined the evidence for so-called levels of causality, or what we are calling "depth" or "underneath" causality.

This evidence is briefly of the following sort. If we consider

[1] For the general theory of holism see J. C. Smuts, *Holism and Evolution* (New York: The Macmillan Co., 1926).

the career of the mind of a man, we find a good deal that can be explained by means of laws intrinsic to that mind itself. Thus if we persuade a man to change his course of action by appealing to his own seemingly forgotten interests or ends, or convince him of the truth of a proposition by demonstrating it, in accordance with logical laws, from premises which he himself admits to be true, we can account for his conduct in terms of principles indigenous to human personality. Yet there are aspects even of behavior of this kind that cannot be explained thus. If a man is tired or ill-fed his thinking will not flow so quickly and so surely as if he is rested and well-fed, and this difference can be understood only through extrinsic laws—not personal, but, as we say, physiological. The decline of the mind is understood not in terms of purpose or of logic, but of arteries and of kidneys; and no man, not even the suicide, dies just because he wants to or thinks it reasonable to do so. So, when a man stumbles and falls his behavior is determined not wholly by laws of personality —say by inattention—or by laws physiological, but by still other laws, which we call physical; if a man is excited we can either persuade him into calmness or give him a sedative. In the social order a man may win a dominant position and perhaps establish a tradition of authority either by his superior leadership or by *force majeure,* and few persons would dispute that every social, political, and international authority has been established and is maintained by a combination of both. From such simple everyday facts as these it is not a very long step to the generalizations of scientific research which tend to establish the existence of at least three levels of law or causality, to wit: the personal or psychological, the physiological or biological, and the physico-chemical.[1]

When the existence of these levels has been established our problems have, however, just begun. The first question that

---

[1] For the general subject of levels of causality consult the following works: A. Schopenhauer, *On the Will in Nature,* tr. by Mrs. Karl Hillebrand (London: George Bell and Sons, 1897) ; E. Boutroux, *The Contingency of the Laws of Nature* (Chicago and London: The Open Court Publishing Co., 1916) ; R. W. Sellars, *Evolutionary Naturalism* (Chicago and London: The Open Court Publishing Co., 1922) ; S. Alexander, *Space, Time and Deity* (London: Macmillan and Co., 1920) ; E. G. Spaulding, *A World of Chance* (New York: The Macmillan Co., 1936) , chap. ix; C. Lloyd Morgan, *Emergent Evolution* (New York: Henry Holt and Co., 1924) .

confronts us is whether the levels are apparent or real—whether the so-called higher can be reduced to the lower and eventually to the lowest, or whether, on the contrary, each is unique and irreducible. According to the first alternative the laws of the higher levels are provisional only, representing earlier phases of scientific research destined to be slowly replaced by physical laws which will finally supplant them utterly. The laws prevailing on the higher levels would be, in the language of Santayana, mere metaphors or tropes, the literal meaning of which should be sought in physical science. And for this reductionist or materialist view there is much accumulating evidence, as everyone who has followed the history of science knows: the dependence of psychological laws on habits, which are physiological, the reduction of organic products to chemical compounds, the growing encroachment of physics on chemistry, paralleling the encroachment of physiological chemistry on physiology and biology. Yet when all is said that can be said for the reductionist hypothesis there remains a residuum of uniqueness and irreducibility, of contingency,[1] on each level; and the more empirical attitude would seem to be to accept this contingency as a fact until it has been proved to be nonexistent. Even though, consistently with our approach to the problem of levels through the underneath causality that appears to determine much of the behavior of the human mind, we should be led to expect that the phenomena on each level would be partly determined by lower levels, yet so long as the determination of human behavior by ends has not been reduced to mere physiological habit or chemical reactions, and life itself has not been shown to be nothing but a complex molecule, the reductionist hypothesis will remain unproved.

Granted the uniqueness of the levels, we find our next problem in the relation between them. One suggestion is that the relation is that of whole and part. But this is, I believe, a mistake. The life of the cell, for example, is not a whole of which the complex molecular constituents are parts. For what is life? Life is a mode of behavior, to some extent the resultant no doubt

---

[1] "Contingency" in this sense is a relative term; the laws differentiating a higher from a lower level are contingent with relation to a lower, in so far as they cannot be deduced from the lower. It follows, therefore, that not all aspects of events on the higher level are predictable from lower-level laws.

of the pattern of the constituent molecules of the cell, but in no sense a behavior whole of which the behaviors of the molecules are elementary parts. The characteristic behaviors of the individual molecules persist alongside the behavior of the cell as a whole; they are not supplanted by, or included in, the latter. And the demonstration that the relation between levels is no whole–part relation is simple if we consider the relation between personality and the levels underneath it. Consciousness is sometimes described as the behavior of the organism as a whole. Let us admit that, viewed from the standpoint of the external observer, from the outside, this is true; but, surely, this behavior does not include as *parts* of itself the behavior of the millions of cells of the body—or, what would be more preposterous, the behavior of the trillions of electrons "underneath" the behavior of the cells! Consciousness is exceedingly complex, much more complex than common sense recognizes, but not as complex as that. The behavior of the organism as a whole—consciousness —is in a measure the *resultant* of the behavior of the electrons on the one hand and of all the cells of the body on the other, but does not *include* them as parts of itself. When I close my hand the act of closing is a single act, which does not include the behavior of the cells or electrons but exists alongside them. As soon as one has come to think of physical phenomena as fields of force, or as types of behavior, rather than in the old-fashioned way as "things," there is no difficulty in conceiving of the different levels as coexisting in the same place; what alone is forbidden, apparently, is the occupation of the same place by different entities on the same level. But we shall have to return to this matter later.

If the relation between higher and lower levels is not that of whole and part, what then is the relation? That it is at least a relation of conditioned to conditioning is shown by all the facts upon which the general conception of levels is based. Some phases of this determination are worthy of special consideration. First, the lower level supplies necessary conditions for the *existence* of the higher: without a body, no personality; without chemical molecules, no cells; without atoms, no molecules; without electrons and protons and the rest, no atom. The immediately lower level is the *conditio sine qua non* of the existence of the next higher level, and of all the levels higher still. Secondly, the lower level partly controls, and therefore partly creates, the activities on the higher level. All the facts with which we began this discussion might be cited as evidence. The lower level does not merely, so to say, permit the existence of the higher, but partly determines what the higher shall be like. According to the reductionist theory, the whole character of the higher would be determined by the lower; but on the theory accepted by us of the uniqueness of the levels, this would not be true. There would be certain characters of items on each higher level which could not be accounted for in terms of the lower, with regard to which, therefore, the higher would be free in their relation to the lower. But now, would determination be one-way only, from the lower to the higher, or two-way, from the higher to the lower, as well? Once having been permitted to exist, and to have its way after a fashion on its own level, would the higher, in its turn, reach down and change the course of the lower? That this is the case can be doubted by no one who heeds the evidence of experience as to the efficacy of human desire and reason in shaping the life of man and modifying his environment. When a man builds a house or a road, he gives to matter a form which it otherwise would not have, and so changes the course of the electrons. It used to seem almost miraculous that this should be so, in the old days when physical laws were conceived of as being absolutely accurate and necessary; but with the newer conception of law as an approximate formulation and as providing only probabilities there is nothing that need disturb intellectual serenity in supposing that personality acts upon the body, and through the body upon inorganic modes of reality, or that life, through its presence, determines alterations in the behavior of the very molecules which provide the conditions for its existence and partly control its destiny. There is causality not only from below, but also from above, not one-way only, but two-way.

Taking human personality for illustration, we may review our reflections on levels and their interrelations as follows. The coming to be of a personality depends upon the next lower level, and therefore upon all still lower levels, for it is obvious that the fertilization of the ovum by the spermatozoon, when the human being begins, is a biological, not a human, process. Nevertheless, it is noteworthy that the determination is not wholly through nonhuman forces, since the choice of the female by the male (or vice versa) in courtship, which is a necessary preliminary to the biological process of fertilization, is, in so far as this choice is governed by considerations of beauty, social position, or comradeship, a human, not physiological, matter. Each level is consequently partly self-perpetuating with regard to what is unique in its own type. Moreover, once the level has come into existence, its development is determined partly in accordance with laws intrinsic to its own mode of existence and partly in accordance with lower-level laws: the growth of the young mind is partly the result of teaching and persuasion in the family and in the school and partly a matter of simple biological maturation. Or consider the origin and growth of a psychoneurosis: it arises undoubtedly as an expression of some biological "organ inferiority," but once having come into existence proliferates according to its own laws and has a reciprocal effect on the organism itself. All of the mind's activities illustrate multiple determination; they cannot carry on without the favoring coöperation of biological and material systems. Thus, if one man tries to persuade another, he cannot speak without the coöperation of physiological processes in brain and speech organs, and his very arguments, though they will have a purely personal aspect, will depend for their procedure on the use of habits of thought which are physiologically based and conditioned (so when a man adds a column of figures he uses, without thinking, number habits formed long ago) ; and the physiological processes themselves cannot occur without the "fitness" of the purely physical environment in providing abundant food and water and air for breathing and the transmission of thought through sound. The fashion in which the three levels are intertwined causally is shown by the triple determination of the effectiveness of a nation: first, through its morale and its inventiveness in technology, science, and the arts, the human factor; secondly, by its fertility and hardihood, the biological factor; and thirdly, by its command over natural resources, the physical factor. Many a human race and culture of exquisite delicacy, failing to secure the enduring coöperation of other levels of reality, has had to surrender to one which at the moment seemed inferior. The rule of force in international affairs, as opposed to the rule of reason, is the rule of nonhuman powers that for reasons which we do not understand are on the side of what seems to us to be unreason. And the death of every mind is determined by such forces. So does man's existence depend upon a nonhuman fate, which the pious among us call the will of God.

We are now prepared to face the last important problem of levels of causality: Is depth causality a disguised form of sidewise or next-to-next causality, or is it *sui generis?* And, if the latter, how shall we picture its action? For example, when the mind acts on the body or the physical environment is the mind a link in the chain of causal processes, fitting like other links into the four-dimensional spatiotemporal world? If not, how does it stand related to them? Now in the situation where the mind reacts to stimuli coming in from the environment or initiates a motor process, as when a man raises his hand, there is obviously causality of the usual next-to-next type between the mind, the sensory nerves, and the physical stimuli in the one case and between the mind, motor nerves, and muscles controlling the hand in the other, but with that we are not concerned; our question is, What sort of causality obtains between the "life" of the sensory or motor nerve cell, say, and the molecules upon which this life is based, or between the psychic process which we call decision and the cortex of the brain? That in this type of case the causal relation is somehow unique seems to be indicated by the fact that the parties to the transaction are in the same place. For personality is where the brain is, and life is where the cellular molecules are. And the significance of this fact lies in the equivalence between identity of location and absence of a time interval between the interacting parties. It means that the influence of the one on the other is instantaneous, that there are, therefore, no intervenient monads, and that the relationship is direct, as if they were parts of a single connected whole. Hence, besides the contact which any monad has with its immediate neighborhood—according to the standard three-dimensional spatial picture of the world—it has the same type of contact with the levels of existence above and below. The mind is in contact with the living brain, the brain with the underlying physicochemical process. Action on any one of these levels instantly entails action within the other levels, because they intersect. When the mind acts the brain and the electromagnetic field beneath act with it at once, and the three function as a unit. The mind, therefore, does not intervene as a new member in the physical series of events, but modifies instantly the character of those events with which it is connected. The biologic and physical levels are larger existences with which the mind overlaps, and which carry on underneath what appears in consciousness. Just as we find our own intentions shaping the material of the mind, so we find this material shaped by other, foreign intentions enveloping us, whose efficacy we experience but whose goals remain unknown to us. In the grip of fever, in strength or weakness, in hunger and in love, in all the tides of personality, we suffer this. It is as if we were a boat, riding the waves, borne onward by the currents from below.

The theory of levels of causality which we have developed enables us to concede the element of truth in the conception of causality by the whole so sharply criticized by us as an unproved assumption. The very conception of levels, as we have seen, arises through reflection upon the fact that there are events, or phases of events, which cannot be explained according to the laws normal to those events. Now the conception of causality by the whole is an intellectual expedient serving very much the same ends. May it not be possible then that the two coincide? This is, I believe, the case. Using the example of life once more, we find that the properties of life, though determined partly by the molecular constituents of the cell, cannot be completely deduced from them; hence, the holists have said, life is the whole which the molecules form, the pattern of the whole accounting for the residual vital phenomena. But this, as we have seen, cannot be the truth, for the molecules are not parts of life; the truth is that life is a higher-level mode of behavior, produced, to be sure, by the lower-level physical elements, but in its turn reacting upon them. In other words, this downward action of the emergent entity on the higher level upon the elements on the lower level is mistaken for action by the whole of those elements. Even so, instead of explaining the peculiarities of human behavior through the "whole" of all the organs of the body, we would explain them as due to the downward control of an emergent entity, the mind, which, although conditioned by the organs, is no mere pattern of them. In this way, I would add, we preserve our monadistic point of view and yet at the same time "save all the appearances" that the holistic hypothesis was devised to account for. Sometimes, however, in order to explain unusual phenomena on a given level we may have to proceed in the other direction: instead of appealing to a higher-level entity, we shall have to appeal to lower levels. Thus the differentiation of the homogeneous fertilized cell, which seems so hard to explain in terms of anything that can be seen in the cell itself, may be due, not to an entelechy, psychoid, or vital force, but to electronic disturbances far below the field of microscopic examination. And in the life of the human mind, also, since there is no level "higher" than its own, so far as we know, I would suggest that the unaccountable facts, namely, those facts that we can explain neither on a human nor on a physiological basis—all the alleged phenomena of mysticism and occultism, if genuine—may be explained through an upthrust from the so-called lowest depths of existence, which are, perhaps, as we shall be led to divine, the highest.

It may serve to clarify and summarize our view of the relation of levels of reality if we apply it directly to the problem of the relation between the mind and the body in terms of the three traditional solutions—interactionism, parallelism, and the identity theory. In its broad implications, our view is clearly a species of interactionism. The human mind, as we conceive it, is a product of the body and the environment of the body. Its whole content of sensation is obviously supplied by the environment remotely and by the sense organs of the body more immediately. But this is not all: its fundamental passions, hunger and sex, and its basic problems and interests are determined by the body and the situation of the body in its environment. To feed and clothe, to protect from danger, to find a mate for the body, and then to foster the new body resulting are the major concerns of the mind, and almost the whole of the knowledge that it seeks and acquires is directed to these ends. We commonly think of the body as the servant of the mind, but it is no less true that the mind is the servant of the body. But, as we know, the relation is a two-way relation, and all the while that the existence and the content of the mind are being created by the body, the mind is exercising guidance over the body and building up the environment, with the coöperation of the body, into a fit habitation for both. The opposing theory, parallelism, to the effect that there is no causal relation between the mind and the body, is, therefore, from our point of view, false. And for us interactionism has none of the difficulties that have led to its abandonment by many thinkers, because we conceive of the body itself as a system of experiences, of generically the same kind as the mind, with which the mind can smoothly interact. Yet there is a certain truth in parallelism. For when we examine the causal relation between the mind and that part of the body upon which the mind most immediately depends, namely, the brain, we find that it is peculiar. In the mind's interaction with other parts of the body and with the environment there is a time interval between the cause and the effect, and the process of causation occurs in the form of a chain of events, but in the case of the mind and the brain no such interval exists, because they are in contact. This means that an event in the mind is part of a whole event of which another part is an event in the brain, the whole event straddling the two. But our account of the matter is not yet complete, for the whole event has a third part in the physical world underneath the living brain. It will be understood without difficulty, I hope, that when we have referred to the brain in the foregoing discussion, we have meant the metaphysical, not the phenomenal, brain: we have meant the activities that are the remote cause of the gray, convoluted shape and the other phenomena—the phenomenal brain—in the mind of an observer, on the basis of which the observer makes his deductions with regard to the locus, the structure, and the behavior of the "real," or metaphysical, brain. Now between the phenomenal brain—which is part of the content of some mind—and the real brain there is a genuine parallelism. For, corresponding to every change in the phenomenal brain, is a change in the activities of the real brain, and vice versa. By reason of this parallelism the phenomenal brain may some day be used as a valid natural language for the interpretation of the events in the real brain. As for the last of the traditional theories—the identity theory—literally interpreted, it is an absurdity, for the relatively simple mental process cannot be identified with the incomparably more complex biological and physical processes underneath; yet here, also, we find an element of truth, since the three processes are intersecting parts of a single whole: the mind has a part in common with the brain, and that same part is a part of nature.

How the process of causation is complicated by the existence of intersecting levels of reality may be illustrated by simple perception. The perception of a rose, it is clear, involves, first, antecedently, a purely physical process in nature. This process then overflows and is continued in a more complicated form in chemical changes occurring in the rods and cones of the retina, with an added living dimension. In this still further complicated form it is propagated chainwise along the afferent optical nerves to the brain, where the final complication occurs in the appearance of visual sensa—the mental phase. Since the mind is in contact with the biologic and physical processes of the brain, and therefore overlaps with them, the visual sensa appear at once in nature, the body, and the mind. When the sensa appear in the mind they receive the conceptual interpretation which refers them back to their remote control in nature, and presently evoke a readjustment of the whole organism to this control, thus illustrating the downward guidance exerted from the higher level of the mind over the lower level of the body. Since the visual pattern of sensa belongs to the physical system as well as to the mind, naïve realism is correct in its supposition that we actually see the physical rose; it forgets, however, that perception distorts the space–time locus of the rose, thrusting it back in time and in space to its causal origin or focus, from which it can be controlled.

If, finally, looking back over the discussion of causality outlined in the last three chapters, we were to try to assemble the essential ideas that have guided us, we should set ourselves no easy task. The picture of causality which any contemporary thinker must offer is far more complex, and its outlines far more indeterminate, than would have been offered one hundred or even fifty years ago. Whereas formerly causality was what we may call monoplanar, it is now multiplanar. Whereas formerly only one species of causal law was recognized, today we distinguish between different species—the statistical law, which expresses an equilibrium, temporarily achieved, among many forces and permits of probable predictions among a class of phenomena for so long as the equilibrium persists, and the true law of nature, a formulation of the intentions and the habits of an individual, and, by analogy, of all individuals like it. The habits and the intentions of individuals render causal laws something more than mere descriptions of events that have actually occurred (as Mach and Kirchhoff and other positivists have conceived them), and make possible their formulation in the contrary-to-fact form—a mode that brings out the necessity they embody. Yet even these laws do not establish prediction with certainty, because every event is the result of the coöperation of many intentions, no one of which guarantees the continuance of the coöperation. From the existence of an intention only probable predictions are possible regarding individual events. Even when we are aware of a stable harmony of intentions, as in the organism, or in well-adapted situations of organism in relation to environment, there is an element of uncertainty, owing to the fact that no situation is completely isolated. Still, if we could know all the forces in action throughout the cosmos, could we not predict with certainty? Not even then, I answer, for there are nodes of conflicting forces all over the world; and when forces stand in equilibrium we have no way of knowing which will dominate. Out of such conflicts arise redistributions of interest creative of events the like of which were never seen before; no prophet could foretell them.

If, however, the same causes operate, shall not the same effects follow? Does not the ancient axiom hold? Yes, the axiom holds, if by cause be meant *vera causa,* a force or intention; for the same cause, the same intention, will create the kind of events that tend to its fulfilment. But the difficulty with the axiom is that, though true, it is irrelevant unless we guard it by making a distinction. If we take it simply, it becomes inapplicable, for there are no absolutely same causes; there is no cause which, having operated, does not change through its operation. It cannot, therefore, by virtue of the very axiom itself, produce unreservedly the same effect that it produced before. Moreover, effects are transitory, and cannot be resurrected in their full individuality. The axiom when applied prevents itself from being simply true. So, in order to save it, we must draw a distinction, and the distinction we must draw is between the essence and the accidents of the cause. An illustration will make my meaning clear. If a man has played the piano we infer that he has an interest in music, and, since interests are creative, we know that musical sounds will appear again in the world, but we do not know on the basis of such knowledge alone, which composition he will play. Or if, because he has played a certain composition often, we can infer an interest in this particular piece, we may know that he will play it again, but we do not know exactly how or when he will play it. The essence of his interest will remain the same, and from this same cause will be produced essentially the same type of event; but in all its concrete fullness, clothed in all its accidental detail, the interest that produced the earlier pattern of sound will never function again and can never produce exactly the same events. Or we know that this child will grow into essentially the same form as that one because the essence of the biological intention is the same in both cases; but no two children ever grow to be just alike. Or, once more, we expect the same chemical reaction from the same combination of elements, but again they are only essentially the same. Moreover, every event is multiply determined, and all the true causes that brought it into being would have to be alike in every concrete aspect for the event exactly to recur. Even as only the essence of the system of causes will recur, so only the generic form of the resulting events will be repeated. The men of the orchestra have essentially the same intention to play the Brahms *First* that they had a year ago, and now, as they are assembled in the hall, "the same cause will produce the same effect"; but the cause is a hundred causes, and each of these is a man whose muscles and nerves have undergone a change since a year ago, and some that were fresh then are weary now, and others that were ambitious to do their best have grown careless. The essence of the old situation has, nevertheless, reappeared, and from the essence of the cause will spring essentially the same effect in sound; but by the very law of cause, it cannot be quite the same. And in the cosmic symphony—the music of the spheres—the matter is no different; there also theme and variation, sameness and difference, necessity and contingency are interwoven, world without end.

XV

The Nature of Value

IN THE history of philosophy we may discern two broad streams, the one springing from the tradition established by Leucippus, Democritus, and Lucretius, the other deriving from Socrates, Plato, and Aristotle. According to the former, value is an incidental, purely contingent aspect of reality, and there might well have been a world entirely void of value—in fact, the world was empty of value for vastly the greater part of its history, until the relatively brief epoch when life and consciousness began upon the earth. According to the other tradition, however, value is essential to reality, and the very conception of existence apart from value is meaningless. It hardly needs to be said that the philosophy of this book belongs to the latter tradition. The unity of value and existence follows directly from the conception of existence as a system of experiences, together with the insight that volition is primary in experience. The history of each monad consists of transitions from desire to satisfaction or frustration. But it would not do simply to set this inference down without discussion, for that would involve assuming too much about the nature of value, concerning which there is little agreement among philosophers. Our inference is valid only if a certain general conception of value as satisfaction is adequate; and the adequacy of this conception must be established over against what seems to us a strange confusion of opposing voices.

In contemporary theory of value there are three main positions: the view that value is an indefinable predicate or quality; the view that it is the expression of a transcendent "ought" or imperative; and, finally, the view that value depends upon what we have been calling volition. This last theory seems to me almost obviously correct, yet one must admit that it is seldom stated in such a way as to cover the whole range of facts and to meet the objections of its critics, who maintain either one or the other of the two alternative views. Yet such a statement is, I believe, possible, and in this chapter I shall attempt its formulation.

We must begin by drawing a distinction between value as a factor in an experience and value as an assigned predicate of a cause or a condition of an experience. Thus an esthetic experience in any one of its forms, like the hearing of the *B–Minor Intermezzo* of Brahms, has value in the sense that there is value resident in the experience itself, while the value one may ascribe to the musical score or the vibrations in the air that mediate the actual acoustic experience is a predicate which does not belong to either intrinsically, but is merely assigned to it by anyone who enjoys the music. Similarly, the experience which occurs when a sensitive mind appreciates the "Venus de Milo" possesses value within itself, whereas the carved marble as a purely physical object possesses no such value within it—although the underlying metaphysical reality doubtless contains a value of its own, which might, for all we know, be the same in kind as ours.[1] Value that is resident in an experience is, I should claim, the only value proper; all other so-called values are fictitious. In other words, intrinsic values are the only values, and they belong solely to states of mind. "Instrumental" or "extrinsic" values, such as are assigned to what are ordinarily called "things," are nominal. Usage may justify us in speaking of the value of a musical score, a table, a block of marble, but philosophy cannot defend the practice.[2]

But what is the value factor in experience? The answer I would give is in essential accord with the type of theory that defines value in terms of interest or desire—value is satisfaction, the appeasing of desire. The primary argument for this identification is the fact that if one considers any experience accepted as containing value—any experience of beauty or enjoyment or insight or love—one always finds satisfaction there; and if one thinks away the satisfaction, one thinks away everything called value. It might be objected that this argument proves only that satisfaction is a necessary condition of value,

---

[1] As Michelangelo believed:

> Non ha l'ottimo artista alcun concetto
> Ch'un marmo solo in sè non circoscriva
> Col suo soverchio . . . .

[2] This statement is, I believe, in agreement with that of Dr. W. D. Ross, as expressed in *The Right and the Good* (Oxford: At the Clarendon Press, 1930) , pp. 75–104.

not that it is value; but so to think would be to miss the point. For what is said is not merely that all experiences which contain value contain satisfactions, and without satisfactions there are no values, but, rather, that when you look into an experience which you believe to contain value and consider the factor of satisfaction there, you discover that what you meant by its value is exactly what you mean by the satisfaction, and that if the factor of satisfaction is lost, what you have been calling its value is also lost. Enjoyments *are* satisfactions of elementary desires; beauty is found to be characteristically a satisfaction through freely created imaginary, or sensuous phenomenal, objects within experience; the intrinsic value of insight is indistinguishable from the appeasement of the curiosity of the investigator. If you look into any one of such experiences you cannot find "good" there as a predicate or factor distinct from satisfaction, as you might find yellow in a yellow leaf distinct from its size or shape. In the esthetic experience there is nothing in addition to the satisfaction, together with the ideal objects and sensuous shapes that mediate satisfaction—no third thing, goodness or good. The total experience is richer than satisfaction, but satisfaction is the value which the concrete whole possesses intrinsically, that is, in independence of the knowledge or the concern of other subjects.

This argument should be conclusive, yet it has not persuaded certain philosophers. To some high-minded thinkers there is something shocking in identifying value with satisfaction for the reason that the values of beauty and nobility are thereby placed alongside the sensuous satisfactions of eating and drinking and the like; as satisfactions, and therefore as values, they would all be commensurate. And, they argue, should we not hold fast to the saying of Kant, that there is nothing in the world or out of it of absolute value, except a good will? Yet, when we look deeper into the matter, we discover that this objection is groundless. For, in the first place, to identify value with satisfaction is not to deny qualitative differences among the desires that are being satisfied. Generic sameness does not destroy specific difference; although the wish to serve the group be still a desire, even as hunger is, it is yet a specifically different desire. On the other hand, I would insist that if value is satisfaction, moral values take their place alongside sensuous values; there is no absolute difference between them. As we go up the scale of values, from the bodily to the esthetic to the scientific to the moral and the mystical, we find that we are moving on a single line; we are not moving on a line perpendicular to the one on which we started. Humble as they are, eating and drinking are still values, and the good life demands them as well as the higher ones. And if we thin out the good life, taking away from it enjoyment, knowledge, and esthetic appreciation, we diminish its value; we cannot give full reverence to a man of good will who is stupid and without sensibility to the beautiful. Nor can we deny that great genius in science or art may compensate in our eyes for a certain decay in moral fiber; on this we must insist against the moral snobbishness of the pietist. Furthermore, to claim that the good deed would still have value even if the good man took no satisfaction in it means either to identify the worth of nobility with its consequences in the lives of other men or to postulate some criterion of moral value outside the moral experience itself. But, I ask, how does one apply this criterion in a given case—how does one know that nobility is a value except through the satisfaction that he does have in a generous act? And if one persists that he does know this independently, I strongly suspect that he is attributing to it, not intrinsic value, but so-called extrinsic value; because, of course, even if the generous deed brings no satisfaction to the doer, it does bring satisfaction to the recipient, who profits from it. There may well be an unadmitted selfishness or utilitarianism in the doctrine of the moral absolute!

That the view which I am defending, that intrinsic value belongs only to experiences, never to objects as such, is a hard doctrine, I do not deny. Prima facie, perhaps, value belongs to objects—the deed is good, the picture is beautiful, the woman is lovely—and this appearance of objectivity is reflected in the judgment of value, which ascribes a worth predicate to the thing itself. But here is a situation where both prima-facie appearance and the usual subject–predicate judgmental form are particularly deceptive. There is, however, a simple explanation of this deceptiveness, most clearly revealed perhaps in the esthetic experience. In this experience value is literally spread out over the object, felt (*eingefühlt*) into it—the yellow of Van Gogh *is* happy; the Strauss melody *is* blithesome—so that the object seems itself to possess value, as a realistic theory would demand. Yet this is possible because in the esthetic experience the object is phenomenal, not independently real, hence is itself a factor in the total experience possessing intrinsic value. Esthetic satisfaction is satisfaction in appearance, or, as Kant put it, in representation; the beauty of the object, that is to say, the satisfaction which the object mediates, fuses with the object. In certain types of social and moral experience the situation is analogous. A woman seems lovely, and, without philosophy, it may be difficult to persuade the lover that her loveliness is not intrinsically her own, for the reason that he tends to associate her charm, which is really his love of her, with her appearance, itself a factor in his total experience. His love and her appearance are compresent; hence his satisfactions seem to belong to her. But as a matter of literal fact, his satisfactions are not predicates of her; a scientific account of her would not include charm as an intrinsic property. The seeming intrinsic worth of a noble action can be explained in the same way. Our gratitude for it coalesces with the appearance or idea of it in our minds, and therefore the value looks as if it belonged to the deed itself. Or else we feel ourselves into the state of mind of the doer and associate his satisfaction in doing the deed with its appearance in our own minds. But, on analysis, we find that there is no value in the action taken abstractly, that the situation is one of projection, made possible by the substitution of phenomenal appearance for the action. Since we know of no external, remote object except through its appearances, this projection of value is universal; but its deceptiveness is clear. It is strictly analogous to the dislocation of secondary qualities in ordinary perception.

The fusion of an attitude with an object, and the subsequent mistaking of the attitude for a quality of the object, occur with regard to other items of experience, also. Thus, we have been told, cruelty is intrinsically evil, and its badness is as intrinsic a predicate as the yellow of an autumn leaf. But, for myself, when I examine such an impulse of my own I can find nothing there except cruelty itself; I cannot find some additional quality which I might call badness. And since the impulse is my own, and is completely given, it is strange that I cannot find the quality if it exists; for I am not as one in a game of hide-and-seek searching for a playmate who may be hidden away in a corner, not directly open to inspection. But if I look into my mind when I have a feeling of cruelty, I do find an enveloping attitude of repulsion—although the Indian who tortures his victim would not find such an attitude in his mind—on the basis of which I condemn the feeling. Now this enveloping attitude is mistaken for an intrinsic attribute of the impulse.

It must, however, be emphatically recognized that, although the object of desire has no intrinsic value as such, it may be a necessary condition of value. Desires are commonly directed upon and satisfied through objects, either of a certain class, as with hunger, or unique objects, as with love. Love would never have appeared in the world without objects of love (need I say it?), or hunger without food. But for all this, we must not confuse a necessary condition for the existence of a thing with the thing itself—the object, which is a condition of value, with value, which is always subject. The object may, however, possess an intrinsic value of its own correlative with the value of the subject experience of which it is the object. Thus to the value ascribed to a noble deed (extrinsic or "false" value) by reason of the benefits which it confers upon members of a group there corresponds an intrinsic value in the doing of the deed, resident in the satisfied love of the person who does it. Or, when love of another sort is "returned," there is an intrinsic value in loving which belongs to the object of love, correlative to the extrinsic value which the beloved has for the lover. But this correlative intrinsic value belongs clearly to the object of desire, not as object of the original desire, but as subject of a new desire. And only persons, or monads, never "things," can possess correlative intrinsic value.

There is an old controversy which has bearing on the conception of value which I am developing, as to whether it should be defined in terms of desire or of satisfaction. In favor of the definition in terms of satisfaction are the cases where value seems to exist without desire, as when we smell the perfume of the orchid, look at a sunset, or taste the savor of sugar or spices; in favor of the definition in terms of desire we have the common experience that the appeasement of desire seems to fall short of desire itself, and may even be disappointing in comparison—being in love seems better than love's fruition. The existence of desireless satisfactions would, however, offer no obstacle to the doctrine of this chapter, which defines the good primarily in terms of satisfaction rather than in terms of desire. Yet I am not convinced that desireless satisfactions do exist even in the cases cited, for it is probable that corresponding desires exist in the deeper layers of experience, unknown to us—we possess the satisfactions, but not the desires appeased; or there may be desires so quickly aroused and so evanescent as to be overwhelmed in the satisfactions that follow. On the other hand, if it were true that value belongs to desire rather than to satisfaction, our definition in terms of the latter would be false; but it can be shown that the facts to which appeal is made are incompletely analyzed and do not bear out the interpretation that is given them. For it is overlooked that the process of desire finding appeasement is complex, like a musical note: it contains overtones of imaginative satisfactions—the poetic element in all desire—satisfactions which are the echoes in memory of past satisfactions, and satisfactions which are anticipations of appeasement, making of every desire something more than mere desire, making being in love as full of value as love's fruition. Desires are not appeased all at once, but in stages, and we tend to forget the appeasements by the way when we reach the ultimate goal. Hence we should not say that desire itself is sometimes better than satisfaction, but rather that the satisfactions that attend the process of fulfilment of desire are often greater than those which attend its final phase.

If value is no intrinsic predicate of an object, may it not, nevertheless, be a relational predicate—not, as I have been contending, a fictitious predicate, but a real quality, as real as any other that the object may possess, only depending for its existence on relation? In particular, may it not be a quality which belongs to the object through its relation to desire? This appears to be the thesis of one of the most widely held theories of value in contemporary philosophy, although the various formulations by its supporters are not all equivalent. For it is one thing to declare that value is "any object of any interest," [1] where, presumably, value would be identical with the object of interest, and therefore would be a substantive; and it is another thing to declare that "the being liked or disliked of the object is

---

[1] See R. B. Perry, *General Theory of Value* (New York: Longmans, Green and Co., 1926), p. 124 and p. 133 n.; see also p. 116.

its value," [1] where value becomes a relational predicate of the object; and it is still another thing to declare that "value is ... a specific relation into which things of any ontological status whatever may enter ... with interested subjects," where value is defined as a relation.[2] In a metaphysical discussion of the matter such differences of statement are not trivial, for it becomes important to know whether value is a substantive, a relation, or a relational predicate. We may, I think, reject the supposition that the writers in question regard value as a substantive, as a thing; we are left, therefore, with the other alternatives. We shall consider each in turn.

We may begin by granting that in all cases of what is ordinarily called extrinsic value there is a relation of an object to an interested subject, and that the attribution of value to the object depends upon the existence of this relationship. Our question is, then, whether the object which stands in this relationship possesses a relational predicate which can be identified with value. When bread is the object of concern of the hungry man or milk of the avid cat, could one find, by the analysis óf the bread or the milk, a property depending upon this relationship which one could identify with value? From the ordinary dualistic point of view of common sense and science the answer seems clear: No, one could not; absolutely no unique property is added to the properties of the bread or the milk through the concern that is taken in them. In the light of Kant's well-known distinction between logical and reflective judgments,[3] it remains true that the judgment, *x* is good, is not a logical judgment, that is to say, cannot be interpreted properly to ascribe the predicate "good" to the object, as genuinely belonging to it. The same situation exists if the ọbject instead of being a physical thing is a person; no analysis of that person could reveal goodness or good as a specific real property of him. Just as we have seen that no intrinsic value predicate can be found in the object, so, equally, no relational value predicate can be found there. It may well be true, of course, that when bread is the

[1] See D. W. Prall, *A Study in the Theory of Value,* University of California Publications in Philosophy, Vol. III, No. 2 (Berkeley: University of California Press, 1921), pp. 215, 227; compare also p. 254: "It [value] is the existence of an interest relation between a subject and an object."

[2] Prall, *loc. cit.*

[3] *Critique of Judgment,* Introduction.

concern of some subject there exist certain physical properties in the bread which would not exist if bread were not the concern of somebody; and, similarly, if one subject be the object of concern of another subject, there may be psychological changes which occur in the former owing to this concern (suppose the person is loved or hated!); but in neither case could these changes be described in terms of the value ascribed to the object. The changes are of a physical or a psychological, not of an axiological, character; no term denoting value need appear in any enumeration or description of them. All that the proposition, x is good, can possibly assert, when x is some object, is that x could, that is to say, would under certain circumstances, conduce to the satisfaction of somebody. When x is an object, the proposition, x is good, is in fact an elliptical expression, which as it stands is meaningless; it must be emended to read, x is good for somebody, and when so emended means, as I have said, merely that x, under certain circumstances, would conduce to the satisfaction of somebody; but this proposition does not imply the existence in x of any property of an axiological character whatever.

If now, reflecting further upon the matter, we take a deeper metaphysical view of the problem, we must be careful not to be misled by, or to place too much reliance on, linguistic expressions. Thus, if we consider the statement, A is liked by B, it might seem as if A must have the predicate "liked by B," which does indeed appear to have an axiological character and which we might therefore be tempted to identify with the value of A. For, generally, when B is related to A, does not B have a generic relational property, "being related to A"? However, even if the truth be granted of the general proposition already insisted on by us in our chapters on relations (Chaps. X–XI), that whenever a relation exists there is a property called by us a relational or acquired property pertaining to each term of the relationship, nothing relevant to our problem can be inferred until we have determined the nature of the relation involved; specifically, in this case, we must determine what sort of relationship exists between A and B when A likes B, for the nature of the relation will determine that of the corresponding relational predicates; and, as we shall see immediately, much that is very unclear metaphysically is hidden under the phrase "being liked by B."

We are thus brought to the consideration of the alternative

interpretation of the relational theory of value, namely, that value is itself a relation, the relation between the subject A and the object B when A is interested in B. No one, I should suppose, would doubt that in some cases a relation of some kind is present in this situation. The question, however, is whether, if present, it is a unique relation that can be identified with value. In many cases there is clearly a causal relation between A and B; this is true when B is a means object and its so-called value obviously extrinsic: as we have shown, the object is said to have value or to be valuable when it could, that is to say, would, under certain circumstances, contribute to the appeasement of some interest of somebody. That is all that its "value" means. A bridge, a steamboat, an automobile, all the common utilities of life, are valuable in this way. But if the object be a complementary rather than a means object, an object in which interest is taken directly and through which it is immediately appeased, is the situation different? Here it is well to distinguish between two situations—one where the object is a phenomenal object or a pattern of sensa lying within consciousness and the other where the object is transcendent to the consciousness of the subject. Let us consider the latter situation first. Suppose I am a spectator watching a football game: here is interest—not in the phenomenal objects lying within my consciousness, not in what I have called the "periphery" (see p. 111) of the players and the ball—but in the players and the ball themselves, who are foci remote and transcendent to me, revealed by the phenomenal objects. What now is the relation between the interested subject and his objects? That here also there are causal relations is beyond doubt—the players, through the mediation of the ideas they arouse in the spectator, incite and satisfy or frustrate his desires.

These causal relations, involved in the situation where A is interested in B, are not, however, to be identified with the value in question, and can hardly be in the minds of those who identify value with an interest relation. For although it be true, as we have claimed, that all causal relations depend upon desire, and come in the end to a coöperation of interests, the interests involved are not solely those of the subject whose values are under consideration, but the interests of nature in coöperation with man. Even when nature's interests are sympathetic with man's, they are not his. In those situations where the value character of the causal relation is evident, as in cases of biological adaptation, upon which, for example, depends the pleasure we take in nourishing food, this is still true. For the causal relation implied is not a relation between the interest and its object solely—not solely between hunger and the food—but includes the purposes embodied in preformed physiological structures. The relation involves factors on the biological level; and though there is the closest coöperation and sympathy between the personal and the biological levels, insuring the preservation of life, the two cannot be identified. A causal chain is not, I repeat, a simple relation between interested subject and its object, but a highly complex relation involving many interests and, as we have seen, many sensa also, in diverse but overlapping monads.

If such causal relations are not the interest relation, what then is this relation? Perhaps we can come closer to an answer to this question if we consider the situation where B is a phenomenal object lying within the experience of the subject A. Suppose, in order to fix our attention upon a concrete case, we have in mind the interest that one takes in following the linear pattern of an oriental rug. In such a case not only the interest but its object are factors in a single monad, and there is no remote object directly involved, for interest is absorbed in the pattern of sensa, and has no concern for the physical rug which may exist behind the sensuous surface within the mind. In such a case it may well seem as if some specific and intimate relation were involved, which we might identify with an interest relation; and so, even when the object is transcendent, it might be true that this relation holds, in addition to the causal relation already discerned, wherever there is value.

In considering this possibility, we must, however, again be careful not to be misled by language. For the verbal expression of the value situation, A interested in B, might induce one to suppose that either there is a specific value relation denoted by the word "interested" or by the word "in," or possibly by the two together, the relation holding between the subject A and the linear pattern B. But careful analysis shows that neither of these suppositions is correct. To begin with, we can restate the expression to read, A has an interest in B, and then, since A denotes the self, which is itself only a system of interests, of which the interest in question is a factor, we may eliminate the term *A* without affecting the logic of the situation, and restate the proposition once more as, There exists an interest *C* in *B*. It follows that the supposititious interest relation between *A* and *B* cannot be the interest which *A* is said to have in *B*, for there is no difference between this interest and *A*—the interest cannot be between itself and *B*. But may not the interest be a relation holding between other terms? If so, between what entities does it hold? Since we have eliminated *A*, we have only *B* left; we have only the supposed relation and the pattern. But there can be no relation with only a single term. An interest is not a relation, but an activity.

Perhaps, however, the interest relation is a relation not between the subject *A* and the object *B*, but between the interest itself and its object, as would seem to be expressed in the little word "in," in the statement, *A* is interested in *B*. But that the word "in" does not necessarily express a relation, that it expresses only the vector character of the interest—its pointing at its object—comes out clearly in those cases where interest has no existing object. Suppose, for example, being homeless, I want a home of my own. Here, of course, there is desire, but there is no existing object of desire, for a desire for a home of my own is conditioned by the nonexistence of a home of my own: if I had one, I could not want one! And, in general, to want what is not is precisely characteristic of desire. As a factor in the state of mind in question, there exists, to be sure, a *concept* of a home of my own; but I do not want a concept of a home, but a real home. As Professor C. H. Langford felicitously puts it, I desire *through* the concept, I do not desire the concept. And when the interest has no existing object it is nonsense to talk of a relation between the interest and the object: there cannot be a relation to nothing. The same analysis would apply if instead of, *A* is interested in *B*, we were to consider the more concrete expression, *A* loves *B*. Despite the fact that "loves" is a verb and therefore might be thought to indicate a relation, loving is not itself a relation but an activity, and the proper logical statement of the situation is, there exists love in *A* for *B*, where "for" indicates the vector character of the activity. Naturally I do not deny that when *B* exists, as is usually the case in love—

though not always, since one may love an ideal or deceased person—there is a relation between A and B, but this is not a specific interest relation, but causality; and causality, as we have seen, is a rather complicated relation between interests, not a simple relation between an interest and its object. When, moreover, as in our example of the interest in the pattern of the rug, both the interest and its object lie within one center, the relation between the two is "compresence"—a relation holding not only between interests and their phenomenal objects, but between any other items within the center; it cannot therefore be identified as a specific "interest relation."

Further evidence against the theories of value under examination is to be found in those experiences where there is value but where desire has no object at all, not even a conceptual or so-called epistemological object. The best example of this is music. In listening to music I may begin to feel an intense longing, growing almost unendurably poignant as the composition develops, and then, dramatically at the end, yielding a perfect appeasement; yet I am not aware of longing for anything particular at all. The tones themselves are not objects of desire (I do not, as one might suppose, long for the return of the tonic or the resolving chord), but embodiments or media for the expression of desire; even as when I say, "How happy I am," the four words in which I express my happiness are not what I am happy about. In the little Bach choral, "Gib dich zufrieden und sei stille," the happiness felt there is not happiness over the musical phrases, but in the phrases. The single example of music would be sufficient to nullify the definition of value as "any object of any interest" or as an "interest relation" between a subject and an object, for in the musical experience there is no object of desire, hence no relation to an object; there is only subject.[1] This result is in conformity with our initial insight that value is the factor of satisfaction in the experience of a subject.

We come finally to a consideration of the theory of value

---

[1] My denial of an "interest relation" has, I believe, a certain analogy in R. W. Sellars' denial of a "cognitive relation." See his *Philosophy of Physical Realism* (New York: The Macmillan Co., 1932), pp. 81 f. For further discussion of the bearing of music on the general definition of value see my *Human Values* (New York and London: Harper and Brothers, 1931), p. 23.

as the expression of a transcendent "ought" or imperative. The evidence for the theory is found especially in the moral experience where we seem to acknowledge values transcending our personal likes and dislikes. The patriot regretting that he has only one life to give for his country, the father sacrificing his pleasures in order to pay insurance premiums that his children may receive higher education after his death are not acting, it is believed, because they wish to, in their own interest, but because they recognize the validity of an "overindividual" imperative. Value is no object or quality of an object, no interest or satisfaction of interest, but a unique "form of objectivity," best expressed in the judgment, *A* is worthy to be. Not any form of existence, but the validity of an ideal of thinking, acting, and feeling is the essence of value. "Its being is its validity." [1] We can best understand this theory if we approach it from the side of its criticism of theories that identify value with satisfaction.

The argument used against such theories may be briefly summarized as follows: First, to define the good as the object or as the satisfaction of desire is circular, because it is assumed in the definition that desire or the satisfaction of desire is itself good, that fulfilment is better than nonfulfilment; and, secondly, this assumption is unwarranted, for do we not distinguish between good and bad desires?—is not, in fact the nonfulfilment of certain desires obviously better than their fulfilment? [2]

The first part of this argument recalls a similar criticism by Professor Moore in his *Principia Ethica*. Professor Moore argued that to define good as pleasure is impossible, for when I say that pleasure is good I naturally intend to mean something, but if pleasure and good are identical all I should be saying would be, Pleasure is pleasure—a silly proposition. The fallacy in this argument is, however, a simple one: the failure to distinguish between a problematic concept, which is the concept to be defined, in this case "good," and one or more definitive or ultimate concepts, the concepts used in the definition, in this case "pleasure." The purpose of all philosophical definition is to replace problematic by definitive concepts; that is all we ever do in defining "beauty," space," "number," "time," "cause," and

[1] See Wilbur Urban, *The Intelligible World* (New York: The Macmillan Co., 1929) , pp. 142, 143, 145.
[2] See *ibid.*, pp. 136, 137, 138. See also Plato *Philebus* 13.

the like. We come to realize that we mean by our problematic or tentative concepts what we mean more precisely by our definitive concepts. There is no circle in the definition, because we do not use our problematic concept in the final definition; we clarify it by replacing it. So when I say that pleasure or satisfaction is good or the good, I am merely calling attention to the fact that what I mean by "good" (noun) is nothing else than what I mean by "satisfaction," or that what I mean by "good" (adjective) is what I mean by "satisfactory," and the proposition has meaning as a definition. And if the definition is correct, I shall find that I can replace in any proposition the terms "good" (noun) by "satisfaction," and "good" (adjective) by "satisfactory." Or, to make use of another example in order to show the underlying principle: Suppose, after exhaustive study, I were to come to the conclusion that beauty is significant form. Would the statement, Beauty is significant form, be as meaningless as, Significant form is significant form? Hardly, for in the one case I am effecting the clarification of a problematic concept, but in the other I am uttering a mere tautology. Of course, once I know what beauty is, then—postulating that the definition is correct—the definition loses its significance unless, as in our hypothetical case, through it I not only substitute a definitive for a hypothetical concept, but also effect an analysis of the concept, that is to say, come to a realization of its structure. And this I do when I define good as the appeasement of desire: I come to the realization that good depends upon desire, yet is not desire, but the appeasement thereof.

The second part of the argument against the view that good is satisfaction is to the effect that this cannot be true since there are bad satisfactions, which shows that good and satisfaction are not equivalent; hence, it is held, the proposition, Satisfaction is good, is not a definitive or a tautological proposition, but a synthetic proposition, and the proposition, Satisfaction is bad, is not a self-contradictory proposition. But this argument is unsound because of the failure to distinguish between intrinsic value, extrinsic value, and what I would call final value. We cannot, I should say, ask of any satisfaction whether it is intrinsically good, for satisfaction is the intrinsically good; to do so would be as meaningless as to ask whether a man is a man or an elephant is an elephant. It is likewise meaningless to ask whether the fulfilment of desire is better than nonfulfilment, when we are thinking of intrinsic good—just as meaningless as to ask whether good is better than bad. Of course, when good is still a problematic concept which we are seeking to clarify or define, then, as we have seen, it is pertinent to ask whether satisfaction is the good; but, once having recognized the sufficiency of this definition, to say that satisfaction is intrinsically good is pointless, unless, to be sure, I mean to say of *this* satisfaction that it is a case of satisfaction or good, even as I might say of this man that he is a man—which is not what is meant. On the other hand, it is pertinent to ask of any particular satisfaction whether it is extrinsically good, that is to say, good for someone else besides the person whose satisfaction it is; and it is pertinent to ask whether the satisfaction is better for someone else than a corresponding nonsatisfaction. The satisfaction which a man takes in injuring me when he hates me is, naturally, not a good for me; and it is better for me that his impulse be frustrated rather than consummated, because his satisfaction would frustrate some one or more of *my* wishes.

In a similar way it is meaningful to ask whether a satisfaction is finally good, that is to say, finally satisfactory. Now when I ask this question I am speaking with reference to my life plan and corresponding life desire—my striving for satisfaction of myself as a whole—asking whether the satisfaction in question would further or hinder it; and the satisfaction will be a case of final satisfaction or not as it tends to do one or the other. Interesting problems touching the unity of the self are involved in this matter, for a satisfaction which I judge not to be finally good is, nevertheless, as a satisfaction of my own, an instance of the intrinsically good; there will therefore be a division within myself—a conflict between good and good, yet a conflict that contains the principle of its own solution, for the very desire from which the "evil" satisfaction springs is taken account of in the life plan that condemns it. Now I suspect that the finally good is what is in the minds of those who define the good as "worthiness to be." But I would stress the point that the final good can be defined only in terms of desire; for the life desire is still a desire, only a deeper stratum of desire enveloping our simpler propensities, encouraging some of these and inhibiting others, making out of them an integral pattern. Worthiness to be has significance only with reference to the matrix self. From the point of view of this self, everything either is or is not what it should be. But the life plan of the matrix self is not subject to review, for, since it is the ultimate source of all valuations, there is no standpoint from which it could be reviewed. I may judge your life plan in terms of mine, and you may judge mine in terms of yours, but there is no way by which we can step outside all life plans and judge them.

There are, however, three possible objections which may still be raised against the reduction of "worthiness to be" to conformity with the life plan: (1) that it makes objective and universally valid moral judgments impossible; (2) that it cannot provide a basis for the hierarchy of values; and (3) that it cannot designate any empirical motivation for overindividual values. Let us consider each of these objections in turn.

We may restate the first as follows: How under the theory proposed, to the effect that the "worthiness to be" of an act is relative to the life plans of various individuals, is it possible to assign a definite moral predicate to an act, since the act may be favorable to the life plans of A and B and C but unfavorable to those of D and E? A radical relativism and pluralism in ethics would seem to be the result. But, it will be insisted, when we affirm that an act is morally good, we are asserting something which either is or is not true, true for all or false for all; and the moral intuition of man reveals to us that this is the case.

To this difficulty I would reply as follows: It would have force if life plans were independent of each other, but in any group the life plan of the individual is, on the contrary, bound up inextricably with the plans of his fellows; what is good for one is largely dependent upon what is good for another. This interdependence is, of course, very obvious—is, indeed, a particular case of the metaphysical interrelationship of all monads. The result is that when we are considering the final "worthiness to be" of an act we are necessarily taking into account all the life plans with which our own is bound; our own life plan demands that we do so. Hence, relative to certain groups of people are judgments that have for these groups what used to be called intersubjective validity, or, as we now call it, social validity. Thus for any group of civilized Americans murder, theft, malicious lying, flagrant neglect of civic or professional duties are unworthy to be, not merely for you or for me, but for all members of the group, because such types of conduct are, in the end, inconsistent with the full realization of the life plan of any one of us. It is hard to conceive what other sort of validity moral judgments could have except intersubjective validity. We can see that this is true if we compare the moral judgment in this regard with the judgment of fact. For what, I would ask, constitutes the universality or objectivity of judgments of fact? Not that everyone is in agreement, for it is notorious that even in what is called science experts disagree. And it cannot consist in the possibility that everyone may agree, because there are some so blind with prejudice or defects of intelligence that they never could agree upon the subtler matters of fact. Not anything of this sort, but the existence of states of affairs to which judgments refer and by means of which they may be tested by anyone who *can* test them, is the basis of their objectivity and their so-called universality. Reality is the basis of objectivity. The case of the moral judgment is no different. A moral judgment will be valid for me if it expresses the nature of my essential self—its potentialities for happiness—and for you if it expresses your essential self; but it cannot be valid for the tiger, in whose nature there is no corresponding system desire, or for the moral idiot or the moron. The admonition, "Serve your group, do justice, practice mercy," has validity for me only if, when so acting, I am happier than when I fail to act so. If someone insistently proclaims that I still ought to serve the group whether I am happy or not, he is either trying to educate me into this happiness or else, perhaps unwittingly, seeking to enslave me in his own interest, since he would himself profit by my moral behavior. And for God to affirm the moral judgment from all eternity would not help; he could not make it valid for me if there does not exist in me a capacity for the ends it proposes. To look elsewhere than in existing desires for the basis of moral judgments is to deny the autonomy of value and to seek to found value on what is not value. But let no one object that to base morality on the desires of individuals is to make it arbitrary and transitory. For this would be a cogent objection only if desires were fleeting, epiphenomenal and unrelated facts, when, on the contrary, they are the permanent, highly organized essence of all centers of experience— the substance of the world. The life desire is as stubborn a fact as a star; the life plan is as much a law governing events as any so-called law of nature.

The second argument against any attempt to explain away the ethical "ought" is based on the existence of a hierarchy of values. How, it may be asked, can values depend upon desire when there is an intrinsic order or dignity—a relation of pure "betterness" [1]—among them, of which the common distinction between the higher and the lower values is an example? Are not the esthetic values better than sensual enjoyment, the values of love better than those of ambition? Or is not the life plan of the saint better than that of the average sensual man, the life plan of the good citizen better than that of the crook? And if there are relations of value among desires and life plans, how can value be based upon the latter?

To these questions I would give the following answers. In the first place, when one satisfaction is better than another it is not better in itself, but better for some subject, which means that it is preferred against its alternative as fitting in with the life plan of the individual. To find a relation of pure betterness independent of preference is as impossible as to find a good independent of desire. To say that one desire is better than another out of all relation to the choices of monads is nonsense. And choice itself issues from a desire that selects among imagined objectives of other desires; and if the choice leads to a fuller satisfaction of the whole self, the selecting desire may then be called of higher order than the desires among which it selects. A is better than B, means, when A and B are values, that to appease the desire which yields the satisfaction A rather than to appease the desire which yields the satisfaction B is in the interest of the matrix self. In the life of a monad there are major interests and minor interests, and the minor are objects of choice for the relatively major. So, for the sake of interest in my health I may prefer to play golf rather than sit quietly dreaming in my chair; or for the love of my friend I may prefer the satisfaction of helping him to the satisfaction of increasing my bank account. In the end all subordinate desires are subject to the desire of the matrix self—the desire of highest order.[2]

[1] Cf. A. P. Brogan, "The Fundamental Value Universal," *Journal of Philosophy*, XVI (1919), No. 4 : 96–104.
[2] For a fuller discussion of these matters see my *Human Values*, chaps. v–vi.

Moreover, it does not follow from the dependence of the hierarchy of values upon desire that the hierarchy is purely a matter of the personal conscience of each individual. It is true, to be sure, that the total structure of desire is as individual, and hence as ineffable, as the total nature of each monad. No man can transfer his conscience to another without remainder. But within the individuality of each life plan the hierarchy of values expresses a law or order among types of objectives of desire—or among types of desires themselves—so far as the subject is capable of them at all. The mystical experience is preferred, and this means is found more satisfying on the whole than any worldly success or sensual enjoyment by anyone capable of both types of experience. The reason why some men do not prefer the higher to the lower is that they are incapable of experiencing both to the full, and cannot, therefore, make a genuine choice. This is the reason why the unmusical prefer jazz to Bach or the average sensual man prefers comfort to beauty. Religion to the secular-minded, music to the unmusical, beauty to the Philistine are mere names, like the names of foreign lands unvisited. This is also the reason why men usually capable of the higher values will prefer the lower under special circumstances preventing the complete realization of the higher; hence the musical person, when tired, may prefer jazz, if not too strident, to classical music. No one can live all the time and under all circumstances on the plane of the higher values; but, so far as he is capable of the higher, no one can prefer the lower to the higher. What is called sin is choice of the lower rather than the higher under conditions that prevent the adequate imagination of the higher, in such a way as to damage the future realization of the higher. The order among values is, therefore, no order external to them, and the imperativeness of duty is no external compulsion. The order is an order within the essential self of the monad, and the compulsion is no other than the lure of its objectives.

When, finally, having worked our way through the dark wood of philosophical controversy and come into the clear, we look for the empirical motivation of overindividual values, we shall have no difficulty in discovering it. For love is the source, and the happiness born of love the justification, for all acts through which the individual identifies his own interest with that of something transcending himself—the devotion of the lover to the beloved, the parent to the child, the friend to the friend, the patriot to the fatherland, the mystic to God. That some philosophers long after Plato's *Symposium* failed to discover this, or, having known it, did not name correctly what they found, will remain one of the curiosities of the history of philosophy—a matter not for metaphysical argument but for biographical interpretation.

XVI

The Eternal

IN THE *Metaphysics* [1] Aristotle defines "first philosophy" as the study of being as being, and especially that part of being which is eternal; as examples of the eternal he cites the heavens, the forms, the Prime Mover, and certain truths. In offering this definition Aristotle was but following tradition, for from its beginning Greek philosophy was a search for an eternal substance underlying change—whether water, air, fire, or, with Plato, Ideas or forms. And almost without exception from the Greeks on down to our own day the philosophers of the Western world believed that something was eternal: God at least was eternal; or, if there was no God, the ultimate particles or energies, out of which matter was thought to be composed, were accepted as eternal. By contrast, contemporary philosophy is hesitant: the twilight that has fallen upon the gods has fallen upon the eternal, also.

The first step toward clearness in this matter is to make a distinction, foreshadowed by Plato,[2] between the timeless and the everlasting or eternal. By a timeless object I shall mean one that is essentially, that is to say, by definition, indifferent to time and not subject to change; and although some such objects exist at one or at several moments in the time series, some perhaps at all moments, others do not exist at all. In one or another of these regards timeless objects differ from events and from finite substances. For an event, although changeless, like a timeless object, must exist and can exist once only and at no other time than it does exist—it is both unique and evanescent—and a finite substance, although like some timeless objects in existing at many moments, is unlike all timeless objects in being essentially an existent and subject to change. Thus the signing of the Treaty of Versailles, being an event, is changeless; for better or worse, it can not become other than it was or happen at any other

---

[1] Aristotle *Metaphysics* 1025b, 1026a.　　　[2] Plato *Timaeus* 37c, 6–38b, 5.

moment of history than it did; and, although the world became its Hall of Mirrors in which to all eternity it will be reflected, it itself flashed into existence, then disappeared forever. But the signers—or, rather, whoever of them have survived—being finite substances, have changed, thinking now other thoughts than on that day of triumph, yet, despite the change, persisting essentially the same "old men" as then, though not for long.

In contrast with all three—event, finite substance, and timeless object—stands the everlasting object, the eternal. Unlike the timeless object it is by definition an existence; and although, like some timeless objects, independent of time in the sense that it is not confined to this rather than to that moment, it is independent thus only because it exists at all moments; it is not, therefore, strictly speaking, independent of time. In this regard it is closer to the event and the finite substance, which, also, are existences. And take away from the finite substance its unique beginning and ending, its possible lapses from existence (as when the mind sleeps), and you get the eternal, of which there is no beginning, end, or intermittence. Our definition of the eternal leaves open the question whether or not it changes; we shall have to discover the answer as we proceed.

Having defined the timeless and the eternal object, let us next enquire whether there is anything that conforms to these definitions. With regard to timeless objects, the answer is clear: universals are timeless objects. This is the almost unanimous doctrine of Western philosophy, from Plato's Ideas to Santayana's Essences or Whitehead's Eternal Objects. Universals have all the characteristics of timeless objects: they are changeless, they may exist at many moments—the melodic pattern, which existed long ago when the composer invented it, will exist again when someone sings it—and yet, so far as their intrinsic nature is concerned, they may not exist at all: anyone who conceives an act but does not execute it, defines a universal that does not exist.

There are, then, timeless objects, the universals, and they are the only such objects we know. But from this truth a strange inference has been drawn: that these objects have a kind of eternal existence, which is yet not called existence, but "subsistence" or "being." The ultimate basis for this belief is as old as Plato (even as the belief itself was originally his), namely: that anything that one can think of, or refer to, must first *be* in order to be thought of, or referred to; the field of reference must be a field of being.[1] This argument, in its turn, rests on the conception, almost universal in Greek philosophy of the classic period, of the passivity and the imitative character of thought and perception. Thinking was believed to be an image, or reflection, of something already there, not in any sense an autonomous creative process. The imitative theory of thought is closely parallel to the imitative theory of art. But even as we have now come to the realization that art is creative, not imitative, so, since Kant, we should have learned the same lesson regarding thought. Thought picks universals out of existing individuals in which they are embodied, just as art selects what it needs from the model, but it also creates them when they are not to be found exemplified, just as art, again, creates what it needs when it cannot find it in the model. That the same universal can be present in the work of thought of many minds offers no difficulty to us, with our doctrine of personal and interpersonal identity. Universals exist only when embodied in thought or experience: when not so embodied they are not, in any sense.

One wonders, in fact, what can be meant by saying that a universal is, or has being. We know what is meant by saying that a universal exists: a universal exists when it is exemplified or embodied; but what is added to the universal "triangle," say, by declaring that it is? Is "being" then a predicate? It is true that I began the preceding paragraph with the statement, "There are, then, timeless objects, the universals," and that is exactly the sort of careless statement, I fear, that misleads the unwary into accepting the realm of being. What I meant, and what perhaps I should therefore have said, was, "Universals are timeless," that is to say, universals are a species—in fact, the sole species—of the genus "timeless objects": "are" denotes the implicative relation in the proposition expressing this fact, not the existential coefficient; in terms of the modern symbolism $\supset$, not $\exists$.[2] One would apologize for pointing out so elementary a confusion if a whole metaphysical theory were not founded on overlooking it.

It is forgotten, moreover, that timelessness is a purely nega-

[1] Plato *Parmenides* 132b.

[2] The proposition is, of course, x is a universal implies x is timeless; in symbolism, $x \, \epsilon \, U \supset x \, \epsilon \, T.$

tive determination, from which nothing can be deduced. All that it means is that no temporal predicate is included in the definition of a universal. You cannot infer from the absence of the property of temporality to the presence of some form of timeless existence. It is as if one were to infer from the statement that Puck is not a man to the statement that Puck is a real elf! Of course I know that it will be objected to what I have written that existence is not meant, but only being. But I ask again, What is being? Existence out of time? As if time were something that existed in its own right, *outside* which something else might exist! *Eternal existence,* perhaps—is that what is meant by "being" or "subsistence"? But eternal existence would not be out of time; it would be an eternal "now," an invariant portion of the present; and since the present includes everything that exists, the eternal would coexist with the varying phases of the temporal world; it would have existed along with each moment of the past, and would coexist with each moment of the future. Instead of existing outside time, the realm of being would coexist with all time, and therefore not be timeless; it would be an everlasting existence, and the timeless and eternal would coincide. But only such universals as are known to be embodied in all individuals that have existed at any time are known to belong to this eternal realm; the rest come and go, recurring, to be sure, but not abiding forever.

In order to show some of the confusions in the thought of those who write of a realm of being in contrast to the realm of existence, I shall examine an argument of Santayana's which impressed me when I first read it as a student and which I find impresses other students still. "That truth is no existence might also be proved as follows," he writes. "Suppose that nothing existed or (if critics carp at that phrase) that a universe did not exist. It would then be true that all existences were wanting, *yet this truth itself would endure;* therefore truth is not an existence." [1] Now let us permit our minds to play about these sentences; we shall find that there are several interesting things to be said concerning them. First, I suppose that we are to understand by "It would then be true that . . ." the same meaning as "this truth itself would endure." Everything turns on

[1] George Santayana, *Reason in Science* (New York: Charles Scribner's Sons, 1906), p. 31 n. The italics are mine.

this equivalence. But when I say, "Suppose that nothing existed . . . . It would then be true that all existences were wanting," am I saying anything more than "If nothing existed, nothing would exist"? For there is no difference in meaning between "Nothing would exist" and "It is true that nothing would exist," or between "Suppose that nothing existed" and "It would then be true that all existences were wanting." In still other words, the statement comes to this, "If nothing exists, nothing exists," or "Nothing exists implies that nothing exists," a sheer tautology—as Locke would call it, a "silly" proposition —from which nothing at all, least of all an important metaphysical proposition, could be inferred. But in answer to what I have written I am sure that Santayana would accuse me of being "malicious," as he has accused Berkeley—of wilfully failing to understand his argument. For I surmise that what he wants us to do is to think away all existences, one by one, until nothing is left, then ask ourselves this question: Would there not, hovering over the silent void, be—or "endure"—the truth that nothing is? My answer would, unhesitatingly, be no. By getting rid of all existences, we would have *ipso facto* gotten rid of all truth, for there is no truth unless there is a process of judgment, and a process of judgment is, needless to say, an existence—unless one means by truth, as sometimes is the case, not the true judgment, but that which makes the true judgment true, in which case, since, by hypothesis, nothing exists, there would still be no truth, since there would not be anything to make any judgment true. Therefore, in asserting that the truth that all existences were wanting would endure you have contradicted yourself; you have postulated a void and have then introduced into the void, surreptitiously, the comment that there is such a void—or else, what is worse, something to make that comment true! You have tried to eat your existential cake and have it, too.

Santayana himself foresees this issue of the argument and tries to evade it by denying that the phrase "this truth itself would endure" means that an opinion or judgment would exist eternally "in the ether," on the ground that "somebody's opinion is not what is meant by the truth, since every opinion, however long lived, may be false." But while it is true that every opinion, that is to say, every judgment, abstractly considered, may be false, even as it may be true, yet if it is true, how can it be false? And, by hypothesis, the opinion in question would be true. Moreover, although truth is not just an opinion, it is a species of opinion, namely, the kind of opinion that conforms to existence. So, if there were nothing at all, there could be no opinion, and also nothing for the opinion to conform to, hence no truth.

There is a more technical way of stating Mr. Santayana's argument. According to the modern interpretation of universal propositions, every such proposition is, in effect, a denial of the existence of a certain class of things; thus the universal affirmative proposition, All A is B , means that the class of A 's that are also not-B's does not exist. Hence the denial of the existence of any class of things, say A , is equivalent to a universal negative proposition; for granted that All A 's are A 's, which is a universal affirmative proposition, then the corresponding universal negative would be, No A 's are A 's, which is equivalent to, A 's that are A do not exist, in turn reducing to, A 's do not exist. If, therefore, we run through the universe and eliminate one by one each class of things, until no class remains, we seem to make true as we go a series of universal negative propositions: A 's do not exist, B 's do not exist, C 's do not exist, Philosophers do not exist, Dictators do not exist, Stars do not exist, Roses do not exist. Santayana's proposition to the effect that nothing exists is equivalent, consequently, to the "logical product" of the members of this series of universal negative propositions: it is a sort of absolute universal negative proposition. Now it is this absolute universal negative proposition that, according to Santayana, would then be true and would endure, in the event that there was nothing. But to this statement of the matter the same reasoning applies as to the less technical statement, for either the assertion, The absolute universal negative proposition would then be true if nothing existed, is simply equivalent to the assertion of the absolute universal negative proposition itself, and therefore says nothing new—which I should say is the case—or else if what is said is that this absolute negative universal proposition would endure even if nothing were left in the world, then the absolute negative proposition is denied, for it could endure only by being affirmed in some existing judgment, in which event it could not be true. If a philosopher, having witnessed the gradual destruction of the world, found himself alone and about to perish, and, surveying the scene of desolation, cried, "After me, nothing," this truth would disappear with him.

The denial of the "being" of universals and truth will, I fear, be branded by some as subjectivism. But, with regard to truth, it is forgotten that three factors are involved: the object, the "essence," and the mind; and as long as the object is what it is, independent of the judging mind, the objective factor in truth is assured, for the application of essences in judgment is not a matter of caprice but is determined by the object, which is the same for all minds. Even if Newton's gravitational formulae had to await the advent of Newton for their existence when he constructed them, the planets whose behavior those laws describe had gone their way long before his discoveries. Not the dependence of truth, but the dependence of the object on the mind, is subjectivism.[1] With regard to universals, the answer to the charge of subjectivism is more complicated. If universals have no being of their own, what becomes, for example, of the validity, independent of the mind, of the deductions from the system of axioms of Euclidean geometry, or of deductions from any other set of postulates? Or are not such simple relations between universals as are expressed in, Two plus two equals four, made dependent upon the existence, always precarious, of a thinker?

Now ever since the time of Locke it has been known that the mind cannot create simple universals, but can only pick them out from objects of experience in which it finds them embedded; on the other hand, however, the mind can bring "simple ideas" (universals) together, as it does in all creative activity. This happens when new postulate systems are constructed by mathematicians. These postulates have, singly, nothing intrinsic to do with each other; they neither belong, nor do they fail to belong, together. Yet when they are brought together interesting relations appear among the universals so defined, and these relations are no more created by the mathematician than are the "simple ideas" between which the relations hold. It is true that the "simple ideas" have no being or existence except as factors in experience, but when they are factors in experience the relations between them are not subject to caprice. They are simply there,

[1] Cf. J. M. McTaggart, *The Nature of Existence* (Cambridge: At the University Press, 1921), I, chap. ii.

within experience. Even so, if a mathematician puts together the various Ideas and simple relations which constitute the system of Euclidean geometry, he finds that they are fertile of further relationships, to be expressed as "inferences" or "deductions"—as a pair of mice of opposite sex are fertile—and will breed as long as he keeps them alive before the mind. There are some universals that will not breed together and some that will: [1] those generally called "inconsistent" [2] are sterile, as are those that have no common genus or are not constructed on a common base. (If I put the parallel-line axiom together with the ethical proposition that esthetic values are higher than simple satisfactions of sensuous propensities, no inferences are possible.) The insight that the same inferences—relations—appear in the experience of all minds that contain the same universals is neither surprising nor significant, since it is a mere recognition of what a universal is: something that is the same—something that is what it is—in any mind at any time, whenever it is in any mind at any time.

By following the way of essences we cannot, therefore, reach a genuine realm of eternal existence. At best there may be certain essences which, being always embodied, are eternal; but our knowledge that this is so could not be deduced from their nature as essences but must be derived from empirical sources of information. Let us, then, try a new path—one that was blazed by Aristotle.[3] To this end we must go back to our reflections on levels of existence. We saw that each higher level was determined both as to its existence and as to the form of its existence by the level beneath it. All levels, therefore, except the lowest, are derivative. That there cannot be an infinite number of levels, but must be a final lowest level, follows from the chain of reflections which, having its inception in Aristotle, we have tried to formulate in our chapter "Finite or Infinite?" (Chap. IX). Until physical research gives us more precise information concerning it we may call this final level the "Omega system." Now have we not here perhaps an eternal realm, in contrast with which all other levels of existence are transient? The race of men are as grass, here today and gone tomorrow, and although the

---

[1] See Plato's *Sophist* 252e.

[2] Inconsistent propositions are believed to *imply* all propositions, but they do not *entail* any propositions.

[3] See *Metaphysics* a 994–995.

varied forms of life have considerable permanence as compared with individuals, they too are transitory; the theory of evolution, all the time that it has given hope of the coming to be of higher types of being, has increased the range of impermanence in the universe by destroying the claim to eternity of the animal species. Even life itself is transient: originating at some favorable moment of chemical synthesis, it too is doomed to perish utterly with the dissipation of heat on the surface of the earth. The science of former days recognized the transiency of chemical molecules, yet pointed to the atom as everlasting. But now the theory of evolution has invaded this department of being, also, and the atom has gone the way of the rest. So far as we know, only the Omega system of the physical world is a type of being that is not known to be transitory.

But can we know that this system is everlasting? It is difficult to see how it could be otherwise. For there could not have been another field of reality to bring the Omega system into existence; since if there had been, that field would exist alongside this field, and not this field but that one would be the ultimate system. The Omega system could not, therefore, have had a beginning. But might not some other field have given birth to the present dominant field, and then passed away, even as the human parent brings its children into existence, and later perishes? Yet how could it perish? For what could destroy it? The human being perishes because the "lower" forms of being, biological and physical, upon which its existence depends, decree its death; but if, as is the case with the Omega system, there are no modes of existence limiting it, there is nothing that could destroy it. But—a final doubt—might not the Omega system evolve into something else that would supplant it, even as the child perishes in evolving into the man? Yet the child is essentially the man, and the man, the child; hence, even so, if the Omega system did evolve, something would remain the same, which itself would then be the Omega system, an eternal present, existing at all moments of time.

The student of Aristotle will not fail to notice that although we have been following the general spirit of his argument we have introduced an important modification into it. For we have not been saying—as Aristotle would have said, and as the science of every generation except our own would have said, holding fast to the conception of matter as a potter's stuff out of which substances are made—that while the organism is built up of cells, and the cells of chemical molecules, the molecules of atoms, the atoms of electrons, only what we may call Omega particles are not built up of anything else; but, following our behavioristic view of natural processes, we have spoken of the *determination* of the organism by the cells, of the cells by the molecules, the molecules by the atoms, and so on. For us there is no stuff, but only modes of behavior, determining and determined. Yet the result is the same; there is an ultimate, all-determining, but itself undetermined mode of reality, which is eternal.

The second approach to the problem of the existence of an eternal realm is through the concept of truth. From our argument to prove that there is no realm of "being" or "subsistence," it might seem as if the approach must prove unpromising, but let us follow the argument and see whither it may lead us.

No empirical propositions, that is to say, no propositions concerning existence, certify their own truth. With regard to any item of existence we may form an indefinite number of propositions with it as subject, but from the mere examination of these, apart from the subject, we cannot tell which is true. The truth of one, and the falsity of the others, is determined by the subject (object) acting as a selector among them. This is evident with regard to propositions concerning items of experience, whose truth may be intuitively verified. In the case of predictive propositions where the future is within the power of the monad itself, the selector is the will of the monad that chooses from among possibilities of fact one that it shall make true. Whether it is true that I shall stay or that I shall return home is determined by my intention in this case. But also, if our general metaphysical hypothesis be correct, the situation is the same in the case of predictive propositions concerning the future of individual monads or groups of monads where the determination of the future is not under the control of each, taken by itself, but of all acting coöperatively. Propositions such as these are of the "if . . . then" form; for example, If I open the back of my watch I shall find works there, If I wind it, it will go, and the like. The situation is not altered, as we have seen, if such propositions are probable rather than necessary or certain. These are a kind of proposition which the positivist and pragmatist have to admit as valid, but for the validity of which they have no explanation. In the pragmatist or positivistic universe they simply hang, as it were, in the air, with nothing to make them true. According to our way of interpretation, on the other hand, the truth of these propositions is based on the intentions of the monads that coöperate with us in determining our experience. Their validity through any period of time depends upon the continued existence of these intentions as habits. Universal propositions, valid within restricted time limits, are based on the negative decisions of groups of monads that there shall not be a state of affairs of such and such a character. According to the modern interpretation of universal propositions, they assert the nonexistence of a class; but such an interpretation does not provide for the continued nonexistence of the class. This defect is remedied only if such propositions are interpreted as the decisions of coöperating creative wills: All crows are black, does not mean, There are no nonblack crows, but, There shall be no nonblack crows. Truths of this type do not, however, take us beyond the limited existence of finite monads, with their temporary plans and purposes.

But there are two types of propositions which appear to direct us toward an eternal realm: historical propositions and propositions concerning the form of the Omega system. That this is the case with regard to the former can, I think, be shown as follows. We may note, to begin with, that historical propositions, like the propositions just examined, do not guarantee their own truth, otherwise there would be no false history and no delusive memories; their truth must, therefore, be guaranteed by something external to them. Unless history is a mere dream or fiction there must be something to make one judgment true and another false, even as in the case of judgments of perception there is a reality which selects among alternative hypotheses. This reality cannot be the events about which history is written, for the events have disappeared; it can be only their echoes. The question then is, What is the duration of the echo? For if the echo is evanescent, the truth based upon it would also be evanescent. But is the proposition that Mussolini marched on Rome valid only so long as it is remembered or as fragile human records endure? Or is it forever true? Is our feeling that once true always true—that the past cannot be changed—an illusion? If this feeling is an illusion, then events might not leave any echoes at all, or, if they did, the echoes might pass away soon after the events; if, however, the feeling is veridical, every event must leave an echo that is everlasting. That the latter alternative is true is my belief, and for the following reason.

I would not deny that we can take the abstraction "event" and the abstraction "echo" and form for ourselves the picture of a world where events would occur and perish utterly, "And like this insubstantial pageant faded / Leave not a rack behind," or, if a trace, transitory, and eventually wiped clean. What I do deny, however, is that this is a picture of our world, for if we fill in the concept "event" and the concept "trace" with anything that we can concretely conceive or imagine we get something quite different. For if an event is a flash of experience, appearing against an enduring matrix of experience which grows under the stress of everything that occurs to it, then it is certain that no event happens that does not permanently change the course of the monad to which it happens; and since monads are not separate but contiguous, every monad is eventually affected by whatever happens to other monads, no matter how distant. The Omega system can be no exception: it must bear on its face the scars and wrinkles of every event. When the ship drives through the sea, making its wake, and the waters close over, calm as before, it may appear as if nothing had happened; but we know that this is delusion: the sea is never calm in the same way again, after the ship has passed. Although, therefore, echoes come into existence at particular moments, they give to reality an enrichment which lasts thereafter forever. Through the echo each phase of reality possesses what we may call a "subsequent eternity," living on in all subsequent phases without end.[1]

So also if there are any physical laws or invariances which hold for all time, as even contemporary physics seems to indicate, or any metaphysical laws, such as those which state the general structure of space, time, and causality, there must be a corresponding form in reality. For a general law is a truth, and, like all truths, implies a relation between a mind, an essence, and an objective state of affairs expressed through the essence, by reason of which the law wins its reality. This objective state

[1] Compare A. N. Whitehead's theory of the "consequent nature" of God, in *Process and Reality* (New York: The Macmillan Co., 1929), pp. 523-533.

of affairs, in the case of absolute general laws, possesses what—
in contrast to the "subsequent eternity" of echoes—we may call
"antecedent eternity," because it has existed at all moments.
Through acquaintance with this form we participate in the
eternal "now." It may be that none of the universal physical
laws today recognized by science are stated with entire accuracy,
and that all the metaphysical principles which we have discovered
are in some degree wrongly expressed, yet they cannot be utterly
wrong. Some form, if not this form, is eternal.

The conviction that there is an eternal form is borne out, I
think, by contemporary physics. To one brought up on the
physics of a generation ago, the suggestions which the physics
of our own day has to offer are, however, surprising. Nothing
in the way of what might be called "material substance" could
be inferred to be eternal. The atom, as we have remarked, is
recognized to be a secondary and transient product of a kind
of evolution. But even matter itself, in the sense of that which
possesses mass, is also believed to be derivative: mass is a product
of radiation and can be created or destroyed. The physical scene
appears as one of varied, unremitting change, which the old
Heracleitean phrase, πάντα ῥεῖ, accurately describes. Yet, just as
Heracleitus mitigated the absoluteness of his statement of the
flux by recognizing the λόγος—a certain rhythm or proportion in
the transformation of one thing into another—so contemporary
physics accepts certain invariances. In the first place, it finds
that there are repeatable operations or experiments. Without
the possibility of repetition of experiment, physics as a social
enterprise permitting one experimenter to check the results of
others would be impossible. There are doubtless individual
variations that cannot be eliminated, but at all events sameness
within assigned limits can be attained. This implies that the
laws of phenomena of a given kind and range are invariable,
within the limits indicated. In the second place, there are
certain "physical constants" in the technical sense, such as the
gravitational constant G, Planck's constant h, and the velocity
of light. These results, it is true, must be taken with reserve in
view of the rapidly changing character of physical theory, itself
the result of the enormous mass of new experimental material
being offered. To sum it up in a sentence: for contemporary
physics the Omega system is eternal with regard to "form," not

to "matter," which is what we should expect in view of our behavioristic, and eventually idealistic, interpretation of physical
reality.

In concluding this argument for the eternal we must consider
the import of those truths on the basis of which the argument
was usually conducted in the past—supposedly a priori logical,
mathematical, and ethical truths. The matter today is not so
simple as it was then believed to be. For, according to contemporary theory, a priori truths are limited to analytic expressions, from which nothing in regard to existence can be inferred.
If, for example, the expression, Two plus two equals four, is a
mere analysis of "four," if the expression, Any two points on a
straight line determine that line, is a mere analysis of the concept
"straight line," if, Red is a color, is a mere analysis of "red," there
is no need to base the truth of these propositions upon any reality
external to the universals "four," "straight line," "red," for these
expressions are founded on our direct acquaintance with the universals wherever embodied or whenever conceived, and no further existence of such universals in other embodiments can be
inferred. The fact is, however, that such expressions are seldom,
as used in living discourse, purely analytic, but contain a con-
cealed reference to the real world, and are therefore empirical in
the broader sense of the term. Thus, what I usually mean when
I assert, Two plus two equals four, is that if we form a class of
any two real things and take the logical sum of that class with
any other class of two real things, then, provided the classes are
disjunct, we shall have a class of four real things. As so interpreted the proposition expresses a law, and a very important law,
regarding the real world, a law which could not be deduced from
the purely formal expression, Two plus two equals four, since
from that expression we do not know that there are any real
things at all, and if there are, we do not know that they are not
so evanescent that no addition operation could be performed
upon them. The propositions of arithmetic and geometry, in
so far, therefore, as they find application to the real world, are
propositions of the same logical and metaphysical type as the
universal law of physics; they, too, express the form of the Omega
system, and presuppose the existence of the Eternal; no extension
of our previous argument is required. The status of ethical
"axioms" is no different: in so far as they are not purely analytic

or definitional, but have application, they are based on the wills of the monads, as we have shown in the preceding chapter. The discussion of their full significance must wait, however, until we have determined the nature of the Omega system more completely, at the end of this chapter and in the next.

The two approaches to the eternal which we have been following arrive, in the end, at the same goal. For, as we have just discerned, if we enter by the pathway of truth, such universal truths as may exist are based on the Omega sysem of the physical world, and it can easily be shown that the echoes upon which historical truth is founded can be conserved nowhere else than in the same system. For historical truth cannot be founded on what we might think to be the nearest echo of an event—its memory or recollection in the life of a finite monad—since memory perishes at the death of the monad, nor on what we might think to be the next nearest echo—a record in a diary or letter or other memoir—since these are highly specialized forms of physical reality, which despite all the efforts of our modern conservators of books in library treasure rooms are destined to disintegrate in time, nor, finally, would a monument of brick or bronze be much more perdurable; only some effect of the event on the Omega system, traceable in accordance with some law of cosmic hermeneutics, would be eternal. Except for the uncertain testimony of the mystics, which we have yet to examine, the Omega system of the physical world is the sole known eternal realm. This conclusion is, in a sense, the same as that of the materialist; but there is, we shall see, a profound difference between his view and ours. The materialist accepts one of two interpretations of the physical world—either a naïve "scientific" interpretation or the interpretation of common sense, while we accept an interpretation in terms of experience. Our chapter "Experience and Matter" offered a prolegomenon to an argument for the interpretation in terms of experience; I wish now to bring this argument to final statement, in doing which we must embark upon a discussion of the meaning of existence. I wish to prove that we have no meaning, no conception, of existence except that of concrete experience; it follows that no other interpretation of the physical universe as an acknowledged system—the Omega system—is possible.

From the time when Kant declared that existence is no predicate it has been recognized that the judgment of existence is peculiar. For whereas when I say, This is a rose, I ascribe a predicate to the entity indicated by the subject of the sentence, when, on the other hand, I say, This exists, I do not ascribe a predicate to the subject, despite the fact that the form of words and the grammatical subject are the same in both sentences. Moreover, it is doubtful whether the sentence, This exists, where "this" is taken to be a pure demonstrative, pointing to something actually discovered, is anything but a tautology, which, since it cannot help being true, is perhaps no judgment at all, since a judgment is by definition something that may be either true or false. Nevertheless, the fact that the sentence is a tautology is interesting, because the reason why it is a tautology throws light on the meaning of existence. It is a tautology because nothing more is said by "This exists" than by just "This": the meaning of "to exist" is precisely to be a *this*—to be concrete, individual, capable of being found or pointed out. If, now, instead of, This exists, I say, A rose exists, my sentence is not a tautology, for it might be false, and yet the same meaning of existence appears: A rose exists, is equivalent to, The concept rose is exemplified in a *this*.

If we accept this meaning of the term "existence," we may define the realm of existence as the realm of *this*'s or, what comes to the same, the realm of exemplifications of first-order concepts. I say first-order concepts, because every concept of order n, if exemplified, is exemplified in a concept of order $n - 1$; therefore only a concept of order 1, if exemplified, is exemplified in something that is not itself a concept—namely in a *this*. Thus the concept "sensuous quality" is exemplified in the concept "red," the concept "red" in the concept of red of a specific hue, brightness, and saturation; but this last concept is not exemplified in another concept, but in a *this*—in this redding of this rose.

Let us now apply this concept of existence to the two current materialistic pictures of the physical world, the "scientific" picture and the common-sense picture. The fundamental defect of the scientific picture is that it is painted wholly in terms of relational concepts. One might be tempted to express its relation to the physical world through the analogy of a landscape painting and a black and white copy which preserves the relations of the elements of the original but abstracts from the colors; but this would not serve, because of the great generality of the relational concepts employed in physics. To get a sufficient analogy, one would have to reduce the black and white copy of the landscape painting to series of number coördinates. It follows that the scientific picture of the world is really no picture, since it employs not first-order concepts, but concepts of at least second order. The scientific description tells us no more of the nature of the physical world than that certain relational concepts apply to it; and these concepts are so abstract that elements of very different kinds could fit them—including Leibnizian monads and the personalities of our human social order, which do, as a matter of fact, fit them. That the social world does enter into the framework of the physical world picture is a most significant truth, as we have remarked, but one which is either forgotten or else misinterpreted in such a way as to drag down social existence to the supposedly lower plane of physical existence; whereas the sole meaning of this truth is that physical categories are of such a character as to include personalities within their range of application, thus showing that they do not in themselves entail the materialistic world picture.

The common-sense picture of the physical world seems, unlike the scientific, to be a genuine picture, for it consists of such apparently first-order concepts as color of a determinate shade, brightness, and saturation, sound of such and such a pitch and loudness, stretches and volumes of definite spread, and the like. It is in fact in almost all respects modelled on the content of given percepts; in its naïve form it is identical with such percepts; in its more refined and sophisticated form it is closely similar. Yet even this picture of the physical world is inadequate, as we have seen, and it is inadequate for the reason that was urged against it by Berkeley, which came to this: that a world of purely sensuous terms, a world that should be a pure expanse of shape of blue, or a pure succession of tones like a melody, or a collection of smells or tastes, or worse than such, a purely neutral expanse of shape or duration, is not anything concrete, not really a *this*, but itself an abstraction, an abstraction from a concrete whole of experience. Even if common sense paints its picture in terms of all known primary and secondary qualities together, recognizing their interdependence, it is no genuine picture after all, for the terms which it employs, being abstractions, are not, as first seemed to be the case, first-order concepts, but second-order ones.

We come then, in the end, to the insight that concrete experience is the only *this* that we know, and no picture of the world in any other terms is a genuine picture. "Star," "sweet," "red," "table," "centimeter," "second," "electron," and the like, are not first-order concepts, but "Stalin," "Mussolini," "Hitler" are. The only world picture that will endure is painted in terms of concrete experience. Either, therefore, we have no notion whatsoever of the external world or any interpretation we put upon it must be in terms of concrete experience. For us, experience and existence are inseparable.

It will surely be objected, however, that science teaches that experience arose at a definite moment of time on the planet Earth, emerging ultimately from a purely physical, unconscious realm of existence. The notion of emergence, so widely exploited in contemporary philosophy, is used against the spiritualistic metaphysics and in favor of the materialistic. For, it is said, the notion of emergence provides for the coming to be of species of existence entirely new; out of the unconscious, therefore, the conscious could have arisen. Yet all that can be deduced from the concept of emergence is the appearance of new species of existence; nothing at all can be deduced as to the nature of existence itself, as a generic concept. We know that our human form of existence began at a certain time and in a certain place on the earth; we know also that it is the latest term in a long series of emergences of new forms of biological reality; but we do not know that it arose out of an unconscious, value-free order of existence. In fact, to say that the conscious came from the unconscious is equivalent to saying that it came from nothing at all. For what is meant by the planet Earth?—what is meant by anything physical? If there is any truth in our chapter "Experience as Substance" or in the foregoing analysis, either we mean nothing by these terms, or we mean fountains of sensa within the concrete experience of some center or else centers of concrete experience in their own right. We deride the pagan notion of Mother Earth as a myth, and, sometimes, the Christian conception of God; but in place of this myth we put another—the scientific picture of the world—one which we may not unfairly call the "myth of the twentieth century."

A last doubt as to the legitimacy of our interpretation of the Omega system may still remain. It may be claimed that our argument is sound against dogmatic materialism, but has no relevance for a truly agnostic position. Even if we have no alternative, by way of interpretation, to construing the physical world in terms of experience, it may be urged that we have no right to any interpretation whatever. Science, our single source of knowledge, provides *knowledge about* the physical world, but no acquaintance with its stuff or substance.[1]

When such agnosticism is consistently held it deserves much respect, but it is seldom so held. Usually it is coupled with a flat denial that the physical world has the characters of experience—as if ignorance, which admittedly does not permit positive statements, yet permits negative ones! It is true that arguments are offered for this negation, the chief being that our knowledge about nature excludes an interpretation in terms of experience because the categories of physics are incompatible with experience: experience cannot have mass, cannot be spatial, and so on. But we have shown, on the contrary, that precisely this is not true, that when space and mass and motion are given their scientific, as opposed to their irrelevant popular, meanings even a monad may possess them. Only when scientific categories are taken naïvely do they favor materialism.

And a consistent agnosticism is, moreover, no final philosophy. For it rests on an indefensible separation of the mind from the external world, in knowledge, and of one level of existence from another. Here I would recall the results of our reflections on the essence of knowledge, to the effect that nature has co-operated with us in the formation of our concepts, so that when we come to the conclusion that the sole concept of existence possible for us is that of concrete experience this conclusion represents no mere subjective belief of our own, no mere myth, no arbitrary fiction, but a message, as it were, or—though I hesitate to use the word for fear of creating misunderstanding—a revelation of nature to ourselves. Nature interprets itself to us in our ultimate beliefs. I am not denying the large share of the subjective in these beliefs, the share of superstition, error, and illusion, but I am insisting on the equal share of objectivity. Belief represents not merely how we picture the world, but how the world mirrors itself in our minds.

If subject and object are associated in the work of the knowing mind, the different levels of existence are also associated one

[1] The view of Professor R. W. Sellars and others—called "critical realism."

with another. The human level is not cut off from the biological, the biological from the atomic, the atomic from the electronic, the electronic from the Omega system. If they were cut off from each other, one would have reason for thinking that when we taste existence in ourselves and when as the result of this tasting we frame the concept of existence as experience we are reporting existence only as it is on our level and forming a concept valid only for ourselves. But the truth is that the levels underneath us are deeper levels of our own existence and are in contact with our own level; the forces that determine us from below are deployed in the very field of our experience. In framing our fundamental concepts we reach down into the lowest depths of existence. We are like divers carrying their treasure up from the floor of the sea; and even as the taste of the water at the surface has the same tang as the water at the depths, so the taste of existence in ourselves is, generically, the same as that of the Omega system.

XVII

The Interpretation of the Eternal

IN THIS, our final chapter, it remains for us to consider whether some concrete interpretation of the Eternal is possible. In particular, we wish to enquire what grounds there are for choosing between the supposition that the Eternal consists of a kind of experience the most elementary and lowly imaginable to man, the like of which we perhaps become in dreamless sleep, and the supposition that the Eternal is not only the most fundamental form of existence, but also the highest form. If the first hypothesis is correct, we are committed, despite our "mentalistic" conception of reality, to an essentially "naturalistic" view of the cosmos and a "humanistic" attitude toward morality and religion. Holding this view, man suffers humiliation in recognizing that his destiny is determined by a realm of being inferior to himself, but at the same time may recover his pride in the thought that he is himself the highest form of existence, for the birth of which, within his own perspective, all other forms were a mere means and preparation. And if not dismayed by his lonely eminence, he may find heroic joy in maintaining his position by unaided skill and courage, until ultimate defeat in death. A free man, he will worship his own ideals instead of God, and in place of the service of the Lord he will consecrate the service of the Group. But if the whole sweep of human thought is taken as the standard, the naturalistic view must be regarded as a deviation from the dominant trend. And, therefore, despite the insistence of the naturalistically minded man that his view, since it is congenial to science, should have first claim upon the attention of the philosopher, we shall begin with the other view, from which, if it fail, we shall have to fall back upon its alternative. We shall ask, Can the hypothesis that the Omega system is a form of existence higher than the human maintain itself in the face of metaphysical criticism?

To propose this question is equivalent to raising the general problem of the truth of religion. For in the midst of the seemingly endless variety of religious experience two beliefs are ever present: the acknowledgment of a superhuman reality and the conviction that this reality is the guardian of human values. These beliefs are found in the lowest as well as in the highest types of religion, in the magical ceremonies of the Australian Bushmen and early Hindus, and in the Christian dogmas regarding God and Providence.   In the practice of any religion three factors are, to be sure, usually distinguished: a rite; a dogma, which is the explanation of the efficacy of the rite; and the conviction that the performance of the rite will serve the interests of the believer.   It is often thought that the rite is the most primitive element in the complex, and one religion at least, that of the ancient Hindus, appears to have been wanting in any theory of the assumed efficacy of the rite.   It is clear, however, that some sort of theory is always latent in the religious experience and is bound to appear in subsequent stages of its development.   And in all religions essentially one and only one theory has been offered—that there is a realm of existence different from the ordinary reality, a holy, supernatural realm which manifests itself in the rite and in its effects.[1]   That the supernatural is thought to be a contrasting reality is shown by the fact that the rite, including magic and all forms of religious exercise and ceremony, is a different kind of procedure from the one—which we may call "technique"—ordinarily used for the satisfaction of desire.   Both may be employed in handling one situation: relatives of the sick man may give him medicine and nursing, and also offer prayers for his recovery; and the same tools or other instrumentalities may figure in both, as when we say a blessing on our food, on our weapons, or even, as at the Palio at Sienna, on the horse which we hope will win a race for us; but the two are not confused.   The rite may be sublimated into the silent prayer of the Quaker or the simple deed of charity of the believer, yet it keeps its distinctive character, for prayer to God is not quite the same as conversation between one man and another, and the believer's deed of charity is done for the love of God and not merely for the sake of the poor.   Among primitive people the rite is communal in character, and it tends to remain so in civilized societies, although, with the development of individualism, religion may become "something that a man does with his loneliness."

[1] Compare Rudolf Otto, *Das Heilige* (Gotha: L. Klotz, 1929).

While perceiving that the rite and its explanation are intertwined, the metaphysician is bound to be more interested in the latter, as containing an affirmation concerning the nature of reality. The explanation depends essentially, as we have noted, upon a supernatural realm of being. Now it is generally recognized that this realm is usually conceived of in terms of personality. Prayer and sacrifice are meaningless except as involving relations with personalities or quasi personalities that may be induced to intervene in favor of the worshiper. Whereas the natural realm is the object of procedures that apparently do not involve personality, it is characteristic of the supernatural realm that it is the object of a way of behaving analogous to our behavior toward our fellows when we seek their coöperation. Just as we entreat them or try to win their favor through gifts and flattery, so we enter into social relations with the gods, hoping to get them on our side; with nature, on the other hand, we do not enter into social relations. To a profounder reflection, however, it becomes clear that the natural and the supernatural cannot be separate. Every rite is a transaction within the natural realm, and every act out of the supernatural realm is an inruption into the natural. In view of this, two different courses have been followed: religion has included the natural in the supernatural, or at least in the power of the supernatural; the naturalistic deviation has excluded the supernatural from the whole realm of being. The impulse to the latter course came from the progress of science in rendering supernatural procedures unnecessary (when medicine will heal, why pray?) and positive evidences for the intervention of supernatural powers less and less convincing. The sphere of that intervention, which from the beginning lay in the region of human helplessness, gradually contracted until, even among the pious, it was confined to chance events—the weather, grave illness, birth and death—precisely those spheres over which naturalistic control has not been established. Eventually, in the eyes of the technically minded, supernaturalism fell to the position of a useless hypothesis, and then disappeared, not because it had been refuted, but because it was ignored. For them, God died, not because they had shown that he did not exist, but because they had lost interest in him. And, finally, a materialistic philosophy was developed to take the place of religion.

Significant, nevertheless, is the fact that, in the face of the contraction of the area of experience assigned to the supernatural and the dominance of the technological point of view in our civilization, the religious interpretation still survives. The dogmatic naturalist explains this as due to the influence of traditional education on the feelings of the child persisting in the man, but it remains a fair question whether there may not be other causes as well, whether, in fact, there may not be some truth in religion which, though obscured by the contemporary naturalistic bias, is yet not wholly lost sight of.

The reasons which have impelled men to accept a religious view of the world have been of two sorts: one philosophical, formulated and consecrated in the so-called proofs for the existence of God; the other of a character which we may call intuitive. In order to explain the kind of difference I have in mind between the two reasons, I would call attention to a parallel distinction in the grounds offered for believing in the existence of our fellow men. There also we find the arguments of the philosophers—such as the proof by analogy—but these are not the reasons why the common man believes that his wife, his children, his fellow townsmen, and his friends exist. If you ask a man why he believes in the existence of his wife, he will probably answer, because he sees her, because he can hear her talk, and because she behaves in a way a person rather than a mere thing would behave. Or if she is not at hand he will say that he has had a letter or a telegram from her, or that some friend has just seen her or talked with her. Now the religious man will offer grounds of a similar sort for his belief in God, grounds, as we may call them, either of mystic vision or of faith. He will say (with the mystics) that he has actually seen God and heard him speak as it were face to face, or else (with the faithful) that he believes because God has spoken to him, not directly but through his prophets, as his word is recorded in the sacred books. The comparison between the religious attitude toward nature and our normal attitude toward our fellows is significant for the reason that even the materialist, in his nonacademic moments, accepts a nonnaturalistic—one might almost say a religious—interpretation of at least one part of his environment, namely the social part. Here at least is a portion of reality the behavior of which he tries to affect by an appeal to desire and reason, rather than by the purely technological methods employed to affect "things." Whoever believes in his fellow men believes in the supernatural. And if the personal, social interpretation is acceptable with regard to one part of the environment, it is, in principle at least, acceptable with regard to the rest. The only question still to be raised is whether the intuitive or other grounds for believing in God are as valid as the parallel grounds for belief in our fellows. Now when we reëxamine our intuitive grounds for belief in our fellow men, we find, as we have shown, that the sole way we have of seeing them, since we do not literally see them, but only appearances of them, is by suffering the control which they exert in our experience. This control must, however, be interpreted through ideas formed after the analogy of our own experiences. In accordance with the fundamental principle of the coöperation of the mind with its object in the process of knowledge, the main drift of this interpretation is sure to be correct, despite a large margin of error due to subjectivity. When the interpretation is correct the minimal meanings expressed in the behavior and conversation of others are the same in their minds and in ours, so that we are enabled, quite genuinely, to look into each others minds. Is, then, the claim to knowledge of God through vision and faith as good as our claim to knowledge of our fellows? Can we look into his mind as we look into theirs?

Since all men experience directly the control of the Omega system—a control of the same generic kind as that exerted by our fellow men—there is a sense in which not the mystic only, but everyone, intuits God. We are as sure, therefore, that there is a God, in the sense of the *ens realissimum,* as we are that there are monads other than ourselves. But what the mystic claims to intuit is something more: not merely the generic will of God, but God's will in its individuality, its oneness, its plenitude of knowledge, its love of man. And he claims that this intuition comes to him, not through the external control which all men acknowledge over their experience, but through a peculiar type of experience which many, perhaps most, people do not have. Now the fact that the mystic experience is peculiar sets a problem to the metaphysician: by the rules of the game which he is playing he cannot accept its evidence at face value, for metaphysics, like science, is a social enterprise based on a common experience. On the other hand, since metaphysics aims to construct a system into which all facts will fit, the philosopher cannot neglect the testimony of the mystic. What in the end he will do with it depends on the type of system he is led to accept on other grounds. For ourselves, we are willing to admit the initial possibility that, with regard to reality, while most of us are as people living with windows partly shut, the mystic is as one who has his windows open wide. We are empiricists; if, therefore, a man tells us that he is experiencing something, we feel that we have no right to dispute his private evidence; only, since we do not have the experience ourselves, we cannot, for our part, build our philosophy upon it. We are prepared, however, to reconsider this evidence not as a primary datum, but as a corroborative reason, if we are forced independently to acknowledge the same sort of reality as the mystic finds.

Our attitude toward the claim to knowledge made by men of faith is similar. For them, God has spoken to us, not directly as to the mystics, but mediately through the word of the saints and prophets. We may fairly ignore all differences in the utterance as recorded in the various sacred books, or in the interpretations of priests and scholars, since such differences may be accounted of no more importance than the differences of meaning gotten by various listeners to a man speaking, or by various readers of the same text; and there is a marvellous unanimity in the message. If God has spoken to men, he could speak only in their language and in accordance with their capacity for understanding, and by only the wisest could he be rightly understood. As philosophers, however, we can no more accept the doctrine of the sacred books ex cathedra than we can take blindly what the mystics say. Since the word of God comes to us at one remove at least, we will listen to it as if it came from God direct only if there is some reasonableness in the message itself consisting in its harmony with what we make out of our own experience; otherwise the holy writers would have no more authority than common men. We will accept their message if we have grounds for believing that the course of our own lives and of history would have been impossible unless governed by a power higher than ourselves. The value of revelation lies in its offering of a hypothesis to speculation. To ask of thinking men that they become as little children in matters of faith is to demand what cannot be fulfilled. For all such men except the mystics the credibility of the religious view of the world depends finally, not upon intuition, but upon reason, in the sense of the organizing function of ideas. Ideas seem credible to us as they formulate the main drift of our experience, physical and historical. For myself, in defending the theory of the origin of ideas as the joint product of the mind and the environment, I cannot suppose that the religious view is utterly factitious, especially when I consider that it has been held with amazing persistence throughout the history of man. It has, I believe, the status of a speculative idea with every claim to initial plausibility.

Moreover, the usual objections to the validity of this idea are weak. The fact that there are persons who have no feeling for the religious interpretation of nature is by itself no argument against its plausibility provided there are other grounds for accepting it. There is no absurdity in the suggestion of the mystics that some people have lost this feeling or are born without the capacity to develop it, even as some are born color-blind or incapable of acquiring an appreciation of music. It is possible that, in the case of large sections of the population, the practical interest in nature may have completely obscured the social or mystical—the sense of companionship which all men feel in youth with woods and stream and sea. We can imagine a development of mind that would lead a man to take a purely practical attitude even toward his most intimate companions. He might come to view his wife as a mere machine and all his dealings with her as machine techniques calculated to produce in her a behavior favorable to his interests. His belief in the existence of feelings and ideas animating her behavior having been lost, his own feeling of sympathy and sense of companionship with a kindred spirit would fade away.[1] He would see her laugh or cry, but instead of laughing or crying with her would consider how this phenomenon might be helpful or baneful to him. If meanings seemed to come to him from her, he would deny that they had any previous existence in a mind other than his own, and would view them as autogenous developments from within, stimulated by intrinsically meaningless sounds heard or gestures seen. If, taking the pragmatic viewpoint, it be rejoined that the mystic

[1] Compare the notion of the "mechanical sweetheart" of E. T. A. Hoffmann and William James.

interpretation of the behavior of our fellows still brings results, but that the mystic interpretation of nature has so far failed in pragmatic value, since no one has ever proved that prayer or any other sort of rite has altered the course of events in a useful way, the believer will interpose that the values derived from the mystic interpretation of nature are not of a practical order. They were expected to be of that order in the beginning, but have ceased to be so considered, in any narrow sense. Men today no longer thoughtfully seek from God relief from sickness, safety from death, or increase in material wealth, but fortification of courage and communion with an eternal presence. The whole range of the miraculous may be discredited, yet these values will remain. And even in primitive civilizations, the motion lost in magical practices was more than compensated for by the heartening effect upon the mind of belief in the existence of favoring, intelligent powers. It may be argued that today, also, because of its influence upon the emotions of the faithful, belief in God does have pragmatic value in the struggle for existence.[1]

Another argument that may be advanced against the religious interpretation is derived from the theory of evolution. If we survey the development of life on our planet, and, correlatively, that of mind, we find, starting from the highest manifestation we know—that in man—a continuous decrease in the complexity on the one hand of mental activity and on the other hand of vital organization, until we meet, at the other extreme, in the unicellular organism, a structure of the greatest simplicity as compared with the human body; and if any mental life at all can be attributed to the cell, it must be of incomparably low order. If then we compare the simple cell with the most complex molecules we know, these with simpler molecules, simple molecules with atoms, atoms with electrons or other constituents of atoms, we descend still further the scale of complexity, until we reach at last the limit of simplicity. The ultimate constituents of the Omega system would, therefore, admitting that they possessed any mental life at all, be animated by a mind of such an attenuated character as to be utterly undeserving of mystic emotions or social appreciation.

---

[1] That belief in God may even have military value was, I recollect, claimed by Marshal Foch, Commander in Chief of the Allied Armies in France during the World War.

But this argument carries no weight against the religious interpretation. For, according to all the higher forms of religion, the control of the Omega system is exerted by a single Will; hence it is irrelevant to compare the human or animal organism or even the simple cell with the single electron; the comparison should rather be made between the organism and the physical world as a whole. When these are the terms of the comparison the latter is immeasurably more complex than the former. It contains incomparably more elements, and its life span, being endless, is incomparably longer. It has not only its own complexity as the system that it is, but an additional complexity as echoing within itself the complexities of organic and molecular systems. The vibration of an electron is but a single event in the life of God; to get the complete life it is necessary to take the whole system of electronic vibrations. The initial fallacy of the argument consists in attempting to apply to the universe the evolutionary concept which has validity only in a small part of the world—the surface of the earth. The simplicity of physical laws—if it be a fact—in comparison with the complexity of the laws of human societies, is no argument against the religious interpretation; on the contrary, it would seem to point to a greater stability, and therefore perhaps greater perfection, in the Omega system.

The result of our reflections up to this point on the nature of the Omega system may be summarized as follows: The objections to the religious interpretation have no demonstrative force; the witness of the mystics cannot be admitted as a primary datum owing to its exceptionality; the testimony of faith, also, is not conclusive, yet gives to religion a certain plausibility in accordance with the principle of the coöperation of the object with the subject in the formation of ideas. Most writers on the philosophy of religion place great weight on one or another formulation of this principle. I find, in fact, that it is the basis of their arguments, and that they use it in almost the same form in which it was used by Descartes in the "Third Meditation." [1] In effect, they argue that the idea which man possesses of a perfect being, together with the emotions and high moral conduct inspired by the idea, could not have grown up spontaneously

[1] See, for example, the argument of John Oman in *The Natural and the Supernatural* (Cambridge: At the University Press, 1932).

within the mind as a pure imaginative creation, but must have appeared there in response to a real environment of the supernatural in general conformity with it. To my thinking, the argument falls short of being demonstrative because of the difficulty of fixing the limits of imagination, and so of error, in human thinking. If, once more, we make use of the comparison between belief in God and belief in our fellow men, we find, despite the analogies which we have pointed out, this signal difference, that while, to be sure, God speaks (*"Gott redet"*) [1] to the man of faith, he does not speak in the same unequivocal way that one man speaks to another. In conversation with our fellows we put forth words with a meaning, and we get back other words that answer our questions with definiteness if we give them the meanings that we ourselves would give if we were to use them; but with regard to the Omega system, though the whole realm of the sensuous is a natural language for communication, we can only guess at its meanings. The romantic poets and the seers think that they know; but do we know that they know? By means of human language we can all look into the minds of our friends; by means of the language of nature we may be able to look into the mind of God, but we cannot be sure what is there. We see as in a glass darkly. Faith may provide a good guess, but it is a guess. Further reasons, I believe, are necessary in order to transform plausibility nearer to certainty. These reasons are implicit in the discussion of the metaphysical functions of God. The decisive question is, Is God a necessary hypothesis for a complete cosmology?

In the history of European thought God has performed three metaphysical functions: of creation, of establishing the unity of the world, and of serving as the locus of truth. I wish to consider each of these in turn, beginning with creation.

It has been said that the apex of metaphysical sophistication is reached when one asks the question, not, Why is there this or that? but, Why is there anything—a world—at all? If one answers by pointing to some existence outside the world as its cause or reason for being, one makes no advance in explanation, because the logic of the question demands that it be asked with regard to the very existence that is offered as explanation; and

---

[1] Karl Barth, *Die kirchliche Dogmatik* (München: Chr. Kaiser, 1932), Erster Band, Erster Halbband, p. 141.

if now a new answer is given of the same kind, one is obviously embarked on an endless regress. Moreover, it is not clear how the cause that was supposed to be outside the world could be outside; for if it had any relations with the world—and how could it act as cause if it did not?—it would belong to a universe that included it and the world as originally postulated, which would then be seen to be not the universe but a mere part of it. If, on the other hand, instead of an existential principle external to the world, one looks to a purely ideal principle of explanation, such as the Platonic Good, there is the difficulty of understanding how the ideal can work. For what is merely ideal is nothing at all. The plausibility of this type of explanation is derived from the surreptitious assignment to the ideal principle of a quasi existence, called "subsistence," the senselessness of which we have demonstrated. For an ideal has no meaning except as an imaginative value picture—the goal of a purpose— and no efficacy except through the purpose which it defines. One must, therefore, either abandon the search for an explanatory principle of the world, or look for it, not outside, but inside. If one looks inside, whatever principle is appealed to must itself be accepted as absolute: it cannot itself be subject to explanation without an endless and vicious regress. In the history of thought God has served as this ultimate principle.

The need for such a principle is suggested by the ensuing reflections, which follow closely a train of thought upon which we have already embarked in other contexts. The sole explanatory ground that we have for events within our own experience is value, the satisfaction of desire. In terms of this ground we can begin to understand the writing of this word or the sound of the theme from the *New World Symphony* which we hum in moments of distraction. It was, however, the fundamental error of the Leibnizian type of monadology to suppose that the entire process of experience of a monad could be explained by appetitions from within; for even the humming of the musical theme and the writing of the word can be fully understood only in the light of satisfactions among the monads that form the group to which we belong. These monads have created in us the impulse to write English words and to hum European music. What we call education is the process through which monads in a group coöperate to build up the satisfactions characteristic of the dominant members. Yet there are events in our experience that cannot be understood in terms of the satisfactions of any human group. The changes in the colors of the phenomenal landscape which confronts the eyes as one looks out of the window, or shifts in the climate, from cold to warm or from clear to rain, cannot be thus explained. Nor can we thus explain more intimate events—the strange impulses that seize us in adolescence and the subtle changes in outlook that settle upon us as we grow older. These changes are determined from below —more immediately in the physiological realm, more ultimately in the physical realm. In the end, therefore, we are faced with the alternative of renouncing all explanation or else of postulating a satisfaction in the Omega system as the ground and reason for these changes. That mere "mind stuff" could find satisfaction in the development of a human being is beyond belief; such a satisfaction could accrue only to a will at least as complex as that of man.

Even more incomprehensible than the growth of the monad on any naturalistic basis is the coming to be of the monad itself. Instead of explaining, the naturalistic philosopher conceals his ignorance with a word—"emergence" or "evolution." For if you start with a mindless system there is no way of explaining how mind can appear in it, however complex you suppose it to become: the water of a metaphysical system will not rise higher than its source. How much more advantageous if we start with an Omega system of highest order and picture the birth of chemical elements as a process of differentiation of its experience substance! While confessing to the "ignorance of the learned," we yet cannot forbear to call attention to the way in which current field theories of matter, which represent chemical substances as nodules within the electromagnetic system, lend themselves easily to this interpretation; and, from the side of concrete experience, we may picture the process within the absolute as somewhat analogous to the dissociation of personality.[1] The creation of matter and life would represent an effort on the part of the Omega system to give freedom to impulses of its own which it found incompatible with a settled way of existence, but although offering them freedom, still providing them care.

[1] Compare William James, *A Pluralistic Universe* (New York: Longmans, Green and Co., 1909) , p. 298.

Alongside the process of creation through dissociation there occurs a counterprocess of creation by association. Of this, sexual reproduction would be an example, two lowly types of monadic existence fusing to produce a new monad; and the formation of complex molecules out of simpler ones might be another example. For this, also, we have an experiential model, in the reintegration of dissociated personalities, as reported in the classical researches of Morton Prince. The neo-Platonic conception of emanation is a much better picture of the fundamental creative process than evolution. Evolution would nevertheless retain its validity in the biological sphere, not however as a causal, but as a descriptive concept. For the ultimate value or reason for the creation of new centers of experience out of the absolute experience no better hypothesis has been suggested than Schiller's, as expressed in his poem "Die Freundschaft":

> Freundlos war der grosse Weltenmeister
> Fuehlte Mangel—darum schuf er Geister
> Sel'ge Spiegel seiner Seligkeit! [1]

The second metaphysical function of God, that of providing for the unity of the world, is implicit in the so-called teleological argument in its various forms and had been recognized by Plato in the *Philebus*. Since the weakness of the usual versions of the argument have been so often exposed, notably by Hume in his *Dialogues concerning Natural Religion* and by Kant, there is no occasion to consider them here. It must be admitted, moreover, that all too frequently the concept of God is brought into a metaphysical system for the purpose of remedying initial mistakes. This appears to be the case in Leibniz' monadology, where, once the monads were defined as "windowless," God became necessary to establish their harmony; and many readers of Whitehead today have felt that with some slight alterations in the definition of "actual occasions" the concept of God could be dispensed with. I shall try to show, however, the need for some entity corresponding to the theological notion of God if the unity of the world is to be understood.

The natural and inevitable type of metaphysical system is some kind of monadology, whether of substances as in Aristotle, of souls as in Plato, or of monads as in Leibniz; even Spinoza

---

[1] Compare the close of the *Phaenomenologie des Geistes,* where Hegel misquotes the lines immediately preceding those cited by us.

gives recognition to this truth in his "modes." For, as we have seen, the thinker finds himself a unified existence, partly identical and relatively self-sufficient throughout his conscious life, one among many others similar to himself. The human group is the model pluralistic world. How reasonable, therefore, to conceive of the universe as a vast society of such units! And if the philosopher looks to science for his material, he finds there also an atomic world. This remains true despite the reconstruction effected by postclassical physics. The old atom has been resolved, but the particles into which it has been analyzed—electrons, protons, neutrons, positrons, or what else—appear to be monadic in character. Even light is now believed to be composed of corpuscles (photons). Recent physics, it may be claimed, has but exchanged old atoms for new. Yet neither in terms of spiritual nor of physical atoms alone can the unity of the world be understood.

To show this, let us consider first the human group of monads. Up to a certain point we can interpret the social order in terms of its membership. In a previous chapter we saw how the political constitution of a society can be explained by the habits of action and sentiments of its members toward each other. By educating the younger members into the tendencies to action of the older a tradition is established, and a tradition is equivalent to a law of nature. On the other hand, the human order is obviously not independent. Habits of action are habits of interaction, and without the interaction involved in language and mutual perception the coöperation of the monads required for social order would be impossible; but human monads, taken by themselves, are much like Leibnizian monads—incapable of interaction. For they can influence each other only through the medium of the bodies which they animate and the intervening physical world. Moreover, the very existence of the units of the social order depends upon a relatively more stable order in bodies and in the landscape which provides the stage for human action: chaos in the body (disease) or chaos in the landscape (earthquake, tornado, or the like) are fatal. The social order is thus doubly dependent, first upon a physiological order, ultimately upon a fitness of the environment. Furthermore, the individuals composing the human group are neither eternal nor self-renewing; they are transitory existences replenished in kind through the agency of the body, which itself requires constant sustenance from the physical world.   If human minds were eternal, or, if not eternal, self-perpetuating through some process of psychic fission or conjugation, and if, moreover, they were in direct contact with each other, so that no intervenient substance was needed as a medium of communication and support for their purposes, then and only then would they be able to carry the full metaphysical burden of their existence.

Of course few if any monadologies have limited existence to the human group, but have enlarged it by including monadic entities drawn from the physical realm.   These new members may be interpreted after the analogy of the self—in the fashion of Leibniz or, more recently, of James Ward[1]—or else may be accepted in their simple material character.   In either case they may appear to have certain advantages over human monads from a metaphysical standpoint.   For, in the first place, they are believed to be perpetual or at least self-renewing; and in the second place, since they constitute the final level of existence, their order would not seem to depend upon anything else and could be believed to sustain the physiological and human orders. Moreover, for the purpose of assuring the autonomy of this order one may interpret it either as a purely statistical pattern emerging out of an original chaos of chance behavior,[2] or else as being due to essential habits of action of the monads with reference to each other, of a kind already employed to explain the order in human society.   Although the former explanation is ruled out by the type of argument set forth in our chapter on causality and probability (Chap. XIII), the latter remains a possibility demanding consideration.   The habits of action in relation to each other of the ultimate constituents of matter would provide the basis for the laws of nature and the unity of the world.

A profounder reflection reveals, however, the insufficiency of physical monadism, even though a spiritualistic interpretation be given the corpuscles in order to save them from metaphysical

[1] James Ward, *A Pluralistic Universe* (Cambridge: At the University Press, 1911), Part I.

[2] See Edwin Schroedinger, *Science and the Human Temperament* (New York: W. W. Norton and Co., 1935), chaps. ii–iii, vi; Bertrand Russell, *The Scientific Outlook* (New York: W. W. Norton and Co., 1931), chap. iv, pp. 95–97.

vacuity. We might begin by criticizing the whole atomistic conception from a purely physical standpoint by calling attention to the possibility that the corpuscles are derivative existences, products of radiation or mere concentrations of energy; but in view of the unsettled state of opinion among physicists we may pass this matter over. What we cannot omit from our debate is the problem of interaction, with all that it implies. For the corpuscles are in constant communication with each other, indeed it may be true that each takes account of all the others in the universe (by the "exclusion principle" [1]); but since they are not usually in contact, any more than human minds are, we are faced with an identical difficulty. This difficulty was recognized by physicists of a generation ago, who postulated the existence of the ether in order to bring the atoms into contact and explain action at a distance. The ether introduced continuity into a world of discontinuities. Today it is no longer in favor, but the "wave" and the "field" perform similar functions. The problem does not disappear when the wave or the field is denied physical reality and is interpreted as a mere symbol stating the probability that, under specified conditions, the corpuscle will be within a certain region and will be possessed of such and such characteristics.[2] For the possibility of interaction and the delay in communication —always the sign of an intervenient substance—remain to be explained. It may be recalled that when we were discussing the merits of a monadistic as opposed to a holistic interpretation of the "wisdom of the body" we were compelled to recognize the importance and necessity of a "circulatory medium" acting as a coördinator of the parts of the organism. The same necessity for a medium of communication that shall also function as a mechanism of coöperation reappears now on the cosmic plane. This medium, which we have called the Omega system, exists "between" the ultimate physical corpuscles and makes of them a single whole. It explains the time required for communication, which, as we showed in our analysis of space, is the same as

1 For a simple account of the exclusion principle see C. G. Darwin, *The New Conceptions of Matter* (New York: The Macmillan Co., 1931), chap. viii.

2 See the discussions of Louis de Broglie in *Matter and Light* (London: George Allen and Unwin, 1939), especially chap. iv, Sec. 2, pp. 187, 189, and chap. v.

distance. Being an existence, the medium must, by the principle of concreteness, have the properties of experience, and that it must be the highest type of existence can be inferred from arguments already given and to be provided in the discussion immediately following.

The third metaphysical function of God is to give reality to the realm of truth. After the discussion of the last chapter, the caution is hardly necessary that the reality in question is not that of the pseudo existence called "subsistence," but a genuine existence that shall be the counterpart of true judgments. If we may assume that we proved an eternal existence of this sort, the problem before us now is whether this reality is of such a character that we could call it God, or whether it might not be of a simple, subhuman quality. That it must be an experience having a complexity of a degree surpassing anything that we can imagine as human, can be shown, I believe, by the following argument.

We have seen that, if an eternal experience exists, it must reflect every event that happens to finite substances; and since we know that such substances have existed for a very long time we can know that, albeit time is finite, the number of events, and therefore the number of echoes of these events, which form the basis of historical truth, must have been enormous. Even if there is some process in the Omega system comparable to our human forgetting, whereby not all events would be remembered individually, there would have to be an organization of such a kind as to make the memory of any event possible. This would exceed in complexity anything that we could imagine as human. And since the realm of historical truth grows with every new occurrence, the complexity of the experience which provides the foundational traces must grow accordingly. We know, to be sure, that single transitory monads, and societies of monads, often suffer involution, passing from relative complexity to relative simplicity; but this cannot be the case with the Omega system; for every stage in the senescence of a transitory substance is a string of events leaving its trace in the matrix of the world, and these traces would provide an increase in complexity compensating for any decrease. Birth, growth, old age, death: these are stages in the life of perishable monads, but the Absolute "has no seasons."

We reach the same conclusion if we consider not historical truth but the other sort of truth upon which the argument for an eternal existence was based—truths concerning the form of the Omega system. Should all the laws that we now know be temporary, we cannot help assuming, nevertheless, that there are eternal laws, and I pointed to the evidence for this drawn from current physics. If the Omega system could be interpreted as a static realm of "things," such laws might be conceived of as pure descriptions; but so-called "things," as we know, are constructions, and all reality is a dynamic process produced coöperatively by the desires of the monads. Being is secondary to doing, and doing is the creature of desiring. The posture of my friend's hand as I see it lying on the table before me appears as a static given existence, but that is illusion; for its posture is determined by the tensions which animate it, and, if I knew enough, I should be able to see that the bony structure and shape of the flesh were determined, not to be sure by my friend himself, but by the appetitions of a biologic system underneath. And the discovery of the Brownian movement destroyed forever the illusion of a static physical reality. It follows that if there are universal physical laws they cannot be descriptions of an existing state of affairs or a mere record of the past (we have covered this ground before); they must be expressions of purposes, of intentions. Only so can they at once be valid now and give us assurance that the future will be as the past. The meaning of any universal proposition, All *A* is *B,* is never merely, *A* that is not-*B* does not exist, but includes the further meaning, *A* that is not-*B* *shall not* exist, "shall" being a temporal, because it is first a volitional, term. Physical laws express the long-range plans of the Eternal, the preconditions of all events to come. Such laws are simple, but it would be a mistake to infer from their simplicity the simplicity of the Omega system, ignoring the infinite detail which they formulate. To do so would be like inferring from the simplicity of the laws of chess the lowliness of the intellectual processes involved in playing the game.

To prove the complexity of the Omega system is, however, not enough in order to demonstrate the existence of a being higher than man; we must, in addition, give reasons for believing that it has a moral nature as well. And, whatever else the heart may claim, we can at least assert on grounds of philosophy that the Omega system has the same ideals that we have. How effective these ideals are in its life and in the world it has created is another matter, to be presently considered. The argument for the sameness of ideals is based on the universal validity of the hierarchy of values for all monads capable of the values in question. From the hierarchy of values alone we could not infer the existence of a supreme moral will, since the hierarchy, as we know it, is the formulation of essential preferences based on human experience; we can infer only that if another being exists who is capable of having experiences of a kind such as the human, it must recognize an identical order of desires; but the evidence that it does exist must come from elsewhere.   Independent evidence for the existence of the Omega system has, however, been given; and that the system is of a nature such that the hierarchy of values applies follows from the fact that all the material of human experience is thence derived. We can be confident, therefore, that God's ideal and ours is the same in essence.

The argument for the existence of God given in the last few pages may be summarized as follows: In order to complete our metaphysical system we have found that we need to postulate the existence of a Being that shall fulfil certain functions. These functions—of ground of creation, of basis of unity, and of truth—can be fulfilled only by a Being of a complexity and order of higher type than man.   There is no pretense, however, that this argument constitutes a proof like the traditional ontological, cosmological, or teleological "proofs."   For it was characteristic of those proofs that they were supposed not to depend upon any special presuppositions; one could offer a man the cosmological proof, say, and expect him to be convinced without enquiring into his philosophy.   The proofs did, of course, have premises, but, whatever they were, they were not revealed in the reasoning. The argument I have given, on the other hand, depends frankly upon accepting the whole framework of philosophy of this book, and I grant that it has no independent cogency.   It is no stronger than the general philosophy of which it is a part.   But if the argument in its wholeness is sound, we have reason to believe that the first of the fundamental theorems of religion is true— the existence of what may not inaccurately be called, adopting ancient phraseology, a Supreme Being.   We turn next to the study of the second theorem, which asserts a special relationship between man and the Eternal—what we call Providence.

Very simply stated, the concept of Providence is the belief

that man is the object of God's special care, the darling of his love. It is easy to dismiss this belief as the mere expression of our arrogance or fear. And in the light of the philosophy which I am expounding, where man is only one and not the highest type of experience short of God, the doctrine has less plausibility than according to the older conception of man's exclusive eminence. Critically considered, Providence can mean no more than that the Omega system works continually to build up in every finite individual a certain fulness of happiness in accordance with its plan. The growth of the individual is providential in the sense that it is determined, first, in its ultimate origin, by the Omega system, and, secondly, by all the influences which come in upon it from its environment, social and physical, conditioned and guided always by the Omega system itself. But the Providence of the Eternal is never a special providence in the sense that it excludes the care of other forms of being. Man can claim the love but not the partial love of the Almighty. The conviction of men of rare gifts and of strong peoples—the Jews, the French, the English, the Germans—that they are the objects of special care is similar to the belief in a special revelation on the part of the great religions, and has no more credibility. As soon as the believers in one religion feel themselves into the faith of another, they come to see that they are on the same basic footing; so, when the representatives of one culture come to understand another, they appreciate its counterclaim. Loyalty to a religion and to a culture are justified, not because they have any absolute superiority, but because, like wife and children, they are one's own. Yet even as there is validity in the revelation of each religion in its testimony to the existence of a superior being, so there is truth in the conviction of a special mission and a peculiar status. For each monad is God's creature and has its place in the cosmic scheme, not all equal, but all unique and irreplaceable. To rephrase Spinoza, "God is revealed alike in the mouse and in the angel, but less in the mouse than in the angel." [1] The sense of a more than human significance in one's life is the mark of the religious as opposed to the purely secular feeling for the dignity of man.

But men today are in a demanding mood: for them the belief in Providence has little worth unless it yields cash value. They

---

[1] Letter XXXVI (XXIII), "Spinoza to Blyenbergh."

wish to know what the Eternal is about in its care for them, and how far they can count on its help.   In earliest days men looked to the supernatural for pragmatic goods, but found in the end that such goods did not come to them apart from the exercise of courage and resourcefulness.   Man must earn his living by the sweat of his brow.   This fact, slowly and painfully recognized in all its disillusioning significance, has been used as evidence that no good things come by the grace of God.   But the inference is invalid, mistaking a necessary for a sufficient condition: it is true that without his sturdy virtues man rates as naught, but it is equally true that apart from the underlying order of nature, established in the Omega system, his virtues avail him nothing. Yet it is clear that getting something for nothing is not in the plan, and in praying for material goods man wastes his pains. Acknowledging this, men pray for other things.   In time of war they pray for victory for their side; but so do they who fight on the other side.   "Yet our side is just: we fight for freedom and humanity, they for their own selfish ends."   In social conflicts, also, both radicals and conservatives, if they be men of faith, claim that God is their ally and justify the claim by the righteousness of their aims.   "If God be just, our cause will win."   So men transfer their demands to the moral sphere, and today God's help is claimed only for the right, or if for worldly ends, such ends must show themselves just.   But what cause is just apart from our effort, intelligence, and courage?   Is it just that the people should own the natural resources of a community if they cannot administer them?   Or do they deserve freedom who cannot rule themselves, or are not willing to fight to win and maintain it?   There is no region of experience where it can be right that we should obtain anything without the exercise of our powers.   One wonders what a human life would be worth to itself or to God without the challenge of problems.   Or is the *summum bonum* of the cosmos the life of the idle rich or a paradise of easy voluptuous joys, won by no charm or wit of ours?

Man's demands on Providence thus undergo readjustment. Man sees now that he can ask only that if he does his best, putting forth all his courage and intelligence, he shall win.   Yet as he looks about the human scene he discovers that he cannot always expect even this.   On the whole, perhaps, he may do so, for victory is usually won by the strong of heart and head; but oftentimes lives full of manliness and eager good will are broken by burdens they cannot bear, or defeated by illnesses against which man has no weapon in his arsenal or by death, with all young hopes put to naught. Then, when having done his best, his own self-help will not avail, he cries unto the Lord. In such emergencies as these he feels, if Providence has any meaning for him, he will be served or saved. And as no assistance arrives from the supernatural realm, although man may still believe because of faith or because he has had the mystic vision, his confidence that philosophy can justify the ways of God is shaken.

We confront, therefore, at the end, as every idealistic philosophy must, the problem of evil, the problem as to why, if the Omega system be the creator of man, and, in creating him, creator also of his ideals of love and justice, it should with such seeming ruthlessness or helplessness, disappoint these same ideals? The only answer that by the nature of the case can be given is to trace the ground of evil in the Omega system itself, for independent of that system there is nothing.

The evil in the world is not pain, which may be the occasion for helpfulness in its alleviation; nor is it struggle or danger, which may be the occasion for resourcefulness and victory; nor is it ignorance, which may be the occasion for teaching and learning, which are pure goods. A world without any of these things would be one so totally different from our own that it is hard to imagine what good it could contain. Even when struggle takes the form of competition, as when two men strive for the love of a woman, for popular favor, or for leadership, it is no evil in itself, because of the values that may be created in the endeavor of each. If competition takes the shape of war between nations, with unspeakable horror and suffering in its train, it is still not evil unmixed, for the same reason. A world without competition would be a world where there was no overlapping of monads causing what happened in one to have effects unwanted in another, no impinging of many monads on the same domain, so that of two seeking control one must give way. It would be a universe of Leibnizian windowless monads, each omnipotent and happy in its little sphere, without effects upon the lives of other monads; or if there were effects, they would be so timed as to meet the needs of the others, coöperating without strain and with perfect knowledge. It is because ours is not that kind of a world, but a world of overlapping and competing monads with restricted areas of control, a world of contingency and ignorance —for even God cannot foretell, since he does not control, all the future—rather than of harmony and exact knowledge, that there is frustration, defeat, disillusionment.   These are evils, but they are also opportunities for goods—without which our world would not seem to us finally good at all—providing for the moral and esthetic values, comedy and tragedy, Aristophanes and Aeschylus.

The evil in the world is not transiency, or even the final vanishing in death.[1] For the good is a process, an activity of appeasement of desire, not a static condition; and when the satisfaction has occurred through the activity it is already past and gone.   Following it a new activity and a new good may then arise, but only through the death of its predecessor.   The good is never anything to be kept, but something to be created anew. In preparing for the new good, or in entering into it as an echo or overtone, the old has fulfilled itself.   It never wholly dies, but its essence lives on in the memories and purposes of neighbors, and when they, too, have gone, in the memory of the Eternal.   Only when there is no new vigorous life grown from the old do men long regret the passing of the old in art, in social organization, in personal affairs.   And it is clear that the new cannot come to be except the old pass away.   The man could not exist alongside the babe, for he is not something that merely follows after the babe, but is the babe grown up.   So a new civilization can spring only from the disappearance of the old, for the theatre of its action is a single restricted neighborhood, within which the new as well as the old must exercise its powers or nowhere; the continuity of a civilization depends upon the sameness of the environment no less than upon the common heritage of tradition.   There could be no France except along the Mediterranean, the Vosges, the Pyrenees, the Bay of Biscay, the Seine, and the Moselle.   It is sheer illusion to suppose that you could transfer it to a new locale and retain the quality of the old.   Canadian France is not France.   And if transiency is the condition for every good, it is the easement of every evil. But for transiency, the anguish of sorrow, the horror of fear, the racking pain would exist forever in all their unbearable vividness, now borne only because we know they finally pass away.

The reason for the eventual death of a monad is the same

---

[1] Contrast A. N. Whitehead, *Process and Reality* (New York: The Macmillan Co., 1929), p. 517.

as the ground of frustration and defeat in its life: the competition for control. The purposes which constitute what we call the physical world permit the deviation we call life, but only for a time, for thereafter their own control would be jeopardized. They permit new monads to arise in place of the old, but could not permit all the old monads to survive alongside the new, because if that were to happen the organic would completely dominate the inorganic. These other values conditioned by the death of our beloved are beyond our appreciation, yet of one thing we can be certain: death is no mere brute fact from which no good results. For, first, in dying the dead give to new monads of their own kind fresh opportunities; and, secondly, they allow the purposes of the physical world to find fulfilment unimpeded by their own. And to reconcile us to our own death we have love, love that creates the child and having created him welcomes and fosters him, and would give him the room that is our room. From the sorrow over the death of the beloved child death itself will free us in our death.

The real evil in the world is the frustration for which there is no compensation through poetry or heroism. It is frustration out of which there springs no victorious effort or dream of beauty, but only the despair of a crushed heart. The world is full of such evil. The mind broken in melancholy, the proud spirit utterly balked, finding no way to ease the shame or employ the mind and make forget, taking flight in self-destruction or living on in complaining misery, such is the sin of the world. Suicide is the affirmation that existence itself in a particular case is evil. It is true, to be sure, that even from such evil good of a kind may follow: the effort of the physician to heal or of the reformer to make impossible the sort of situation that was its soil; and we do not know what song some superhuman bard may sing with our agonies as theme. The interpretation of nature as an existence higher than ourselves provides room for all sorts of compensations outside the range of our personal and social experience. It may be that there is a victory celebrated there for each defeat of ours. The agonies of drowning men or of young soldiers dying on a lonely barricade may yet be heard and may not go for naught. But even so, the evil in the world would still be evil, when it occurred. For all evil is personal evil, the frustration of personal desire, which can be adequately compensated for only by some satisfaction in the self that suffers.   The willing sacrifice of a free spirit, given for its own pure faith or vision, is no final evil; but the pain of an imprisoned mind, even though it become the occasion for the most intense scientific, poetic, or merciful interest on the part of another mind—albeit that mind is God's—remains evil still.   The monadic, democratic nature of existence renders compensation of this kind forever incomplete.

In the end, God is responsible for the evil in the world.   The theologian will not admit this; and because he will not admit it, he has tried to show that evil is illusion.   But every such attempt has proved to be a failure.   This may be the best of all possible worlds—the only one that could have issued from God's nature— but, as Candide proved, it is not therefore a wholly good world. The misery of Candide remained an evil for him, even though God did his best for him .   God is responsible for evil because all existence proceeded from him.   The primary material of the world was once part of God, and in it lay hidden the competition and disharmony that are the root of evil.   In creating the world, God rid himself of these, but he left them there in his children. It is absurd to blame the evil wholly on man's freedom, for at least God permitted such men as we to be, with our freedom and our limitations.   But if God is responsible, should we then with Job curse God and die?

There are as many standpoints for judging the universe as there are monads in the universe; none of these is absolute.   If for any one of these life is intolerable, then it is intolerable.   But if that one were possessed of sympathy and would look abroad, it would find that to others life is a joy; and then it could not view the world as utterly evil.   So, contrariwise, when any monad in its joy feels the misery of another, then its joy is stained.   Yet to curse God for this stain would be to ignore all that religion teaches both of God and of his relation to the world.   For the meaning of Providence is that God is seeking at every moment to lift the world out of the evil that was an inevitable accompaniment of creation.   Creation entailed the Fall, and the Fall the plan of salvation.   And since God's sympathy is boundless, he himself suffers for all the misery of his creatures.   This is the meaning of atonement, that God experiences in his own life the like of every pain that followed his creative act.   What in the creeds are called his mercy and forgiveness are rooted in his

knowledge that our failures are his own.   Yet he remains omnipotent still, in the sense that there are no external limits to his
power.   The limits of God are within his own nature: the original sin, of conflict and division.   To believe that this will ever be
healed in the created world is to live in illusion.   For the basis
of evil is metaphysical, and what is metaphysical is eternal.   But
in the creative process, in which we are co-workers with God, we
are given the opportunity for victory and love, for beauty and
for virtue, which is its own reward.   To ask for more is to ask
for what God himself cannot give.   To ask for more is to show
that one is tired and sated with activity.   Final peace is death.
To understand that in creation born of love is happiness is the
wisdom of Plato and of Christianity; to know that to be is to
suffer and that death is peace is the wisdom of Buddhism.   And
in this peace the misery of every creature finds surcease.

INDEX

Index

Music, 88, 133, 239–240, 290–291, 304, 311
Mysticism (or mystical experience or mystics), 3, 4, 224, 331, 327, 336–337, 341, 354
Myth, 330–331

Natural history, 16
Natural language, 30, 112, 167, 342. See also Language
Natural piety, 53
Naturalistic world view (or naturalism), 333, 335
Necessary connection (or internal necessity), 6, 59, 198, 231, 235–239, 241, 244, 248, 252
Neighborhood, 125, 232–233, 278, 355
Neurath, O., "Physikalismus," 15 n.
Neutral entities, 7, 21
Newton, 131, 147, 319
Next-to-next causality, 276, 285
Next-to-next relations, 276, 278
Nicod, J., Foundation of Geometry and Induction, 119
Nietzsche, Friedrich Wilhelm, 134
Nisbet, R. H., "The Foundations of Probability," 259
Nominalism (or nominalist), 70–79, 80–84, 90–93
Nonrepeatable factors of experience, 50–51, 60
Novelty, 132
"Now," the eternal, 325
Number: of events, 176, 178, 187, 192; of moments, 187; of monads, 192; of numbers, 180; of points, 176, 187, 192; of traces, 180, 187; of truths, 187
Numbers: infinite cardinal, 172; irrational, 172; real, 185

Object, 6. See also Phenomenal object and Scientific object
Objective immortality, 68
Occasional versus efficient causality, 102, 274
Oman, J., The Natural and the Supernatural, 341 n.

Omega system, 320–321, 323–327, 330, 332–333, 337, 340–342, 344, 348–352
Order: of events, 146, 163–164, 169; social, 346; spatial, 126; of values, 310–311
Organism, 276, 279, 282, 341
Origination, 232
Otto, Rudolf, Das Heilige, 334 n.

Parallelism: of events, 151–153, 155; of mind and body, 287–288
Participation, 224
Particulars, 71, 209–211
Passing away (or passage), 131–132, 134, 137, 139, 150–151
Past, the, 135, 141
Past events: existence of, 131, 141, 158–159; order of, 157–159, 164
Past moment, 154–155
Patterns: of control, 120; of sensa, 16, 102
Peace, 358
Pearson, Karl, The Grammar of Science, 40, 40 n.
Peirce, Charles: 194, 252–254, 276; "The Doctrine of Necessity Examined," 253 n.
Perception: 30, 103, 289; Greek theory of, 315; Hume's use of, 28
Perceptual relations, 126
Periphery of a focus, 111, 301
Perry, R. B.: General Theory of Value, 298; Present Philosophical Tendencies, 101
Personal identity, 60, 62, 64, 66, 68
Phenomenal object, 65, 97–99, 103, 107, 110, 113, 121, 167, 219, 228, 235–236, 253
Phenomenal world, 104
Philosophical concepts, 24
Philosophy, 3, 5, 10, 16, 26. See also Metaphysics
Physical world (or physical system), 12, 15, 157, 282, 326, 341, 347
Physicalism, 15

Physics, 7, 15–16, 165, 325, 346
Picture, 5, 7, 13, 17–18, 228, 246.
  See also World picture
Plato: 3, 5, 32, 41, 52, 65, 88, 93,
  132, 248, 292, 312–313, 345, 358;
  Cratylus, 132 n.; *Parmenides,*
  315 n.; *Philebus,* 5, 305 n.; *Re-
  public,* 65, 248 n.; *Sophist,* 52,
  52 n.; *Symposium,* 312; *Timae-
  us,* 5, 313 n., 320 n.
Platonic existence, 45, 68
Platonic good, 343
Platonic "Ideas," 23, 77, 313, 314
Platonic philosophy, 323
Platonism, 71
Plotinus, *Fifth Ennead,* 21 n.
Poetry, 356
Point, 115, 117, 120–121
Polarity, 5, 37
Position, 120–122, 277
Positivism, 4, 9, 15
Positivists, 4, 10
Possibility, 260
Possible, status of the, 174–175,
  245, 260–261
Pragmatic goods, 353
Pragmatists, 19
Prall, D. W., *A Study in the The-
  ory of Value,* 299 n.
Predicates, *see* Concept, Proper-
  ties, *and* Qualities
Prediction (*or* prophecy), 20, 21,
  160, 232, 236, 248, 250–251, 260,
  267–268, 290
Present (*or* present moment), 20,
  135, 140, 151–154, 159
Price, H. H., *Perception,* 98 n.
Prince, Morton, 234, 345
Principle of concreteness, 7, 349
Principle of individuation, 115
Probability, 249–269
Problem of knowledge, 6
Proper name, 89
Properties: axiological, 300; ex-
  trinsic, 88; generic, 4; intrinsic,
  86–88; original and acquired,
  220
Proposition: regarding the future
  (predictive), 9, 10, 13, 19–21,

256–257; historical, 9, 21, 323;
  impossible, 246; inconsistent,
  320; distinguished from judgment, 31; necessary, 244–246;
  negative, 21, 318; preposterous
  9; probable, 21, 255–261; true
  246, 255, 322; universal, 323
Providence, 351–353, 357
Psychology, 16

Qualities, 102, 219–224, 329
Quantity of probability, 261–263

Radiation, 232, 272
Radical empiricism, 9
Ramsey, F. P.: 83; *Foundations of
  Mathematics,* 83 n.
Realism, 70, 73
Reality, 6, 21, 177, 335
Reality feeling, 35
Reason, 339
Recording mechanism, 157
Reductionist theory, 281, 283
Reference to an object, 36
Reflexive relations, 61–62, 195
Reichenbach, K., 254, 264–265;
  Wahrscheinlichkeitslehre, 254 n.
Relational factors of experience,
  79, 81
Relations, 194–227 *passim. See
  also* Asymmetrical relations, Cog-
  nitive relations, Definitions, Mo-
  nadism, Monism, Reflexive rela-
  tions, *and* Symmetrical relations
Relativity, 151, 162, 167, 170
Religion, 333–336, 339–341, 357
Remote control, *see* Control
Repetition, 88, 325
Res cogitans, 68
Resistance, 39
Revelation, 338, 352
Rite, 334
Ross, W. D., *The Right and the
  Good,* 293 n.
Royce, J.: 131, 136–137, 173, 200,
  202, 204, 220–221; *The World
  and the Individual,* 131 n., 173
  n., 220 n.
Russell, Bertrand: 7, 71, 73, 174,